*For female movie villains… past, present, and future.
Cinematic Thrills, Unforgettable Women.*

MOVIE VILLAINESS 101

The Deadliest Women in Cinema…
Ranked

Andy Phillips

ACTION
GIRL
BOOKS

MOVIE VILLAINESS 101
The Deadliest Women in Cinema… Ranked

First Published 2026 in United Kingdom by Action Girl Books
First Edition Copyright © 2026 Andy Phillips

ISBN 978-1-917698-03-0

Cover Design by Action Girl Books
Using AI source images and post processing in GIMP

More information is available at:
https://actiongirlbooks.co.uk/

Introduction

It was a female unmasking that started it all.

Picture the scene: a red-garbed ninja sat on a golden throne in an island lair, surrounded by henchmen and burning skulls. As a child in the 1980s, I never suspected it was a woman under the hood. I fell for the ruse completely, and experienced my first surprise villainess as she revealed her face to the stunned male hero. I imagine gamers who played the original *Metroid* and earned the true "Samus is a girl" ending will appreciate the impact of such a moment.

Since then, I've sought female villains, but that introduction has rarely been surpassed. A fan for over thirty years, I've been delighted with many women foes, grudgingly content with others, and had my fair share of disappointment. In 2021, I had the idea to review and summarise my favourites, and so came up with the idea for *Movie Villainess 101*.

101 is American terminology for an introductory course, so might seem an odd choice given I'm British. But the overall tone of this series is educational, and I'm hoping to introduce readers to at least one example they didn't know before. I'll be summarising a hundred movies on the ranking

tiers, plus the introductory villainess to start things off. Who else could that be but China / Scarlet Leader from *Unmasking the Idol?*

After researching other internet sites, I've found many articles about female villains and a plethora of top lists. These vary in quality, but all focus on mainstream movies, and the same names come up repeatedly. While this is understandable, I feel not including other sources (direct-to-video, TV movies, lesser-known cinema releases) is a mistake, as so many "unknown" villainesses outshine A-list counterparts.

The problem – though a good one to have – is that my DVD / Blu-ray / digital collection is extensive, and there are too many female villains to cover. But I wanted to include as many as possible, so I eventually decided on themed reviews. These focus on one primary villainess (or pairing) with honourable mentions for others that are linked. It could be the same actress in another role, other movies in the same franchise, or an overarching theme (such as female cat burglars, witches, or tournament fighters).

For example, I cover the Connery era James Bond villains at #70. Fiona Volpe from *Thunderball* (1965) is the main ranked entry, with honourable mentions for female villains in the same era. James Bond is a substantial source (or was until the recent movies) for multiple series entries that feature on the list. A lot of my choices are subjective, and I haven't seen everything, so apologies if your favourite doesn't make the cut.

The List

I published written reviews on my blog between 2021 and 2023. These summarised the overall movie, any female villains of note, and themed honourable mentions. I've reproduced the content here, with edits to clean up grammar, spelling, and flow. And there have been a few additions and changes for the 2026 edition.

To avoid potential copyright issues, the reviews are text-only, with no images. My blog posts include screenshots, but those are inappropriate for a commercial publication. To compensate, I will provide descriptions of outfits and key visuals.

A few points to cover before we begin:

- Most genres are featured. The exceptions are pornographic or softcore flicks, which I consider detrimental to females. Some erotic thrillers with "real" plots and actors, such as *Basic Instinct* (1992) which features nudity in relative moderation, are on the list.

- Most entries are about female antagonists, but some are notable anti-heroines and female criminal protagonists such as assassins or bank robbers. While debatable, my overall aim is to cover as much material as possible, and I felt the need to include those examples.

- Whether I could add meaningful commentary was the major factor when choosing villainesses to rank. Those without sufficient screen time or notable scenes feature as honourable mentions. Lifetime films about jilted ex-girlfriends rarely make the cut, but those with more original storylines or great confrontations do.

- Movies are mostly from the 1960s onwards, with only a couple of classic "golden oldies". *Double Indemnity* (1944) at #26 is the only black and white movie. This is a personal taste, but I'm mostly a fan of modern material. Old films can have memorable female villains, but I prefer to discuss what I know best.

There's also a bias towards my favourite genres: action, thriller and science fiction, and a tendency to favour the golden age of 1990s B-movies.
- My original list included only movies from 2022 or earlier. There are a few recent ranked entries and honourable mentions, but a limited selection from 2023 onward (after a few revisions).

The review format changed several times, and my prototype was *The Mummy Returns* (originally ranked at #42). My second effort – *The Hunstman: Winter's War* (#57) – was much better. Because of quality issues, I started a redux series in April 2023 to clean up content and work in some additional honourable mentions.

Ranking different genre villainesses is difficult, so ultimately I put them in the order I enjoyed them. The ranking table got long and clunky as reviews piled up. So I split the list into four tiers. Superior, Epic, and Legendary, and Goddess, using a video game style breakdown.

With that preamble out of the way, it's time for the opening villainess review. No ranking since it's part of the introduction and sits outside the list. But it needs a number: **Movie Villainess 101**.

Unmasking the Idol (1986)
China / Scarlet Leader (Shakti Chen)

Movie

Judged as a movie, this bizarre spy adventure is dire stuff. However, its villainess is a "must include" since she started my love affair with female baddies. I remember watching this film on VHS rental in the 1980s (back when we rented videos from brick and mortar stores) and never seeing it again for years on TV. It took me almost two decades – and help from the online community – to put a movie title to my early childhood memory.

It's hard to describe what the film is actually about, with so many elements in this "throw in the kitchen sink" approach to filmmaking. Secret agencies, ninjas, a secluded island with horror-themed decor, an informant dressed like a 1930s explorer, a pet baboon with martial arts skills... and those are just the highlights. Previously released on DVD only, the title is now available on Blu-ray thanks to Vinegar Syndrome.

The film plays like a parody of James Bond, straight from the opening sequence where ninja hero Duncan Jax recovers a microcassette from a hotel room safe. Hardly grand stuff, but there is a stunt jump into a swimming pool and a dramatic escape via an inflatable balloon. Then come the title credits, complete with a cheesy song, and a casino scene where the tuxedo-wearing hero places bets on 00 and 7 at roulette. And of course the good guy has to deliver the "Jax. Duncan Jax." introduction.

Ninja movies are also spoofed with masked men (and the occasional female) duking it out. Perhaps continuing the roulette theme, the good guys wear black and the baddies red. Jax is a reluctant agent for a mysterious organisation based in a high-tech building with old-fashioned computer systems. There's also a pool room for relaxation with women in bikinis for company.

Plot elements appear out of nowhere only to be discarded. The secondary antagonist is a guy in a white suit named the Baron / Goldtooth. Jax wants revenge against him, but that's forgotten, and the Baron has a dastardly plan to exchange gold for nuclear weapons that we never see. There's hidden treasure on the island (the titular idol) that Jax somehow knows about, but it's never explained how. While this mess is a must-watch for any female villain aficionado, it's best to switch your brain off.

Villainess

What makes this woman so special? Picture Ernst Stavro Blofeld replaced by a masked villainess (who nobody knows is female), and you get the Scarlet Leader. Like the iconic Bond foe, this criminal mastermind has an inner sanctum with a piranha pool for body disposal. Add an army of ninja henchmen and a throne adorned with golden skulls, and it's a great lair. There's also a treasure vault and a control room, as you'd expect.

Before the Scarlet Leader is even mentioned, the unimaginatively named China meets Jax at the roulette table and later sleeps with him. The Chinese woman enquires about ninjas and watches the hero in action with a sinister expression, so attentive viewers will peg her as the masked villain. Especially since the bad "guy" uses a voice disguiser, and China mysteriously vanishes after the prologue. But those viewers who've never experienced female unmasking (like this child in the 1980s) will fall for the ruse.

The villainess shows how evil she is when two old folks crash-land near the island. Too bad the piranhas are hungry, so the woman gets a wheelchair ride down a water slide and a muscular henchman tosses her husband in soon after. The fish get a second meal when the Scarlet Leader uncovers a traitor – a woman in tribal attire who's far too clumsy. Her fate: lowered into the death pool while the villain laughs sadistically through her voice box.

Most other scenes are rather bland. The masked ninja meets with the Baron to discuss the never-seen nukes and issues radio orders after Jax and his army invade the island.

This leads to a confrontation between the hero and the villainess. She gets the upper hand, but Jax asserts himself. Eventually, the Scarlet Leader quits and reveals herself to be China. Cue wide-eyed surprise and a dumb "Scarlet" joke before the villainess drops a smoke bomb to make her escape.

Jax and his team clean up the opposition – including a tough henchman who's dealt with too easily – and recover the secret treasure. They escape in hot-air balloons, providing a comical sequence where the unmasked China flies past with a playful wave. Jax returned in a sequel named *Order of the Black Eagle*, but this is Scarlet's only appearance.

Honourable Mentions
Theme: Ninjas

2012: *Supernova* (2009) – Kwang Ye (Allura Lee)

The first honourable mention is almost a dishonourable one and proves that even a masked villainess can't save a dire movie. Produced by Asylum, it's no surprise the result is a poor-quality mockbuster, a sci-fi disaster in more ways than one. Expect to see woeful special effects, cheap action scenes, and a beautiful woman meditating during a meteor shower.

When the title supernova threatens Earth and lays waste to the solar system, our only hope for survival is a team of international scientists. The "experts" are an American named Kelvin, a vodka-drinking Russian, and a smart Chinese woman. Stereotypes, anyone? Their plan hinges on antique computers and nuclear weapons, while a digital doomsday clock ticks in the background.

As the hero's wife and daughter evade bad guys and

cheap CGI weather, a ninja spy (all in black, of course) sabotages computers in the base. It's obviously a woman behind the mask, so her identity is obvious long before the reveal. Attempts to make the Russian alcoholic seem guilty are laughable, and the two fight scenes are dark and poorly staged.

After seventy minutes of mind-numbing drivel, the Chinese scientist is revealed as the traitor we all knew she was. The third fight (in space this time!) is an improvement in that we can actually *see* the action. And there's a half-decent scuffle before the hero finishes the villainess with an electrified cable.

Mask of the Ninja (2008) – Kisei Shirasuna (Crystal Kwon), Kumioko (Jodi Long)

A made for cable actioner that sadly doesn't include any unmasking scenes despite the promising title. Kisei gets a grand introduction during an intro montage sequence that names the primary villains. Dressed in revealing attire and carrying a colourful war fan, she doesn't seem a fearsome ninja lieutenant, but this woman is deadly.

In this movie, ninjas operate in plain sight and go up against police officers in force. Detective Jack Barrett (Casper van Dien) has his hands full protecting a young woman named Miko (Kristy Wu) after her father is killed during an attack on their mansion estate. Stakes become even more personal when the assassins kill Barrett's partner.

The evil ninjas are after dangerous technology, and Miko is the key. That leaves a couple of loose ends to tie up: a corrupt security officer and a hacker. Kisei deals with both men, starting with the security guy, whom she attacks in a parking lot and tortures for information. Of course, she is a sadist who enjoys mutilating her victim while grinning in delight. The hacker, who likes female company, is a much easier target. Unfortunately for him, Kisei interrupts her seduction with a deadly poison-coated fan and a snarky comment.

The biggest set piece is a full-on ninja assault on a police station. We're talking about a complete massacre with a bunch of armoured baddies slaughtering their way through offices of cops. Bullets have no effect on the ninja, leaving the police defenceless against katanas and throwing stars. Kisei is annoyingly not involved much, dressed as a cop to gain access but no kills. Miko and Bennett escape, so the boss is angry, and it looks like that will end the villainess' involvement.

However, Kisei gets a reprieve. She fights the hero in a brief encounter and leaves him alive, only to get knocked off a motorcycle and die without a word. There's also a secondary villainess: Miko's stepmother, Kumioko. This isn't much of a revelation since we knew somebody was feeding the bad ninjas information and there was nobody else in a position to do so.

Kumioko fights with Miko, who's suddenly proficient in hand-to-hand combat. And the bad girl ends up with a knife in her chest. Uninspiring stuff with a weak villainess.

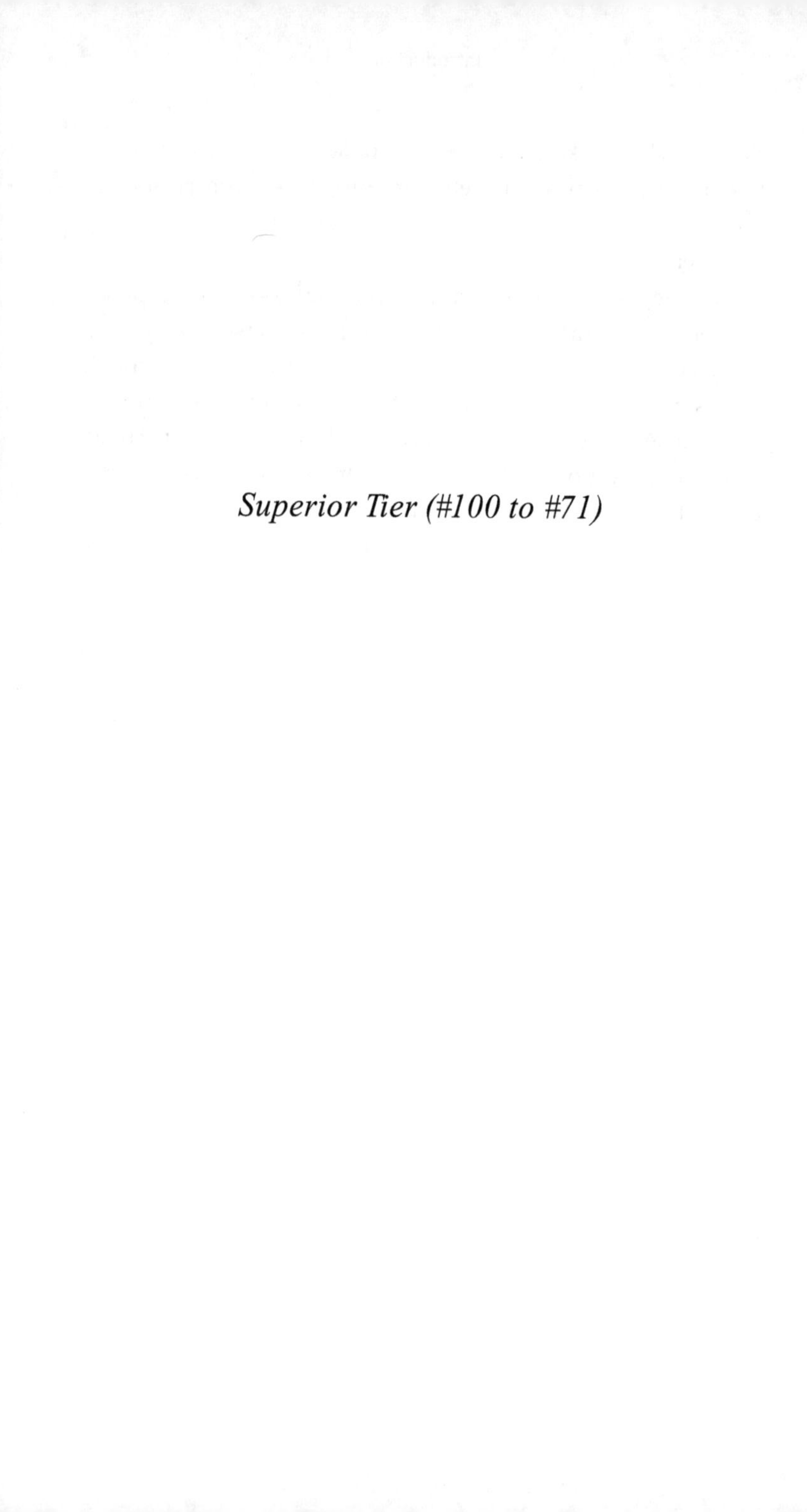

Superior Tier (#100 to #71)

Clue (1985) - Ending A
Miss Scarlet (Lesley Ann Warren), Yvette (Colleen Camp)

Movie

Clue is the lowest-ranked entry on my list, but I consider all these villainess selections to be at least "superior", and many didn't make the final cut. The movie is loosely based on the classic whodunnit board game (known as *Cluedo* in the UK). Set in 1950s New England, events take place – like all good murder mysteries – in an isolated, spooky mansion. It's a splendid setting, suitably spacious and creepy, with a multitude of secret passages and dark areas for potential killers to hide.

The story begins with six guests arriving. They use aliases that match the game characters from the classic American version: Mr Green, Colonel Mustard, Mrs Peacock, Professor Plum, Miss Scarlet, and Mrs White. All six have connections to Washington, D.C. and mysterious pasts they want to keep secret. Three staff members are also present: the butler Wadsworth, the maid Yvette, and an unnamed female cook. The hired helpers are as suspicious as the guests, and any of them could have murderous intent.

Shortly after dinner, it's revealed a seventh guest named Mr Boddy is blackmailing the rest, and that the whole gathering is a setup arranged by Wadsworth to expose him. Things take a sinister turn when Mr Boddy presents the others with six weapons (also based on the board game) and makes a deadly proposal: that someone kill Wadsworth to keep the matter secret. Turns out this wasn't the best plan, as the blackmailer ends up a victim. And it was a dumb move to switch off the lights, which the killer used to their advantage.

And so begins a rather chaotic and darkly comic murder mystery. Other nameless characters, such as the motorist and the cop, are introduced. For those counting, there are six "extras" that get bumped off, each in a different location with a unique weapon. This is a plot device to keep the six primary suspects on the table as potential killers, and to mix in some action amidst the snooping and bitter accusations.

The humour is hit and miss. Some of the better scenes have guests attempting to conceal the murderous goings-on from the visitors. The section where the suspects split into pairs to search the mansion works especially well. However, repetitive gags, such as Mr Green saying "I didn't do it" whenever a body is discovered, become tedious after a while. There's an overlong recap towards the end where Wadsworth enthusiastically recounts events in annoying detail, complete with overacting and high drama. While funny to start with, eventually you want the annoying butler to take his guests' advice and just get on with it.

However, all this is preamble to the ending. Or rather, three endings. The ambiguous conclusion is what most viewers will remember the movie for. When released in cinemas, only one of the three different endings was shown. These were later edited together and separated by title cards for the home video version, and have since become known as endings A, B, and C based on the order.

Villainesses

For villainess fans, the first ending is arguably the best. The motive and movements fit better than endings B and C, and the killers are exclusively female.

Ending A has Miss Scarlet as the main killer, with Yvette the maid as an accomplice who kills Mr Boddy and the cook. That's before her scheming employer strangles her. Miss Scarlet also murdered the motorist, policeman, and a singing telegram girl, who were all revealed to be part of a complex blackmail plot. Miss Scarlet's confessed motive is that she's a proud capitalist. Yvette was uncovering the other guest's secrets, which Miss Scarlet planned to sell. Except for the motorist, we get to sell all the murders re-enacted.

Police arrive in force to arrest Scarlet, but not before she takes part in possibly the best joke of the movie. This revolves (literally) around how many shots were fired during the movie, and whether any bullets remained in the gun. Turns out Miss Scarlet can count and Wadsworth can't, as he discovers to his detriment when he proclaims the gun empty before shooting a chandelier. Oops!

Honourable Mentions: *Clue* Endings

Unlike other reviews, the honourable mentions are from the same film, covering endings B and C. Villainess fans will be pleased to know all three conclusions have at least one female killer.

Clue (1985) - Ending B - Mrs Peacock (Eileen Brennan)

Ending B is the least satisfying, mainly because there's

only a single killer. Even for a comedy, this is not plausible given the number of murders and the need to avoid detection. And despite six victims, no murders are shown in flashback, unlike endings A and C. This makes ending B feel somewhat tacked on, as if it were filmed last and less effort was put into it.

After a lacklustre reveal, the best part is the villainess' arrest when the police chief arrives disguised as an evangelist and boldly states "The Kingdom of Heaven is at hand!" That's the cue for dramatic floodlights to switch on and a small army of cops to descend on Peacock to foil her escape. But overall, it's a disappointing climax.

Clue (1985) – Ending C – Miss Scarlet (Lesley Ann Warren), Mrs Peacock (Eileen Brennan), Mrs White (Madeleine Kahn)

Ending C is the fan favourite, and often regarded as canon based on the "what really happened" title card. From a comedy perspective, it works well because it's chaotic. In this resolution, all the guests except for one commit a murder, often to remove blackmail evidence. The exception is Mrs White, who strangles Yvette just because she annoyed her. Wadsworth reveals himself to be the real Mr Boddy and the mastermind behind the whole thing. Yes, the butler did it.

Unfortunately, the lack of a single main villainess makes it all feel unsatisfying, and the killings come across as random rather than meticulously planned. Ultimately, Mr Green is unveiled as an undercover FBI agent and takes down the real blackmailer in a brief shootout. Then the six killers are arrested together.

Rank #99

Star Wars: Episode II – Attack of the Clones (2002)
Zam Wesell (Leeanna Walsman)

Movie

If this were a series about male villains, Darth Vader – one of the most iconic bad guys in cinema history – would be top 10 material for sure. But since I'm reviewing female baddies, there are few to choose from in the *Star Wars* franchise. Discounting the miscellaneous women who've appeared as Imperial commanders and the like, I can think of only two.

Female leads have become more prominent in action movies over the past decade, and *Star Wars* follows this trend. Jyn Erso in *Rogue One* (2016) proved to be a fantastic heroine in the well-regarded spin-off prequel to *Episode IV – A New Hope* (1977). However, female villains remain a rare breed in this galaxy, and those that have featured are not especially memorable. A shout-out to *Solo* (2018) for including a masked rebel pirate who turns out to be a woman (with a voice disguiser, naturally), but she couldn't be considered evil. There's also a late reveal that a seemingly sweet companion is actually a Sith agent, but it's a onetime appearance. So we're still waiting for a true female badass.

Villainess

There's not much competition for *Star Wars* villainesses, and Zam almost wins by default. That said, there are memorable scenes in *Attack of the Clones*, even though Zam is a minor character who only lasts the first quarter or so of the movie. Unfortunately, she's then eliminated by an allegedly more important male villain.

Zam is a bounty hunter working for the bad guys who want to conquer the galaxy. No limit to their ambition, and anyone who's seen the original trilogy will know they succeed. Which makes the heroes' efforts moot, but they have to fill up three movies somehow and make it a struggle for the Dark Side. Technically, Zam works for Jango Fett, father of Boba from *The Empire Strikes Back* (1980), and she's a footsoldier in it (presumably) for credits.

The villainess gets an explosive introduction when she attempts to assassinate Senator Padme Amidala on her arrival to Coruscant. When the bomb kills the Senator's decoy instead, Jedi Master Obi-Wan Kenobi and his apprentice Anakin Skywalker are assigned to protect her. The mercs are not about to be deterred, and Jango orders his underling to "try something more subtle". That means killing off Padme with poisonous, slithery worm-like things. I'm sure the creatures have a more ominous name in the *Star Wars* universe, but they're never given one in the movie.

After the Jedi arrive in the nick of time to save the imperilled Senator – a habit of heroes – we're treated to one of the best scenes in franchise history. The two main characters pursue the would-be assassin in an airborne speeder chase through a planet-covering capital city. This is especially memorable as their quarry proves to be slippery and dangerous, with Zam shooting Obi-Wan off a flying drone and performing daredevil moves as she attempts to give her pursuers the slip.

During the sky chase, Zam is revealed to be a changeling, a humanoid creature able to alter her appearance. After a crash landing, the final confrontation takes place in a bar. This sequence is disappointing as the villainess remains in the same human form throughout. I'm assuming changelings can take on any guise within limits, so I would have liked Zam to be more deceptive considering that Anakin has already seen her face.

Instead, she foolishly goes after the master Jedi and gets cut down rather easily by his lightsaber. The villainess' demise is okay, though nothing special. Just as she's about to name her superior, a helmeted mercenary offs Zam with a toxic dart, and she reverts to her natural form. Before the Jedi can track the killer, he jetpacks off into the sky, setting up the main plot of the film.

Overall, I've ranked Zam low on my list because of her limited contribution. The role of women in this film series is worthy of discussion, but the wait for a notable female foe goes on. Until then, Aussie actress Leeanna Walsman can claim she's played the best villainess in a *Star Wars* movie.

Honourable Mentions: *Star Wars*

Star Wars: Episode VII – The Force Awakens (2015) – Captain Phasma (Gwendoline Christie)

Okay, so perhaps she's not *terrible*, but people expected so much more from Gwendoline Christie as the statuesque silver stormtrooper. After her memorable stint as warrior woman Brienne of Tarth in *Game of Thrones*, fans understandably had high expectations. Then *The Force Awakens* was released in 2015, and we got to see Phasma do… well, not very much.

When she featured in *Episode VII* – and her appearances were fleeting – Phasma stood in the background and gave a few orders to her troops. Armoured eye candy is *not* what we expected. As for actual combat, there was none. Phasma gets captured by the heroes without a fight, and we're left with a *very* unsatisfying off-screen resolution with her character thrown in a trash compactor (according to Han Solo).

Star Wars: Episode VIII – The Last Jedi (2017) – Captain Phasma (Gwendoline Christie)

The good news is Phasma sees some action in Episode VIII and didn't get the off-screen death we all feared. Maybe the filmmakers resurrected her to avoid fan backlash?

This time, the silver-clad giantess poses a threat, though she's absent for most of the film. Phasma engages in combat, fires blasters, and fights hand to hand with the hero Finn in an epic confrontation. Still, there are a lot of cutaways to CGI-heavy hero versus trooper battles, and the all-too easily defeated commander is jettisoned into space. Which left *Star Wars* and villainess fans wondering what might have been.

Two barely honourable mentions, and even that feels generous.

The Blues Brothers (1980)
Mystery Woman (Carrie Fisher)

Movie

Film buffs will always remember Carrie Fisher for the iconic role of Princess Leia in the Star Wars franchise. Besides starring in *The Empires Strikes Back* in 1980, she also played a mysterious female assassin in this classic comedy adventure.

For those unfamiliar with the story, it's a lighthearted musical about the title brothers, Jake and Elwood Blues. Played by John Belushi and Dan Aykroyd, they literally see the light and undertake a "Mission from God." Their goal is to reform their old band and raise enough money to save an orphanage from closure. Dressed in matching black suits, hats, and dark glasses, the Blues could be mistaken for government agents, but these two are definitely anti-authority figures.

It's not long before the brothers make enemies of the police. Bad news for Jake, only just released from prison. The list of vengeful foes grows after they steal a gig from a rival band and wreck a fascist group's parade. By the end of the film, even the military has Jake and Elwood in its sights. Plenty of antagonists, but the Mystery Woman is the standout villain.

Villainess

The character's credited name is appropriate, as the assassin's true identity is never revealed, although she gets an explanatory monologue near the end. Before that, the Mystery Woman makes it her personal mission to murder the two brothers. And it's clear from the get-go that she's really ticked off, because she doesn't even bother with small arms and brings out the big guns straight away.

The cigarette-smoking villainess' introduction sees her aim a rocket launcher and unleash a volley at the brothers while they're on the steps of an apartment building. She misses the men somehow, but destroys the entrance and leaves the brothers buried in a pile of rubble. They dust themselves off, showing no concern as if this is perfectly normal. Maybe it is for these two, who seem to attract chaos wherever they go.

Murder attempts played for laughs become a recurring theme. As police raid the apartment, the Mystery Woman gives the brothers a loud wake-up call by detonating explosives, which causes the entire building to collapse. On a holy quest, the brothers are not about to be deterred by minor inconveniences like their apartment being reduced to a pile of bricks and scrap metal.

As you've probably gathered, the humour in the movie is very dark. This extends to the name of the salon where the female assassin works: *Curl Up and Dye*. There, she brushes up on her weapons knowledge, specifically an M-79 flamethrower. The Mystery Woman tries to roast the Blues alive as they make a call from a phone booth (back in the 1980s when they still had those), but only blows up a nearby propane tank. We then get a funny scene where the kiosk launches into the air and comes crashing down, providing the brothers with some loose change.

Unfortunately, that money is nowhere near enough to save an orphanage, so Jake and Elwood perform a well-advertised gig at a packed venue. And so the people after the anti-heroes – practically everyone by this point – know where to find them. The brothers sneak out through the basement, which deceives the boneheaded cops but not the Mystery Woman, who's there waiting with an assault rifle and a motive rant.

Actually, it's Jake who's been her main target, and Elwood was collateral damage. It all stems from the assassin's ex-lover standing her up at a wedding, and now she wants payback. Hell hath no fury like a woman scorned, as the saying goes.

Jake and the assassin kiss and make up before he promptly dumps her again by pushing her to the floor. This woman is not about to take another rejection lying down, and so chases after him. In her last appearance, the Mystery Woman fires wildly at the fleeing brothers as they drive off into the night.

Honourable Mentions: Notable Henchwomen

China White (1989) – Henchwoman (Saskia Van Rijswijk)

If I had to give an award for the best female villain entrance, it would go to the unnamed blonde brute in this rather generic 1980s action movie. As two guys are being interrogated by a ruthless crime boss (Billy Drago), a tall female in stiletto heels walks in, trampling broken glass underfoot. The camera then pans up to reveal a scary villainess wearing a short-sleeved leather top and sunglasses. She doesn't need to say anything – it's obvious what her role is.

Sadly, the movie is otherwise dull, though I located a DVD copy to give this henchwoman a deserved review. There are no heroes in this tale, just criminal gangs in Amsterdam and a high body count as hoodlums fight violently over territory. Before the last half hour, we see little of the Terminator-like bodyguard, who remains silent while the main villain schemes and threatens.

Characters in this film die in gruesome ways, and the henchwoman gets the best execution when she roughs up a surprisingly brave prisoner by kicking the bound man in the chest. That had to hurt, but he refuses to talk, so the villainess beheads him with a fire axe. While that scene alone earns an honourable mention, the climactic action set piece involves a shootout at the docks and the blonde's desperate attempt to kill off a main character. When firearms don't work, the tough woman resorts to martial arts, but it's a rather brief fight even if she proves a resilient opponent. After so many brutal deaths, she deserved a better demise than a plunge into the ocean.

Death Ring (1992) – Ms Ling (Elizabeth Fong Sung)

This movie is easier to find, but sadly suffers from similar flaws as *China White*. The henchwoman to the main villain (Billy Drago again) appears to be a secretary at first, before she's established as a competent martial artist. A promising start, but she only gets two tame fight scenes in the closing minutes.

Before that, Ms Ling is window dressing who does her best to look menacing. Often this involves handling weapons without actually using them, or passing them to other bad guys who like to hunt humans for sport. Yes, this is another one of those *Most Dangerous Game* type movies, probably the most copied scenario after *Die Hard*. Two beautiful blondes show up as sadistic assistants, but they have no dialogue and exist only to show the villain's poor taste in women.

The males get the interesting stuff (machete, spear, garrote), while Ms Ling makes do with a pair of knuckle dusters. After screaming hysterically and mouthing some timid insults, she's taken out by the hero's girlfriend all too easily.

Quiet Fire (1991) – Hector (Dorothy Herndon), Jax (Laura Vukov)

Continuing the theme of under-used henchwomen (two in this case), this 1990s direct-to-video movie stars Lawrence Hilton-Jacobs as Vietnam vet Jesse Palmer, and real-life female bodybuilders as hired muscle that deserved far more screen time.

Quiet Fire includes every cliché in the book: a shady politician involved in arms deals, corrupt police officers on his payroll, a martial artist whose best friend dies just after passing on key information. Plenty of gun battles, explosions, and sexy women, and yes... even a standoff where the villain's pistol is empty. A fight in front of electrical junction boxes... you already know how that will end.

After the local thugs fail to eliminate Jesse, the politician brings in outside help. Hector and Jax get an easy kill: a sleazy male assistant who'd messed up too many times. They then target the hero and his girlfriend and somehow miss with a sniper rifle despite having a clean shot. In an unexpected development, the girl is not kidnapped in exchange for the incriminating data, but murdered in a shootout.

Time for Jesse to go all ninja and deal with the problem.

After he deals with some lesser thugs, Hector and Jax are the last obstacles between Jesse and the politician. Hector is disposed of with a throwing star, then it's a fight with the leather-clad Jax. She dishes out a good beating to Jesse, but disappointingly goes down with a single punch. No kill, hero? This is the woman who assassinated the love of your life, remember?

Cobra (1986)
Nancy Stalk (Lee Garlington)

Movie

Action movie buffs often hail the 1980s as a golden era. Back then, films received adult certificates, uncut violence was expected, and macho men uttered one-liners while taking down bad guys. No pesky character development was required. *Cobra* is a cult fan favourite because it adheres to this template.

Lt. Cobretti (Sylvester Stallone) is the typical action hero: a cowboy cop who drives a classy car, wears cool shades, and chews matchsticks while dealing out lethal justice to criminals. "Cobra" is the man superiors call when they need tricky situations dealt with. Naturally, the same bureaucratic bosses then blame the hero for being reckless.

Like many gritty cop movies, *Cobra* is set in Los Angeles. The opening scenes establish the tone: a statistical voiceover by Stallone (thankfully brief), a psycho biker cult clinking bladed weapons together, and a lunatic terrorising supermarket customers with a shotgun. Said nutter serves as an introductory villain for the hero to blow away. The triumphant cop holsters his pistol: a fancy weapon with a cobra painted on the white handle.

The main baddie is the appropriately named Night

Slasher, who's attacking random civilians to usher in a new world order. A motive as nonsensical as the plot, but action movie fans won't care. The guy has a fancy knife and an army of psychos to back him up. Cobra is on the case, and the streets of L.A. are about to turn even more violent.

Villainess

Cobra thinks there's more than one killer. His boss thinks he's off the mark. Guess who's right, and we get two Night Slasher attacks in quick succession to validate the hero's theory. Like many action movies, there's a lone female in the stocking-masked gang, and that would be Nancy Stalk.

Just as psycho as the men, Nancy smashes a car windscreen with a sledgehammer in the first attack. For the second murder, she's unmasked and distracts a female motorist while the Night Slasher sneaks up behind. As the villainess disposes of the body, a woman drives past and witnesses the crime in progress. Ingrid Knudsen (Brigitte Nielsen) is a fashion model, and her career is an excuse to show dancing scenes with robots (don't ask) and a montage of Cobra following leads while *Angel of the City* plays in the background.

Despite having little screen time, Nancy Stalk comes across as brooding and dangerous. There's a creepy scene where she flirts with the Night Slasher while he sharpens his oversized, spike-handled knife. An additional threat comes from the villainess' reveal as a police officer whom Cobra and his partner trust implicitly, though it's not clear why they're so easily taken in. There's obviously a mole in the department, and Cobra spies Nancy making suspicious telephone calls more than once. The villainess' assigned role is an informant lurking in the background, with action mainly left to the Night Slasher and his biker army, but things improve for the finale.

After Cobra prepares for war and Nancy shows her true colours (which the cops should have seen coming), there's a long shootout / chase scene. One helmeted biker has long hair, raising hopes of a secondary minor villainess, but the solitary female baddie rule applies. The motorcyclists don't last long, and Cobra wipes out the gang single-handedly.

Nancy gets more action in the showdown, wielding a shotgun and chasing the terrified Ingrid through a steel mill. There's the standard hero versus the remaining bad guys climax, but it's obvious only the Night Slasher will put up a worthwhile fight in the inevitable last confrontation. At first, Nancy appears to get a rather lame death when Cobra shoots her in the back, but the villainess returns to disarm the hero (after a lengthy tough guy monologue!). Sadly, the resurrection is short-lived, and Nancy gets shot by the Night Slasher when Cobra uses her as a human shield.

Honourable Mentions: Criminal Gang Members

Deadly Target (1994) – Mei (Lydia Look)

Gary Daniels is another action star who always plays lone hero types, though his movies usually disappoint in the female villain department. This pedestrian flick has a Hong Kong cop (with no regard for police procedure) team up with an American counterpart to tackle an ambitious triad boss intent on wiping out the competition.

There's a minor henchwoman in the opening scene, but she's considered expendable by the main villain and dies within the first ten minutes. Mei is a more important criminal enforcer who murders rival gang members and anyone else who gets in her way. The villainess has some memorable scenes, notably a murderous, gun-toting rampage at a charity fundraiser. One guy takes cover behind an overturned table, but that offers no protection against Mei's armour-piercing rounds.

Sadly, this is another villainess who peaks too soon. Casino dealer Diana Tang (Susan Byun) becomes romantically involved with the hero and predictably faces off with Mei in the climax. Despite no apparent martial arts background, she's still able to defeat the villainess twice, during a home invasion and later in the climactic battle on a cargo ship. The fights are *very* unconvincing and feature cutaway shots of Daniels doing his thing before Diana finishes Mei after a brief struggle.

Ides of March (2000) – Alexandra Krystofich (Lydia Chin), Muse (Tracy Phillips)

Also known as *Ultimate Target*, this is another Gary Daniels vehicle that remained unreleased for many years until a version surfaced on YouTube. The trailer promised a lot of action and two female villains, but the end product was a slow-burning, dialogue-heavy yawnfest. For much of the runtime, Alexandra and Muse talk with other assassins around a table. The best way to experience this movie: fast-forward through the silly character introductions and unremarkable flashbacks to the final fight scene.

There we get the rocket launcher attack that made it into the trailer and Daniels' encounter with the two hitwomen. Neither puts up a great struggle, but they certainly look the part as leather-clad killers. The hero is a superior martial artist and makes quick work of his outclassed foes, but the fight scene is fun while it lasts.

Ride or Die (2003) – Tommy Wong (Miranda Kwok), Fake Venus (Meagan Good)

Another cliché-ridden direct-to-video actioner (see a pattern here?), with Duane Martin as private investigator Conrad "Rad" McRae. Expect plenty of gun battles (with dual wielding the norm), disposable bad guys, explosions, and attractive female extras. Vivica A. Fox is tough-talking weapons specialist Lisa, and there are cameos by well-known B-movie actors, notably Daniel Dae Kim as a Triad boss and Gabrielle Union as a domino-masked woman.

Rad investigates the murder of rapper superstar friend and teams up with his widow Venus to take on a corrupt record producer who doesn't even feign innocence. Tommy Wong gets a badass introduction as the henchwoman when she takes down the hero PI in a restaurant without breaking a sweat. Frustratingly, she disappears until a late showdown, when she returns clad in leather, but this time Rad easily bests her in the return fight.

Tommy wouldn't earn an honourable mention by herself, but after surprise villain Venus – who's *not* the widow – is revealed as a criminal mastermind, she disposes of the false big bad and turns her dual pistols (that cliche again) on Rad in the final shootout. After lots of gunfire and traded insults, Lisa finishes the treacherous woman off with explosive underwear in a rare moment of originality.

Rank #96

Fatal Reunion (2005)
Lisa Calders / Dana Declan (Juliet Landau)

Movie

I wanted my list to be as inclusive as possible, so I've included several Lifetime movies, with *Fatal Reunion* being the lowest ranked. Technically, these films are independently produced, but I'm referring to female-driven made-for-TV flicks as "Lifetime movies" because it's a lot easier and tidier to write.

As is usual for this genre, there's an opening murder sequence with a mysterious figure in a black hooded outfit offing some poor woman. So, nothing too original to start with. After that, we're introduced to the main character, Jessica, played by Erika Eleniak (which satisfies the casting requirement of a well-known B-movie actress as the lead).

Jessica is unhappily married (surprise!), and believes her husband, Russell, may be cheating. So – in typical double-standard fashion – Jessica reaches out to old classmate Marcus Declan via an online reunion site. Anyone who's ever seen a Lifetime movie will know such situations never end well, and it isn't long before Marcus comes on to Jessica. After she rejects him, Jessica receives harassing phone calls in the middle of the night.

Fatal Reunion is a slow-burner, with hardly any

interesting scenes in the first two acts. The director's weird scene transitions don't help. For some inexplicable reason, the camera pans off to the side, often to uninteresting background props or up towards the sky. We're talking about almost every interlude here, which becomes flat out annoying.

Rare standout moments include Jessica pole fighting with a harsh instructor (which will obviously become important later) and finding herself on the wrong end of a loaded crossbow. Someone poisons the family dog, and the protagonist's two children get completely forgotten about. But things pick up towards the final act, and the exciting, drawn-out climax is my main reason for ranking this movie.

Villainess

It's not until approximately the sixty-minute mark that we're introduced to the real killer. A brunette stranger shows up at Jessica's house and introduces herself as Lisa Calders, an attorney from Dallas, Texas. Intelligent viewers may peg "Lisa" as the villainess from the moment she walks on screen, given we've never seen the stalker's face and the newcomer's Southern US accent is creepy enough to arouse suspicion. But Jessica and her husband Russell welcome Lisa with open arms and don't do a background check until it's too late.

Lisa offers to help the couple trap Marcus but advises they keep the cops out of it (a further clue something is off, in case another is needed). There are several meetings between the women, and it becomes obvious the villainess (we can stop pretending already) is drawing her victims into whatever scheme she's cooked up. Jessica escapes a further attempt on her life, this time a hit and run by a masked driver, and goes to the police. Naturally, they don't believe her claims and imply that the husband is responsible.

The movie climaxes in a barn when Lisa lures Jessica to a meeting. Russell, who finally figures the "lawyer" is an impostor, races to the rescue. Or that's his plan anyway, because instead he discovers her holding Jessica and a tied-up Marcus at gunpoint. Then the villainess reveals her real identity: Dana Declan – Marcus' wife – who doesn't take too kindly to his perceived infidelity.

Juliet Landau is credited as Lisa Calders (her alias), probably to keep the reveal a surprise. Of course, the DVD cover gives the game away, as it shows her character wearing black gloves and holding a pistol.

The last confrontation is suitably long, with plenty of improvised weapons. With Marcus and Russell incapacitated, the two women battle it out. Jessica survives multiple strangulation attempts before she gets to put her martial arts practice to use. The heroine grabs a metal bar that happens to be lying around, deflects one blow, and impales the villainess. One of the better Lifetime death scenes – far superior to the tame resolutions that plague the modern era – which makes the tedium beforehand worth sitting through.

Honourable Mentions: Lifetime Movies

Deadly Sorority (2017) – Jubilee Swan (Chloe Babcock)

Another movie I considered, this surprisingly clever mystery thriller aired as *Too Close to Kill* in the UK. For once, Channel 5 made sparse edits.

The plot centres around the murder of a new sorority pledge, with many dodgy characters for prime suspect Samantha (Greer Grammer) to investigate. Some are clearly red herrings, such as the boyfriend who later winds up dead. The obvious candidate is a teaching assistant named Victor. Why? He *isn't* obvious, and no evidence points to him. In 99% of TV mysteries, he would be the killer, but not this time.

Instead, a relatively obvious suspect – bitchy sorority head Jubilee – is the villainess. An impressive narrative feint implies a college professor's wife is the murderer. The genre-savvy heroine picks up on this and escapes after throwing hot tea in the woman's face. Sadly, the amateur sleuth's instincts are wrong, and the actual killer reveals herself soon afterward.

The knife-wielding psycho threatens Samantha, and there's a rather brief confrontation before police arrest the villainess, but the above-average resolution earns an honourable mention.

A Neighbor's Deception (2017) – Cheryl Dixon (Isabella Hofmann)

2017 was a good year for TV movie endings, because we got a surprisingly exciting conclusion to what seemed a pedestrian thriller. The plot is as generic as they come: a woman romances a guy with a mysterious past, only to find her life in danger.

After a drawn-out stalk and slash scene at the beginning, main character Chloe (Ashley Bell) moves in next door to the suspicious Gerald Dixon (Tom Amandes). The heroine suffers from panic attacks – a plot device to ensure nobody will believe her later – and Gerald conveniently reveals he's a psychiatrist. Cue inevitable warning signs, a shadowy stalker breaking into Chloe's house, amateur detective work, and near misses with the psycho doctor.

A secondary character gives Chloe dirt on Gerald. Can

you guess what happens next? The guy is killed off almost immediately with the overused backseat garrote MO. This one's longer and more realistic than usual, but annoyingly, it's mostly filmed with a long-distance shot. So far, so average, and you'd never suspect an exciting and violent finale was on the cards.

After Chloe learns Gerald's wife Cheryl has mental issues, the villainess decides her nosy neighbour is a threat. The black-gloved killer attacks Chloe in her bathroom, leading to a drawn-out strangulation with multiple life attempts that goes on for several minutes. Yes, you read that correctly. Minutes, not the usual five seconds.

Eventually, Chloe frees herself only to be captured again. The heroine wakes up in a chair, restrained and forced to endure Cheryl's insane ranting. Then, after the villainess and the slightly more sane Gerald have a violent difference of opinion, the murderess puts a plastic bag over Chloe's head to suffocate her. Did the producers forget this is a TV movie? Eventually, the husband comes to the rescue at the last moment, and Cheryl goes down fairly easily considering what transpired before.

Killer Photo (2015) – Sarah Miller (AnnaLynne McCord)

Another so-so Lifetime movie with a good ending, this thriller (also known as *Watch Your Back*) earns an honourable mention thanks to an intriguing premise and a decent twist that makes sense. An elaborate prologue murder has a woman follow a trail of red heart balloons and greeting cards, only to find a mysterious assassin waiting with a silenced pistol.

Fast forward two years, and businesswoman Sarah Miller could be the next target. Viewers hoping for a killing spree will be disappointed, as the story focuses on Sarah's relationships and dull office politics. Characters act weird just to create potential assassin candidates, and suspects include a company rival and a devoted assistant. Someone photographs Sarah and plants listening devices in her house, and it appears ex-cop Vincent Stirrup (Brent Stait) is the hitman when he leaves a mysterious package in the Millers' letterbox.

However, appearances can be deceptive, and ultimately it's revealed that Sarah is the hitwoman and Vincent a good guy tracking her. In retrospect, her odd behaviour – refusing to involve the police and caring more about a man's camera than an accident victim – makes perfect sense. Scenes of the protagonist working out, handling firearms capably, and throwing darts with lethal accuracy will seem obvious hints on a repeat viewing.

The female assassin dishes out a couple of martial arts beatdowns and gains the upper hand on her cover story family. The confrontation with the husband goes the obvious way when the villainess claims he doesn't have what it takes to squeeze the trigger. Fortunately, the assistant does, and the movie ends with Sarah receiving the same post-mortem photograph treatment she gave the opening victim.

All-American Murder (1991)
Tally Fuller (Josie Bissett)

Movie

Murder mysteries are tricky to cover as the villainess is not usually revealed until the end, so making the 101 list requires original elements, a great reveal, or a very entertaining movie. The main character of this darkly comic tale is Artie Logan (Charlie Schlatter), a social misfit with a long track record of getting kicked out of academic institutions. When he transfers to Fairfield College, people are naturally wary. Except for the dean's flirty wife, who quickly invites the newcomer into her bed.

Artie's life changes for the better when he meets Tally Fuller, who's possibly the ideal woman. Smart, attractive, respected, a star cheerleader on the team – all-American qualities to be sure. Artie and Tally soon become romantically involved, go on dates, and even share a spooky love scene in a graveyard. Their bliss was never going to last, though, considering the movie title. Sure enough, Tally is burned alive and thrown over a balcony while Artie looks on.

At least we're supposed to think it's Tally, but savvy mystery buffs will know that when corpses are charred beyond recognition, there's a good chance the dead person is somebody else. Which means the final act twist is not hard to guess if you have experience with murder mysteries. But before the "surprise" ending, we get an entertaining thriller, with more victims along the way.

The lead detective is P.J. Decker, played by Christopher Walken. In a major surprise, he's not the villain. Decker is unorthodox in his methods, as he ably shows when he provokes a criminal into violence and fires a disabling gunshot into the man's knee. Luckily for Artie, Decker believes his innocence plea and gives him twenty-four hours to prove it. Time for amateur detective work on campus, as Decker constantly turns up and reminds Artie how much time remains.

Villainess

What makes Tally more interesting than most villains, and my reason for including her on the ranking list, is the backstory that unfolds as Artie digs into her past. The image of the perfect all-American girl is eroded over the course of the film, with Tally revealed to be a drug-taking shoplifter who slept with the dean and star football player to get ahead. Most notably, the hero uncovers a videotape of Tally blackballing Wendy (a student helping Artie) out of the sorority and encouraging her fellow pledges to follow suit.

There are plenty of red herrings, from Tally's jealous boyfriend to the dean, who has many skeletons in his closet. And what mystery would be complete without a creepy janitor with a personal "shrine" to Tally in the basement? In the final half hour, the psychotic killer goes on a murder spree and whittles down the suspect list, racking up five victims before the denouement. This tests Decker's patience, and the supportive cop becomes increasingly uncertain of Artie's innocence.

First to die is the janitor, who gets a drill bit through the forehead after Artie confronts him. Three more victims follow in quick succession to liven things up. The murder methods are creative, with the most bizarre involving a snake left in a car that poisons and strangles the dean's wife. Not long after that, her equally unfortunate husband gets blown up with a hand grenade whilst working out. The scene where Artie discovers what's left of the body, and Decker finally arrests the obvious suspect, is straight out of a gory horror movie.

The ending is suitably climactic, with Wendy lured to a secluded location and attacked by the masked killer. Artie rushes to the rescue, but needs Decker to make a dramatic last-minute appearance to save him. Then the hero rips off the psycho's mask, revealing the supposedly deceased Tally as the murderess. This part is a disappointment, as the unmasking, while on-screen, happens all too quickly.

With the killer exposed, it's time for her motive rant. Tally had grown tired of being prominent, so wanted to disappear, but first needed to "remove" those who knew about her shady past. Tally – not quite done yet – attacks Artie with a blowtorch as she's being led away, but only burns her own face. Quite a karmic outcome, considering how Tally killed her double.

Honourable Mentions: Mystery Killers

Stringer (1992) – Sheila (Laura Reed)

Released in the US as *Prime Time Murder*, this mystery thriller features an all too obvious culprit, but at least the setup is more interesting than usual. Frank Simmonetti (Anthony Finetti) is the titular stringer, a freelance video reporter who sells footage to local TV networks. Prepared to risk his life to settle his debts, Frank scares off a rookie partner who doesn't enjoy being shot at. The "hero" has more success with Jack Mitchett (Tim Thomerson), an ex-cop not averse to dangerous action when the situation warrants it – such as confronting a shotgun-armed lunatic who's convinced his hostage is an alien. Crazy intro? It's that kind of movie.

Frank is determined to catch a serial killer who preys on homeless men and leaves poker chips by their bodies to signify moving on to a better life. Jack believes they're hunting a "compassionate" psycho who murders out of remorse, so maybe Frank shouldn't get too cosy with a charity worker named Sheila. Sally Kirkland has an extended cameo as a network editor, and suspicion falls on local beat cops who seem to hang around murder scenes. But there aren't many suspects, and Sheila is the only person who fits the profile.

After Jack gets attacked during a sting operation, Frank searches old videotapes for clues. Evicted and without his partner's support, he turns to Sheila for help. Since the person the hero trusts most is usually the killer in these films, it's no surprise Frank finds a recording of a shadowy figure wearing a telltale necklace. Sheila arrives and does the standard psycho routine: a crazed explanation before she stabs Frank in the chest. Then, the murderer cuts the phone line before her victim can raise the alarm.

The ending is worth waiting for – or at least fast-forwarding to – with Sheila and Frank in a prolonged struggle on the floor. She's on top holding a knife, while the wounded hero struggles to fend her off. Eventually, he knocks Sheila out and tosses away the weapon, but she comes back for another try when Frank makes it to the door. Then another cop shows up to finish the villainess off.

Whisper Kill (1988) – Winifred Rogers (June Lockhart)

Another mystery thriller with an interesting premise that elevates it above usual TV movie fare, *Whisper Kill* is about a serial killer who telephones their victims before they commit the murders. The main characters are newspaper reporters Dan Walker and Liz Bartlett, played by Joe Penny and Loni Anderson. After two men are stabbed, the hero establishes a connection between the victims and Liz, which makes her the prime suspect. Of course, that doesn't stop Dan from getting involved with a beautiful woman.

The ongoing whispered threats and murder scenes are the highlights, as the masked killer strikes in dark locations. The first victim is attacked after his sabotaged car breaks down, another dies near a phone booth in a park (probably the best kill of the bunch), and a sting operation goes horribly wrong when a third male receives the familiar back seat killer treatment.

There's an interesting subplot where Dan and Liz use phones at the same time the whisperer makes a call. But obvious people are rarely guilty in TV mysteries, and the "least likely culprit" rule applies. The murderer turns out to be Liz's mother, Winifred Rogers. Her motive is nuts, some nonsense about shielding Liz against the men in her life. Think your solution *might* be a tad extreme, Mom.

The anticlimax has the killer ditch her black outfit, gloves, and ski mask (for no apparent reason), and target Dan while wearing a blonde wig – all to fool him into thinking she's Liz. This seems pointless if Winnie planned to kill the reporter anyway and is arguably a lame excuse to trick viewers. We get a brief shootout as the local police chief comes to Dan's rescue... and that's it. Someday we'll get a great masked killer and reveal, but this is another letdown.

Rank #94

Mission: Impossible – Ghost Protocol (2011)
Sabine Moreau (Léa Seydoux)

Movie

Ghost Protocol is movie number four in the long-running spy franchise that started way back in 1996. Since then, the stunts have become increasingly extravagant and the stakes ever higher. In this outing, the Impossible Mission Force (IMF) led by Ethan Hunt (Tom Cruise) is after stolen nuclear launch codes (that old plot device). Extra complication: the agents were disavowed after a disastrous mission in Moscow.

This film is best remembered for an incredible sequence in (or rather outside) the iconic Burj Khalifa Hotel in Dubai, the world's tallest building at the time of filming. Tom Cruise performs his own death-defying stunts, climbing the skyscraper's exterior and swinging about on a cable. After those antics, whatever came next was always going to seem tame. But another highlight is a "double meeting" sequence where the IMF deceives a female assassin into handing over the all-important data.

Despite eight *Mission: Impossible* movies to date, the series has a poor track record for female villains.

Villainess

An agent makes a daring getaway, but lowers his guard as a seemingly innocent woman approaches. A fatal error in judgement, since the smartly dressed blonde is a remorseless contract killer who eliminates him with a silenced pistol. She retrieves important documents, later revealed to be the nuclear codes, which she plans to auction to interested terrorist parties. How's that for an opening sequence?

The murdered man had a partner called Agent Carter (not to be confused with the Marvel comic character), who arrived too late to save him. Naturally, she's out for revenge, and her personal stake adds more tension.

Like many low-ranked villainesses, Sabine doesn't have much screen time but makes a memorable impression. The aforementioned double meeting is imaginative and suspenseful. Agent Carter must pose as Sabine, and the hatred for the real assassin is clear. Meanwhile, Ethan and another male IMF agent impersonate terrorists and meet the real Sabine. This is all a complex ruse to acquire diamonds from the villains and purchase the launch codes.

Thankfully, none of the IMF agents wear a mask for this sequence. They planned to, but their latex face-generating machine broke down. A definite plus, as I felt this gambit was overused in previous instalments. But despite the commodity exchange going down without a hitch, Sabine discovers the IMF team are impostors when she spots a contact lens camera. Should have planted an old-fashioned bug, Ethan.

This leads to a confrontation between Agent Carter and Sabine in a corridor, with the assassin captured a little too easily. Fortunately for villainess fans, she escapes, and there's an exciting (if brief) fight between the two women.

Ultimately, Carter kicks the assassin through a smashed window. Since the location is the Burj Khalifa, it's a very long way down.

Honourable Mentions / Discussions: *Mission: Impossible* Franchise

Mission: Impossible (1996) – Claire (Emmanuelle Beart), Max (Vanessa Redgrave)

Probably the second-best movie in the franchise for female villains, not bad for a first attempt. This was a low-key affair compared to later IMF missions, with Ethan assembling a rogue team to steal a covert file from CIA Headquarters in Langley, Virginia. The "big" action set piece is Tom Cruise on a cable harness, albeit only a few metres above the pressure-sensitive data vault floor.

Nearly all the original IMF team wind up dead or are revealed to be traitors. This includes the deceptive Claire, who is disappointingly inactive for a field agent. While she detonates a car bomb to murder a fellow operative, this is only one possible version of events (shown in flashback), so her accurate body count may be zero. In the end, she's reduced to a woman that Ethan and the main turncoat bad guy, Jim Phelps, argue over. Then she gets shot, and that's it.

Redgrave is much better is the arms dealer Max, a menacing figure even if she does leave the muscle work to her bodyguards. In her introductory scene, she verbally fences with Ethan, coming across as humourous and threatening. Her subsequent appearances and arrest are anticlimactic, though.

Mission: Impossible II (2000)

This John Woo film is widely considered the worst in the franchise. With no female villains, there's not much to say here. The treatment of Thandie Newton's character is demeaning and hasn't aged well. She plays a thief, but rarely gets to show off any heisting skills. Insultingly, she's discovered by the bad guys because of her own incompetence after she makes a mistake no professional would. Eye candy with gratuitous sexualised shots, and a love interest who gets taken hostage. Ugh.

Mission: Impossible III (2006)

Improving on the lacklustre second movie wasn't hard, but the strong female characters in this entry were a pleasant surprise. Besides two IMF agents (Keri Russell and Maggie Q), Ethan's wife (Michelle Monaghan) also gets to play tough girl. Russell's character is killed early on, but Q is a natural action star and remains a presence throughout, involved in covert espionage and a big shootout on a traffic-jammed bridge.

No real female antagonists, sadly. An unnamed woman serves as a translator and head of security to the main baddie, but she's eliminated off-screen after failing him. This is only revealed when she's fitted with a mask to deceive Ethan into thinking his wife was the victim. Because her role is so brief, another character needs to remind us who she is.

Mission: Impossible – Rogue Nation (2015)

Before movie five, no female character had lasted more than one, but that changed with the badass Ilsa Faust (Rebecca Ferguson). An MI6 agent with her own agenda, she flips between assisting the IMF team and betraying them.

She excels as friend and foe – a skilled operative proficient in unarmed combat, firearms, and motorcycle chases.

The plot revolves around a mysterious organisation called The Syndicate (who comes up with these generic names?). And Ilsa looks the part whether she's infiltrating a classy opera, performing bike stunts, or prepping for an underwater heist.

Mission: Impossible – Fallout (2018) – The White Widow (Vanessa Kirby)

Ferguson returns as the mysterious MI6 agent. Once again, it's never clear whose side she's truly on as Ethan gets sucked into a scheme to free the main baddie from Rogue Nation.

As a bonus, there's also the White Widow, an arms dealer played by Vanessa Kirby. While her impact cannot rival the franchise's other Vanessa (Redgrave from the first film), it's implied the women are related. More shady than villainous, but we'll take it.

Mission: Impossible – Dead Reckoning Part One (2023) – **Paris (Pom Klementieff)**

An extended honourable mention for the seventh entry, which gives us Paris, a crazy assassin who speaks French (appropriately), wears face paint, and brings a sword cane to public venues.

By now, Ethan has saved the world six times. Time to go up against an old nemesis who murdered his first love… and an artificial intelligence with a God complex. Everyone but the hero thinks they can control the mysterious "Entity" that communicates through sinister blue pulsing circles. As daft as they sound, these images show up everywhere from secret US intelligence briefings to a Venetian nightclub party.

The central plot device is a cruciform key in two halves that unlocks the original source code on a sunken Russian submarine. The keys change hands so often it's a miracle they don't get lost entirely. Usually, it's pickpocket Grace (newcomer Hayley Atwell) who steals the precious gold crosses from under her rivals' noses. She becomes the latest IMF recruit when they need a woman to impersonate the White Widow.

As for Ilsa Faust, she returns to assist Ethan and gets a little too close for her own good. After faking her death in the Middle East, chief baddie Gabriel kills her off for real. A disappointing exit for a standout character, even if Grace is a capable replacement operative during the Orient Express finale.

Paris' first appearance establishes her as dangerous when she threatens a guy with a concealed pistol. From then on, she's often a silent enforcer in the background while Gabriel does the talking. But when situations call for it, she goes crazy and kills people.

In Rome, Ethan and Grace are chased by Italian police and American agents, but Paris – in a hijacked armoured vehicle – is the primary threat. With no regard for subtlety, this woman enjoys creating carnage, demolishing any parked vehicles in the way. It takes a dramatic reverse escape through a narrow tunnel to shake her off.

Not a woman you want to meet in a dark alley, so pity Ethan when that situation unfolds in Venice. Lured into a trap, he's attacked my a male thug – who doesn't last long – and the female assassin. Fortunately, Paris can't swing her sword in the narrow space, but she's still a dangerous unarmed combatant. Her attacks are furious and relentless. Until Ethan knocks her down, grabs a metal pole, and...

spares her life. Yes, we're headed down that familiar redemption path.

But Paris hasn't converted to good – or even neutral – just yet. She jumps from a bridge onto a moving train, disables an engineer, and visits the US Director of Intelligence. His security men frisk her, but this deadly woman doesn't need weapons to eliminate them. Gabriel chats to the American, then murders him. And turns on Paris because the Entity warned of her betrayal. Ever heard of a self-fulfilling prophecy?

The female assassin escapes death, only to return and save Ethan and Grace in a literal train wreck ending. Perhaps there's a metaphor there, because Paris was a near-perfect female villain until the last act.

Mission: Impossible – The Final Reckoning (2025)

In reality, this is *Dead Reckoning Part Two*, a supposed final outing that ties up loose ends from previous instalments. A minor character from the original vault heist returns as a seasoned CIA operative in Alaska. We also say farewell to Luther, who's been a team member since the beginning.

Things are more ridiculous than ever before. Ethan retrieves the source code from the sunken Russian sub, swims naked through ice-cold Arctic waters, then Grace revives him with a kiss of life. Averting nuclear Armageddon, the heroes defeat the all-seeing AI by capturing it in a plastic container. Reality was never a series strong point.

Other than a prison scene where Hunt springs her, Paris is a good girl. She sees a fair bit of action, notably a battle with Russian commandos in an arctic safehouse and the climax at an underground doomsday vault. Quite telling that in an action movie with strong female characters all over the place, women can command aircraft carriers, be secret service agents who save the life of Angela Bassett's President, but there are no female villains at all.

49

Rank #93

Crime Lords (1991)
Jennifer Monahan (Susan Byun)

Movie

In summary, a generic action movie with an equally generic plot. Two Los Angeles cops, grizzled veteran Elmo Lagrange (Wayne Crawford) and his womanising partner Peter Russo (Martin Hewitt), have little in common, except for a boss they both dislike. Because of that, they're assigned unglamorous duties as car theft investigators. That doesn't stop the duo from getting into a world of trouble, however, and they soon uncover a crime ring with links to Hong Kong (still a Crown Colony of the UK back then).

During a chop shop raid, there's an all guns blazing shootout, and Lagrange pursues a female villain down a dark alley. He doesn't get a good enough look at the mystery woman to identify her, but does land face first on her tattooed thigh. No time for gawking, pervert, and the smitten cop only narrowly avoids a fatal gunshot before the high-heeled villainess makes her escape.

Not willing to accept the resulting suspension, the two partners jet off to Hong Kong on an unofficial visit to get some payback. There, they have a few misadventures, including detention at the airport for bringing in a firearm, and a run-in with some muggers (including a female, though it's only a minor role). Much of the action is amateurish, with questionable camera angles and shoddy editing. But the last half-hour – where Monahan becomes the primary adversary – is worth it for villainess fans.

With no money or place to stay, the heroes find themselves "guests" in a police cell until they're bailed out by the shifty Inspector Thornberry. No surprise he has organised crime connections, which includes prime suspect Ling (James Hong) who Russo recognises from the US chop shop. Then we're formally introduced to the villainess. Officially, Monahan is Ling's translator, but clearly she's far more involved in the criminal operation.

Villainess

The two heroes fall out (would it be a buddy cop story otherwise?), leading to an encounter between Lagrange and a muscular henchman armed with a cut-throat razor. He's your typical heavy who doesn't speak much, the kind of guy villains send to deal with bothersome cops. Meanwhile, Russo does some detective work before he gets caught snooping. Confronted by Ling and Monahan, Russo acts the corrupt cop, but his ploy is hardly convincing.

Time to find out what Russo knows, so Monahan plays the charming seductress. Once she's through with the flirting and questions, the villainess leaves Russo in the care of a masseuse with an evil expression. Russo should have paid more attention to those vibes, since the razor-blade henchman creeps up behind and collects his ear as a trophy.

Monahan has no qualms about dating older men, since she also seduces Lagrange to find out what *he* knows. Fortunately, Lagrange is more switched on than his partner, and he catches the deceptive charmer in a lie after she claims Russo returned to America. Too bad she forgot about the time zone difference when she forged the fax. Monahan convinces Lagrange she's not a bad person (!) with a ludicrous claim she's working undercover, and they end up in bed. Then the "stupid" cop pulls down his lover's stocking, and the telltale thigh tattoo gives her away. A candidate for the most unorthodox reveal of all time?

Lagrange punches out the villainess, but perhaps he should have killed her, as this woman is too ambitious to remain an underling. After the resourceful cop escapes a sniper attack and defeats Mr Cut Throat with help from a teenage girl, it's time to rescue Russo from the bad girl's clutches. Lagrange witnesses just how ruthless Monahan is when she executes a criminal with a headshot.

Uncovering a plot to smuggle gold out of Hong Kong disguised as car parts, the heroes must contend with Ling, Thornberry, and a small army of thugs. That's until Monahan decides to go into business for herself and eliminate her former partners. It's fitting that she's the last villain standing, because she always came across as a key player and Ling as a figurehead.

There's a decent standoff between the villainess and Lagrange, but the ending lacks tension. The hostage teen makes an easy escape, prompting Monahan to jump into a vehicle and chase her quarry. Thanks to active sprinklers and wide camera shots, we don't see the villainess' face often, perhaps because it's a stunt driver behind the wheel. The scene ends with Monahan getting shot, leading to the expected crash and explosion.

Honourable Mentions: Gang Leaders

No Code of Conduct (1998) – Shi (Tina Nguyen)

Another female gang boss I considered for my list (she only just missed out), Shi takes no nonsense from either her underlings or pesky cops. The plot of this direct-to-video action thriller is average, with Martin and Charles Sheen (real-life father/son) as er... a father and son detective duo. They have to deal with violent criminals, corrupt police officers, and government officials. The usual antagonists, then.

Shi's best scene is a shootout outside a motel where she eliminates an undercover vice cop and takes on an approaching unmarked car with a handgun. Unflinching – this is one badass female villain. If that's not enough, there's also a lengthy vehicle chase where the heroes pursue a van through narrow alleyways, while Shi leans out of the passenger door and takes potshots. Plus a torture scene where the villainess threatens a kidnapped woman and shows absolutely no mercy.

The main negative: Shi appears timid when talking to her businessman boss, completely out of character for an underworld enforcer. And the final gun battle, where she's taken down by a single headshot, is poor quality compared to earlier action sequences, with barely any buildup before it's all over.

Avarice (2022) – Reed (Alexandra Nell)

An Australian home invasion thriller with standard plot elements, plus the added gimmick of a physically fit, trained competition archer as the protagonist. A great skill set (and weapon) to have when your husband is taken hostage by mercenaries led by a ruthless woman.

The movie offers no major surprises. The two "hidden" bad guys are so obvious they don't even hide it, and it's a full hour before the heroine Kate Matthews (Gillian Alexy) takes up her trusty bow. From that point on, the action is relentless. After Kate dispatches a couple of thugs with precision arrows, their leader Reed kills Kate's father just to make a point. The villains are after money (what else?), and in the modern electronic era, that doesn't require a bank vault raid.

Reed is a threatening presence, practically oozing nastiness in every scene she dominates. Technically, she's a hired thug too, but doesn't hesitate to "fire" her boss when he becomes a liability. It was always going to end in an ultimate confrontation between the two women, but it's all over far too quickly. And of course it's a last-ditch grab for an arrow to make the last kill. Despite the drawbacks, it's a pleasant surprise to find a good – if not great – villainess in a modern action movie.

Rank #92

Sudden Death (1995)
Carla (Faith Minton)

Movie

Of the many *Die Hard* scenario movies I've seen, *Sudden Death* is one of the craziest, but undeniably fun. The premise was unoriginal even back in the 1990s: a lone hero trapped in a building with nasty bad guys, and the only person who can save the day.

Our hero is Darren McCord, played by Jean-Claude Van Damme (a mainstream action star at the time), and the setting is a National Hockey League Stanley Cup Finals game in Pittsburgh. The Vice President is a Penguins fan, so the criminals take advantage and infiltrate the event disguised as employees. Then they occupy the VP's box and demand he transfer vast sums of money from secret accounts before the game ends. Naturally, a dramatic late goal ties the contest and buys some much-needed sudden-death overtime.

It's an overused storyline, but *Sudden Death* has set pieces on its side. Villain deaths are all suitably over the top, often involving Darren using his skills as a firefighter, a job he quit after a young girl tragically died. Makeshift weapons include a flamethrower (a water pistol filled with flammable liquid) and a dart gun fire extinguisher.

In a totally insane sequence late on, Darren dresses up as a Pittsburgh Penguins player and skates onto the rink. Heck, he even makes a dramatic save. Then, a helicopter falls vertically through the open stadium roof and explodes on the ice. But the hero's fight against the "killer penguin" – a henchwoman in a mascot costume – is the standout scene. And despite a premature demise, I simply had to include this villainess on my ranking list.

Villainess

The actress has a wrestling and stunts background, so looks the part of the brutish henchwoman. She makes an intimidating choice and is convincing in her fight scenes, compared to the frail beauties that populate modern action films.

Other than the infamous penguin encounter, Carla doesn't feature much. Her first two kills – the real mascot Joan (who later turns up dead in a closet) and an inquisitive woman in the women's restroom – both occur offscreen. Darren's daughter, Emily, stumbles across the villainess' latest victim when she leaves her stadium seat. The terrified girl flees before Carla can silence her, only to be captured moments later.

Emily watches the sociopath villainess shoot a Secret Service agent in the head (after he understandably mistakes Carla for a guy) and put several more bullets in his chest to make sure. The terrorist has already shown she has no problem murdering a child, and only an empty pistol clip saves Emily from execution.

After Carla delivers her young hostage to the main bad guy, she's sent after Darren. This doesn't take long, as he's tracked Emily to the kitchen. He's already suspicious after finding his daughter's discarded baseball cap, and Carla's lies are unconvincing. With the hero alert to danger, he spots the shadow of Carla drawing a gun and disarms her.

The fight scene between Darren and the "killer penguin" lasts over three minutes for those timing it. While Carla's choice of costume is bizarre, the padding offers substantial protection from Darren's punches. The villainess, skilled in martial arts, lands quite a few blows of her own. Kitchens are always a great location for fights, with sharp cleavers, boiling fat, and trolleys to use as weapons. Don't forget the tray, potato masher, and meat cutter. Did I mention this is a long fight?

Fed up with Carla shrugging off his attacks, Darren adopts the video game approach and goes for her weak spot. The hero pours spicy food into the mascot's beak where the eyeholes are, disorienting Carla to gain the upper hand. Tough women never go down that easily, so Carla gets a great death scene when Darren kicks her onto a processing machine. The mask strap gets caught around her neck, strangling the villainess as the hero watches on.

Honourable Mentions: Van Damme Movies

Timecop (1994) – Fielding (Gloria Reuben)

This is a mainstream Van Damme movie about a time-travelling policeman, mostly set in modern times. Among the bad guys is a sole henchwoman with one decent scene and little screen time. Sarah Fielding is an internal affairs agent working with the hero. Except she isn't, because she's in the pocket of a corrupt US senator. Not sure why the traitor is so shocked when the lead bad guy murders someone in cold blood. Wake up – you're expendable too.

Fielding beats up Walker in a one-sided encounter. He drops the chivalrous "won't fight a woman" line, but knocks her down with one punch, anyway. The senator shoots Fielding once she's outlived her usefulness, and the repentant traitor reflects in hospital before another baddie kills her.

Eventually, Walker restores the timeline, and Fielding becomes a good girl, so none of that ever happened. An honourable mention… just about.

Kill'em All (2017) – **Almira (Mila Kali)**

Perhaps the ultimate "one-scene wonder", Almira is the only positive in this direct to video actioner. In an establishing flashback, the sexy female assassin poses as a prostitute and displays a fair amount of skin. The beautiful killer uses a blade-on-a-rope (disguised as a wristband) to stab a crime boss in the chest, leap over his chair, and garrote him. Not finished, Almira defeats two bodyguards hand to hand (or should that be legs to neck?).

A terrific beginning with so much promise, but what follows is terrible. Hardly any action and a silly plot with Van Damme pitted against a hit squad in a hospital, told in flashback by a nurse. The civilian supposedly has martial arts experience, but you wouldn't know it from the badly choreographed fight scenes. Almira's death is a lame, almost comical, strangulation.

Except the "nurse" is really an operative or assassin herself (the explanation is vague), and an unreliable narrator. The actual death scene – shown later on – has the impostor kill Almira with a far more efficient neck snap. So, a slight improvement, but not much.

Derailed (2002) – **Galina Konstantin (Laura Elena Harring)**

Another low-budget action flick with Van Damme (he's

made a few), this features three female villains, though only one of note. The extended honourable mention goes to the antiheroine thief who assists the good guys despite her own self-serving agenda. A stealth expert and martial artist, Galina is a far more charismatic character than this movie deserves.

Jacques Kristoff (Van Damme) is the main hero, but the female cat burglar takes centre stage during the opening credits. Between black screen title cards, we're treated to a daring heist with the hi-tech operative deceiving guards in Slovakia and breaking into a supposedly secure facility. After three minutes of thievery clips and fancy gadget use, Galina steals a metal box marked with a biohazard symbol. It's a while until we learn the vials contained within hold a smallpox viral strain, and before that there's the matter of escaping the authorities.

A shady contact assigns Jacques the job of escorting Galina to Germany. Her cover is a theatrical performer, and she even pulls off a high-wire stunt to evade a small army of troops. More acrobatics follow with a light show as a backdrop, then Van Damme finally sees some action. The exit route is a train (you probably guessed that from the title). Once aboard, the sexy thief tries to seduce Jacques in the cabin, but he's wise enough – and devoted to his wife – to refuse her advances.

The passengers soon have far greater concerns when armed mercenaries take over the train and come after Galina and her mysterious package. These are cookie-cutter villains who murder unarmed civilians to show their nastiness, led by a bland guy called Mason. Jacques and Galina escape, setting up the usual *Die Hard* scenario. The burglar uses more acrobatic moves to subdue a terrorist, but nothing as fantastic as the opening theft.

The lead villain has a lover accomplice called Natasha

(the usual mean sadist), and after some background smirks, we get the inevitable catfight with Galina. Jacques battles a male baddie, but instead of annoying cuts between the two fights, we get a bizarre split-screen showdown. Too bad the women only exchange a few blows and it's over in thirty seconds.

A vial shatters during a scuffle, contaminating the train. What follows is a convoluted mess with weak action, bad special effects, and passengers looking gloomy as the virus spreads. Mason kills Natasha for her incompetence (so much for love), which leaves an unnamed female terrorist for Jacques to dispose of far too easily.

The unsatisfying conclusion has Galina ill with smallpox and sidelined for the final action scenes. Van Damme, of course, saves the day and miraculously cures the passengers. As for Galina, she goes back to thievery and pulls off a (sadly low-tech) heist in the closing scene.

Rank #91

S.W.A.T.: *Under Siege* (2017)
Simone (Monique Ganderton), Ellen Dwyer (Adrianne Palicki)

Movie

What it "says on the tin" basically – a S.W.A.T. team under siege. Who would have guessed? Expecting to recover drugs on a joint raid with the DEA, things get complicated when they discover a chained-up prisoner with a scorpion tattoo on his back. And even messier when mercenary villains, led by the suave Lars and his ruthless lieutenant Simone, want to capture "Scorpion" because he has valuable information.

It's established early on that there's an insider when a mystery caller offers to give up Scorpion for fifty million dollars. Lars would rather spend money on his private jet and henchmen, so he decides to take Scorpion by force. Since the traitor uses a voice disguiser and many female operatives are on the team (close to a 50/50 split), there's a good chance of a second villainess besides the obvious Simone.

And indeed there is, although there are two traitors on the S.W.A.T. team (and that tired excuse of police work not paying well), with the caller revealed to be male. A clever subversion of the expected trope, but don't get too disheartened because the final villain is a woman. The subplot mystery of who's feeding the baddies information works well, maintaining the tension in between the frantic action.

Villainess – Simone

Ganderton has a martial arts and stunts background, and so is believable in her fight scenes. These don't happen until the last third of the movie, but the actress performs well in dialogue-heavy scenes and comes across as menacing. The occasional sinister smile when required, and her body language suggest a woman with no problem killing anyone who interferes.

A male hacker gets too distracted by the beautiful henchwoman (with her semi-revealing black leather top, who can blame him?), and Simone quickly establishes her authority by rubbing his shoulders. Sounds sexy, but her toying behaviour makes him uncomfortable. Simone's best non-action moment comes when she threatens their S.W.A.T. team's families unless they surrender Scorpion. Her evil smirk afterwards is pure gold.

Monique's most memorable scene is the inevitable catfight with Ellen Dwyer, a federal agent working with the cops. The two women hold nothing back, and Fiorentine doesn't ruin action by cutting away. The uninterrupted fight lasts approximately a minute, and the two combatants are evenly matched. Ellen gets the upper hand, but she's knocked out from behind before she can finish Simone off.

The villainess returns to fight the male hero Travis with a baton and becomes a nearly unstoppable whirlwind of fury. Sadly, this scene *is* interrupted, and the action flips between another confrontation between Scorpion and Lars. After her decent contribution, Simone gets a mediocre death scene when she charges Travis and he sends her flying off the roof.

Villainess – Ellen Dwyer

Lead female Ellen is characterised as badass fairly early on, equally proficient on the firing range as taking on male opponents unarmed. The skilled agent shows markmanship and fighting skills before her villainous reveal. As noted above, she's mole number two, but the overly confident male turncoat outlives his worth and Lars cuts his losses.

Viewers who paid attention to the pre-credits sequence, where an unknown assailant attacked Travis in a forest, will already suspect Ellen. Since that scene hasn't happened ten minutes from the end, and only one person is alive besides Travis and Scorpion, it's not a great shock Ellen is indeed working with the bad guys.

This leads to a gun battle where Ellen recovers a microchip with Scorpion's data, and a chase through the aforementioned forest. Adrianne Palicki is surprisingly physical in her tussle with the hero and lasts a little longer than expected before she's disarmed and arrested.

Honourable Mentions
Theme: Mercenary Henchwomen / Traitors

The Package (2013) – Monique (Monique Ganderton)

No, it's not a typo. Monique Ganderton plays a henchwoman who shares her first name, which sums up the lack of imagination in this mundane action thriller. With B-movie heavyweights Steve Austin and Dolph Lundgren as a debt collector and criminal underworld boss, badass moments as expected, but generic gun battles hardly set the pulses racing. There's an unneeded romantic subplot with a woman who just gets forgotten, and the final fight between the two leads is an anticlimax.

A mercenary group *really* wants the titular package, enough to cause carnage in small-town America with civilians caught in the deadly crossfire. Monique, a thankful highlight, is a sadistic interrogator with a beef against the hero after he kills her fiancé. Bad move, considering she's a torture enthusiast who murders a disposable henchman with a head scissors move to show off.

After spending most of the movie talking on the radio, Monique finally gets in on the action. She tests out various sharp blades before opting to choke her prisoner with a garrote. Her eagerness to exact revenge on the hero proves her undoing, allowing him to escape, and the villainess dies in a blink-and-miss-it shootout. Still, it's another memorable tough-girl role for an actress who seems to specialise in them.

Gridlocked (2015) – Gina (Trish Stratus)

Another action-packed tale about a police unit under siege, this one features Dominic Purcell as a tough cop babysitting a bad boy actor. Except his community service turns deadly when armed criminals raid a remote training facility. Vinnie Jones shows up as a villain (what else?) and Danny Glover plays another guy "too old for this shit." A welcome cameo before he bites the dust halfway through.

No romance to distract us from the gun battles and fight scenes. Gina rejects the actor's sleazy advances, and the actress' wrestling background makes her a convincing action heroine. Back in the 1980s and 1990s, a lone female in a testosterone fest would always end up being good, rescued by the hero in exchange for evidence. These days, said scenario means she *can* be evil, even if Gina wastes a few minor baddies to fool us.

After pretending to be heroic all film, the greedy woman betrays her fellow officers for… yes, money. She frames an innocent cop as the mole and explains her motives before she bumps him off. After Gina's reveal and failed attempt on the actor's life, a brutal fight ensues. This tough woman shrugs off attacks that would fell lesser foes, including a gunshot to the face. But the unlikely hero gets the better of the treacherous cop, and a second headshot proves decisive.

U.S. Seals II: The Ultimate Force (2001) – Sophia (Sophia Crawford)

Patriotic nonsense with American military heroes, but Isaac Fiorentine as director usually heralds above-average action and enjoyable hokum. Former U.S. SEAL Casey Sheppard (Michael Worth) leads a team of misfits against an ex-colleague who betrayed him. Haven't we seen this plot somewhere before?

A *Dirty* Dozen-style setup, with an ex-convict, Japanese civilian Kamiko (Karen Kim), and mercenary assassin coaxed into service to foil the standard nuclear weapon extortion plot. The villain's island base is contaminated with explosive methane, a convenient excuse to ditch firearms and focus on martial arts and swordplay.

Some impressive fights, but no shocker the team gets wiped out – save the two leads – or the greedy merc betrays Casey for a more lucrative pay offer. Plus points for having the henchwoman involved in the action. From the very start, when Sophia snaps a sentry's neck to show her strength, she's never far from the main villain's side. The tough woman forgets about the explosive threat when she slices open a vent shaft with her katana. All brawn and no brains?

Kamiko is established as a swordswoman herself early on, and thus it's inevitable that she and Sophia will face off. Their lengthy fight has some cutaways to other action, but thankfully the last section is unbroken. The women prove worthy opponents until Kamiko triumphs, slaying the villainess with an acrobatic backward thrust.

Rank #90

Exposure (2001)
Anne (Susan Pari)

Movie

Quite a few direct-to-video movies made my list, including this one with Alexandra Paul (of *Baywatch* fame) in a supporting role. Photographer Gary Whitford (Ron Silver) sets off a deadly chain of events when he discovers a beautiful woman sheltering on his property. She's wrapped in orange fishnet, which triggers flashbacks to Gary's dark past as a war correspondent. Back then, a brutal military regime executed his lover and left her body wrapped up in... take a guess.

The trespasser is Elaine Drury, a legal secretary played by Susan Pari. Yes, the same actress as the villainess. This is one of those "evil twin" twists to fool the audience and cut down on expenditure. The reveal in this film works better than most, since the bad sister remains a constant threat throughout.

Before the well-choreographed encounters between Gary and the mysterious hooded psycho, there's an intriguing setup where he and his friend Paul persuade Elaine to become a fashion model. For extra spice, Gary has an intimate history with Paul's wife, Jackie (Alexandra Paul's character). Do thriller heroes ever have normal relationships?

After someone murders Elaine and leaves a message in blood referring to the "Holy Trinity", Gary finds himself targeted by the psycho who clearly didn't approve of the victim's modelling career. The dead woman's boyfriend, Brad, serves as a red herring, though it's obvious he doesn't fit the religious angle. Evil twin reveal incoming.

Villainess

Keeping with the religious theme, a mysterious woman leaves a note in a Catholic confession booth. Then the preachy lunatic murders Paul in his office and makes several attempts on Gary's life. The best of the bunch is a knife attack in a deserted parking garage.

The villainess targets Jackie, and after a lengthy fight, the killer is unmasked as Elaine's twin sister, Anne. The devout Christian's parents disowned her after Elaine's picture appeared on an advertising billboard, and the deranged Anne became convinced it was the devil's work. Which led to her killing spree.

After the priest recounts the story to Gary and Jackie, he becomes expendable, so it's no surprise the psycho slasher kills him moments later. The contrived finale has the stalked couple split up for no reason other than dramatic tension. Like all worthy villainesses, Anne proves difficult to defeat. There's a fantastic moonlit lake encounter where Jackie thinks she's drowned the murderer, only for her to resurface and resume the attack.

Anne tracks Gary to the same shed where he found Elaine, and the villainess becomes the third woman in this movie to get wrapped in a fishnet. Talk about telegraphing the outcome. With Anne entangled and weighed down, Gary pushes her into the lake. No miraculous recovery this time.

Honourable Mentions: Knife Attacks

Primal Doubt (2007) – Marianne Thorne (Jamie Rose)

Another movie with a masked, knife-wielding psycho, but a few decent moments weren't enough to earn it a ranking slot. Yet another story where an unhappily married woman arranges an ill-fated date, a plot any Lifetime devotee will know only too well. The outcome is more unpredictable than normal, as the guy isn't the villain. Instead, someone slits his throat, and it appears the cancelled date was the motive.

While the angry husband is an obvious suspect, the opening murder featured a hooded figure who looked distinctly feminine. After the assailant slices up the best friend in an office (seen as silhouettes through a murky glass door, arguably the best kill scene), the only genuine candidate is the heroine's psychiatrist, Dr Marianne Thorne.

Other than that, the movie is average. It doesn't help that the main character is so unlikable and refuses to admit she was cheating. The villainess' reveal is a mess, too. The masked Marianne murders an assistant, only to appear unmasked in a different outfit a minute later.

To add insult to injury, it's clearly not Jamie Rose under the balaclava. Differences in eye colour and skin complexion suggest a stunt double took her place. The ending is a clichéd stinker, with the police coming to the rescue at the last moment.

Ultimate Desire (1993) – Adrienne (Mary Stavin)

In a new review for this compilation, I first watched this movie back when Channel 5 (UK) aired uncut erotic thrillers on Friday nights. Unfortunately, the sexy villainess times are long gone.

Restored in wide-screen format for streaming services, the film is far tamer than I remember. A serial killer stabs topless, blindfolded women and douses their bodies in expensive perfume named *Desire*. The exotic MO provides a novel twist, but the murders are bland and bloodless, with the psychotic slasher reduced to a shadow on the wall.

Perfume magnate Grace Lantel (Deborah Shelton) isn't happy some lunatic is tarnishing her brand, but fortunately her security consultant Lauren (Kate Hodge) is an ex-cop. The prime suspect is Gordon Lewis (Martin Kemp) who has a revenge motive, British accent, and a letter opener that resembles the murder weapon. Lauren's police liaison thinks he's guilty, but it's too obvious, surely?

The actual murderer is a shop assistant who appeared in three quick scenes. Her nonsensical motive: she was a former employee of Grace and loved her. After Adrienne stabs her ex-boss, she attacks Lauren. A decent climatic catfight, demise, and stunt balcony fall. Compared to the low-budget tripe that infests TV movies today, that merits an honourable mention.

Rank #89

Nothing Underneath (1985)
Barbara (Renee Simonsen)

Movie

A scissor killer targets fashion models in this Italian giallo, also known as *Sotto il vestito niente*. It's *another* movie where the ending is the best part, and the super creepy villainess shines in the denouement. Bob Crane is a Wyoming park ranger, and his twin sister Jessica has travelled overseas to become a model. The siblings have a psychic connection, and Bob can sense whenever Jessica's in danger.

When he "sees" a black-gloved, scissor-wielding psycho head towards his sister's hotel room, he panics. Despite Bob's best efforts, he fails to warn Jessica and so travels to Milan to investigate. The psychic device is messy because it's never explained why Bob sees things from the killer's perspective when his mental link is with Jessica. Obviously, the filmmakers need to hide the assailant's identity, but this could have been handled better .

With no body, Bob has trouble convincing Commissioner Danesi (Donald Pleasance taking a hiatus from the *Halloween* series) that his sister is dead. Until the scissor attacker offs a second model in her hotel bathroom. The suspects include an abusive lover who knew the models, and a weird photographer employed in the fashion world. But any mystery fan knows the answer is rarely so obvious.

Villainess

The real killer is another fashion model, whose earlier gym workout established her as physically capable. Barbara is clever and resourceful, seducing Bob to discover what he's learned. And there's a "bluff" where the supposed victim gets nervous when someone loiters outside her room. Savvy viewers won't be so easily deceived, especially those who notice a long-haired feminine figure hiding behind a clothes rack during the third murder scene.

The gloved killer stole diamonds from the second victim's room, apparently the connection as the latest dead model also has a valuable gem stash. These are revealed to be payoffs to cover up an ill-advised game of Russian roulette, which went horribly wrong. With an increasing chance of death every time a suicidal woman pulls the trigger and five "players", it was likely somebody would bite the dust. Guess these fashion models are greedy *and* stupid.

The stolen gemstones are a red herring, however. Barbara's actual motive is that Jessica became distant after the fatal shooting, and now the psychotic woman wants revenge on the models and host responsible. Barbara copies Jessica's handwriting and sends a fake telegram while disguised as her dead lover. This fools Bob for a while, and he's about to fly back to America when he experiences psychic visions of an apartment building.

Shortly after Bob locates the killer's lair, Barbara returns and reveals herself as the murderer. The creepy villainess has kept Jessica's corpse nailed to a chair and even talks to the body. But it's not long before the psycho model discovers Bob and attempts to kill him off. In the final sequence, Barbara exchanges her scissors for a power drill. The DIY tool becomes a deadly weapon in her hands, especially since Bob injured himself on the way in.

The wounded Bob evades Barbara's attacks by dodging and throwing items, fending the strong woman off until she pins him down. As she's about to drill a hole in his face, Danesi arrives and disconnects the power. With Barbara disarmed and outnumbered, she decides tragic suicide is the only way out and pushes Jessica's chair-nailed corpse through a window. Music plays in the background as events conclude in slow motion, and surely Barbara deserved a better ending than this.

Honourable Mentions: Model Serial Killers

Evil Obsession (1996) – Liz (Stacie Randall)

This direct-to-video thriller features prominent B-movie actors, including Brion James as a tyrannical acting coach who might just be a psychopath. Corey Feldman stars as crazy fan Homer, who sends love letters in crayon to actress Margo (Kimberly Stevens). Worried for her safety – justifiable when twelve models have been slain in Los Angeles – she hires a private detective.

The murderer binds their victims with medical rubber tubing, removes their underwear with a scalpel, and dissects them on an operating table. So, when receptionist Liz tells the PI her father was a doctor, it's a major clue. The male stalker has a creepy shrine to Margo, but no reason to slay the other victims. In the end, he's revealed to be a harmless nutcase, and the detective races to save Margo from the killer's blade.

The climax is uninspired, since we see Margo lured to

the acting studio, and in her next scene, she's being prepped for invasive surgery. No real confrontation, just a single fatal gunshot from the detective. Then the "surgeon" is unmasked as Liz. Lack of a confessed motive makes for a refreshingly different resolution, and viewers are provided with enough details to infer Liz was jealous of successful actresses and models.

Murder in Miami (2014) – Rachael (Caroline Gutierrez)

More model slayings in this low-budget thriller, and oddball photographer James Romero (Joseph Myers) is the suspect. The pre-credits murder, where a black-cloaked intruder bludgeons a woman with a baton and tosses her off a high-rise balcony, is the best part of the film. Before the half-way point, there's a shower attack homage to Hitchcock's *Psycho,* and a lesbian bondage session that ends with a double murder. The topless host is strangled and her tied-up subject gets a kitchen knife through her vagina (!).

All the death scenes are heavy on nudity but light on gore, with cutaway shots and implied violence. The second half is a padded-out snoozefest. Naked women galore, and overlong stock footage transitions that must waste ten minutes in total. Watching trees and buildings is mind-numbing, and the murder storyline gets forgotten for a silly subplot involving drug dealers who supplied the victims.

When James teams up with a woman called Rachael, there are no more killings. Figured it out yet? Rachael plays the helpful assistant and sidekick to James' amateur sleuth, only to get kidnapped late on. Next up is a "comedy" scene where a chain of people shoot each other, only to get a bullet themselves. When the juvenile stuff is over, Rachael unmasks herself and provides a weak motive that suddenly makes a minor character important. James takes down the villainess with a single gunshot, the last action before the credits roll.

Rank #88

G.I. Joe: The Rise of Cobra (2009)
Ana / Baroness (Sienna Miller)

Movie

A few villainesses covered so far have notable finales in their respective movies, but dull lead-ins. *The Rise of Cobra* has the opposite problem: a strong opening that establishes the Baroness as a powerhouse to be reckoned with, but a weak conclusion where she switches sides.

The overall tone is a blend of flashy action and science fiction, bordering on fantasy. An arms manufacturer develops a nanobot warhead that eats through metal (and produces evil green smoke as a byproduct). Just the weapon any terrorist would want in their arsenal, so the evil organisation Cobra sends in a commando team led by a brunette in black leather.

The movie essentially serves as an origin story, with a lot of time spent introducing various characters and their backstories. Macho military man Duke once knew the villainess as the blonde Ana. Naturally, these two have a tragic romantic history, and were engaged until her brother was killed on a mission Duke led. And now she hates his guts.

Thankfully, an elite unit known as the G.I. Joes arrives to save Duke's ass. These guys (and one gal called Scarlet) wear high-tech armour and carry futuristic weapons, and want Duke to join them. He accepts the offer and learns Ana is now an elite Cobra operative known as the Baroness. One of many codenames in this enjoyable, over the top adventure.

Villainess

The Baroness as a physical badass, and the forest encounter is only the first of her skirmishes with the good guys. Whether dual-wielding sonic pistols or kickboxing in her stylish leather outfit, this woman is more than a match for Duke and his crew.

A key figure in the Cobra hierarchy, the villains entrust her with their most important missions. When she leads an infiltration team into the Joes' base, she takes on Scarlet in a surprisingly intelligent and well-staged fight. Even with optical camouflage, the heroine loses to a combination of wits and martial arts. Despite Duke's best efforts, the Baroness escapes with the warheads. This round goes to Cobra.

The villainess has a double life as a lavishly dressed noblewoman (hence her title) and devoted wife of a scientist. This is a ruse to gain access to his laboratory, and the operative proves a mistress of deception. Once hubby has activated the warheads, he's of no further value to Cobra, so they eliminate him. Never trust a beautiful woman in black.

The standout action set piece is a chase through Paris, where Duke and his partner pursue a vehicle on foot. That's made possible by "jumping" suits that enhance their athletic ability, leading to an entertaining if silly sequence with car crashes and explosions. Females don't get sidelined in modern action movies, so it's no surprise Scarlet rides a motorcycle through Parisian landmarks. Think you're a badass? The Baroness controls missiles and an EMP gun!

Duke chases his ex to a rooftop extraction point while she fires an automatic rifle (and smashes every glass window in sight). That gives Storm Shadow (the evil ninja in white) the opportunity to launch a nanobot warhead at the Eiffel Tower. It's a race to recover the disarming device from the Baroness as the famous landmark collapses. Then the triumphant villainess gloats with Duke now Cobra's prisoner.

If things had continued on this trajectory, the Baroness would have made the top 40 legendary tier. But Ana discovers she was manipulated by her brother (still alive and now the evil Cobra Commander), and breaks free of his supposedly infallible mind control. How Ana does this is never explained, since she still believes her brother is dead and has no incentive to rekindle her romance with Duke.

After all the buildup and villainy, Ana turns good. When the heroes locate Cobra's underwater hideout and launch an assault, the redeemed villainess co-pilots a minisub and fires torpedoes, but we'd rather watch her fight for an evil cause. In the closing scene, Duke visits the imprisoned Baroness and promises not to give up on her. Sienna Miller quit the franchise after this, but for seventy percent of *Rise of Cobra*, we had a fantastic villainess.

Discussions: G.I. Joe

G.I. Joe: Retaliation (2013)

Producers decided on a soft reboot for the sequel, and almost none of the original cast returned. The Baroness is a notable absentee in Cobra's ranks, and Duke dies in the first act. Many characters in the first film wore full-face masks or had ambiguous fates. Convenient – one suspects the franchise was already in the contingency planning stage, with the option to recast expensive actors or change narrative direction.

If the French had it rough in *Rise of Cobra*, London suffers worse in *Retaliation* when the entire city is destroyed. The villains (and American filmmakers) don't like Europeans much, eh? Amidst all the carnage and fresh faces, a red-garbed ninja named Jinx is the replacement tough girl for Scarlet, and her evil female martial artist counterpart poses no real threat. They dropped the awesome leather-clad villainess for *this*?

Snake Eyes (2021)

The good news is that the Baroness returns for this origin story reboot. Bad news? We see very little of Úrsula Corberó, as the primary focus is the title character and his backstory. An interesting plot angle has Snake Eyes starting off as a villain and Storm Shadow the more heroic adversary until a late role reversal.

Before the expected development, Snake infiltrates a ninja clan, who test him with three trials. The most ludicrous is a pit full of CGI giant anacondas, psychic creatures that can sense a person's purity. Cobra are reduced to minor antagonists, and while the Baroness looks evil in her black leather outfit and high heels, she's barely involved.

There's an annoyingly brief confrontation with Scarlett (Samara Weaving), then the Baroness forms a temporary alliance with the heroes. Until things get too dangerous, and the villainess (can we even call her one?) bails. Truly pathetic stuff.

Movie

Many movies on my list are from the 1990s, the "golden age" for direct-to-video and a treasure trove for female villains. This was especially true for the erotic thriller genre. That term has become synonymous with softcore pornography, but believe it or not, these movies once had recognisable B-list talent and actual plots.

Sensation, starring Eric Roberts, Kari Wuhrer, and Ron Perlman, is a fine example. One nude scene has the main female character relaxing in a bathtub after canvas painting, surrounded by multicoloured floating blobs. Erotic imagery is present even when people are clothed, with surreal portraits of naked women and fertility statue antiques in the background. Modern viewers can watch the movie in wide-screen HD after its restoration from the original film footage.

The storyline is bizarre, but definitely original. Lila Reed (Wuhrer) is a graduate student hired by the mysterious Dr Ian Burton (Roberts) to study psychometry. That involves detecting imprints or "sensations" from objects and reliving the experiences of previous owners. Interesting study material, but Lila discovers some items belonged to a murdered student named Carrie Reiner, putting herself in danger.

Creepy men in Lila's life include her pushy boyfriend, a stranger she meets in a bar, the eager Detective Pantella (Perlman), and Dr Burton himself. When Lila moves into Carrie's old apartment, the landlord Mitch takes a voyeuristic interest in his new tenant and watches her shower through a skylight. No shortage of suspects, then.

Savvy viewers will write these off as red herrings, and as usual, it's the one person who isn't presented as sinister who turns out to be the killer.

Villainess

The murderess' motive is generic: a jilted lover and colleague. Why do scorned women always go crazy in these flicks? Paula's infatuation with Burton is obvious from the moment she first enters his office. It's later revealed she gave Dr Burton an alibi for Carrie's murder, claiming they were together. A clever deception that also gives *Paula* an alibi. She's playing you, doc.

Given that the killer strangles her victims with a leather cord, the 6'2" Claire Stansfield was a good casting choice with her towering physical presence. In most scenes, she dwarfs her male co-stars. The actress is also attractive and convincing as the femme fatale the story requires, including a topless sex scene with Eric Roberts.

Paula doesn't appear much, however. Her only victims are poor Carrie (seen in the opening title sequence and psychic visions) and Lila's best friend, Maryann, who dies because of a borrowed coat and mistaken identity. The late death in a fountain plaza occurs entirely off-screen, except for when the black-gloved murderess grabs her prey.

A tense finale has the ski-masked murderess break into Lila's apartment, bludgeon Detective Pantella, and attempt to strangle the protagonist. This leads to a struggle and a dramatic reveal where Lila rips off the intruder's mask. There's a brilliant reaction shot of Paula after she's exposed, one of the greatest female unmasking scenes in movie history. No hyperbole – it's that good.

Some viewers have debated whether a male double played the killer in the climax. Personally, I'm inclined to believe it is actually Claire Stansfield under the mask, given her tall build. A shot of the killer's feminine arms suggests the actress played the part, and the eyes match in close-ups. Seen from a side angle, the body shape is that of a woman. And pausing the improved HD version confirms this.

Stansfield is convincing as the not obviously female intruder, so it would have made sense to use her ski-masked guise more often. We'll have to make do with the incredible buildup sequence where she stretches her leather cord... and the bland finale that follows her reveal. Dr Burton arrives, discovers the truth about his lover, and they struggle. After the murderess grabs a pair of scissors, Ian shakes her off, then Lila grabs the detective's gun and blows the psycho away.

Honourable Mentions: Claire Stansfield / Masked Killers

Drop Zone (1994) – Kara (Claire Stansfield)

The versatile actress had another villainous role in 1994, as the sole female member of a criminal skydiving gang. This Wesley Snipes vehicle is fast-paced and entertaining, and the reliable Gary Busey plays the chief baddie (doesn't he always?). His corrupt agent plans to steal valuable data from high-rise office buildings, and only a cop and hero skydiver, Jessie (Yancy Butler) can stop him.

Kara doesn't speak much, but gets action aplenty. In her

most notable scene, she parachutes onto a police station, impersonates an officer, and shoots a cop to access the evidence lockup. The tall henchwoman comes across as an intimidating and efficient killer, so it's frustrating to sit through her non-action scenes.

With one woman on either side, it's no surprise Jessie takes down Kara. Unfortunately, the heroine is a few inches shorter than her Amazonian opponent, so their physical duel is not very convincing. However, the villainess' memorable and original demise – when Jessie smashes her head through a photocopier – makes up for any shortcomings.

Doorman (1985) – San Lu (Haru Aki)

Movies where the hero literally unmasks a villainess are rare, which earns this otherwise pedestrian thriller an honourable mention. A black-gloved killer prowls an apartment building, offing doormen so quickly that three are dead within twenty minutes. The murderer is a martial arts expert with a death touch technique, somehow able to snap a man's neck with one hand. Kill scenes are laughably inept, bloodless even by TV movie standards.

Terry Reilly (Bradley Whitford) is a doorman (uh oh!) and budding mystery novelist who teams up with Linda (Sharon Schlarth) to solve the crime spree before he becomes the next victim. Unfortunately, Terry's recited novels are much more riveting than the actual plot. The murderess has an unfathomable motive, something about stolen packages and a criminal double-cross. Many subplots turn out to be irrelevant, and the padded-out credits show clips of *every* character with dialogue. That includes the principal cast, minor roles, and extras who barely feature.

After Terry arranges a meeting with resident San Lu,

the masked ninja-like killer attacks him in the parking garage. That rare moment of excitement is over in five seconds, and it's a long wait until their next – and last – encounter. A brief kung fu scene, then Terry unmasks the callous San Lu, who gets a decent bad girl speech before a frustrating off-screen death.

Rank #86

Demolition High (1996)
Tanya (Melissa Brasselle)

Movie

An unlikely hero trapped in a building with terrorists planning extortion. Sound familiar? Yep, this is another *Die Hard* scenario movie. A fair number of these films made my list because they often include above-average villainesses. The setting is (unsurprisingly) a high school, and the hero is Lenny Slater (Corey Haim), a recent transfer from New York City who's quite handy in fistfights.

Lenny isn't popular with the school bully, but they put aside their quarrel and team up with a timid girl to battle the bad guys. The rough kid must be a fan of the 1980s TV series *MacGyver* because he fashions makeshift weapons from whatever materials are lying around. He'll need those skills, since the enemy leader is planning to launch a stolen missile at a nuclear power plant.

The movie is competently made (by B-movie standards) and moves along at a brisk pace. No plot twists to floor the audience, but an undemanding watch. A digitally restored version is available on DVD and many streaming services, worth watching for action lovers and Haim fans. Stacie Randall, an on/off action star in the 1990s, offers "support" as an interfering FBI agent.

Villainess

The sadistic henchwoman dressed in black is a stock character in these films, but Tanya is better than most. She remains a constant presence throughout the runtime, and there aren't many action sequences where she doesn't play a part.

Many characters exist simply to show how evil Tanya is. These include a security guard who chats her up, a cop who pulls the villain's van over after they steal the missile, and a nameless thug who gets captured by Lenny. All get blown away by the villainess' nickel-plated Desert Eagle.

Tanya makes it clear she wants a larger share of the take, so it's no surprise she considers Lenny's hostage expendable. Fortunately, the hero evades Tanya and disposes of her with a fire extinguisher and calligraphy pens (which make a crude launcher). At least he thinks he's won, because the wounded woman comes back with a fire axe to finish the job.

The henchwoman's death scene is below par compared to what came before. A police sniper shoots Tanya in the back after she gets the better of Lenny. It would have been more fitting if the resourceful kid had devised another ingenious way to defeat Tanya for good, but overall Melissa Brasselle plays a solid, if not spectacular, female foe.

Honourable Mention: *Demolition* Series

Demolition University **(1997) – Elia (Michelle Maika)**

The producers re-used many plot elements from the original. Lenny the hero, a bully sidekick, terrorists take over a building (surprisingly *not* a university) and a cruel henchwoman. Elia, while not as sadistic as Tanya from *Demolition High,* is still a cold-blooded killer. *Die Hard* in a water treatment plant – another location to cross off the list.

Elia's introduction is pretty lame. She infiltrates a guarded research lab wearing a masked ninja outfit and garrotes two stronger army guys. Don't expect any realism. The choke scenes both last five seconds with no resistance from trained soldiers. We get a decent unmasking (though it's obvious the attacker is female), followed by a poorly staged shootout and a deadly nerve agent heist.

Overall, the sequel is more amateurish than its predecessor, with an annoying subplot where an American traitor flirts with Elia. Viewers will root for the villainess when she calmly executes the cocky American late in the film. Elia is so confident in her aiming skills she's not concerned about harming his hostage (her own brother, no less). Or that her target might drop a vial of nerve agent and kill everyone in the room.

Lenny's final "fight" with Elia is poor stuff. An easy knockdown, then a weak comeback where she garrotes the hero only to drop her weapon for no obvious reason. The hero sets the villainess on fire, raising hopes of a spectacular death, but she goes out with a whimper.

Full Exposure: The Sex Tapes Scandal (1989)
Debralee Taft (Jennifer O'Neill)

Movie

Don't be dissuaded (or fooled) by the raunchy title. It may sound like a late-night softcore flick, but this is an NBC TV movie from the late 1980s. No nudity except rear shots of Lisa Hartman, though the film received an 18 certificate for its UK DVD release. One assumes the sex videos, which feature a dominatrix and whips, were enough to classify this as adult material.

A masked intruder murders a prostitute but flees when the flatmate returns earlier than expected. A stolen videotape gets left behind, and clearly contains footage someone is prepared to kill for. The foolish witness isn't deterred by dead bodies and auctions the tape with the help of an adult film producer. Powerful men would prefer to keep their kinky private lives secret, so it's a lucrative if dangerous play.

While two bidders are prepared to pay over $100,000 (a lot of money in 1989), the leather-clad, masked killer prefers more direct methods. The intruder gatecrashes the auction and wastes the competition with a shotgun. Great stuff, although violent for TV, and another potential reason for the age rating.

Duplicate tape recovered, but there's still a copy out there, plus loose ends for the shooter to deal with. The two main characters, Lieutenant Thompson and rookie DA Sarah Dutton, must solve the murders, but find their investigation obstructed by an obviously corrupt police chief and judge. Are they on the tape by any chance?

Villainess

The investigators soon discover a connection between the dead prostitute and a modelling agency run by Debralee Taft. Since an unnamed bidder was absent from the auction massacre, it's easy to infer Debralee is the culprit or somehow involved. She claims to be a legitimate businesswoman, but her evasive answers to Thompson's questions – and a hulking bodyguard named Earl – suggest she's hiding something. After an undercover policewoman is killed on her way to Debralee's office, Thompson agrees to Sarah's plan to pose as a model.

Debralee makes the list because she's an unusual villainess. Instead of a typical psycho, this is a scheming businesswoman quite prepared to kill people herself. Jennifer O'Neill brings gravity to her performance, leading to a foreshadowed but welcome reveal in the last twenty minutes. The greedy flatmate gets shot with a silenced pistol, and the murderess in black leather goes after Sarah, who now has the all-important tape.

Sarah's house is the setting for the showdown with Debralee and Earl. While never explicitly confirmed through dialogue, it's likely Debralee committed the murders since her black jacket matches the killer's. Earl has a shotgun, but voiced his objection to the killing spree. The predictable outcome sees the bodyguard shot by Thompson and Sarah cornered by the homicidal villainess. There's a distraction, a chase where she fires a few shots, and a last-moment rescue by the hero.

Honourable Mentions: TV Movies

Weep No More, My Lady (1992) – Judy (Cécile Paoli)

This TV movie has imaginative murders and a mystery killer who wears two different masked outfits, but the pacing is ponderous, with all the exciting bits saved for the last half hour. The story, based on a novel by Mary Higgins Clark, is set in a Parisian chateau. So it's strange that a Japanese theme runs throughout, right from the opening credits that include animated images of kendo fighters.

The main plot is rudimentary, and annoying side characters help stretch the runtime to ninety minutes. An actress named Leila (Francesca Annis) is driven mad by creepy phone calls, which strains her relationship with sister Elisabeth (Kristin Scott Thomas) and husband Ted. Leila has vocal arguments with her family in public, so when a scuba diver drowns her in a nearby lake, everyone assumes she's run away. Except for Elisabeth, who's determined to uncover the truth.

After the slow opening act, there's a tense sequence where the kendo-masked killer eliminates a female assistant with a bow and arrow. The murderess then reveals herself – and a typical jealous lover motive – to a nosy guest too inquisitive for her own good.

Elisabeth replaces her dead sister in a movie production, and Judy takes a stunt diver's place to make one last attempt on the heroine's life. The killer dons a scuba mask as dramatic music plays, but what should be an exciting climax is a total dud. Gloomy underwater action shots, and a pathetic resolution where the film director saves

Elisabeth.

Ladykillers (1988) – Morganna Ross (Lesley-Anne Down)

This TV movie from the late 80s is difficult to find, so my review is based on an average quality broadcast scan with mediocre sound. The novel scenario takes a well-worn premise and gender-flips it. A mysterious blonde-wigged assailant slashes a male stripper while he's performing on stage at *Ladykillers* nightclub. Forensics have a hard time identifying the murder weapon, which turns out to be an artist's tool used for sign painting.

Lieutenant Flannery (Marilu Henner) is a tough homicide cop, and an early scene has a female PR agent sneak up on a showering man and pretend to strangle him with a scarf. In this movie, it's women in charge and the males who get topless. This includes a mass strip scene at the police station when Flannery and club owner Morganna audition detectives to go undercover as a dancer.

After a near miss when the slasher almost kills a second stripper, an ex-prostitute gives Flannery a crucial lead. In an original turn of events, the heroine rushes to save her boyfriend. Morganna is revealed as the murderer, and the struggle in a burning lounge is above average for a TV thriller. Furniture gets knocked over as the two women wrestle, then the villainess gets the standard "tossed through a window" treatment.

Rank #84

Momentum (2015)
Alexis Faraday (Olga Kurylenko), Ms Clinton (Shelley Nicole)

Movie

When compiling my list, one goal was to vary the content as much as possible. So I included protagonists who commit serious crimes, and anti-heroines just as ruthless as the bad guys, even if their intentions are noble. The main character in *Momentum* fits into both categories.

For viewers who prefer outright villainy, there's a cold-blooded – and especially hard to kill – henchwoman. More than enough to justify placing these deadly women in my rankings.

Anti-Heroine

The protagonist is a professional thief, and straight from the outset, it's clear she's not a woman to mess with. Make that *person*, because the armed robbers are masked during the opening bank heist in Cape Town, South Africa.

The crooks wear sleek black outfits with body armour and voice modulators. Those conveniently light up in different colours, so we can tell the four apart. In one bizarre moment, a drugged-up robber quotes *Dirty Harry* to a terrified security guard while sounding like a robot.

The voice distortion and form-concealing outfit might fool the hostages into thinking the heist crew are all male. But anyone who's read the blurb in advance or seen this trick before (most viewers, I suspect) won't be deceived. But we still get an awesome reveal moment after the crazy robber shoots it out with Alex and her mask comes off in the struggle.

While the protagonist has a moral compass (no killing innocents), she is ruthless. When the bank manager doesn't cooperate, she punches out his tooth, then forcibly re-inserts it to bypass a biometric security lock. And Alex has no problem executing her treacherous crew member, even if the lunatic had it coming.

Olga Kurylenko as a tough girl with a mysterious past? Familiar territory by now, but the actress plays these parts well, which explains why producers keep casting her.

Villainess

The villains are "cleaners" (translation: professional killers) employed by an unnamed senator. The big bad is played by Morgan Freeman, who always seems to be cast as a politician. James Purefoy is the evil Brit (there had to be one) and the antagonist with the most screen time.

His character is Mr Washington, whose team includes the equally ruthless Mr Jefferson, Mr Monroe and Ms Clinton. These are either code names based on former US presidents or one amazing coincidence. Since Clinton is female and the film predates 2016, perhaps the filmmakers assumed a certain woman would become president, which seems presumptuous now.

Clinton is a skilled fighter who kickboxes Alex's partner into submission. The bad guys want a data drive stolen during the heist, which holds vital information about the

Senator's plans. After Washington's crew torture the poor guy to death, Alex retrieves the MacGuffin and goes on the run.

Somewhat refreshingly, Ms Clinton is more professional than sadistic. Mostly calm, with the occasional smile and snarky comment to suggest she enjoys her work. Like the other cleaners, she's a competent operative. Alex often evades the opposition through ingenuity, rather than their being hopeless.

However, the expected confrontation between the two women never transpires. The climax – in an airport terminal – has the crippled Alex outsmarting the villains by detonating a bomb. A risky move, but the security staff identifies Clinton as the threat. Probably because she strikes first and beats them up while Alex grapples with Mr Washington.

The cleaners are difficult to kill. Before this point, the baddies have survived explosions, a knife to the back, and stab wounds. So the outnumbered Ms Clinton was never going down easy. She takes out several men despite starting the fight unarmed. Until a more sensible guard shoots her. Yes, that's right – killed by an unnamed character. Original, perhaps, but unrewarding.

As for Alex, she outsmarts Mr Washington and makes a memorable anti-heroine. Too bad the movie failed at the box office, and the sequel setup – with the senator still at large – will probably remain unresolved.

Honourable Mentions: Professional Killers

The Courier (2019) – **Agent Simmonds (Alicia Agneson)**

Olga Kurylenko has made a name for herself as an action star. In this movie she's a motorcycle courier with –

yes, you guessed it – a mysterious past. Mostly set in London, the story begins when she delivers a package to a safe house. Bad move, since it's a disguised cyanide dispersal device. Say goodbye to a key witness.

As in *Momentum*, the main villain directs his business from overseas. Gary Oldman is the big-name baddie: a criminal boss sporting an eyepatch. His inside woman is Simmonds, a corrupt Interpol agent who murders her colleagues for financial gain.

Despite being fourth on the credits, Alicia Agneson's character dies in the first twenty minutes. Presumably, her prominent position is because she has multiple dialogue lines in a movie where most characters don't speak. Before the villainess leaves us, she shoots the courier (and stupidly assumes she's dead), gets her ass kicked in retaliation, and ends up on the losing side.

A disappointment, but the treacherous agent looked fantastic in a gas mask.

Full Disclosure (2001) – Michelle (Penelope Ann Miller)

Michelle is a secondary character, but still features prominently on the movie poster. Why? The ruthless and efficient hitwoman is the most interesting part of this dull political thriller.

Reporter John McWhirter (Fred Ward) investigates the murder of a prominent businessman. The muddled conspiracy surrounding his death leads to many encounters with recognisable B-movie actors. Christopher Plummer's FBI boss is the definition of shady. Rachel Ticotin is a Middle Eastern love interest, and Virginia Madsen has an extended cameo as John's newspaper editor.

Plot elements go nowhere, notably the Algerians behind the assassination, who don't feature at all in the second half.

Before they disappear, they hire Michelle to tie up loose ends, which gives viewers something to get excited about. The blonde woman is a cold professional who murders and tortures people as if it's normal. After she eliminates the assassins, John is next on the list.

Fortunately, the reporter has a secret hiding spot in his apartment, allowing his female guest to surprise Michelle. The disappointing duel has the assassin chase the woman, and John uses her own silenced pistol to kill her. Then some postmortem shots to remind us how great the character was.

Rank #83

Strategic Command (1997)
Mira (Gina Mari)

Movie

Royal Oaks Entertainment produced several low-budget action flicks in the 1990s. They always open with stock intro music and usually have Michael Dudikoff in the lead role. In this one, he's a biologist named Rick Harding who conveniently has a military / martial arts background. Helpful when boarding a hijacked plane mid-air with a special forces unit as backup. Rick's mission: defuse a nerve toxin bomb before the terrorists use it to attack the US.

If this sounds familiar, it's because the plot is identical to *Executive Decision* (1996). In that, Kurt Russell is the scientist (no martial arts) and Steven Seagal's commando is a decoy hero who dies halfway through. The heroes approach the hijacked commercial airliner in a stealth plane and use a connecting tube-like thing to access the cargo hatch. The sequence midway through *Strategic Command* is a carbon copy.

For added tension, the main character's wife is on board the plane, which feels convenient and contrived. But since the inspired clone (or knockoff, if you're feeling less generous) has a female hijacker – and a nasty one – in Mira, it's worth checking out for villainess fans.

Villainess

Before the mid-air antics, the terrorists raid a chemical storage facility and steal a fictional nerve agent called Bromex. It's obvious these guys are bad because they wear black commando outfits, and the lone female, Mira, has a sleeveless top to emphasise her sexiness. She sure looks like a sadistic henchwoman, a role confirmed when the leader Gruber (any relation to Hans?) produces a human eyeball. Mira smiles in delight as they bypass a retina scanner.

Some toxin is accidentally released, and a disposable guy is sealed in an airtight chamber. His vomit is supposed to be stomach acid, but resembles milkshake. The terrorists make their escape, and there's a decently staged shootout with casualties on both sides. And a surprise early fight between Harding and Gruber, but the hero can't win yet, otherwise there would be no movie.

After the villains hijack a 747 with the Vice President on board, Mira acts the tough girl and headbutts the uncooperative VP. She's eager to execute some hostages purely for fun. This is one psycho lady, who gets *very* excited when Gruber murders a press liaison to convince the authorities he's serious.

Mira's best moment comes when the Secret Service attempts to retake the plane. A female agent holds the villainess hostage, then a traitor turns the tables. After the would-be heroine surrenders, Gruber orders her execution, and Mira is happy to oblige. The smiling villainess' reaction – where she pants and draws back her hair – is downright evil.

After the heroes sneak on board *Executive Decision* style, Mira investigates the cargo hold. Harding escapes the henchwoman on this occasion, but a confrontation is coming. The showdown on the doomed airliner is weak, with shaky-cam fight scenes. It's Harding against Gruber and Mira versus the traitor (who's developed a conscience and joined the good guys).

The unlikely hero overpowers Mira and forces her against a fuselage door. Then he opens it, depressurising the cabin and sacrificing his own life to defeat the villainess. There's a scene a little later where Harding kills Gruber with the nerve agent. The sadistic Mira deserved an equally nasty fate, but went out with a faint scream.

Honourable Mentions: Hijackers

Passenger 57 (1992) – Sabrina Ritchie (Elizabeth Hurley)

British actors playing villains is nothing new in Hollywood. This film gives us two: Bruce Payne's psycho hijacker and Liz Hurley as his accomplice Sabrina Ritchie. She seems to be an innocent flight attendant, but that accent is a giveaway.

Sabrina reveals her treachery when she offers a meal to two unsuspecting FBI agents and serves up bullets from a silenced pistol. Too bad that's her only decent moment. After that, Sabrina has occasional dialogue and holds a crew member hostage. The hero knocks her out with one punch, and she's arrested when the plane lands. Anyone hoping for a decent climax will be very disappointed.

Hijacked (2017) – Sadie (Greer Grammer)

Also known as *Altitude*, this movie features a villainess with a wonderful introduction. Sadie – yet another fake flight attendant – is part of a criminal gang hunting a former associate. There had to be a simpler solution than hijacking a passenger plane, but it suffices as an excuse plot. The action heroine is hostage negotiator Gretchen Blair (Denise Richards, cast against type).

After Sadie breaks a jokey attendant's neck to show off her martial arts prowess, she tricks her way into the cockpit. There, she injects the pilot with poison and stabs his co-pilot with her heeled shoe. An awesome double kill, but the film doesn't build on this impressive opening.

The fight scenes are poorly choreographed and edited, and the two "confrontations" between Gretchen and Sadie don't amount to much. Eventually, the villainess is sucked out of the plane. In hijack movies, you can guarantee at least one baddie will die this way. But it's predictable and unconvincing.

Hijacked (2012) – Liesel (Ashley Cusato)

Yes, there are two generic B-movies with the same title. This one has more star power, with Randy Couture as CIA agent Paul Ross, who teams up with Dominic Purcell's bodyguard to foil a hijacker extortion plot. The target is a private jet owned by a wealthy businessman, and – to make things personal – Ross' girlfriend Olivia is on board. This appears to be a plot contrivance, but is later revealed to be a setup.

The villains are bland, leaving it to the henchwoman Liesel to offer the best action. Though her role is mostly limited to sinister facial expressions and the occasional tough-girl speech, she gets two great kills. Liesel is sadistic and trigger-happy. That goes for all the hijackers, since the businessman wants the hostages murdered as part of his diabolical scheme.

The opening party scene has a British spy played by Vinnie Jones (in a rare good guy role) don a tuxedo and do a not-so-great 007 impression as he flirts with a sexy woman. The awkward romance gets cut short by a phone call, then the MI6 agent and Ross later discover the female tied up during an armed raid. A trained operative should spot the warning signs, but he's stupidly caught off guard. The villainess seems to enjoy her deception before she blows his brains out.

After the mercenaries board the jet with help from an inside woman (who's nowhere near as smart as she thinks), Liesel enters a private cabin through a hatch. She surprises a couple in the middle of passionate sex, takes a moment to enjoy the view, and finishes them with a silenced pistol. Her best scene in the movie, and while it's possible Liesel gets an off-screen kill later on, the shooter isn't confirmed.

After a string of "act tough but don't do a lot" scenes, Liesel engages the heroes in combat. Sadly, the henchwoman doesn't have the fighting skills you'd expect, and is easily captured. For the last act, Liesel is a prisoner until she's released to help defuse a bomb. She has no idea how to disarm it, but escapes and aims her gun at the careless Ross. Then the inevitable happens: Olivia shows up to put a bullet in the villainess' back.

Man of Steel (2013)
Faora-Ul (Antje Traue)

Movie

Another movie in the never-ending deluge of Hollywood reboots, this is a solo outing for Superman. One difference from earlier adaptations is that the hero doesn't work at the *Daily Planet*. He only takes on his Clark Kent "disguise" in the film's last scene.

When reworking a franchise, it's a good idea to revisit the previous movies, reuse the ideas that worked well, and ditch the rest. That appears to be the strategy. *Man of Steel* combines the origin story from *Superman: The Movie* (1978) with the rogue Kryptonian villain arc from *Superman II* (1980). As in the latter film, the main villain is General Zod, with Michael Shannon taking on the role previously played by Terence Stamp.

Besides the obvious improvement in special effects and scope, the pacing is superior to the 1978 film, where the villain's plot only came into play later on. And Zod doesn't have to share the stage with the overused Lex Luthor. In the DC Extended Universe movies, that character was saved for *Batman v Superman: Dawn of Justice* (2016).

The first act centres on Superman's struggle with his identity and reporter Lois Lane's investigation into his mysterious past. Things ramp up when Zod and his Krypton followers arrive on Earth, with a nefarious scheme to terraform the planet and wipe out humanity. With superhuman powers of their own, the villains are worthy adversaries and don't need to rely on kryptonite to weaken the hero.

Villainess

Ursa and Faora-Ul are two distinct characters in the comics, but they fill the same role as Zod's second in command. Overall, I prefer the villainess in *Man of Steel* because her physical confrontations are better staged.

Faora appears in the Krypton-set prologue as part of Zod's rebellion. Following their defeat, the rebels are sentenced to the Phantom Zone until (as in *Superman II*) a cosmic event frees the villains. Superman is the son of the man who imprisoned them, so the vengeful general travels to Earth.

Zod and his underlings brush aside tanks and gunships and make a televised demand that the authorities turn Superman over to them. It's then that the villainess introduces herself, leading to an explosive series of action set pieces. These culminate in a one-on-one battle with Superman. Rules about male/female fights have been relaxed over the last forty years. They are now expected to be brutal, and this one certainly delivers.

The winner is debatable, as both Superman and Faora are invulnerable to each other's attacks. Neither pulls any punches, as entire buildings get destroyed during an epic fight that lasts several minutes.

Arguably, the most memorable encounter is when an ordinary soldier challenges Faora with a knife. Brave and foolish, and it would have meant certain death save for a last-second intervention from Superman. In the finale, the soldier commits suicide by crashing a spaceship (with Faora on board) into an alien device, a heroic act which returns the villainess to the Phantom Zone.

Honourable Mentions: Detective Comics (DC)

Superman II (1980) – Ursa (Sarah Douglas)

It wouldn't be fair to discuss Faora without mentioning Ursa. The character was created especially for the movie franchise because of a shortage of female villains in the source material. It's actually she who first encounters the humans during a lunar mission.

A spaceman is understandably shocked to see an unsuited woman float down and survive in the vacuum of space. Curious, Ursa pulls off his NASA badge, which ruptures his suit. Collecting trophies becomes a thing, and she adds a sheriff's star and general's stripes to her black outfit.

Ursa gets physical in confrontations with Superman, but never has a one-on-one battle like Faora in the reboot. Some of the action is tame by today's standards, but Douglas still makes a fine villainess. She also has the honour of being the last villain standing after Superman strips his foes of their powers. Lois Lane gets to deliver the knockout punch, accompanied by a fitting one-liner.

Wonder Woman (2017) – Dr Maru (Elena Anaya)

The female villain's role in the first *Wonder Woman* movie is relatively small. Dr Maru (better known as Dr Poison) is a scientist who develops a corrosive gas which could impact the outcome of World War I. Hardly a minor contribution, but she's a secondary antagonist to Greek god Ares.

Maru has a creepy aura thanks to the mask she wears to hide disfigurement. She also chuckles with the fake, big bad Ludendorff after gassing a room full of German officers. Then the real villain shows up in an overblown CGI finale, and the lethal poison plot becomes an afterthought. In the end, Maru's fate is ambiguous after Wonder Woman discovers the value of love and spares the villainess' life.

Wonder Woman 1984 (2020) – Barbara Minerva / Cheetah (Kristen Wiig)

The female antagonist in the sequel – Barbara Minerva, aka Cheetah – gets a lot more screen time, though she doesn't take on her villainous persona until the third act. For most of the movie, the chief bad guy is Maxwell Lord: a power-mad businessman obsessed with a mystical artifact called the Dreamstone. The crystal has the power to grant its user a single wish, though it takes something they value in return. Things become desperate when Lord becomes the Dream Stone and abuses its power for his own ends.

Before all that, the timid Barbara wishes to be like Diana Prince (Wonder Woman), which grants her superhuman strength at the cost of humanity. The adverse effects can be reversed by relinquishing a wish, but Barbara embraces her powers and becomes the iconic feline foe.

Cheetah – and Wonder Woman herself – see little action until the second half. One of the villainess' best moments is when she confronts a man who molested her and enjoys her revenge as only an evil person could. Like the first DCU film, the ending is CGI-heavy, and this time two women battle it out. The confrontation is brief, and Barbara reverts to her human form when it's over.

Charlie's Angels: Full Throttle (2003)
Madison Lee (Demi Moore)

Movie

A sequel to a re-imagining of an old TV series, which *itself* has since been rebooted. Perhaps audiences are growing tired of the whole remake thing, as the latest attempts were commercial failures.

The movie with Cameron Diaz, Drew Barrymore, and Lucy Liu as the secret agents hasn't aged well. From a modern viewpoint, the heroines are overly sexualised with many instances of male gaze. But *Full Throttle* addresses the imbalance by adding topless men into the mix.

These films are better at humour than plot development. Given that jokes often fall flat, this should give some idea of how obvious the twists are. Plenty of action, though the fights are cheesy with impossible stunts involving CGI and obvious wire work. The first *Charlie's Angels* film had its critics, but had a decent box office return. Hence, no change in style for *Full Throttle*.

If viewers switch off their brains and don't take the movies seriously (is that even possible?), there is much to enjoy. Both entries feature a major villainess and the expected catfights that come with her. While the sequel is weaker than the first film, Madison makes my list because of her more interesting backstory.

Villainess

The *Charlie's Angels* films directed by McG have similar themes. There's a mission that's not what it seems, a supposed ally that turns out to be manipulative, and a last act reveal for the villainess. The sequel adds a dark-haired female antagonist (seen from behind) early on. So when a former Angel named Madison Lee enters the picture, it's obvious she's the bad girl.

A Mongolian warlord is the main villain in the opening teaser where the heroines rescue a US marshal (Robert Patrick). However, it soon becomes apparent that these are minor players in a much bigger scheme. The dark-haired lady is after two titanium rings, decoders that reveal the identities of people in witness protection.

The marshal had one ring, and a Justice Department official is guarding the other. Bruce Willis has a short-lived cameo as the second man. He discovers his entire detail dead in an aircraft hangar (somehow they got slaughtered with absolutely no noise). The stealthy masked assailant hangs from the plane's roof, like something out of *Splinter Cell*, and holds a gold-plated Desert Eagle to the official's head. This is someone who kills with style.

The Angels track a surfer henchman to a beach. An excuse to show attractive women in bikinis, including Madison and a *Baywatch*-style entrance. The assassin is eliminated by the acrobatic Thin Man (returning from the first movie). There's a history involving Drew Barrymore's character and an Irish mobster against whom she testified. Given who's playing the US marshal, it's no surprise he's a turncoat. In summary, a convoluted mess of minor villains and subplots.

Madison reveals herself as the principal antagonist when she blows the marshal away with a pair of Desert Eagles. In case you'd forgotten, those were the weapons used by the masked killer. The villainess likes her golden guns and uses several in the action sequences that follow. This, together with her black outfits and egotistical boasts, makes her a stylish foe who should have been revealed much sooner.

Madison is a formidable opponent for the Angels, countering their dodge moves with gunplay. One on one, the heroines are no match, and even all three acting together struggle to defeat the villainess. Only after a lengthy finale do the agents beat Madison in an abandoned theatre. She gets a good death scene when she falls through the floor and accidentally shoots an exposed gas pipe.

Honourable Mention: Charlie's Angels

Charlie's Angels (2000) – Vivian Wood (Kelly Lynch)

The first Charlie's Angels movie also featured a villainess with stylish attire, though Vivian didn't wear her skintight black catsuit until the finale. She's proficient in unarmed combat and goes toe to toe with the Cameron Diaz character. The downside is that nothing stands out about her character. She's a secondary foil to the chief bad guy, more of a henchwoman than a villain in her own right.

Vivian's reveal is handled better than Madison's. While viewers may suspect a plot twist is on the agenda, there are no giveaway shots of a mysterious female pulling the strings. So the client isn't that suspicious before her heel turn.

Rank #80

***Entrapment* (1999)**
Gin (Catherine Zeta-Jones)

Movie

One of many late 1990s films to use the "Millennium Bug" as a plot device, this is a slick heist thriller with great performances from the two leads. *Entrapment* is notable for being one of Sean Connery's last film roles. His only major features after this were *Finding Forrester* and *The League of Extraordinary Gentlemen*. Plus, there's *that* bendy laser-dodging sequence with Catherine Zeta-Jones.

Oddly, the infamous set piece – the theft of a gold mask as a payoff for an even bigger score – occurs at the film's midpoint rather than the climax. The action-packed climax is set in Kuala Lumpur on New Year's Eve. The target? A whopping $8 billion from a banking terminal in the iconic Petronas Towers.

For the benefit of younger readers, the Millennium Bug was a computer flaw where date years were stored as two digits. This would have caused issues come 2000 with 00 interpreted as 1900. In the end, the glitch was resolved with no major consequences, so the panic seems silly in hindsight.

Entrapment has one of the cleverest film usages: an integrity test of electronic banking systems. A plausible occurrence in real life, although they probably didn't run them at the last second.

Villainess

Virginia Baker (Gin for short) is an insurance investigator from New York. She's after aging professional thief Robert "Mac" MacDougal (Connery). He's suspected of stealing a Rembrandt, a daring office skyscraper heist that involved a remote controlled winch, and Gin is determined to get her man.

The *Thomas Crown Affair* setup is inverted when Gin reveals *she* stole the painting and needs Mac's help for a job. He's not impressed, which might have something to do with her overconfident ego. She has a habit of declaring an outcome "perfect" being messing up. Gin wastes no time in using her feminine charms on the much older Mac. He admires her form during a training montage scene, as she bends sexily between ropes substituting for lasers.

Many film critics criticised the "implausible" romantic relationship. But it's about Gin's thieving ability (Mac sees his younger self in her), and not simply her beauty. The old-timer desires to return to daredevil heists, and the initial deceptive flirting develops into genuine affection.

After Gin dodges lasers for real and steals the golden mask from Bedford Palace, things get tense when Mac accuses her of setting him up. Until she lets him in on her grand plan. Suspense builds well, with various side characters up to no good (notably Gin's boss and a shadowy acquaintance of Mac's).

The Malaysian heist is disappointing at first. The thieves crack a high-security vault that requires less effort than stealing the mask (or even the Rembrandt). But then Gin says "perfect" – just before she triggers a system integrity alarm. A dramatic escape follows, with the thieves swinging from lights under the sky bridge and sprinting through tear gas.

Gin and Mac separate and promise to meet at a train station. It's then that the old man reveals *he's been playing her* all this time, though he reconsiders and helps her escape. After they outwit the authorities, the lovers embrace in a surprisingly moving moment.

Honourable Mentions: Cat Burglars

B.L. Stryker: Grand Theft Hotel (1990) – Dawn St. Claire (Loni Anderson)

This is technically an episode of the *B.L. Stryker* TV series, with Burt Reynolds in the title role. But since the runtime is ninety minutes, and this aired as a TV movie in the UK, it meets the inclusion criteria.

Buddy Lee is after a cat burglar with a penchant for stun guns and dramatic helicopter escapes. No surprise the masked thief ends up being female (don't they always?), but her all-black outfit is impressive. Loni Anderson's role as beautiful socialite Dawn St. Claire seems superfluous, so most viewers will peg her as the villain. For the middle act, she's demoted to the sidelines while Stryker pursues other leads.

Unfortunately, we don't get an unmasking reveal, or another robbery with Dawn in her masked outfit. A black-clad thief shoots a guard, but that's a male copycat. The final heist takes the whole movie to happen, and then Dawn shows up unmasked to steal a jewelled necklace. She triggers the fire alarm to evacuate the hotel, but what self-respecting cat burglar would risk showing her face?

Return of the Pink Panther (1975) – Lady Claudine Litton (Catherine Schell)

Also, the return of Peter Sellers as Inspector Clouseau after a long break (his last movie was *A Shot in the Dark* way back in 1964). The infamous pink diamond is the target of a dramatic heist following the cartoony credits. In an impressive – and inventive – robbery scene for the era, a black-clad thief uses a crossbow, rope and lubricant to evade laser beams and guards.

The prime suspect is Charles Litton, aka The Phantom, with Christopher Plummer taking on the David Niven role from *The Pink Panther* (1963). Most scenes are played for laughs (this is a comedy, after all). Subplots include Clouseau's boss Dreyfus descending into homicidal mania and the innocent Charles trying to figure out who set him up.

His wife stole the jewel, though a male stunt double was probably used to film the thief's zipline getaway. The scheming Claudine has several encounters with the clueless detective and can't contain her laughter, but her post-reveal role isn't that memorable.

The Real McCoy (1993) – Karen McCoy (Kim Basinger)

Yet another example where the thief is masked at the beginning and never again. That's four examples on this page alone (yes, it happens in *Entrapment* with the Rembrandt theft). Some advice for filmmakers: cat burglars are supposed to wear masks during robberies.

The Real McCoy has a villainess protagonist, though Karen is arguably an anti-heroine as she's coerced into planning a heist by a crime boss. When threatening her doesn't work, the bad guy takes her son hostage as leverage. So Karen teams up with an inept thief (Val Kilmer) to turn the tables.

Basinger plays the mother/criminal mix well, and there's plenty of minor heist action before the big vault raid. Karen breaks into the villain's mansion to rescue her son, but seasoned viewers won't expect her to succeed. Lack of tension is a recurring problem, even with the bank heist finale. Nothing goes wrong, and Karen outsmarts the villains too easily.

Rank #79

Killer Dream Home (2020)
Morgan Dyer (Eve Mauro)

Movie

Many modern Lifetime movies have female villains, but it's a case of quantity over quality. Motives are unimaginative (how many jilted lovers are there in America?). Three murders, a low body count in the 1990s, would be a veritable bloodbath today. And the climaxes are weak or nonexistent.

Thankfully, some producers understand what's expected in these films. Time to champion The Ninth House, a partnership between writer/director Jake Helgren and producer Autumn Federici. Movie titles are typical for the genre: *Deadly Matrimony*, *Psycho Party Planner*, *Psycho Sister-in-law*, *Psycho Stripper*... Yes, death and psychos abound. What makes them stand out are the unpredictability factor and exciting finales, truly a lost art in the 2020s.

Jake Helgren has a horror background, and that shines through in his final products. Expect darkly lit scenes, creepy supporting characters, red herrings, and a few people to get bumped off before the end credits.

Sourcing these movies in the UK is difficult. With no official Lifetime network, these films often turn up on the free-to-air Channel 5 for afternoon showings. That means

114

censorship of violence, which is a big problem with Ninth House productions. The murder sequences are the best parts, and better shot than most TV movies – if only we could watch them. *Killer Dream Home* isn't available in Britain, but I sourced enough footage from online clips to review it.

Villainess

Ninth House varies its casting and includes actors who aren't known for Lifetime movies. Eve Mauro is a fashion model and an unfamiliar face, which helps to keep things fresh, even if her psycho is suitably over the top.

Morgan really wants her dream home: a lavish mansion with exquisitely decorated rooms, a swimming pool, and even an elevator. As the movie title suggests, she's prepared to kill for it. So, she breaks in and drowns the owner in her bathtub. Lunatic Morgan wears a red raincoat instead of the traditional black hoodie favoured by Lifetime villains. Points for originality straight from the outset.

When the property comes onto the market, it's purchased by Josh and Jules Grant (John Deluca and Maiara Walsh) with the help of realtor Renee Rivera. Unfortunately, the happy couple makes the mistake of hiring a psycho woman as their interior designer. As is so often the case, the main characters are a little slow on the uptake, and it's left to the supporting players to snoop. Best friend Bliss (Brooke Butler) is suspicious from the start, leading to many confrontations with Morgan and a simmering hatred between the two women. Which you know is going to end badly for Bliss, but it's a while before we get there.

Morgan is physically attractive (she even gets a swimsuit scene) and uses that to her advantage. She seduces her landlord, who thinks he's onto a winner. Until he wakes up and discovers kinky pictures plastered over the fridge, and a letter from Morgan "suggesting" he ignores a late rent payment. Murder is her solution for those who interfere, and Renee becomes the obligatory mid-movie victim to keep up the pace.

Like any decent Lifetime villainess, Morgan has some crazy chick lines. Her best is when she calls Bliss a lapdog and threatens to bury the mole. This is a preamble to the finale, where Morgan shows up pony-tailed and dressed all in black like an action movie henchwoman. In case Jules and Josh haven't figured out she's insane, Morgan delivers a barmy frame-up monologue served with extra ham and cheese.

Ninth House keeps viewers guessing who'll survive until the end. They do a good job with a minor character who appears to die before he makes a heroic comeback. Being the best friend is usually deadly, so it's no real surprise Bliss meets a gruesome end. Morgan strangles her in the elevator, though the choice of weapon (a tape measure) is inventive.

Far too many Lifetime baddies are arrested or escape justice altogether. Ninth House continues to buck the trend by killing off the villain. Morgan is eliminated with her own nail gun. Not bad, but it would have been nice to add in a stunt double and balcony fall (like *Deadly Matrimony*) to cap things off.

Honourable Mention: Ninth House Productions

Babysitter's Nightmare (2018) – **Audra Monrose (Arianne Zucker)**

Another Ninth House production, this is arguably a horror movie in disguise. It's available to stream in the UK, but (to my knowledge) has never aired on TV. The opening murder scene, where a masked killer suffocates a babysitter, is brutal and graphic for afternoon television. Another woman is stabbed with a broken wine bottle – good luck getting that past the censors.

Babysitter's Nightmare (also known as *A Stranger Outside*) is a typical female alone in the house scenario. Technically, the main character is *not* alone, since she has her child and best friend for company. As expected with this production team, there's a high body count and a bizarre killer guise. The murderer likes to cosplay as Darth Sidious from *Star Wars*, with the same black robe and face-shadowing hood.

The villainess is a vengeful woman whose own child died, so she targets innocent nurses in retribution. There's a great ending to look forward to – a prolonged 20-30 minute sequence with the killer defeated after an epic struggle. Lifetime filmmakers, please take note. This is how to shoot a climax.

Rank #78

Species (1995)
Sil (Natasha Henstridge)

Movie

This sci-fi thriller is best described as a high-budget B-movie. The opening credits scream Syfy channel, but the creature designs by H.R. Giger (better known for the *Alien* franchise) elevate this to an above-average romp.

The plot: a manhunt for an escaped alien/human hybrid. Scientists thought engineering a female guinea pig would make her "more docile and controllable" (their words). Nobody seems to have told them that women are the deadlier sex, and watching a few femme fatale movies beforehand might have suggested a rethink.

After things go wrong (shocker!) and the hybrid escapes, project lead Xavier Finch (Ben Kingsley) hires a team of specialists to track her. This includes a psychic empath (Forest Whitaker), a biologist (Marg Helgenberger), a social studies expert (Alfred Molina), and – naturally – a covert ops military guy (Michael Madsen).

Sil isn't content to remain the prey, however. After the escaped child transforms into an adult, she searches for a male mate. And given that just one hybrid leaves a trail of dead bodies and destruction, that wouldn't be good.

Villainess

Species was Henstridge's first film role, and it's no coincidence the actress is a stunning beauty and appears in many topless scenes. For the early sequences in the research lab and the initial manhunt, Michelle Williams plays the child Sil. Even in this form, the alien hybrid is dangerous, capable of high speed and killing a much larger male. Then Sil grows up, and her real mission begins.

Los Angeles is the hunting ground and – as the culture specialist points out – an ideal location for Sil to blend in. She's very particular about her mating habits, and violently rejects her first choice when she senses he's a diabetic. The hybrid has more luck with the second man, whom she lures into a hot tub for passionate interspecies sex. Unfortunately for Sil and the companion who's promptly drowned, the tracker team arrives before he impregnates her.

Sil can change between human and alien forms, seemingly at will. There are some decent creature effects as the hunted woman becomes a green-skinned predator. The best part of the movie is when she goes on the offensive and becomes the huntress. Deciding the military man would be a suitable mate, she fakes her own death. The humans are too quick to believe their quarry is dead (don't they watch these films?), especially since the hybrid has proven elusive and dangerous.

After changing her appearance, Sil continues her hunt. She's adept at infiltration, and even converses with the biologist in a restroom. Her third attempt at sex, with the social expert, is successful. The pregnant hybrid eliminates her mate and escapes underground with the trackers in close pursuit.

The ending sequence is unimpressive. Sil stays in creature form throughout and doesn't carry the same threat the disguised woman did. In a thankfully brief sequence, Sil gives birth and the heroes burn her disgusting offspring alive. The enraged mother is harder to kill, but the confrontation is weak. It turns into a Michael Madsen show, with the other characters reduced to inactive supporting roles.

Species spawned several poorly regarded sequels, though the original received some acclaim. Henstridge signed up for a trilogy, but only appears briefly in *Species III*.

Honourable Mention: Aliens

Aliens (1986) – Alien Queen (N/A)

Okay, so it's debatable whether a creature can truly be a villainess. But this iconic antagonist, and the epic confrontation with the one-woman army Ellen Ripley, deserve an honourable mention.

The standout segment is the iconic battle, which goes on for several minutes. Like a video game final boss, the creature is a bullet sponge. She (it?) shrugs off entire magazines of ammo that would shred her minions in seconds. Explosive rounds merely prompt the Queen to abandon her lower body and chase the heroine to a spacecraft.

Even 35 years after release, the creature effects stand up to modern viewing. They didn't use CGI, which can date quickly. Ripley in a mechanical versus the Queen's second form is no less exciting. While the creature is predictably jettisoned through an airlock, the death scene with the defeated monster floating through space is satisfying.

Final Move (2006)
Iris Quarrie (Rachel Hunter)

Movie

Chess-themed serial killer movies have been done before, but *Final Move* adds a paranormal element. Psychic Dan Marlowe (Matt Schulze) assists Detective Krieg (Lochlyn Munro) with his investigation. It appears someone is copying the recently executed "Chess Piece Killer" Thomas Page. Marlowe previously identified him from a vision, but did he make a mistake? Cue lots of murders as the duo go on a psycho hunt, and – yes – a city map is used as a chessboard. Why does that always happen?

The annoying colour palette – a horrible orange tint – makes some scenes difficult to watch. The opening murder is well staged, but the other killings are over too quickly. Some are only shown in psychic visions, green-filtered and filmed on shaky cam.

Another problem is that the villainess is too easy to spot. There's an attempt to fool us into thinking an African American chess player is the bad guy, but the masked killer is clearly Caucasian. On the plus side, the film moves along at a brisk pace. The subplot about Marlowe's strained relationship with his wife is well done, though it's obvious the murderer will target his family.

Villainess

An FBI agent helping with the investigation (or pretending to), Iris is a rare example of a female serial killer with a high body count. She tasers a woman after taunting her over the phone, hangs a man in an elevator, and tosses a judge through a top-floor window. Can't complain about a lack of variety.

The opening murder is the most impressive. After making some nasty (voice distorted) threats, the masked psycho attacks her victim, roughs her up, and electrocutes her as she writhes in agony. When the police search the crime scene, they find a chess piece in the victim's hand.

The killer leaves messages for Marlowe, phones him, and even breaks into his house. This hints at a personal connection, and despite the police arresting several suspects, viewers will suspect Iris after she attempts to seduce the married Marlowe. Her response to his rejection is to bed another man, have forced sex, and call him Danny. The director may as well hang the guilty sign around her neck.

After the elevator hanging, the killer escapes to the roof and makes a dramatic escape on a zipline, with the cops shooting in desperation at the fast-moving, black-clad figure. The assailant is masked, but on reviewing the footage of a rooftop shootout, it seems to be Rachel Hunter (or a close match) under the hood. Points for that.

Krieg grows suspicious of Iris when CCTV footage places her at the latest kill scene, but Marlowe is reluctant to accuse her. Iris attempts to throw the police off by claiming another suspect assaulted her. Since this happens off screen, it's no surprise the attack turns out to have been staged. When Krieg and Marlowe find the suspect dead, they should identify Iris as the killer.

In the climax, the masked killer lures the men to a warehouse. She shoots Krieg and confronts Marlowe, with his kidnapped wife and daughter strapped to an explosive-rigged chair. When the black-clad Iris removes her balaclava, it's no surprise she's the copycat chess killer, but good to have an actual reveal.

There's an average confrontation between the villainess and Marlowe where she taunts him only to get shot. The hero's choice of post-mortem line is oh so predictable: "Checkmate."

Honourable Mention: Masked Assailants / Zip Lines

The Last Stand (2013) – Magnet Girl (Diane Lupo), Agent Ellen Richards (Genesis Rodriguez)

Two relatively under-used villainesses in this (kinda) comeback action thriller for Arnold Schwarzenegger. He plays a sheriff who must defend a town when an escaped crime lord and his private army roll in. Expect lots of shooting, explosions, fistfights, and general mayhem.

The black-garbed Magnet Girl, who remains masked throughout, is the point woman for the villain's dramatic breakout. She presumably gets her name from the sequence where she descends atop a crane electromagnet and airlifts a prisoner transport van. She matches the police for firepower, riddles one officer with assault rifle rounds, and keeps the rest pinned down as she ascends. Sadly, this is her only action sequence, and she disappears with no explanation soon after.

Agent Ellen Richards is a weak addition: an FBI agent on the crime boss' payroll. She's revealed as a turncoat early on, but doesn't do much except be the main villain's passenger during his ride to the border. Ultimately, he gets fed up with the woman and kicks her out of his car. She then disappears, only to return at the end and get arrested.

Rank #76

Blast (2004)
Luna (Nadine Velazquez)

Movie

Another *Die Hard* on an X movie, and this particular X is an oil drilling platform off the San Diego coast. Terrorists posing as environmentalists stage a shipping accident, arm themselves with automatic weapons hidden in Christmas presents (!), and take over the facility. The unlikely hero is a tugboat captain with former military experience, who joins forces with an FBI plant to battle the bad guys.

The production budget is large enough to hire some name actors. Vinnie Jones plays a villain (he usually does), and Vivica A. Fox is a tough-talking agent. She has a subplot of her own to contend with: a traitor on her team. And yes, she gets a badass moment when she arrests him.

The villains are after money (who knew?), and their plan is to set off an EMP (electromagnetic pulse) device launched by missile. While *Blast* goes through the obvious plot points – lone heroes against an army of bad guys, a botched raid by US special forces – it's an entertaining ride.

Villainess

Surprisingly, Luna is *not* the only female among the terrorists, though she is the only woman to see any real action. She soon ditches her Christmas outfit for the more usual leather top, and straps on an LMG. That's a light machine gun for those unfamiliar with weapons. And she has a metal finger-blade and martial arts skills to fall back on. We get it – she's a tough girl.

Luna's role in the first half isn't that memorable. She hunts an escaped child through the lower structure, sits around taking orders, and provides verbal support. Her first fight is against the hopelessly outmatched FBI agent. Things get more interesting later on, when Luna finally gets to fire her oversized weapon in a kitchen shootout. A shame that's the only time she uses the LMG, and she somehow doesn't hit her target.

After the villains arm the EMP, the heroes attempt to avert disaster. Luna has repeated fights against the FBI agent, whom she takes a dislike to. The villainess is acrobatic and slippery, dodging automatic weapon fire by somersaulting. While a skilled opponent, the henchwoman survives because the heroes don't finish her when they have the chance. Eventually, the FBI guy gets smart and drops a metal plate on her.

Honourable Mentions: Combat Henchwomen

Crash Dive (1996) – Bolanne (Elena DeBurdo)

Another Michael Dudikoff-led B-movie action thriller, *Crash Dive* is one of his better efforts. When a nuclear submarine is hijacked by terrorists posing as shipwrecked sailors, only he can save us. The lone female in the villain ranks is Bolanne, a beautiful Eastern European who strips naked to seduce a crew member. Sex in the shower, then the nude assassin chokes him with a barbell.

Apart from that excellent kill, there are some decent

henchwoman moments. Bolanne frees her captive leader with a throwing knife, snakes around menacingly, and stabs a man helping the hero. The end fight is longer than usual (about a minute), and the good guy has to work for his victory.

Triple Threat (2019) – Mook (JeeJa Yanin)

This aptly named henchwoman is a member of a mercenary group hired to eliminate a bothersome woman who makes the mistake of campaigning against crime. The pay mistress is a mysterious executive who gives orders by mobile phone. While the big bad isn't particularly interesting as a villainess, Mook is a memorable inclusion, even if she dies before the halfway point.

The film features several high-profile action stars: Tony Jaa, Scott Adkins, and Michael Jai White. Brutal action, a high body count, and explosions galore – what did you expect? Most loud bangs come from Mook, who's overzealous and trigger-happy with her grenade launcher. She specialises in clearing obstructions and dealing area of effect damage.

Mook gets three high-carnage, all-out assaults: a jungle compound, a TV studio, and a police station. On the third raid, she meets her match and loses to the hero. Then he gives Mook a taste of her own medicine and blows her to smithereens.

Blood Widow (2014)
The Blood Widow (Gabrielle Ann Henry)

Movie

When discussing teen slashers, the iconic villains that spring to mind are Jason Vorhees from the *Friday the 13th* series and Michael Myers from *Halloween*. Female slashers of this mould – the silent, mass-murdering type – are rare. Many horror films with a villainess opt for a psychological, supernatural, or jealous psycho archetype. The low-budget slasher *Blood Widow*, and its title character, are a refreshing change.

The movie has few locations, with the entirety taking place in two houses and their surroundings. And the level of acting… best not to mention that. However, the gore effects are better than expected and the kills bloody. The pace is excellent, and other than character development that goes nowhere, there is very little filler material. Most scenes are stalk or slash (or a mix of both), with some backstory interludes. Like Jason and Michael, the masked killer prefers murder to explanatory monologues.

The movie should suit horror fans, provided they can overlook its shortcomings.

Villainess

All credit to the filmmakers for choosing a classic slasher-style outfit. The villainess looks the part in her studded leather outfit and white face mask. Gabrielle Ann Henry plays the Blood Widow, but we only see part of her face when the mask is damaged in the final sequence. Which makes her a terrifying foe – a purely evil, emotionless killer who slices her way through hapless teenagers.

She racks up plenty of victims, starting with a random photographer who wanders into an empty house (as you do) and meets a sticky end in the psycho's basement. Then teenage couple Hugh and Laurie purchase a property next door. When their friends visit for a social gathering, you can predict the outcome.

Next to die are two partying teens and dumb redhead Harmony, who thinks it a good idea to meditate in candlelight in the creepy house. She gets gutted because of her stupidity, then the villainess goes on the offensive and slaughters the rest of the cast. This includes the final girl (!) who's crazy enough to return for payback after knocking the psycho out.

Exposition is provided when Laurie searches the empty property. We learn through photographs and a diary that the Blood Widow's real name is Tiffany, and she was abused as a child. Why is that always the reason? Weird dolls and masks lying tell us she's a *very* disturbed young lady.

It seems the producers intended a *Blood Widow* franchise, and there was a movie listed on IMDb called *Blood Widow Lives*. Sadly, this never materialised, though an improved sequel with such an iconic female slasher would have been welcome.

Honourable Mention: Masked Slashers

Coda (1987) – Dr Leslie Steiner (Arna-Maria Winchester)

Also known as *Symphony of Evil,* this Australian slasher is let down by its slow-burning opening, but things get good in the last hour. If *Blood Widow* had a female Jason Vorhees, then the villainess in *Coda* does her best Michael Myers impression, stalking women in a white face mask.

The murderess targets students, though her motive is never explained. There is an attempt at a summary in the closing scene, but the reasoning ultimately boils down to "she was crazy". Obviously! The villainess' reveal is telegraphed, with only one major character as a credible suspect. At least there was no out of left field reveal.

Another issue is the killer seems to have problems... well, killing people. Leslie requires multiple attempts to murder her victims. Notably, she strangles one woman and drowns her in a lake, then gives up and leaves her alive! Well, at least the psycho's mask is cool.

Night School (1981) - Eleanor Adjai (Rachel Ward)

A golden oldie (for slasher fans), also known as *Terror Eyes,* and now available in restored high definition. The killer's black motorcycle leathers and dark-visored crash helmet won't fool seasoned viewers, but there's still a fantastic unmasking moment near the end.

A nutcase decapitates women with a kukri and dumps their severed heads in water, whether that be a toilet, pond, water-filled trashcan, or local aquarium. The obvious suspect is a voyeur with mental health issues who stalks Eleanor through the seedy nighttime streets of Boston. The familiar "make her seem a victim" trick – who are they kidding?

The investigation switches to an anthropology lecturer familiar with cleansing rituals, but his exchange student assistant, Eleanor, is the culprit. An overlong shower scene and a British accent are not-so-subtle clues to her guilt. Madly in love, the teacher responds to her confession by donning her leathers, and after a chase, he suffers a fatal accident. Case closed, but the lead detective has doubts.

Great kill scenes - such as the loony biker spinning a merry-go-round and springing from a closet to confront a female scuba diver - make this a memorable nostalgia trip. There's also a surprisingly effective scare when the cop's partner plays a masked killer prank in the closing scene.

Shredder (2001) - Evil Skier / Shelly (Candace Moon)

The credited villainess' name aptly describes her: a psycho dressed in a black outfit and reflective goggles, who hates snowboarders (or shredders) enough to slaughter an entire group of them. Typical slasher fare with idiot kids who don't realise there's a killer out there for the first hour, but surprisingly light on nudity. Themed weapons include an ice pick and an icicle, adding some much-needed originality.

Years ago snowboarders hounded a teenage girl, leading to a fatal accident. Her sister is alive, so horror fans will make the connection long before the reveal when she unmasks herself in an icebreaker truck. A fake European who was involved in the girl's death and her resentful father are obvious suspects, which means they aren't guilty to any intelligent viewer.

In a rare gender flip, a male is the last survivor after his bitchy girlfriend's dying words are "I never loved you."

Nobody will mourn her death. This "final boy" scenario is a bluff because a girl thought dead returns to blast the psychotic Shelly into the icebreaker's spinning blade. An honourable mention for an entertaining, if flawed, low budget production.

Rank #74

Sky High (2005)
Gwen / Royal Pain (Mary Elizabeth Winstead)

Movie

When putting together my list, I focused on action movies with some thrillers and horror entries. Comedy isn't my favourite genre, but I'm aiming for variety. This Walt Disney family adventure has a lot going for it, and a strong moral tale at its core. And the inclusion of a masked villainess is welcome!

Sky High is about school kids with problems. Not that original, you might think, except these children have special powers. The title institution – that floats in the sky – is an academy for superheroes. Students learn how to build ray guns, save imperilled citizens, and all the other good guy stuff.

One prevailing theme is the two-tier education system. Impress during induction, and you're chosen to be a hero. If not, then you're a sidekick (also known as hero support) and treated as inferior. Will Stronghold is the offspring of two superhero parents, but he has no powers and so becomes a sidekick. That's until he develops super strength during a cafeteria fight with a pyrokinetic arch-enemy. Then he's transferred to the hero group, and his problems really start.

Villainess

The chief antagonist is a mysterious armour-suited villain known only as Royal Pain, whom Will's parents defeated many years ago. But great foes aren't so easily disposed of.

Guessing the villain's identity is relatively easy. Royal Pain uses the voice disguiser trick, which usually implies a female. Will has two girls in his life, so a decent chance one of them is bad. Girl #1 is Layla (Danielle Panabaker) who's a good variant of Poison Ivy with the power to control plants. Girl #2 is Gwen Grayson, a teaching assistant who seems charming at first. Then she reveals her true colours and deceives Layla into abandoning Will at a house party.

The event is a cover to steal Royal Pain's pacifier, a suitably high-tech beam weapon. If Will had any doubts about Gwen's intentions, those are erased when he discovers his girlfriend's photo in the school yearbook. Long ago, she was called Sue Tenny, and is shown holding the pacifier in lab class.

Will races off to save the day and must foil Royal Pain's diabolical plot. She wants to turn the Sky High kids into babies and re-raise them as villains. Suitably dastardly, eh?

No surprise that the school bullies and bitchy cheerleader (who makes multiple copies of herself) side with the villainess. Naturally, Will teams up with the sidekicks whose maligned powers prove useful. And the theme resurfaces when Royal Pain / Gwen / Sue Tenny reveals her motivation was derision as a sidekick. Maybe the school should rethink its policy.

There's a fun climax where Will battles Royal Pain, and the sidekicks (make that heroes) overcome the villainess. As this is a family movie, their efforts are recognised, and the villains imprisoned to set up a potential sequel. So far there's been talk of one, but nothing ever materialised.

Honourable Mention: Family Movies

Mr Magoo (1997) – Luanne LeSeur (Kelly Lynch)

Another comedy adventure produced by Walt Disney, adapted from a cartoon about a short-sighted, accident-prone hero. The movie received backlash from the disabled community because of its negative portrayal of visual impairment. That said, this Leslie Nielsen vehicle is a fun romp, even if most of the humour is mediocre slapstick.

That criticism doesn't apply to the villainess, who's above average. Luanne is a jewel thief with a habit of double-crossing her partners, and a mistress of disguise for good measure. She's played by martial artist Kelly Lynch, foreshadowing her *Charlie's Angels* role a few years later.

Luanne wears some silly outfits, notably a bikini, a shiny silver catsuit (just because) and – most crazy of all – a "money suit" with wads of cash sewn into black fabric. Well, this is a comedy. Thankfully, the villainess' high-kicking antics are lively, and she makes a good adversary. She beats up a small army of guys while unarmed at a crime boss' wedding, but she's no match for Mr Magoo, who wins purely by accident.

Rank #73

Colombiana (2011)
Cateleya (Zoe Saldana)

Movie

A villainess protagonist entry, with a female assassin out for – what else? – revenge. Despite the tragic backstory, the central character is firmly in anti-heroine territory (if not villainy) because of her cold-blooded style and ruthless executions.

As plots go, *Colombiana* is standard fare, yet another tale of retribution that plays out predictably. But the lead is more interesting than most.

Villainess

The opening twenty-five minutes showcase Cataleya as a young girl (Amandla Stenberg in these scenes), and she's a fiery one. Her father has ties to the criminal underworld and is targeted by a rival. Good thing he's trained his family in weapon use, then. This includes his wife (handy with automatics) and teenage daughter. She soon proves she's no easy prey by skewering a henchman's hand to the dining table.

Even at a young age, Cataleya is a force to be reckoned with, navigating the streets and shanty towns of Bogota with confidence. After she eludes her pursuers, our anti-heroine bargains her way into the United States (with financial data from her father), gives the authorities the slip, and meets up with a family friend in Chicago. The contact is – of course – a criminal, whom Cateleya asks to train her as a killer.

After a time skip to adulthood, Cateleya orchestrates a fake DU crime and gets locked up in a police station. All part of her plan to murder a criminal under guard by US marshals. This nimble killer is a grown-up version with even more intelligence and athletic skill. After an imaginative sequence, where she escapes custody and disables a vent fan, we get a cold execution by the remorseless protagonist.

Things settle down after that, with three subplots converging. The first involves a police detective piecing together the assassin's many murders (and assuming the killer is male). The second is the prerequisite romance present in female assassin tales. She may as well give up, because these never play out happily. Third, there's the relationship between Cateleya and her adopted father / mentor, which breaks down since she's obsessed with revenge. To the point of leaving calling card tattoos on her victims.

To keep things zipping along, there's another assassination, this time at a luxury villa with a glass-covered shark pool (!). This enables an over-the-top death scene with a crooked financier fed to his own pets by the merciless hitwoman. Subplots are then wrapped up. The boyfriend takes a photo, which leads to a police raid on Cateleya's apartment and a daring getaway. The reckless woman's antics get her mentor killed, which really pisses her off.

After Cataleya blackmails / tricks the detective into helping her, she learns the main villain's location from a corrupt agent. Putting a man in the crosshairs of a sniper rifle is a good way to break down his resistance.

The big finale has Cateleya assault the big boss' mansion estate with enough firepower to wipe out a small army. The bodyguards don't last long, except for the tough lieutenant, who puts up a bit more of a struggle. Throughout all this, the main baddie hides in a safe room. After the massacre, he makes a run for it and thinks he's got away in a van. If he had checked the rear before setting off, he might have seen the assassin's hounds. Feeding her targets to hungry animals is this woman's speciality.

Honourable Mention: Assassins

Menno's Mind (1997) – Loria (Stephanie Romanov)

A direct-to-video sci-fi thriller, and another anti-heroine firmly in villainess territory. The reluctant hero is a computer programmer (Billy Campbell) drawn into a rebel operation to expose a corrupt politician. This dodgy official plans to win an election through subliminal mind control. Virtual reality is a familiar plot device, and the atrocious computer graphics weren't even good in the 1990s.

The female lead is the black-garbed Loria, who's more of a vicious henchwoman than heroine. She has no issue with killing security personnel, often in brutal fashion. When she's done eliminating two rent-a-cops with neck snaps, she threatens the nerd at gunpoint. Loria even forces her captive to download her dead lover's memories into his brain.

The only reason to root for Loria is that the bad guy (Corbin Bernsen) is even nastier than she is. Fittingly, she sacrifices herself to save the programmer and is reunited with her lover in cyberspace. Don't expect the story to make sense – it's that kind of movie.

The Alternate (2000)
Mary (Brooke Theiss-Genesse)

Movie

A B-movie where most of the budget was apparently spent on recognisable actors, this action thriller is laughable at times. Eric Roberts plays an ex-CIA man known only as The Replacement and does the *Die Hard* thing when bad guys kidnap the US President. For the last act, there's just one villain: The Leader (Bryan Genesse), who takes on the authorities and hero all by himself.

The Alternate (also known as *Agent of Death*) features extended cameos by Ice-T and Michael Madsen. The former is a glorified security guard who spends most of his screen time behind a desk. He's probably Secret Service, though it's not specified. This guy is terrible at his job, since it only takes a team of five to infiltrate a hotel, disable the agents on duty with blowpipes, and abscond with the President.

Turns out this is a fake kidnapping orchestrated by the campaign manager to increase popularity. Except the Leader and his henchwoman Mary fancy a bigger payday, so the hostage situation becomes real.

Madsen's character is the "guy on the outside", who stands about in his tinted shades and manages (more like botches) special forces raids. The hotel has no alternative access routes, a lame excuse to keep all the action in one location. Good job that the Replacement offers some actual resistance.

The last half hour is especially silly, as the Leader comes after the Replacement with a flamethrower. This leads to average shootouts and poorly staged fights between the two men on the hotel roof. Fortunately, the female villain is more memorable, otherwise the film would be entirely forgettable.

Villainess

No, the actors' names are not similar by coincidence. Brooke Theiss-Genesse is the real-life wife of Bryan Genesse and seems to have a martial arts background. Or trained a lot before filming, since she's very able in her lengthy fight scene, one of the rare highlights.

Viewers are first introduced to the athletic Mary during a training sequence. She gets plenty of action here, dropping from the ceiling and mowing the opposition down with blanks. Not long after, she swaps those for real bullets and shoots it out with the Replacement. The hero is forced to leave the President behind, and the Leader sends his top (and only!) ally after the one man who can stop them.

Mary's initial attempt doesn't go so well. She steps into an obvious trap: loose wires in a pool of water. The villainess turns on the power, goes all shaky and collapses. Many first-time viewers probably cursed this "wasted" opportunity. Fortunately, there's much better to come.

See, this woman doesn't go down so easily and comes back for round two. She now has a metal rod to even things out and enjoys working over the Replacement. The fight lasts almost two full minutes, and there's no cutaway shot to another scene. Pure brilliance for any villainess fan. Both parties exchange blows – this is a woman who can receive damage and dish it out. She lands some heavy strikes and ultimately gets the better of her opponent.

Mary, like many action villainesses, gets cocky and lets down her guard. This allows the Replacement to grab the henchwoman as a human shield when the Leader shows up. And so Mary gets taken out by her own team. With a better demise, this villainess would have ranked much higher. But this fight is a must-see.

Honourable Mentions: Tough to Kill

Tagget (1991) – Mrs Sands (Sarah Douglas)

The actress, best known for playing Ursa in *Superman II*, has a brief but brilliant role in this conspiracy thriller. Her brutally efficient hitwoman kills an old man, beating him with a stylish wooden cane after a clandestine meeting. Then the assassin goes after the hero, a crippled Vietnam veteran who suffers from paralysing flashbacks.

Mrs Sands plans to stage Tagget's suicide, but he outsmarts her by switching off the lights. Action continues with a shootout and a drag-out fight on the floor. The crippled hero angle works well and gives the hitwoman a physical advantage in the struggle. But the hero overpowers the assassin, then knocks her through a window and over a balcony rail to her doom. At least she put up a good struggle.

Post Impact (2004) – Sarah Henley (Joanna Taylor)

The villainess in this post-apocalyptic sci-fi thriller is a British ex-SAS (Special Air Service) agent who wastes no time seducing the hero (Dean Cain). This includes a steamy sex scene in a shower (in uncensored versions).

The world has entered a second ice age after a comet impact, and a satellite microwave beam weapon has fallen into rebel hands. It's up to Dean, the Brit, and a team of soldiers to recover it. Henley is depicted as brutal, gunning down people without remorse. A second female is a romantic interest, so no surprise that Henley is a plot twist villain.

After a brutal knife fight in a control room, the hero tosses the traitor through a window. Unlike Mrs Sands, a high fall doesn't kill this woman, and she returns for a second go. There's more combat, some boasting, and Henley is shot. *Another* long drop, then a sharp icicle falls and skewers the villainess. The best demise of the three reviewed here, but the action scenes are average.

88 *Minutes* (2007)
Lauren Douglas / Lydia Doherty (Leelee Sobieski)

Movie

Note: This review is based on the director's cut version.

A mystery thriller based on the "real time" concept, with one minute of screen time per minute of actual in-universe time. Technically not true for the prologue (set many years earlier), but the rest of the film plays out in real time. This includes the titular 88 minutes the murderer gives the main character to live.

The hero is Jack Gramm (Al Pacino), a forensic psychologist and university lecturer. His testimony helped convict the serial killer Forster, who strung his female victims up by their ankles using cables and pulleys. He then cut their arteries and let them bleed to death. Now there's a copycat with a vendetta against Gramm, who murders the women in his life to frame him.

It turns out the 88 minutes refers to a tragic event in Gramm's past, where he left his young sister alone and she was murdered. An answerphone tape recording of the crime lasted the same length, and it appears Forster and his copycat accomplice are making things personal.

There are many suspects in the movie, primarily Gramm's students and a mysterious guy in black leather.

No prize for guessing he's a red herring, and with everyone else eliminated come the climax, it's easy to pick out the killer.

Villainess

That murderess is one of Gramm's students: the inquisitive Lauren, who tries to throw him (and viewers) off the scent by faking an attack on herself. Savvy watchers won't be fooled since we never see the attack take place and Gramm finds no sign of the phantom suspect. To provide even more hints, a montage shows a murder victim where Gramm considers only female suspects. So even the hero has twigged that threatening callers who use voice disguisers are usually women.

Lauren dons biker gear and a dark-visored crash helmet to bump off the "leather guy" at Gramm's apartment. The outfit is standard attire for someone who'll later be revealed to be female. The villainess then goes after the women in his life: the helpful student, a colleague the good doctor slept with, and the university dean. With help from his trusted assistant, Gramm identifies Lauren as Lydia Doherty, an attorney working with Forster. She's one of his psycho groupies who worship serial killers (a besotted female lawyer represented Forster in the prologue trial).

After the unsurprising reveal that Lauren/Lydia is indeed the killer, Gramm confronts her in a university office building. For literal leverage, the murderess has the dean suspended over the balcony edge by a rope/pulley setup and holds the cable. If Gramm shoots her, the hostage dies, and the killer also has the student hostage as backup. Lauren recounts her scheme with sparse black and white flashbacks that should have been longer or more detailed.

Lauren insists on giving Gramm the full 88 minutes she

promised. This proves her undoing since the doctor tipped off his FBI agent friend, and he shows up to shoot the villainess in the back. With the threat taken out, Gramm grabs the cable and saves the dean, which sends the villainess plummeting to her death. Overall, it's a decent confrontation capped off with an average demise.

Honourable Mention: Real Time

Nick of Time (1995) – Ms Jones (Roma Maffia)

Another real-time movie, this one stayed true to the concept from the opening titles to the end. Johnny Depp plays an average accountant, and Christopher Walken is a menacing villain known only as Mr Smith. He and his accomplice, credited as Ms Jones, kidnap the hero's young daughter to coerce him into killing the Governor of California.

The plot plays out mostly as expected, with Depp's character attempting to warn people of the intended assassination. His efforts are moot, and end with Mr Smith making timely threats or the person involved in the conspiracy. Eventually, the hero enlists the help of a Vietnam veteran to thwart Smith's plan and rescue his daughter.

Ms Jones is always secondary to the charismatic Walken, but has a few worthy scenes. In her most memorable scene, she threatens the daughter with a gun hidden behind a seat cushion. The villainess outlines the various firearms she could be packing and the nasty effects. There's a good scrap between Ms Jones and the Vietnam vet, which culminates in him knocking her out with a detached false leg.

Epic Tier (#70 to #41)

Rank #70

Thunderball (1965)
Fiona Volpe (Luciana Paluzzi)

Movie

James Bond movies have a winning formula: action, romance, and humour. Over the decades these films have delivered, except for the occasional misfire. Every iconic hero needs worthy adversaries, however, and there have been many standouts in the series. Including females.

If I ranked my favourite female villains, there could easily be half a dozen entries from the Bond franchise. Since I'm aiming for balance, I've chosen four "headliners" and will cover the other films as honourable mentions and discussions. Fiona Volpe is my lowest-ranked pick, and this review also summarises the Sean Connery Bond films and George Lazenby's solo outing.

The plot of *Thunderball* is generic, involving the theft of nuclear weapons by a criminal organisation and a ransom demand. Main bad guy, Blofeld, holds conferences with electric chairs in case his underlings should fail or betray him. These plot elements will be familiar to anyone who's seen *Austin Powers*, where the tropes were spoofed. Bond stumbles across the fiendish plan by accident whilst recuperating at a clinic, and embarks on a mission to save the world. That scenario seems to recur a lot.

The movie is infamous for ambitious and overlong underwater sequences. With the slowdown, this is a poor setting for action set pieces. The last act – a battle between henchmen in black scuba gear and the goodies in orange – is a boring drag. Thankfully, the villainess' scenes all take place on dry land.

Villainess

While the main villains are faceless Blofeld and Largo (Adolfo Celi), Fiona is almost his equal with a major role in Spectre's evil scheme. In an early scene with an accomplice who's too greedy for his own good, she comes across as a no-nonsense authority figure. This is moments after she plays the femme fatale with an airman she lures into a deadly trap.

Fiona's talents extend to assassination when Blofeld orders a man killed as punishment for failure. Fiona does the deed in style, intervening as her quarry pursues Bond's Aston Martin DB5. Not to be outdone, the female killer has her own gadget vehicle: a motorcycle fitted with rocket launchers. Those make quick work of her target. Not long afterwards, there's a decent reveal where the helmeted biker is revealed as Fiona. But it was almost certainly a stunt double for "her" earlier scenes.

Fiona and Bond don't meet until the halfway point, when she picks the stranded agent up and gives him a high-speed ride. The villainess is vilaring in this sequence, openly displaying her Spectre ring. Later on, she seduces Bond and brags she's immune to his charms. And unlike Pussy Galore in *Goldfinger*, there's no final act shift of allegiance this time around. Fiona even makes the point in a defiant speech.

After Bond escapes Largo's henchmen, the final

encounter takes place in a bar during Mardi Gras. Bond hides by dancing with a female patron, but Fiona soon takes the woman's place. She intends it to be his last fling and has a concealed henchman ready to shoot Bond in the back. However, the hero expects this move and pivots Fiona around at the last instant, so it's her shot instead. Cold-blooded execution of female villains would come much later in the series, but we're still treated to a one-liner.

Honourable Mentions / Discussion: Sean Connery / George Lazenby Bond Movies

Dr. No (1962) – Photographer (Marguerite LeWars), Miss Taro (Zena Marshall)

The first official Bond movie set the tone for those that followed. Dastardly villains operate from elaborate lairs, and women are beautiful, seductive, and frequently dangerous. The weakest of Connery's films from a villainess perspective, but there are two female foes worth a mention.

Marguerite LeWars has the honour of playing the first-ever Bond villainess, though the photographer is never named. A freelancer working for a mysterious enemy, this woman shows her evil side by licking a lightbulb after snapping shots of Bond in Kingston, Jamaica. When caught, the photographer refuses to talk, even when Bond's allies threaten to break her arm. She even smashes a lightbulb in her questioner's face, drawing blood. Tough cookie, this one.

Miss Taro is a more traditional femme fatale, relying on her sexy voice to deceive the spy. That might have been more effective if he hadn't caught her eavesdropping. Still, Bond never turns down an opportunity to bed a beautiful woman, even one with dark intentions. Of course, the hero merely bides his time – and enjoys himself – until the authorities arrive.

From Russia with Love (1963) – Rosa Klebb (Lotte Lenya)

The second film has the series' first major villainess, even if she answers to Blofeld. The notorious man with the white cat is still faceless at this point, leaving Klebb and henchman Red Grant to do Spectre's dirty work.

Klebb lost out to Fiona Volpe when I selected my pick from the early Bonds, but she makes a sinister spy. Her character is manipulative and controlling, especially with Bond girl Tatiana Romanova. Though prominent early in the movie, Klebb vanishes for the middle act, only to return and stab a fellow operative with a poisoned blade concealed in her shoe.

Her attempt to kill Bond doesn't go so well, resulting in a poorly staged fight. After Tatiana shoots the villainess, Bond utters a darkly humourous one-liner, a trait that would continue throughout the series.

Goldfinger (1964)

The first truly extravagant movie in the franchise, there are many iconic elements, notably a charismatic title villain and his henchman Oddjob (don't forget the killer hat). There's also an epic finale at Fort Knox, where an all-female pilot squadron takes out tens of thousands of US troops with nerve gas.

Other minor villainesses include a treacherous beauty in the pre-credits sequence and an old lady guarding a checkpoint (who's handy with a machine gun). A female sniper makes an appearance and takes a potshot at Bond. She's after Goldfinger, but misses by some distance, only to meet her end shortly afterward.

The main female character is Pussy Galore, the villain's personal pilot. A damn good one (in her words) and a judo expert. Bond still overpowers the feisty woman, seduces her, and converts her to the cause of good. So she exchanges the deadly nerve gas for a harmless alternative, and *Goldfinger* – while a classic movie – is not the best from a villainess perspective.

You Only Live Twice (1967) – Helga Brandt (Karin Dor)

This movie takes Bond to Japan, but he displays the same weakness towards women. Almost getting killed by a Chinese agent in the pre-title sequence doesn't dampen his enthusiasm for Oriental females. In fairness, the "assassination" was staged to fake Bond's death.

Blofeld returns, this time played by Donald Pleasance. The minor villains include businessman Osato and Spectre number eleven, Helga Brandt. After the henchwoman seduces Bond in a cabin, she traps him in a crashing aircraft and bails out mid-flight. Any 007 fan will know that elaborate attempts will fail, and what that means for Spectre operatives. Here, Blofeld feeds Helga to his piranha fish.

A gruesome death to frighten Osato (not that *he* succeeds either), followed by a ninja commando raid in a spectacular volcano lair. Some good girl action, but no female villains, unfortunately.

On Her Majesty's Secret Service (1969) – Irma Bunt (Ilse Steppat)

George Lazenby starred as James Bond for the first and only time in a movie most famous for its tragic finale. Telly Savalas is Blofeld, with Irma as his main henchwoman. This lady comes across as a strict, bossy type and wouldn't look out of place as a school headmistress. Many of her scenes take place in a Swiss Alpine clinic where Bond frolics with female patients, arguably the weakest part of the movie.

After a slow buildup, things kick into gear about halfway through with some great action sequences on the snowy slopes. For the descent, Blofeld leads the pursuit, but Irma takes over with a secondary team after Bond reaches the presumed safety of a village. Don't be so naïve, 007 – it's never that easy to escape.

Irma is overshadowed by Diana Rigg as the ill-fated Teresa Bond. The hero's fling blossoms into genuine romance, and the lovers tie the proverbial knot. Most aficionados know how this story ends – with an injured Blofeld and Irma tracking the couple down. Since the main bad guy is injured, the henchwoman fires the fatal shot, a single wicked act that makes her a notable villainess in the franchise.

Diamonds Are Forever (1971) – Bambi (Lola Larson), Thumper (Trina Parks)

After the downer ending to Lazenby's brief tenure, Bond entered the 1970s with this campy entry. Charles Gray is a much softer Blofeld with hair. He's obsessed with world domination, and so scared of Bond's vendetta that he's got multiple doubles. Tiffany Case is among the weaker Bond girls, reduced to little more than a bimbo by the time the credits roll.

Diamonds Are Forever is best remembered for its secondary villains. There's a great elevator fight between Bond and a smuggler, and a humorous pair of hitmen in Wint and Kidd. They have a thing for trading one-liners after they kill someone.

For villainess fans, two physical bodyguards in Bambi

and Thumper, and like everything else in this movie, their scenes ooze camp. This is Bond's first proper fight with female opponents, but the ending is weak. The two women dunk Bond in their swimming pool, only to be easily overpowered moments later.

Never Say Never Again (1983) – Fatima Blush (Barbara Carrera)

Sean Connery returned for this unofficial remake of *Thunderball*. He shouldn't have, because the updated version is inferior in almost every respect. The characters are unimpressive, with no official series actors present. Edward Fox is a comical version of M who's dreadfully out of place, Max Von Sydow is a lacklustre Blofeld, and Rowan Atkinson has a terrible cameo as a hapless diplomat.

For the villainess, we have Barbara Carrera as the poor woman's Fiona Volpe. Her first assassination – throwing a snake into a man's car – is a pale imitation of the biker/ rocket original. Carrera overacts in nearly every scene, giggling whilst wearing increasingly ridiculous outfits. She fails multiple times to kill Bond, using truly bizarre methods (remote controlled sharks, anyone?). In the end, Bond defeats her with an exploding pen with about forty-five minutes to go. Normally, such a premature exit would be disappointing, but it's a relief here.

Bloodfist IV: Die Trying (1992)
Lisa (Cat Sassoon)

Movie

This 1990s action flick stars Don "The Dragon" Wilson, a B-movie regular who often headlined mid-budget productions. Several of his films featured female villains, though most were forgettable. The henchwomen were usually defeated easily with little screen time, so this entry in the *Bloodfist* series is a welcome exception.

The plots of the six entries are mostly unconnected. This one has Wilson's character, a repo man called Danny, pursued by criminals after he repossesses a car containing a box of Easter chocolates. The villains really want their property back, so they show up at Danny's office and massacre his colleagues. No, these guys aren't worried about snacks, but want the nuclear triggers hidden inside.

Various people take an interest in Danny, including the police, the FBI, and two shady CIA agents with their own agenda. The storyline then becomes confusing with the various groups working against each other, and many people impersonating someone else.

Villainess

One of those charades involves a woman masquerading

as a babysitter. Danny thinks she's harmless until he discovers the body of the real babysitter in a closet. This leads to the first fight sequence between Wilson and Sassoon. The martial artist villainess switches between kicks and uses improvised weapons. Eventually, the two fighters wrestle over a hot electrical hob, which burns Lisa's wrist, and Danny knocks her out.

Then the police show up and assume Danny is the bad guy. Lisa takes advantage and kicks the gun out of his hands. He's able to escape with an acrobatic dive through a window before the woman takes out the shell-shocked cops with lethally accurate headshots. As introductions go, it's impressive.

Disappointingly, Lisa vanishes after that encounter, and most of the middle act revolves around Danny's attempts to evade the authorities and track down the bad guys. Several B-movie stars appear, including James Tolkan (Mr Strickland from *Back to the Future*) and Gary Daniels.

When Lisa returns, she's dressed in a suitably evil black outfit and smokes a cigarette. Cat Sassoon comes across as menacing, so it's unfortunate the actress died at a young age. Lisa shows her ruthlessness after two henchmen recover the wrong box of chocolates. Instead of her fists, the villainess uses a switchblade to cut the throats of the lackeys with one swipe.

After that double execution, it's the restaurant finale. Lisa tries to kill a woman Danny's working with, but her burn marks give her away, and the villainess gets sprayed with mace before she can strike. After Danny destroys the triggers (which *really* annoys the bad guys), he encounters Lisa for the last time. In a one-sided affair, she pummels him with kicks, including a rather painful one to the crotch!

Promising, until Danny turns the tables and knocks Lisa out in bland and unimpressive fashion. A disappointing end, but Lisa's screen presence and the babysitter fight land her a ranking spot.

Honourable Mentions: *Bloodfist* Series

Bloodfist VI: Ground Zero (1995) – Tori (Cat Sassoon)

Cat played another villainess in the series: a traitor officer working with terrorists to steal – you guessed it – nuclear weapons. Don Wilson's character is a military courier who must stop them. Viewers hoping for a repeat of Cat's impressive displays in *IV* will be disappointed. No martial arts, which is a waste, but this woman is ruthless and trigger-happy.

After Wilson thins the terrorist ranks, Tori gains the upper hand by equipping night vision goggles and shooting a power relay. This plunges the underground bunker into deep red as emergency lights come on. A clever tactic, but it makes the action scenes difficult to follow until Wilson outsmarts the henchwoman by blinding her. Once again, he knocks Cat's character out with a single punch, and it's not even on screen.

Moving Target (2000) – Kate (Lisa Duane)

Bloodfist IV was remade and set in Ireland, with all the picturesque scenery that implies. This could be called a copy, with identical situations and dialogue to the original. Many elements are familiar: an overweight detective, a CIA agent duo, and a staff room massacre. Wilson is a tourist caught up in events when he purchases a six-pack of beer. Want to guess what's hidden inside?

The bad guys aren't as memorable, with an unknown replacing Gary Daniels and the redhead Kate instead of Lisa.

She's an inferior martial artist, and only impresses in the double execution by knife scene. Yes, that's repeated here too. Her opening fight – in disguise as a hotel maid – is over in a minute with barely any combat. Her final encounter with Wilson is not much better, and we get a single knockout blow even tamer than Lisa's.

Rank #68

***Happy Death Day* (2017)**
Lori Spengler (Ruby Modine)

Movie

Teen slasher movies have been done to death (pardon the obvious cliché), so it's always welcome when someone injects a dose of originality. This 2017 film mixed familiar genre staples (girl in peril, masked killer, everybody a suspect) with the time loop plotline from *Groundhog Day* (1993). The resulting crossover had the heroine Tree reliving (and dying) the same day until she solved her own murder.

This setup allows Tree to meet many sticky ends at the hands of the mascot-masked psycho, instead of the plot immunity normally afforded to final girls. One nice element was Tree's progression from hapless screaming victim to determined investigator, and then to leather-clad badass by the finale.

It takes a dozen minutes – with plenty of exposition – before the first kill, when Tree stupidly wanders into a darkened tunnel to investigate a music box. Only to get knifed by the murderer. The heroine goes through a period of denial before she wises up and avoids the death trap. Taking refuge at a party isn't a bad idea, but it doesn't save her from a second skewering.

Many characters are presented as potential killers,

including boyfriends and sorority girls. Tree crosses most off her suspect list, usually when she sees them (or their body) at the same time as the murderer. There's an attempt to pin the killings on a crazy serial killer, but it's not hard to figure out he's just a red herring and who the real psycho is. Despite the predictable outcome, this is an entertaining romp with a nice twist on the usual slasher affair.

Villainess

The girl behind the mask turns out to be Tree's roommate, Lori. She conveniently works at the hospital where the serial killer was a patient, making him an ideal patsy. Seasoned horror fans will peg Lori as the killer long before the reveal, given her open hostility to Tree. Her motive is a wacky mix of jealousy over Tree's affair with a doctor / teacher and "just because".

Despite the insane monologue, Lori's kills are inventive. Besides basic stabbings, Tree is drowned in a fountain and incinerated in a flaming police car before she figures out the mystery. The villainess' initial plan was to poison her victim with a birthday cupcake, but Tree doesn't eat it until she thinks she's won. Then the day repeats, and she realises the nutcase male isn't the killer.

There's a decent deduction speech with Lori unmasked as the villainess, and the climax is suitably crazy. Tree and Lori have a massive dorm room fight, which culminates when Tree grabs a light fixture and swing kicks the murderess through a window.

Honourable Mentions: Teen Slashers

Happy Birthday to Me (1981) – Ann Thomerson (Tracey Bregman)

A more traditional slasher flick from the early 1980s, and a quirky one. The varied kill scenes include a scarf thrown into a spinning bike wheel and, most infamously, a shish-kebab through the mouth. Production values are higher than usual for teen horror, too.

The main character is Ginny, a girl with a traumatic past. About two-thirds of the way through, she's revealed as the killer. Or so it seems, since the actual murderer is her friend Ann wearing a latex mask. This is a cop-out, as the lead actress plays the role prior to the reveal. The motive is a confusing revenge tale about a birthday party years ago, Ann being half-sister to Ginny, and an affair with Ginny's father.

The climax is completely out there, with dead bodies arranged around a birthday party table. After such a bizarre setup, it's disappointing that the struggle between Ginny and Ann is brief. This ends with Ann stabbed in the chest and Ginny with plenty of explaining to do.

Girls Nite Out (1982) - Barney / Katie Cavanaugh (Rutanya Alda)

A creepy villainess dressed as a university mascot is the highlight of this 1980s slasher (also known as *The Scaremaker*). An inmate at the local nuthouse commits suicide, inspiring an unknown killer to "borrow" the bear costume (after they stab the owner), attach razor claws to the furry gloves, and turn a scavenger hunt into a student hunt. On the dark campus, the teens are easy pickings.

Production values are high for the era, with an impressive college arena scene and dozens of extras when the police are finally called. Before that, the killer phones the student radio station and whispers about whores in a cackling, gender-neutral voice. The head of security dismisses it as a prank (surprise!) until he connects the murders to the dead inmate's twin sister.

The cafeteria lady is the killer, suffering from a split personality. A creepy outfit and some eerie kill scenes are undone by the "resolution" that resolves nothing. The security guard confronts the insane slasher, who opens a freezer to reveal the body of her brother wearing a bear claw.

After that "what the hell" moment, the credits roll, leaving Barney's fate ambiguous. Where's a gutsy final girl when you need one? Honourable mention for the bear, shame about the ending.

Silent Thunder (1992)
Python (Sandahl Bergman)

Movie

Another late female baddie reveal, but this is an ordinary revenge tale about a family man hunting the psycho trucker who killed his son. No surprise that the father (Stacy Keach) and his lad argued just before the tragedy, and now the hero wants to make amends.

Also known as *Revenge on the Highway*, the film is based on the true story of Claude Samms, and the production is dedicated to his son, Paul. Some plot elements are almost certainly dramatised, but the setting and villainess are relatively unique. Sadly, the title is only available on VHS, but image quality doesn't matter for a text review.

Much of the movie focuses on Claude's relationship with his wife, which becomes strained as his quest for justice turns into a personal obsession. Frustrated with the police, Claude takes justice into his own hands. In his anger, he nearly shoots an innocent man before he comes to his senses. Then, Claude gets a breakthrough when a witness to an earlier murder comes forward.

While early action is lacking, the finale is enjoyable. An extended truck duel between Claude and his nemesis lasts over ten minutes. Since the movie predates the CGI era, there's impressive stunt work, and plenty of tire screeching and explosions in the satisfying climax.

Villainess

The villain isn't fully shown until the last fifteen minutes, with most shots focusing on their distinctive yellow truck or partial facial features. The deep-voiced antagonist – known only by their handle, Python – enjoys causing fatal motor accidents. One couple narrowly escape in the pre-credits scene, before a woman and her car are completely incinerated partway through.

Anyone familiar with "disguise a woman as a man" movie trick will suspect the psycho is female. As an extra hint for villainess fans, Sandahl Bergman is listed in the credits. She *always* plays someone bad and hasn't shown her face with twenty minutes to go. Which means...

After the lady trucker reveals herself, she confronts Claude in a seedy bar. The male regulars start out on Python's side, but they abandon her after she smashes a bottle and threatens to slash Claude. Seems violence is okay for these guys, but murder isn't on the agenda. After that, it's truck against truck as the hero and villainess go tire to tire in an epic last encounter. This livens up the movie, which had been pedestrian before that.

Python smirks and laughs while causing carnage, with Claude equal to the challenge. One destructive scene has the villainess and her juggernaut truck crash through a police barricade, leaving burning cars and chaos in her wake. After a prolonged road chase, both drivers ditch their trailers for the last stretch. Claude gives the villainess a taste of her own medicine, causing an accident of his own as he topples the opposing vehicle. In the climactic scene, Claude stands over the wounded Python and shows no sympathy for her plight.

Honourable Mention: Natural Disguised Voices

Serial Cops (1997) – Rachel Quinn / Alone (Terri Hawkes)

Also known as *Papertrail* and *Trail of a Serial Killer*, this mystery thriller features another deep-voiced female psycho. It's a fairly average tale livened up by tense physical encounters between the hero and the hooded murderer.

Much of the plot centres around a psychiatrist and her therapy group, all of whom are potential suspects. Both the lady doctor and the cop are taunted by the killer – known only as Alone – who mutilates their victims and makes things personal.

The ending is a cop-out, with a previously unseen woman revealed as the murderer. Before that, she'd "appeared" as a faceless caller phoning in during the therapy sessions. After that non-twist and a dull chase through a darkened building, viewers hoping for some improvement will be disappointed. In a weak confrontation, the cop dispatches the villainess with a single shot. An honourable mention for some decent kill sequences, but there's little else to recommend here.

Rank #66

Fair Game **(1995)**
Rosa (Jenette Goldstein)

Movie

This is the second movie adaptation of Paula Gosling's novel to make my list. *Cobra* (1986) has a lower-ranked entry at #97 – and a different plot, though both feature women in peril. Best known for starring Cindy Crawford as the lead and being a box office flop, this is a routine actioner. But 1990s movies are a reliable source of female villains, and *Fair Game* doesn't disappoint.

Crawford plays Kate McQuean, a civil case lawyer who stumbles across a plot by ex-KGB operatives to pull off an electronic bank heist. Obviously they're not keen on nosy women poking around, so they blow up Kate's luxury apartment. Except she escapes unscathed (imagine that!).

Then a cop (William Baldwin) gets involved and becomes a one-man protection team. Of course, there's an ex-girlfriend he's fallen out with, which leaves him free to romance Kate, so it's no surprise we're treated to a sex scene before the climax.

Hollywood loves to use Russian bad guys, and Steven Berkoff hams it up as the main villain with his usual thick accent. His henchmen are technically savvy, which maintains tension in the deadly cat-and-mouse game. Not a great movie, but serviceable enough as light entertainment and better than its reputation suggests.

Villainess

Better known as the tough cookie Private Vasquez from *Aliens*, Goldstein plays a villainous brute in this one. She spends most of her screen time either looking menacing in the background (which she does well) or in a hi-tech van while the Russian technical whiz does his thing.

Rosa gets some early action after the Russians track Kate and her bodyguard to a "safe" house. The police make the mistake of ordering pizzas with her credit card, giving Rosa the chance to impersonate a delivery woman and murder a detective with a silenced pistol. Naturally, the hero proves more difficult to take out, so there's a lengthy shootout with Rosa and her goons. The villainess shows her toughness by kicking in a door and surviving while her team is wiped out.

It's a while before Rosa returns to the fray, but she beats up a nerdy sales guy who assisted Kate. Hardly a worthy opponent for a woman of her prowess. Thankfully, Rosa offers Baldwin his hardest fight of the film in the final act. When she and a mook attempt to eliminate the pesky annoyance while wearing all-black commando gear, the hero guns them down after surprising them.

If he thought it would be that easy, Rosa had the foresight to wear a bulletproof vest. This leads into a moderately lengthy fight, with Rosa proving more than a match for her male opponent. She gives him quite a beating before he responds in kind. They made villainesses tough in the 1990s, so Rosa shrugs off these attacks and turns the tables. Despite her having a gun and knife, the cop defeats her, leaving one wishing for a slightly better demise –

though I've seen far worse.

Honourable Mentions: Tough Assassins and Mercenaries

Killer Wave (2007) – Woman Assassin (Valérie Wiseman)

This two-part sci-fi miniseries was later released as a three-hour movie on DVD. As is typical for this sort of film, fiction overrides science, with a "story" about some nonsensical plot to create tidal waves in the Atlantic. Cue poor special effects and an overlong potboiler that could have been told in half the runtime.

The heroes are two scientists (gender-balanced, of course), and the businessman villain hires assassins to stop their investigation. One hitter is a six-foot she-hulk (Wiseman should have got more roles like this) who shows up at a remote cabin to battle the hero. He struggles to even hurt her as the muscle woman shrugs off his timid attacks, and it takes makeshift weapons to take this foe out. Only a couple of minutes of screen time, but one of the few highlights for sure.

Patriot Games (1992) – Annette (Polly Walker)

Less of a toughie and more of a femme fatale, Annette is a member of an IRA splinter group up against Tom Clancy's hero Jack Ryan (Harrison Ford in the first of two outings). After he stops an assassination attempt on the British royal family and kills the group leader's brother, he and his own family become targets.

Action shifts between Britain and America (with some scenes in Africa), and Annette is mostly in the background. The villainess is a brunette but disguises herself as a redhead for spy work. Her best scene is an early hit on an

IRA idealist, whom she bumps off after sex. After that, she drives vehicles and becomes the hero's most important lead, before a showdown raid on Ryan's home.

Like Rosa, the villainess wears commando gear, but the closest thing to a fight is getting knocked out by Ryan's wife. Don't expect a grand finale – she goes out tamely after the vengeful main villain turns against his own team.

Thor: Ragnarok (2017)
Hela (Cate Blanchett)

Movie

Man of Steel and the DC Universe were covered earlier, so it's only fair to include an entry from the Marvel Cinematic Universe (MCU). The X-Men movies feature a plethora of female baddies, but that's a separate franchise and earns a much higher ranking spot. In the MCU, Hela stands out as a notable villainess.

Ragnarok is the third Thor-led movie, though he played a prominent role in two Avengers crossover films. The hero's treacherous brother Loki is up to no good again, and a cataclysmic plot begins when their aging father Odin passes away.

Besides the main antagonist, Thor battles two secondary foes. The first is a fiery horned demon, whom he defeats in the prologue, and the second is the self-proclaimed grandmaster of a "junkyard" planet. Thor is stranded there for the entire middle third. It's this segment that is most disappointing, as Jeff Goldblum's villain is pitiful. As with other Marvel films, another big-name hero shows up. On this occasion, it's Dr Banner / the Hulk who battles Thor in a vast arena before joining forces.

Ragnarok introduces Valkyrie, who (unsurprisingly) is a

female Asgardian warrior turned bounty huntress. Her character arc is predictable. She progresses from Thor's foe to his reluctant helper, then to an all-action heroine by the finale.

Villainess

Any woman called the Goddess of Death is likely to rack up the kills, and Hela doesn't disappoint. Not daunted by Asgard's army, she massacres them solo to prove how powerful she is. Before the wipeout, Hela claims an even greater scalp when she destroys Thor's legendary hammer Mjolinir bare handed. After such an iconic first encounter, it was always going to go downhill.

While Thor is stuck on planet junkyard, Hela does bad girl stuff. This includes raising an undead army from the crypt beneath Asgard's palace and taking a pet giant wolf for company. Hela narrates her own backstory over camera shots of painted murals. This is mostly about how she and her father, Odin, conquered other realms before he became an advocate of peace. A flashback from Valkyrie shows the warrior women defeated by the evil tyrant in a battle long ago.

Thor returns to Asgard, and it's God of Thunder against Goddess of Death. Their fights live up to the billing, with plenty of barbed dialogue from Hela. She even cuts out Thor's eye before they're through. To defeat his powerful foe, Thor has Loki summon the demon (remember him from the prologue?), which destroys Asgard and the villainess along with it. So, the result is Hela taken out by a third party, but she manages a Pyrrhic victory.

Honourable Mentions: Marvel Cinematic Universe

Black Widow (2021) – Antonia / Taskmaster (Olga Kurylenko)

Marvel's Phase Four has left fans unimpressed, and this is another mediocre entry. The promising setup focuses on a young Black Widow, her sister, and an all-female team of black-clad assassins. Add a masked villain – Taskmaster – and this should be a winner.

Too bad the family drama bogs down the middle third. When a mind-controlled pig is the most interesting part, there are serious problems. Eventually, the filmmakers realise this is supposed to be an action movie, and we get an epic climax on a floating sky base.

If you're hoping for a great reveal, get ready for disappointment. Taskmaster is a badly scarred woman we don't recognise, so it's kind of Black Widow to tell us she's the big bad's daughter. All very uninspired, and the last fight is unimpressive, making this a disappointing solo outing.

Ant-Man and the Wasp (2018) – Ava / Ghost (Hannah John-Kamen)

Ghost is another Marvel masked adversary who possesses the ability to phase through solid objects. While her reveal is expected given the publicity around her character, the backstory is much better this time. Ava has a moral standpoint, since she was experimented on as a child. Now she's seeking a cure for her condition, which brings her into conflict with the heroes.

With a combination of fighting skills, interesting powers, and character development, Ghost is a worthy addition to Marvel's villainess roster. Some action is repetitive, with far too many shrinking and enlargement scenes, but there's plenty to enjoy.

Rank #64

The Red Wolf (1995)
Elaine (Elaine Lui)

Movie

Another *Die Hard* scenario, set on a cruise liner with Hong Kong action for added spice. The hero is an ex-cop turned security guard (Kenny Ho), and his backup is Christy Chung as a pickpocket turned reluctant sidekick. She's the early antagonist who shows her good side by returning a stolen wedding ring, but then the terrorists – led by a treacherous first officer and singer Elaine – make their move.

The bad guys are after uranium locked in a safe. It's not explained why that would be on a cruise liner, and this entire plot is abandoned after a power cut stops a hacker in his tracks. So much for that, then. *The Red Wolf* has a ludicrously high body count, with scores of hostages mowed down by the trigger-happy terrorists. These guys prefer to use prisoners for target practice instead of bargaining chips.

Action scenes vary from routine to imaginative, and the hero utilises the environment to his advantage. There's some comedy mixed in, notably when the pickpocket sings in a dressing room, only to be disturbed by the villains. She puts on a wig and pretends to be a bust (!) – bonus points for originality.

The movie is chaotic, but the fast pacing and above-average fights make for an entertaining diversion.

Villainess

The villainess first shows up as a ballroom singer, and is quite good, though this lady prefers beating people up and killing them. Her first victim is a ship's officer who has the safe keycard. Elaine plays the typical femme fatale, then burns his wrist with a cigarette and easily overpowers him… and clearly enjoys it.

If the villains were hoping to be discreet, killing people indiscriminately wasn't the best approach. They're soon discovered by the cop and pickpocket, who team up to battle the hijackers. After a hectic shootout, the cop literally bursts into the ballroom through a high window… and that's when Elaine drops the nice girl act and goes all psycho.

One of her meanest scenes is where she shoots a guy having a heart attack for pure amusement. It's the newlyweds from earlier, and the bride is gunned down during an ill-advised revenge attack. Amid all this, Elaine finds time to threaten a distraught woman with broken glass. Another shootout follows as the psychopathic woman chases fleeing hostages on the decks.

The inevitable happens, and the pickpocket faces Elaine in a fight. Lots of weapons are used, and there's a comical tone shift that doesn't quite work. Ultimately, the villainess is covered in paint, which the heroine sets alight. The on-fire Elaine screams, and her prolonged death scene goes on far too long (even though this bad girl deserves a horrible death).

Honourable Mentions: Sea Hijack Movies

Counterstrike (2002) – Monica Chang (Marie Matiko)

Another Asian villainess in this TBS Superstation-produced movie, also set on a cruise ship. The Taiwanese bad girl and her associates are after nuclear launch codes and attack a summit during the US and China. Up against them are two brothers who (yawn) don't get along, one a secret service agent and the other with the ATF.

It's a while until Monica's reveal, and then she only kills one guy during the entire film. Since she's an actress who battled the leading lady / hero's girlfriend earlier, it's no surprise the women duke it out during the finale. The karate fight is not well choreographed, and TV movie limitations show through. At least this section doesn't have annoying fade to black transitions.

The good girl sees off the villainess by throwing her over a guardrail. Other than that part, there's nothing special to see, and it's all pretty forgettable.

Final Voyage (1999) – Max (Claudia Christian)

This is another actioner from the director of *Demolition High* (covered at #86), but while we get a villainess in leather, Max is unfortunately no Tanya. The heroes are a bodyguard and a spoilt rich woman, who must deal with Ice-T's hijackers who've targeted – you guessed it – a cruise ship vault.

The villainess' introduction is impressive, seen in silhouette as she bumps off two crew members below deck. Several executions follow, all supplemented with cold-blooded dialogue. Anyone expecting a good showdown should prepare for disappointment. There are a few brief shootouts and a pathetic fight with the heroine. After murdering over half a dozen crewmen, taking out a rich brat is apparently too difficult.

1st to Die (2003)
Chessy Jenks (Angie Everhart)

Movie

James Patterson's *Women's Murder Club* novels were adapted for ABC TV in the late 2000s, but before that, the first book got the NBC miniseries treatment. Inspector Lindsay Boxer (Tracy Pollan) and her partner investigate the murder of a high-profile groom and his bride shortly after their wedding. Initial enquiries lead to inevitable dead ends, then Lindsay discovers the deceased couple are missing their rings, and a serial killer is only just getting started.

Other main characters are an assistant district attorney, a newspaper reporter, and a medical examiner. The four women create an informal discussion group (the murder club) and set about solving the crimes. The killer bumps off three unlucky couples before Lindsay uncovers a solid lead. This leads her to crime author Nicholas Jenks (Robert Patrick), who becomes the prime suspect.

All the physical evidence points to him, as does footage of a bearded male recorded at a brutal nightclub slaying. Following his arrest, fresh evidence suggests Jenks is being framed by a female killer. As expected from a Patterson crime novel, there are many twists before the resolution.

A dull subplot involves Boxer's worsening blood disorder and doesn't add much to the story. The romance with her partner is mostly predictable, but plays an important role later on.

Villainess

Chessy has little dialogue and is often a beautiful background figure whenever the police question Jenks. His fitness instructor ex-wife becomes a suspect when the club realises they're after a female perpetrator. However, she turns up dead after Jenks escapes police custody.

The final showdown (for Chessy, at least) has Jenks and the police confronting her in a museum. There's a very good unmasking scene as the murderess removes a well-designed prosthetic face. Chessy's background in makeup allowed her to impersonate her husband effectively, and – for once – they didn't swap actors halfway through the reveal scene. There's some minimal action before Chessy is killed in a shootout that also claims the life of Boxer's lover.

Since there are ten minutes left, viewers assuming a final twist will be right, and it's expected the Robert Patrick character ends up being the villain. The revelation is that he controlled Chessy into committing the murders, which is far-fetched as anyone that unstable would make a poor proxy. Boxer finishes the baddie off in a bruising confrontation that she barely survives. Too bad they didn't include more action for the wife.

Honourable Mentions: Male Disguises

Inner Sanctum II (1994) – Sharon Reed (Sandahl Bergman)

A murder mystery whose solution should be obvious

from the outset. Does Sandahl Bergman ever *not* play a villainess? This sequel to *Inner Sanctum* (1991) has some decent kills, but all the action is reserved for the final half-hour. Abundant sex in this erotic thriller, but only one scene I'd class as overlong and softcore, so it's still eligible for inclusion.

The heroine – who killed her treacherous husband in the first movie – is having nightmares about zombie hubby screwing her sister Sharon. Yes, there's some weird stuff here. Her live-in nurse and family do their best to look suspicious, and a time-filler side plot about a secret fortune pads out the film until things get interesting.

In the space of about 20-30 minutes, there are four murders and a meat hook-wielding "zombie" stalker who unmasks herself as Sharon. A decent catfight follows, ending with the murderess pushed through a high window. Had the first two-thirds been that thrilling, this could have earned a ranking spot, but it's too little too late.

NetForce (1999) – The Selkie (Odile Broulard)

Based on a Tom Clancy novel, this is – you guessed it – a techno-thriller about a US cybersecurity force. The antagonists: a criminal group attempting to destroy the Internet. As you've probably gathered, the computers in this movie bear no resemblance to real life. Virtual reality sessions take place in actual locations, and the hero converses with a digital AI "ghost" of his murdered boss. Naturally, the enemy hacker has no trouble breaching White House security.

There are two female villains. One is rarely seen and lets her male counterparts do all the shooting. Her only noteworthy scene is when she's part of an assault team wearing gas masks, before she dies in an explosion.

The other villainess is more interesting: an assassin and mistress of disguise, who makes several attempts on the main character's life. Early on, she infiltrates a hotel suite as a hooker to bump off a mafia don. To escape, she wears a male prosthetic mask that's surprisingly realistic. She later impersonates the heroine, but the last fight is tame, and the disoriented hero defeats a supposedly professional killer.

Die Hard 4.0 (2007) (aka *Live Free or Die Hard*)
Mai Linh (Maggie Q)

Movie

With all the *Die Hard* clones on my list, it's only fair to include the series that started it all. The franchise is better than some for female villains, but the first two movies – the original 1988 action classic and its 1990 sequel – pitted the hero John McClane against only male baddies. However, the other three entries featured villainesses worth mentioning.

By the time McClane made it to 4.0 – *Live Free or Die Hard* to American audiences – he'd battled terrorists (or thieves masquerading as them) in a Los Angeles skyscraper, Dulles Airport in Washington DC, and New York City. With events escalating to ever grander proportions and John perpetually in "the wrong place at the wrong time", it's no wonder he's gone bald. To make matters worse, villains have become technically savvy, and McClane is... old school to say the least.

A group of cyber-terrorists hacks into the US government systems to cause chaos over the Independence Day weekend. Being villains, they eliminate underlings once they've served their purpose, and so the American teenage hacking population takes quite a dent. One guy (Justin Long) survives, and by chance McClane is the cop bringing him in for questioning. This veteran is an excellent ally to have on your side, even if he isn't computer literate.

The baddies led by Thomas Gabriel (Timothy Olyphant) aren't especially memorable, but the action comes thick and fast. A little too thick in the final sequence, which sees the hero targeted by a fighter jet (!). An entire highway is demolished, but John miraculously survives to say his trademark sendoff line.

Villainess

The female villains in the third and fifth instalments had their moments, but their contributions were disappointing. And while the bad girl in 4.0 is seen off 60% of the way through, the Asian hacker and martial arts expert Mai Linh is the most formidable of the bunch. Plus, she proves very hard to kill, which is always a bonus.

Early indications aren't promising, with Mai wearing headphones doing generic techie stuff. After sitting on the sidelines for the first half hour, Gabriel sends his lover / lieutenant to lead an assault on a utility control station. The villainess poses as an FBI agent, which conveniently gives her the excuse to wear body armour. She shows her ruthlessness by executing on-site personnel with a silenced pistol. And when she beats down a gate guard, that's a good sign of things to come.

Not long after the raid, McClane and his sidekick show up to investigate. John has no trouble eliminating Mai's mooks, but the boss lady soon turns the tables and gives him a proper battle. This is pleasantly brutal, and the hero shows his foe the lack of respect she deserves. He even tears out a lock of hair as he knocks her out. Perhaps he should have killed her though, because Mai soon recovers and kicks McClane through a window.

While the villainess strong-arms the hacker into

compliance, the hero returns in an SUV (!) and drives himself and the villainess into an elevator shaft. Even that doesn't stop this woman, because she climbs back up and fights McClane in the vehicle. Eventually – after a few advantage shifts – the hero escapes his predicament and sends the persistent henchwoman plummeting to her explosive doom. One of the better male vs. female fights on the list, enough to elevate Mai to the middle tier.

Honourable Mentions: *Die Hard* Series and Clones

Die Hard with a Vengeance (1995) – Katya (Sam Phillips)

After two serious action movies, the series broke with tradition by opting for a revenge plot (or so it seems at first) and a more humorous outing. Samuel L. Jackson provides comic relief as Zeus Carver, which makes this entry a fan favourite. The cops are actually intelligent, even though the main villain – Jeremy Irons as Simon Gruber – is even smarter.

Like almost all *Die Hard* villain plots, this is ultimately about a heist. In this case, the theft of gold bullion from the Federal Reserve Bank. The mute villainess Katya gets a brutal introduction when she drills her way into the vault and slices up a guard. After that, she mostly stays in the background until the climax. It turns out she's the lover of the tough henchman *and* in a secret relationship with Simon. Guess she likes the main baddie more, since she murders his competition during a double-cross.

After a brief, non-explicit love scene, Katya pilots Gruber's chopper during the showdown against the heroes. She's incinerated after McClane brings down a power line, a great send-off capped by *that* trademark line.

A Good Day to Die Hard (2013) – Irina Komarov (Yulia Snigir)

The final *Die Hard* film has the shortest runtime at approximately 95 minutes, which is merciful because it all feels tired and pedestrian. This time around, McClane is in Mother Russia to help his estranged son and – to nobody's surprise – things soon get messy. John Junior is a spy on a mission to liberate a political prisoner, and the man's daughter Irina is working with the baddies.

The prisoner ends up being a villain too, and plans to steal enriched uranium from a secret vault in Chernobyl. The plot is just as stupid as it sounds, and Irina doesn't feature much until the end. There she finally gets to dress in black, shoot a gun, and pilot a gunship. Another helicopter showdown to finish things off, and Irina gets the honour of being the last main villain of the franchise. A pity her death is an unsatisfying suicide crash, a failed last-ditch effort to eliminate those troublesome McClanes.

Skyscraper (2018) – Xia (Hannah Quinlivan)

Almost every setting has been used for "*Die Hard* on an X" films, and some have even dared to reuse the lone hero in an office building plot. In fact, there are two films called *Skyscraper*. One had Anna Nicole Smith in the lead and was expectedly awful, so won't be discussed further. The other starred Dwayne Johnson as an ex-hostage negotiator turned safety inspector, who uses his artificial leg in inventive ways.

A group of criminals sets the world's tallest building on fire, forcing the hero to battle them and rescue his trapped family. Plenty of clichés abound, but the blend of *Die Hard* and *The Towering Inferno* (1974) is original enough to maintain the viewer's interest. The movie is not overlong and packed with stunts, and there's a decent (if under-used) female baddie in the mercenary Xia.

The villainess' best scenes are early on, where she murders scores of people with a silenced pistol and knocks out the hero. After that, she's mostly absent, and never sets foot in the title skyscraper. The hero's wife and Xia have a catfight that's very brief, and the villainess gets arrested. That's right – not even a deserved karmic death for this cold-blooded killer. She's the only baddie to survive, which smacks of double gender standards.

A Bride's Revenge (2019)
Lori Parker (Hannah Barefoot), Caroline / Rose Parker (Kendra Carelli)

Movie

As you've probably gathered, this is a Lifetime movie about… a bride seeking revenge. Technically, Lori is a *former* bride dumped on her wedding day after the groom, Ian, decided she was too psycho to marry. It's no shock she goes over the edge and stalks Ian's new fiancée Miya. While wearing a bridal gown, no less.

There are several positives that elevate this above standard Lifetime fare, enough to earn a ranking slot. The tempo remains high, and within the opening five minutes we're treated to a cancelled wedding, a creepy mock invitation, and a knife-wielding female stalker dressed in white. The obvious suspect has an alibi for the attacks, which implies an accomplice. Since the antagonist's face is masked by a veil and Miya works in a salon with two female assistants, both women are potential suspects.

The film's main issues are its weak climax and finding a decent copy in the UK. Too obscure for a physical release, and while the movie has aired in the Channel 5 afternoon slot, the early screening time means censors edit out more graphical parts. For *A Bride's Revenge*, this includes knife shots (but not the detective referring to the weapon!), Lori bashing her head against a mirror, and Miya getting bludgeoned with a brick. All the exciting bits. Fortunately, Johnson Production Group has uploaded an unedited version on YouTube.

Villainesses

There's no doubt who the main villain is, with Lori acting completely psycho from her first scene. She does all the crazy woman stuff required: taunting the heroine, loony-eyed stares, self-harm, and threatening her boyfriend just because. Lori somehow convinces the police Miya is insane thanks to a doppelgänger bride / accomplice. The outfit is an original take and contributes to the eerie stalking sequences. Nothing like a woman in long white gloves and a trailing dress sticking a knife into a wedding cake. Before she offs her victim, in this case Ian's mother.

Hannah Barefoot knows what's required for this type of movie and provides multiple insane rants to keep viewers entertained. Lori's best moment comes at the mother's funeral when she adds salt to Miya's wounds and then accuses *her* of being unstable.

Besides the bridal gown, Lori wears a more traditional evil black outfit when she kills the family dog (!) and makes an unfriendly hospital visit to murder a patient. Enough to cause Miya's relationship to deteriorate, but fortunately Ian sees Lori is the truly crazy one. His suspicions are confirmed when his ex-girlfriend injures herself in front of him. After Miya digs up information about a suspected arson that killed Lori's parents. Yes, there's a crazy backstory, like always.

It's revealed that Lori has a sister named Rose, which explains her alibi for the earlier bride attacks. Suspicion falls on Miya's friend Sandra after she shows off rose-tattooed fingernails, but nobody will be surprised this is a red herring. Lori's actual sister/accomplice is the other coworker, Caroline. This all leads to a showdown at Lori's house, where the psycho siblings capture Miya.

The finale takes place in a creepy mausoleum. Lori is suitably menacing and jealous during this encounter, demanding Ian commit suicide in front of his mother's crypt, but the villains are both defeated easily. The accomplice is shot in the back during a struggle. And Lori? She falls down a short flight of steps and breaks her neck before reaching the bottom.

Honourable Mention: Masked Lifetime Villainesses

Ruthless Realtor (2020) – Lynette Dee (Alexandra Peters)

This Lifetime thriller also benefits from good pacing and a great masked outfit for its villainess. The psycho's wardrobe is all black, with a creepy gas mask that resembles something from the First World War. Her attire allows for stunt double use in the opening beat-down scene. No skimping on action – it comes across as brutal.

The prime suspect is the realtor of the title: Christy Burson as Meg Atkins. It turns out she isn't so ruthless, just a disturbed young woman set up by the actual killer, Lynette. An obvious plot twist, given that the attacker uses chemicals to kill her victims and Lynette works in a pharmacy. Plus, she seems really interested in the property her parents once lived in, and is *very* disappointed when Meg sells the house to another couple.

After the opening, action is sparse, but for once the police are useful. That's no consolation to the officer guarding the property, who becomes the standard mid-film victim to ramp up tension. Maybe this guy should have been the stereotypical useless cop after all.

The ending sequence is eerie for a TV movie, as Lynette uses a sledgehammer to break down a basement wall and reveal the skeletal remains of her parents. As a bonus, we get three unmasking scenes: one real-time and two more in flashbacks. The struggle that follows the lengthy monologue is melodramatic, and the villainess is taken out a bit too easily. But nowhere near as tame a finale as Lori's.

Indiana Jones and the Last Crusade (1989)
Elsa Schneider (Alison Doody)

Movie

Another iconic franchise with a patchy record for female villains. There are very few women at all in the series, let alone baddies. The timeless classic *Raiders of the Lost Ark* (1981) features a feisty companion in Marion Ravenwood. Despite many damsel in distress moments, she also proves capable and resourceful. The prequel *Indiana Jones and the Temple of Doom* (1984) has the *much* more annoying Willie Scott, a lukewarm romantic interest who screams whenever the situation calls for it. In fairness, that happens a lot.

For the third film, we got a *Raiders* redux of sorts. Indy battles Nazis in the late 1930s and chases around the globe after another legendary religious treasure. This time out, it's the ultimate prize: the Holy Grail. The gift of eternal life is handy when almost everyone wants to kill the hero, whether they be German troops, a religious sect, or double-crossing backstabbers. Locations include Utah for the teen Indy prologue, the scenic city of Venice (and not so scenic catacombs), an Austrian castle, Berlin, and Hatay.

Such an epic quest deserves a companion, and since the female is a villain, Indy works with his father, Henry (Sean Connery). Their relationship, which starts frosty but develops into mutual respect, is a highlight.

Villainess

After the exciting prologue, the main plot kicks in with the hero tracking his father, who disappeared while in Venice. For the opening third, Elsa is Indy's companion as they search the catacombs for the tomb of a Crusader knight. The "helpful" woman is thankfully less wimpish than Willie. There's also some expected romantic tension and an exciting boat chase along the city's famous canals.

It's only after Indy finds his father in Austria that Elsa reveals she's in league with the Nazis. Her villainous turn is surprising, given it's rare for the lead female in a 1980s movie to be bad. While there's clearly a traitor involved, we'd already been introduced to a man called Donovan. Being played by Julian Glover, it's no surprise he ends up being a villain. The twist is that there are *two* traitors for the Joneses to contend with.

Indy has his father for backup, though he's lacking in encouragement and proves a hindrance on more than one occasion. Returning from *Raiders* are Marcus Brody (even less helpful) and Sallah for comic relief. The heroic quartet has many perilous encounters, and the action sequences are well done.

Elsa seems to work with the Nazis out of personal greed, but shows distaste for their more barbaric methods, especially book burning in Berlin. Despite some reluctance, Elsa shows no remorse, and anyone fearing she might turn good should perish the thought. This villain is a woman of intelligence rather than action, which she leaves to the guys, but while Elsa is Donovan's lackey for much of the film, she's a lot more evil in the finale.

After Indy guides the villains through booby traps to

save his wounded father, they find a twelfth-century knight guarding the grail. Or rather, grails, since there are many fake ones on display. Elsa offers to help Donovan choose, but his trust is misplaced since he drinks from a false chalice and disintegrates. The villainess' screams won't generate much pity. She knows her history, and this was likely an intentional double-cross to keep the prize for herself.

Elsa's greed gets the better of her, and she ignores the knight's warning not to remove the cup from the temple. As the structure collapses, Elsa falls into a chasm. Rather than take Indy's generous outstretched hand, the villainess opts to reclaim the grail and plummets to her doom. A nice parallel follows with Indy in the same position. Fortunately, he listens to his father and chooses life over glory.

Honourable Mention: Indiana Jones

Indiana Jones and the Kingdom of the Crystal Skull (2008) – **Irina Spalko (Cate Blanchett)**

The divisive fourth instalment gives us a female main antagonist for the first time... and the longest movie title on my ranking list. Cate Blanchett is back on mature villainess duty as evil Soviet psychic Irina Spalko, leading KGB agents on a mission to find the lost city of El Dorado. That's the place in South America with streets and buildings built from solid gold, for anyone not versed in treasure hunter myths.

The film is a mixed bag with inventive sequences and... some not so good parts. The opening shootout in Area 51 gets things off to a thrilling start, with a battle in the secret warehouse where the ark from *Raiders* is stored. Marion Ravenwood makes a welcome return, and the Peruvian jungle section is decent. Then Indy escapes a nuclear blast by sealing himself in a fridge (yes, that infamous sequence). And there are alien beings with magnetic crystal skeletons (!) that somehow defy the laws of physics.

Spalko is an expert sword fighter, so naturally fights Indy's son, who's also had fencing lessons. Blanchett's role is surprisingly physical – with a fantastic jungle jeep chase – but she's absent for much of the movie and doesn't generate the expected menace. When she tries to mind control Indy, he resists her easily, and the titular crystal skull is more threatening than the villainess.

In the end, Spalko stands in the lost city demanding knowledge and gets sucked through a dimensional portal. If this sounds vague, it's because the last twenty minutes are utter gibberish plotwise. Repeat viewings don't improve the weak conclusion.

Spalko is an intriguing foe, but had the potential to be so much more. And since *Indiana Jones and the Dial of Destiny* (2023) only gave us a misguided female CIA agent, Elsa remains the top female villain.

Rank #59

Stone Cold Dead (1979)
Olivia Page (Alberta Watson)

Movie

If a movie stars Richard Crenna and it's not *Rambo*, the chances are he's playing a cop. The actor played Frank Janek in a series of TV movies, and the lead role in this 1970s thriller about a sniper who targets prostitutes working the sleazy streets of New York. It's a well-paced tale with a dark atmosphere and enough mystery and red herrings to puzzle armchair sleuths.

The movie is available on Blu-ray – with a very good picture transfer – but there are differences with the version that previously aired on UK TV. The biggest change is the opening murder of Linnea Quigley's character in the shower, which now doesn't occur at all (but still makes it onto the front cover!). That scene wasn't in the original version and was added later for sensationalism. There's no missing sniper footage, because the killer was off screen for the axed pre-credits sequence.

To pad out the runtime, there's a subplot about Sergeant Boyd (Crenna) pursuing a pimp named Kurtz. This bad guy is a 1970s caricature with oversized glasses and a messy blond haircut, and oozes sleaze every time he appears. To bring him down, Boyd enlists help from an undercover policewoman, and since she's not the main female character

(Monica Page played by Linda Sorensen), it's not too hard to guess she bites the dust. Ironically, it's a sniper who kills her after a bent cop sells her out, but not *the* sniper terrorising the red-light district.

The pimp plot is wrapped up a bit too neatly. Rather than a showdown between Boyd and Kurtz, we simply see him arrested after the fact and rotting away in a prison cell. Thankfully, they're saving the drama and thrills for the climax with the main villain.

Villainess

For someone who ends up being the murderer, Olivia has little screen time until the last twenty minutes. This keeps the actual killer under the radar while her photographer boyfriend is made out to be guilty, but some extra backstory before the reveal would have better established her character. Instead, we get second-hand accounts from Olivia's mother, a woman Boyd is on/off dating and a potential suspect.

Olivia still makes my list because the film and its antagonist are relatively unique among the horde of serial killer movies that plagued the era. Instead of the usual knife-wielding slasher, we have the "sin sniper". This psycho lurks around fire escapes, wearing a trench-coat that conceals a sniper rifle with an attachable camera. The obvious Canon product placement is questionable, as the killer photographs victims and taunts the police with the pictures. And yes, there's a threatening message made from cut-out newsprint letters.

With plodding police work by Boyd, it's good that scenes where the shadowy sniper assembles her weapon are so effective and accompanied by creepy music. The killer takes out three prostitutes before the climax, which effectively rules out Kurtz. What pimp would murder his source of income? The desperate Boyd enlists Olivia's help to trap her boyfriend, unaware she's the assassin.

The climax begins at a cemetery when Olivia reveals herself as the sin sniper to her shocked mother. Boyd and the police show up to arrest her, and the murderer shows off her sharpshooting skills. Cops should use cover more effectively, considering she's a sniper.

The final chase sequence is suitably long, with Olivia proving a slippery opponent. The sniper ditches her raincoat for an all-black outfit and her trusty rifle for a sidearm. After a shootout in a tunnel, Boyd corners his quarry on a rooftop. Unwilling to surrender, the villainess takes her own life. By the end, everyone Boyd cared about is dead or badly injured. No happy resolution, which suits the dark tone just fine.

Honourable Mention: Richard Crenna Movies

Terror on Track 9 (1992) – Leslie Renner (Joan Van Ark)

Crenna TV movies are hard to find, as most were never released on DVD or video streaming sites. The only sources are VHS tapes and third-party footage... and hoping the footage is watchable. Fortunately, I found a passable version of this Frank Janek film that features the series' best villainess.

A murderer dresses up as a prostitute and stalks women in the eerie confines of Grand Central Station, New York. This high-heeled psycho injects their victims with heroin and spreads golden glitter around their bodies. Why do serial killers have to be so weird?

Janek is hindered by an inquisitive TV news reporter who paints the police in a negative light and internal office politics. And a female FBI profiler who starts off hostile, but finishes in romance territory. Procedural describes this movie, with the usual false leads that don't play out. One suspect is a wig maker who sold his goods to the killer and now knows too much. Cue a visit from the shadowy woman in red, an off-screen lethal injection, and a sinister "Too Late" message in glitter.

Eventually, Janek identifies the killer as an Amish woman abused by her father. She's Leslie Renner, the same news reporter who's been hounding him. After a great setup, the weak finale has the murderess mentally break down live on air. But the movie deserves an honourable mention for its creepy stalking scenes, and a female clothed killer that's *not* a male cross-dresser.

Lady Bloodfight (2016)
Svietta (Ng Mayling)

Movie

If the title sounds like *Bloodsport* – the 1988 martial arts movie starring Jean-Claude Van Damme – that's probably intentional. This is basically a female fighter remake with Amy Johnston as Jane Jones, an American who travels to Hong Kong to find out what happened to her father. Since this is a movie, it could never be a simple disappearance. He vanished after fighting in the kumite, a brutal fighting contest, and a shady businessman is involved.

In a familiar storyline to any martial arts fan, Jane becomes the student of Shu. This enigmatic woman has an ongoing feud with another trainer over a dead relative and who's responsible. Since their kumite duel ended in a draw, both women accepted the compromise to train a fighter for the next tournament. Shu's rival takes on Ling, a young thief who's also nimble in combat. This proxy battle becomes the focus, though Ling is not evil enough to qualify as a villainess.

Lady Bloodfight fares better than other female-led martial arts movies because the producers had the sense to include some actual fighting. This may sound obvious, but there are many films that don't make good use of a talented cast. The fights are bloody, and apart from the bizarre magical /

fantasy elements – such as Shu's healing water dance (!) – this is a brutal depiction. Tough females in action, and many deadly encounters before the credits roll.

Villainess

Ling is an antagonist with a heart, and while she has barbed verbal exchanges with Jane, there needs to be a brutal, sadistic opponent in a film like this. Enter Svietta, a former Russian convict covered in tattoos. Mercy is not a word in her vocabulary, and she has no qualms about killing her outmatched foes.

Most of the key female characters get establishing fights: the two trainers in the previous kumite, and various young women turning the tables on attackers in spectacular fashion. Jane disposes of unwanted male attention when she knocks down a guy in a diner, and again after he foolishly comes back for more. Svietta doesn't need to fight. Her fellow prisoners give her a wide berth in the shower, deciding it best to leave this psycho alone. A wise strategy, because losing to this woman is deadly.

After forty-five minutes spent setting up the plot, the kumite gets underway, and a nervous Jane fights first. Despite nearly stepping outside the ring, she wins her bout. Ling also shows her fighting prowess while Svietta watches in silence. The Russian brute beats her first opponent to a bloody pulp, despite the contest being over long before that. Psychological warfare? It certainly has the desired effect on the audience.

As eliminations – including some literal ones – continue, Jane befriends a cocky Australian fighter named Cassidy. Anyone familiar with tournament movies will know what's coming. Next up is the weapons round, which provides plenty of opportunity for injury and death. Jane knocks her opponent out with a bladed staff, but Svietta isn't so lenient with Cassidy. The Aussie's fighting skills don't match her boasts. The evil woman wins this one easily and slits her beaten foe's throat before she can crawl to safety.

That sets up a semifinal encounter between Jane and Svietta. The Russian is so despised by the other competitors that Ling finds time to give the heroine a pep talk. That all seems pointless when Svietta overpowers Jane. The judges are about to call the result when the "defeated" fighter rises to her feet. Revenge is a powerful motivator, enough to give Jane the adrenaline she needs to take her opponent down.

After mystical healing from Shu, the heroine defeats Ling in the final. Then, the shady businessman gets his comeuppance, and since he was behind the death of Shu's boyfriend, the trainers and their students make amends and found a martial arts school. Routine and predictable, but the well-staged fight scenes make the movie worth watching.

Honourable Mention: Tournament Fighters

Pushed to the Limit (1992) – Inga (Christl Colven)

Before *Lady Bloodfight* came along, naming a decent all-female tournament film was a challenge. Women usually appeared as fighters in otherwise all-male fields. Quite telling that the "best of the rest" is this mediocre offering with wrestler Mimi Lesseos as... herself. She enters the kumite for revenge after ruthless drug traffickers kill her brother. One day, there will be a fighter with a more original background.

Action is limited, with all kinds of filler involving dancing in Las Vegas and boring family scenes. When we get some fight sequences, they're poorly choreographed with frequent cutaways to mundane side events. The villainess is an Amazonian henchwoman who breaks her opponent's spines by standing on them after her victories.

Sadly, Inga sounds more interesting than she is. Things liven up when Mimi snoops around the main villain's house, but she inevitably ends up back in the ring and defeats the henchwoman in the marquee fight.

Rank #57

The Huntsman: Winter's War (2016)
Freya (Emily Blunt), Ravenna (Charlize Theron)

Movie

This follow-up to *Snow White and the Huntsman* (2012) is superior entertainment, and offers more lively action and likeable characters. Charlize Theron can always be relied upon to provide a great villainess, but the first movie was as dull as her evil queen's barren landscape. Kristen Stewart's title heroine doesn't return, which might have something to do with her lacklustre performance. Chris Hemsworth is promoted to hero, which is no bad thing.

Fans of strong female characters will find much to enjoy in *Winter's War*, which serves as both a prequel and a sequel. Besides the two evil queens, the Huntsman gets a warrior companion and lover in Jessica Chastain's Sara. A ratio of 3:1 of female to male top billing is welcome, considering the token roles for women in decades gone by.

The movie begins approximately ten years before *Snow White*, with the Huntsman and Sara as children captured by Queen Freya. She's the sister of Ravenna and rules her own icy kingdom. It will come as no surprise that the romance, like so many in fantasy worlds, ends tragically. The focus then shifts to events after the first movie, with Ravenna defeated and Freya searching for the fabled magic mirror.

Villainesses

Freya is the main villain for acts one and two, and the prequel section does a good job of establishing her character. This lady is literally an ice queen, whose magic powers awaken after her child is murdered. The person responsible is seemingly her lover, but most viewers will deduce early on that Ravenna is behind it. Especially since she lurks in the corridor beforehand, but the proxy killer is enough to deceive her naïve sister.

Freya has a cold attitude toward love and human life. She captures young children to train as her personal army, which includes the Huntsman and Sara. Years later, the queen learns of their forbidden romance and disobedience. So she orders Sara's execution, and forces her lover to watch through an impenetrable wall of ice.

Shifting forward in time, the Huntsman – now a lone wanderer – is rescued from attackers by a masked figure. The audience will probably guess their identity before the reveal, but Sara gets a badass unmasking scene. Freya's wall of ice created different illusions for the two lovers, but neither died. And guess what? They team up to track down the magic mirror and save the world.

Freya's army captures the heroes, and the queen tests Sara's loyalty. The heroine appears to betray the Huntsman by shooting an arrow through his heart, but anyone hoping for three female villains will be disappointed. He survives because of the old "concealed object obstructing a projectile" trick. The life-saving item is a pendant that signifies their love is well and truly alive.

Freya's delight at acquiring the mirror proves short-lived as it responds to her inevitable query, "Who is the fairest of them all?" by summoning her evil sister back from the dead. She's now a shapeshifter construct made from gold, which makes this incarnation of Ravenna especially hard to kill.

In the climactic battle, the Huntsman and Sara attempt to assassinate Freya, only to discover the original evil queen has returned. Ravenna can't resist revealing her involvement in the murder of Freya's child, so everyone teams up against the big bad for the denouement. Even those odds prove a challenge until the Huntsman targets the source of the power – the magic mirror – and shatters it.

In a spectacular death scene, Ravenna solidifies into an inanimate golden shell and breaks into tiny pieces. Fans of the 1996 *Tomb Raider* game will find this reminiscent of Lara's fate should she step on Midas' hand. Freya's death and her overall character arc are much more tragic. She perishes from a mortal wound, with just enough energy to acknowledge the heroes' true love.

Blood Run (1994) (aka *Outside the Law*)
Paige / Felicia (Ashley Laurence)

Movie

In the wake of *Basic Instinct,* many erotic thrillers were produced, almost always themed around male detectives getting too close to female suspects. This one has the bonus of a masked villainess, if only for the opening murder scene. When a mystery psycho stabs a woman to death, douses her in gasoline, and sets her aflame, suspicion falls on her drug-dealing boyfriend. But once that red herring is cleared, the next candidate is the victim's lesbian lover, Tanya (Anna Thomson).

The lead detective is Brad Kingsbury (David Bradley), who has a distanced relationship with his ex-wife (don't they always), and a school-age daughter he doesn't see much because of work. Brad's partner Paige has a thing for him, but not vice versa. Yes, everything happens pretty much as expected for this type of movie. Cops come to blows as the evidence mounts against Tanya, but that doesn't stop Brad from getting in too deep. A couple of dates, followed by passionate sex. Things move fast in Los Angeles.

Another victim shows up: a Russian guy killed off screen with little fanfare. He exists only to move the plot forward, since he also knows the prime suspect, but he's barely mentioned afterwards. Of course, there's an interview scene where femme fatale Tanya smokes a cigarette.

She looks increasingly guilty once the police uncover a backstory involving suspected arson, which fits the MO of the recent killings. Kingsbury protests her innocence, but his conviction wavers as all other plausible suspects are dead. Another cop called Geoffreys is determined to prove Tanya is the killer, and even breaks into her house to compare a button recovered from a crime scene with her clothes.

Villainess

It's easy to figure out who the masked killer is given everyone else is too minor a character or likely too obvious. When we find out the arson victim had a sister named Felicia, Paige becomes the prime suspect. There's an attempt to throw the viewer off by claiming Felicia is dead, but since this comes from Paige anyway, it's unconvincing. Kingsbury finally pieces things together when a witness contradicts his partner's story, which leads to an exciting if predictable finale.

Before that, Paige gets a great "unmasking" scene when Geoffreys visits her house hoping for sex, only to discover a buttoned coat that matches his evidence. Too bad the murderess expects this and removes the bullets from the cop's revolver in advance. No masked killer, but a woman with a silenced pistol who gloats before pulling the trigger is an effective substitute.

Paige breaks into Tanya's house, takes her hostage, and sets up a sadistic birthday party for the daughter. Kingsbury arrives to get the expected twisted monologue from the killer. The last encounter is rather tame. Tanya recovers the disarmed hero's weapon, shoots, and misses despite being at close range. All rather contrived, setting up a confrontation where the hero takes down the psycho with a thrown knife.

Honourable Mentions: Silenced Pistol Kills

Act of Piracy (1988) – Laura Warner (Nancy Mulford)

Yet another waste of a great villainess, this is a ponderous action thriller with little action or thrills. Gary Busey – playing a good guy for once – is a Vietnam veteran searching for his children after modern-day pirates kidnap them from his luxury yacht. Arnold Vosloo shows up as a henchman, but the adversaries are unremarkable and the excitement stalls after the opening half hour.

The best character – the treacherous lover – is killed off far too soon. Before that, Laura gets a memorable sequence when she eliminates the yacht's entire crew with a silenced pistol. Starting with a perplexed guy whom she offs in her cabin. This scene lasts several minutes, with the white-dressed professional assassin sneaking about below decks and showing plenty of intelligence and skill.

Laura single-handedly captures the vessel and almost caps the hero when she surprises him on deck. Sadly, he survives, which gives the chief villain an excuse to toss his henchwoman off a hotel balcony. A stupid course of action, since it brings the police – and eventually the hero – to that location anyway.

Professional Affair (1995) – Heather (Kim Stetz), Sophie (Shannon Elliot)

This review is light on detail, as I could only source a German-dubbed DVD. The plot is easy to follow, with a private detective hired by a mob boss (Robert Z'Dar) to recover money stolen from a henchman. That scene – where a scantily clad escort undresses, pulls out a silenced weapon, and pumps the guy full of lead – is enough to put the film in honourable mention territory.

The prime suspect is a woman named Heather, and inevitably the detective falls in love with her. This is despite her revisiting the crime scene in the same outfit worn by the murderess. She also shows off a silenced gun to her co-worker Sophie (as the detective watches via a hidden camera) and seduces men at every turn. Heather seems to be exonerated when a black-clad figure attacks the PI in his motel room, and that person – after a fight and shootout – is revealed to be Sophie.

However, Heather is the killer after all. She and her detective lover keep the cash after they blow away the mob boss in a poorly staged finale. Guess the money and sex make up for letting a murderer off the hook.

Decoy (1995)
Katya (Charlotte Lewis)

Movie

Moderate budget action with two name actors – Peter Weller and Robert Patrick – each known for a star-making film franchise and a career's worth of direct to video roles. Jack Travis (Patrick) is a tough mercenary who survived a bullet to the head thanks to some rich guy named Wellington. The shady benefactor has now called in that debt and wants Travis to babysit his daughter while a billion-dollar business deal goes down.

Naturally, things aren't what they seem. And the title is a clue for those slow on the uptake. Travis enlists his pal Baxter (Weller), an equally crazy guy who's into the spiritual meditation thing. The two heroes spend most of the movie trekking in the woods and protecting the young woman. Cue annoyingly dark scenes and blurry action shots of people running past trees. But there's a lot of action for genre fans to enjoy, with few distractions. *Decoy* is a movie that doesn't pretend to be something it's not.

Travis and Baxter discover the woman they're guarding isn't really Wellington's daughter (big surprise), and the whole charade keeps a business rival occupied. That opposition is an even nastier man called Jenner, who takes things by force and has a personal hit squad – and a leather-clad henchwoman – to deal with such matters.

Villainess

Before she dons more appropriate bad girl attire, the villainess shows up at Wellington's estate in a sexy evening dress. Guards should never trust a beautiful woman, a mistake the front gate sentry learns the hard way when Katya fires a dart from a wrist-mounted contraption. The clever and rather unique device sadly becomes an ornament, since it's only used in the prologue.

Katya and her team dispose of Wellington's thugs with ease and leave a video message that sets the main plot in motion. The villainess is obviously Jenner's "go-to" woman, since he hires her squad to retrieve the daughter. And the savvy operative uses the "minor complication" of Travis to negotiate a higher price. By now, she has changed into black leather, the standard for any self-respecting henchwoman.

To show how ruthless she is, Katya offs a mole in Wellington's camp with a high-powered automatic rifle. That weapon is useful for clearing dense forestry, and during the prolonged chase that follows. Katya is a female villain with plenty of screen time who prefers violence to talk, though she makes a few snide comments in a posh English accent. Some of her combat tactics are questionable. She often stands in the open and makes herself an easy target, but the chief henchperson is immune to return fire.

The best scene is where the female mercenary and her crew attack a bus the heroes have commandeered. Plenty of bullets are fired with no notable casualties, which only happens in action movies. Katya mixes up the weapons, tossing grenades in a skirmish and a weighted lasso to capture the decoy daughter. She's a good match for Baxter and Travis… until the disappointing finale.

After resolving a complex romance / revenge subplot, which ends when Baxter offs Wellington, attention shifts to a nondescript office building. This location provides a lot of glass to shatter once the bullets fly. While Travis deals with a lesser thug, Baxter gets the honour of fighting Katya. Don't expect too much, because the final encounter is bizarrely shot and rather lame.

The villainess is wearing a weird cloth and strap outfit, which looks plain silly. After a brief tussle, the action switches to first person with shots of Baxter throwing punches and Katya kicking towards her off-screen target. After that broken mess, the hero takes the villainess down with a single blow. A pity, because Katya was headed for a much higher ranking spot.

Honourable Mention: Female Assassins / Mercenaries

Timebomb (1991) – Ms. Blue (Tracy Scoggins)

A solo female mercenary on an otherwise all-male team is a common occurrence. While many roles are token, occasionally a villainess stands out. This action thriller stars Michael Biehn – another *Terminator* actor turned B-movie star – as Eddie Kay, a watchmaker with mental health issues. Turns out he was part of a military experiment to create assassins with false identities, and his former teammates want to silence him.

The programmed killers have code names based on colours, and Ms Blue is as beautiful and deadly as you would expect. Action scenes with the female assassin are rare, but decently staged when they happen. Her best attack is in a parking garage, where she gets into a knife fight with Eddie. She also shows her sadistic side when confronting the heroes in a hotel room.

Ms Blue's fate is ambiguous, and she's absent from the final showdown. But Tracy Scoggins has a great screen presence – even for sections with no dialogue – and so earns an honourable mention.

Rank #54

***Alien Fury: Countdown to Invasion* (2000)**
Ava Zurich (Chyna)

Movie

A cheap sci-fi production with a storyline to match. The main character is a police detective (Dondré T. Whitfield) who investigates a murder, only to stumble across an impending alien invasion. *Alien Fury* was distributed by Paramount Pictures and notable cast members include Paul Shulze and Stephen Tobolowsky. Hiring them probably exhausted the budget, but the terrible special effects are mercifully sparse.

The plot starts off simply but quickly becomes convoluted. A shady military agency fakes an alien attack to avoid funding cuts, except there really are extraterrestrials out there. The infiltrators look like humans (of course they do) and act normally. Except they need extra nitrogen to survive, so they carry inhalers. Cue a mini-mystery with multiple asthma sufferers suspected of being aliens, complete with bluffs and counter-bluffs.

The detective doesn't know who to trust and is the only person who can expose a splinter group's scheme to trigger an interplanetary war. Despite the story being a mind-boggling mess, the movie is never dull, and a muscular henchwoman is a definite bonus. Ava is a villainess who sticks around for the duration and doesn't need male assistance to kill people.

The movie is hard to find, with no official DVD release and few VHS copies. An uncut version aired on the Horror Channel in the UK (now defunct), which provided the source material for this review.

Villainess

This professional wrestler / actress was slated to play the T-X in *Terminator 3*. While that never happened, Chyna's relentless security officer offers a taste of what might have been. The movie begins with a nerd attempting to escape an office building while pursued by a shadowy female figure. It's not long before Ava mounts a motorcycle and cuts off the man's escape. The villainess shows off her physicality by dragging the wounded employee into range of a high-voltage hand taser. And rather than stun her victim, this weapon is lethal.

The inquisitive detective has a few run-ins with Ava before another guy smuggles out incriminating evidence. The villainess pursues him, though it's an unfair contest since she chases a pedal cycle on her motorbike. A woman in black leather, racing through the city streets, is a menacing foe. The employee proves more elusive and escapes the assassin thanks to a convenient tram crossing.

The main villain is an alien called Templer, but he mostly talks and leaves the physical stuff to his Ava. She enjoys killing people – all in a day's work for this ruthless woman. Given her wrestling background, Chyna is well cast as the muscular brute. Fittingly, she outlasts the other villains and is the detective's final opponent.

After Templer is killed by his wife (later revealed as an alien herself), we get the fight that's been coming the whole film. First, Ava tries to kill the troublesome cop with her sidearm, then we get the usual heroic gusto when he challenges her to a fair fight. Ava happily accepts these terms and pummel the detective. The muscle woman has the upper hand throughout and is only defeated after the cop grabs Ava's taser and uses her own weapon against her.

Honourable Mentions: Motorcycle Assassins

Romeo Must Die (2000) – Motorcycle Fighter (François Yip)

A stylish villainess in an otherwise forgettable affair, Yip's leather-clad killer still merits a mention. The movie is a loose adaptation of Shakespeare's *Romeo and Juliet*, set in modern-day Oakland. Jet Li is Han Sing, a man out for revenge after his brother is murdered in an ongoing gang war. Aaliyah – in her debut, and one of only two films she made before her death – is an innocent woman caught in the crossfire.

As expected, there are plenty of martial arts, with a pacifist hero and inventive fights to add originality. The unnamed villainess is a biker assassin who attempts to eliminate the heroes after they uncover the villains' plot. For the first part of the lengthy chase scene, the rider wears a dark-visored crash helmet, but genre-savvy viewers will *know* it's a woman.

After another biker is taken out, the second puts up more of a struggle, surviving a crash to confront Han on foot. Once she's revealed as female, the good guy gets all chivalric and refuses to hit her. Fortunately, the heroine provides an inventive solution and acts as a proxy fighter to strike the blows. The assassin's brief appearance ends when she's knocked back onto a wooden stake and impaled through the heart. We see her death in graphic detail thanks to a bizarre X-ray shot, but that's it for female villains in this one.

Crusader (2005) – Leila (Laia Blanch)

A European production set in Barcelona, this conspiracy thriller has plenty of star power, including Michael York and Bo Derek. The plot is fairly standard, but the villainess is above average and plays a larger part in proceedings than you might expect.

Hank Robinson (Andrew McCarthy) is an ambitious television reporter who pilfers footage of a terrorist attack from a dead rival. This gets him in the good books with media mogul McGovern (York), who offers him a dream job with his major network. Too bad he's a pawn in a much larger game involving a frame-up, fake anarchists, and a hostile takeover. Be careful what you wish for.

Hank's most prominent adversaries are two motorcyclists who eliminate loose ends. One of the "hitmen" is revealed to be female early on. The second doesn't show their face until much later, but sadly – from a villainess perspective – is a male. Hank's informant (the titular *Crusader*) uses a voice disguiser, but don't get excited. It's just the same guy playing both sides.

Leila gets several merciless kills in the opening attack, plays the femme fatale, and pursues Hank through a dark room with a silenced weapon. Her contributions get worse as the movie goes on, and what should be a tense stadium encounter is ruined by cutaway shots to prerecorded sports action. Whenever important side characters die, it's the male assassin who does it. Leila is seen only briefly. Often she taunts Hank and shows a nasty streak, but more action would have been preferable.

For the finale, it's the male again who gets the most screen time. Earlier in the movie, we'd been shown a malfunctioning camera crane. So it's no surprise this machine is used to defeat Leila after an all-too brief catfight with the heroine. Familiar stuff, and another villainess who deserved a better send-off.

Last Run (2001)
Kerlov (Viki Kiss, Edit Illés)

Movie

This post-Cold War spy thriller is as routine as they come, but still offers action aplenty. And the primary antagonist, Kerlov, is a deadly Russian sniper and mistress of disguise rolled into one. Frank Banner (Armand Assante) is a former extraction specialist who led a failed mission during the last days of the Soviet Union. A fellow agent – his wife – was killed during that operation, so Banner is not eager about returning to the field. That's until an ex-colleague falls victim to the nemesis sniper, giving Banner the opportunity for payback.

Get used to dead bodies, because many supporting characters – and a high percentage of the main cast – bite the dust. All the spy tropes are in force: items concealed in bibles (twice!), ambiguous motives, shifting allegiances, and impersonations. Any espionage fan will feel right at home. Except for the sniper (who goes missing for the entire middle act), the villains are forgettable. Middlemen in suits and a politician seen only on TV are hardly formidable opposition.

Banner's mission to extract former KGB agent Bukarin (Jürgen Prochnow) takes him from Austria to Ukraine, with attractive scenery along the way. A pleasant distraction while we wait for Kerlov's return, and lots of potential vantage points for a lurking sniper. Camera shots of high windows and church steeples suggest an imminent attack. These are bluffs, and the grand confrontation doesn't happen until the last ten minutes.

Villainess

No mistake – two actresses play the female villain, and even share a curly bracket on the end credits. One could be an action stunt double or another performer to portray Kerlov in disguise, and it's unclear who the lead is. Hence, I've credited both on my ranking list.

The female assassin makes an impact during the opening sequence, gunning down Banner's team and the love of his life from an apartment window. During this attack, the sniper is masked, and it's not obvious she's a female. This unseen villain tactic continues into the next sequence, where a former colleague approaches Banner in a cemetery, and they are targeted by their old foe.

The shootout among the tombstones is suitably dramatic and well staged, with Kerlov disguised as a priest. The sniper's weapon is superior at long range, but Banner uses cover to close the gap. With this still being early on, the shooter vanishes, leaving only shell casings behind. It's then that the "priest" discards their cap and cloak to reveal long hair and a woman's bra. Before that, we'd been given mild hints such as smooth hands loading a sniper rifle, but now Kerlov is confirmed to be female. Like any decent tough girl, she rides a motorcycle and makes a speedy getaway.

The next encounter comes within a few minutes, when the assassin disguises herself as a policeman (the gender flip is intentional) and attacks from a speedboat. Banner gets within range this time, but Kerlov eludes him once again. After all that excitement, viewers hoping for a film-long duel will be sorely disappointed. In fact, we only see the disguised assassin once before the finale: when she watches Banner in a restaurant. Instead of a latex mask, she adopts a spectacled "Clark Kent" approach to remain incognito.

Kerlov is masked for the final shootout, and her face covering suggests a stunt double. The action is amateurish, and people stand in the open waiting for the roaming sniper to pick them off. Bukarin joins the long casualty list, leaving Banner to chase and fight the assassin alone. Long-distance shots make the encounter feel anticlimactic, and there's an obvious actress switch when Banner unmasks his foe. First, Kerlov is a brown-haired woman, then a brunette wearing a white wig.

Banner quickly disarms Kerlov, who's swapped her rifle for a combat knife, and drops the villainess off a rooftop. Usually there's a body shot to confirm the kill in moments like this, but the camera remains on the hero.

Honourable Mention: Snipers

Dragon Heat (2005) – Yuet (Maggie Q)

A shootout with the hero in a cemetery. Sound familiar? Rest assured that Maggie Q's turn as a deadly sharpshooter is well worth a watch. The plot is straightforward: a team of cops against an equally well-trained criminal group. A microfilm contains financial information, but the plot device is barely mentioned. It's an excuse for blood and bullets, and a series of one-on-one battles.

Character backgrounds are established with flashback images, which become distracting once shown multiple times. Many action regulars feature, including Sammo Hung and Michael Biehn. The unnecessary drama sections drag on, but the combat set pieces are relentless. Early on, the masked gang attacks a police convoy. Yuet makes only a fleeting appearance, but things improve quickly. The villainess is proficient in martial arts (she *is* played by Maggie Q) and kicks ass in a nightclub.

Since there's a sniper on the police team, it's no surprise he and Yuet go head to head. The first of two epic encounters takes place in an alleyway and on the overlooking rooftops, with casualties on both sides. Maggie Q has a great screen presence and knows how to sell an action role, so it's little wonder the DVD cover features her prominently. There's a glorious moment where a policewoman acts all tough and blows away a baddie, only for Yuet to show her who the most dangerous female is.

Then comes the final confrontation in a cemetery. For the battle of wits and accuracy, Yuet strips down to a combat vest and screams furiously as she charges headlong into battle. The cop emerges the victor and kills his foe with a close-range shot. Then another cutaway to past images ruins the villainess' death scene.

Der Clown: Payday (2005)
Mona (Xenia Seeberg)

Movie

A continuation of the German television series of the same name, about a clown-masked vigilante taking on criminals above the law. Admittedly, I'm not familiar with the original material, but newcomers will appreciate the abridged intro outlining the key players. The native German audio is far superior to the English dub, but even basic language skills suffice since the film is an all-action affair.

After his former girlfriend and partner was killed by hockey-masked thieves, Max Hecker (aka the Clown) gave up his crusade and became a mall security guard. This is not purely remorse, as Max spies on the hiding spot where the big bad stashed stolen documents. Should the villain ever return, the Clown has his old mask and a small arsenal of weapons ready to exact vengeance.

The robbers turn the tables early and inform a reporter about an upcoming heist. This leads to the first of many action sequences, where we're introduced to the villainess Mona. The masked female has a prominent role, gunning down police officers as her crew raids an armoured truck. The gang leader is a guy named Zorbek, but Mona is evidently his number two. Their true target is not the van, but the reporter lady, who's the sister of the murdered woman the Clown wishes to avenge.

So begins a deadly game of cat and mouse, centred around a daring plot to steal gold bullion from a reserve vault. The pace rarely drops, which is good because this is not a movie to overthink. There are many ludicrous situations where suspension of disbelief is required. Perhaps having the hero wear a clown mask is a hint not to take things that seriously.

Villainess

The villainess carries out the opening robbery wearing a hockey mask with narrow eye slits. It's a great unisex all-black outfit, and if Mona weren't shown masking up, it could have been a pleasant surprise female reveal. She's a bloodthirsty lunatic and happily drops a grenade into heavy traffic to cause a massive Autobahn pileup. The effects team goes overboard, and police cars fly at all angles through dense smoke.

When things settle down – just a little – Mona shows a romantic interest in a fellow robber, a hunk who should know better than to mess with Zorbek's lieutenant. The action is relentless and becomes even more intense when the heroes assault the villain's base. They're holed up in a swimming pool / leisure centre, an excuse to have a vehicle crash through the window and make a loud splash.

Xenia Seeberg also played a villainess in the action comedy *Schwarz & McMurphy* (2001) (also known as *Die Großstadt-Sheriffs*). Another tough henchwoman, but I've only seen clips and not the entire film, which is notoriously hard to find. Thankfully, we have *Der Clown* to make up for that loss.

Mona wears a black leather jacket, impractical high heels, and a short skirt. Her weapon of choice is an automatic rifle, which she loves to fire at every opportunity. And there are lots of opportunities, notably when she and Zorbek return to the mall to recover the documents. In a deadly game of hide and seek, Mona patrols the concourse and taunts the masked hero. And plenty of glass breaks in the crossfire that follows.

The stolen plans are essential to Zorbek's scheme. The gold reserve's access point is underwater and requires the villains to breach a dam with explosives. Despite the onsite military personnel, the thieves gain access with ease. It's a shame that Mona doesn't wear scuba gear, though. Mona is a woman who loves gold, perhaps too much from the way she runs her gloved hand over the stacked ingots. Think there's a betrayal coming?

Time for more action set pieces. First up is a highway chase with the reporter woman strapped to a truck grille. The Clown pulls off a daring high-speed rescue with the help of his helicopter pilot assistant. Zorbek and Mona get frustrated with the vigilante hero, as he effortlessly dodges gunfire and explosions that would kill any normal person.

The finale takes place at an airfield as the villains attempt to escape on a gold-laden cargo plane. Actually, Mona and her lover robber decide to abandon Zorbek, but the guy should know better than to trust a woman in black leather. The fool gets a fatal lesson when Mona guns him down to claim his share of the loot.

There's a long chase with Mona in the aircraft cockpit, laughing crazily as she orders the pilot to ram the reporter's car. The villainess outlasts Zorbek, who's seen off when the clown throws him from a helicopter. Just when Mona thinks she's escaped, the hero dumps a stack of gold ingots onto the cargo plane. This triggers a fuel explosion, and the occupants are engulfed in flames.

Honourable Mentions: Treacherous Robbers

Wedlock (1991) – Noelle (Joan Chen)

Vaguely set "sometime in the future", this sci-fi thriller moves at a snippy pace and offers an over the top, psychotic backstabber of a villainess. Frank Warren (Rutger Hauer) is an electronics expert betrayed by his partners, Sam and Noelle, after a diamond heist. Unfortunately for them, Frank stashes the loot beforehand and is transferred to a low-security unisex prison. No guards are needed because the inmates are fitted with Wedlock collars, which explode when separated from their partner by more than a hundred yards.

The early portion plays out like a typical prison thriller, and Frank falls foul of the local thugs. Scheming Warden Holliday wants the diamonds and puts Frank in solitary when he doesn't co-operate. In this place, that means sensory deprivation in a sealed tank, but the anti-hero is a tough nut to crack. Not one to give up, Holliday allies with Sam and Noelle and hires Frank's Wedlock partner Tracy (Mimi Rogers) to stage a dramatic getaway.

As expected, the central gimmick comes into play. Frank and Tracy have many near misses where they end up separated, but return within the distance limit just in time. Sam and Noelle assist the escapees, hoping Frank will lead them to the loot. The villains corner the fugitives in a brewery and eliminate Frank's friend to remind us they're dangerous psychos. Noelle shoots the wounded Sam purely for thrills and a greater share of the take.

Being an electronics whiz, Frank defuses the collars before the finale. Which is handy because Holliday has a remote detonator to blow them up whenever he chooses. Instead, it's the warden and Noelle who fall victim to their own treachery since Frank plants the bombs on them instead.

Reindeer Games (2000) – Ashley / Millie (Charlize Theron)

A Christmas heist thriller with far too many plot twists, *Reindeer Games* starts off intriguing but becomes a mess by the climax. On the upside, Charlize Theron stars in an early villain role, and playing a cold-hearted bitch is her forte.

Convicted felon Rudy (Ben Affleck) and his cellmate Nick are two days from release when Nick is stabbed during a prison riot. Against his better judgement, Rudy assumes Nick's identity and gets romantically involved with the dead man's pen pal, Ashley. A bad idea, because Ashley's brother Gabriel (Gary Sinise) shows up and forces Rudy to assist with a casino heist. The dangerous psychos want "Nick" to provide insider knowledge, so the impersonator must improvise to keep himself alive.

Ashley seems to be a timid and vulnerable woman, but this is all an act, and she reveals herself to be Gabriel's girlfriend and not his sibling. The heist – when it finally happens – is a complete disaster. The Santa-suited crew are amateurs who've never committed a robbery, the inside info is bogus, and the body count high. Ashley arrives after things get messy, now in full-on villainess mode. She's an equal partner to Gabriel, who gives the gang orders and is just as psychotic.

It's then revealed that Nick faked his death and orchestrated the whole thing. His master plan: go to prison for two years, set up an unknown felon with Millie, and hope his patsy remembers their late-night chats about casino security. Why not forgo the prison sentence and hire a professional heist team? Because we need a final act twist, and it doesn't matter how ludicrous it is.

Charlize Theron has some decent moments to make this tosh bearable, such as shooting Gabriel in cold blood. There's also a satisfying demise where Rudy hot-wires a car and rams the treacherous Millie off a cliff.

Tick Tock (2000)
Rachel Avery (Megan Ward), Carla (Kristin Minter)

Movie

Most films in the 1990s and 2000s that featured lesbians had them be villainesses, and this twisty thriller is no exception. *Tick Tock* has a novel storytelling mechanic: a plot twist, time rewinds to an earlier point, and we witness events from another character's perspective. The result is a cleverly evolving story set in Bakersfield, California.

Rachel Avery is a trophy wife to the domineering Holden (David Dukes), and her best friend and lover Carla is a scheming photographer. Initially, the theme appears to be blackmail, as Carla sets Rachel up with a guy named Travis Brewer (Linden Ashby). He demands money to keep the kinky snapshots secret, but doesn't realise the two women are in cahoots to murder Holden and frame Travis for the crime.

Extra players are revealed through flashbacks, including a private detective whom Holden hires to follow Rachel and identify her secret lover. This is a ploy by the scheming women, who use the PI to create an alibi for Rachel while Carla commits the murder. She does the deed fully nude except for surgical gloves, which is an inventive way to keep blood off her clothes. The unusual murder weapon is an ivory tusk Rachel tricks Travis into handling.

The detective has an appointment at Holden's place, where he's supposed to discover the body. Rachel and Carla gloat in the restroom over successfully duping the two men. But like all brilliant plans, the diabolical murder plot comes apart in the middle act.

Villainesses

Carla is the planner and drives the most important events. Rachel is more reluctant, even though she will inherit her husband's money. When the detective misses his intended appointment and Travis discovers Holden's body, the fall guy cleans up the murder scene. Carla repeatedly claims, "This is even better than we planned" every time something goes wrong. And a lot does, so get ready to hear those words a lot.

Rachel and Carla have a narrow miss when they recover the corpse and get pulled over by a deputy sheriff. Rachel passes an alcohol test with Carla watching – in true smoking, femme fatale fashion – and the lovers keep the faulty trunk closed. Unfortunately for them, their joy is short-lived when they find the Avery residence occupied by Holden's daughter Anne, who's introduced by... another time rewind.

Rachel becomes increasingly stressed and angry as the plan falls apart. She abandons the frame-up plot when she sees Carla seduce Travis at a remote cabin. Then, an enraged Rachel knocks Travis out with a shovel. Things go downhill when Carla finds the dead body has fallen out of the trunk. Who said murder was easy?

While Rachel finds the missing cadaver, she runs into the private detective – now hired by Anne to investigate Holden's disappearance – and he detains her. Carla comes racing to the rescue and runs down the pesky PI at high speed.

When the schemers attempt to frame Travis *again*, he's ready and waiting with a revolver. Carla feigns an argument to gain the advantage, but Rachel's patience with her co-conspirator runs out and she shoots Carla fatally in the chest. The finale has Rachel escorting the handcuffed Travis through the woods at gunpoint, only to find the gun she stole from the detective is faulty.

After a chase and struggle, Rachel bashes Travis' head in with a shovel. However, the dying man freed himself from the handcuffs and secured her ankle to his wrist. Thus, the conniving murderess dies alone in a secluded woodland area. The epilogue features a news report that names Travis as a suspect in Rachel's kidnapping. Months – or maybe years – later, the last shot shows undiscovered skeletal remains.

Honourable Mentions: Lesbians

Hourglass (1995) – **Dara Jensen (Sofia Shinas), Kami (Colette O'Connell)**

Another psycho-lesbian pairing, Dara and Kami are the highlight of this terrible thriller. C. Thomas Howell plays fashion mogul Michael Jardine (no connection to the detective from the Scottish TV series *Taggart*), who's as unlikable as they come. Not good when we have to cope with his insane rants and crass attitude for the entire duration. Trust me – you'll root for the mysterious villainess who murders everyone in his life.

The film borders on unwatchable with dull boardroom segments, difficult to follow dialogue, and bizarre sequences. This includes a house party where people dance around Jardine's father as he sleeps on a life-support machine.

Dara is a scheming murderess skilled in martial arts, with a varied wig collection that comes in handy for her many disguises. Highlights include her sparring with Jardine in a health centre, the opening strangulation of his wife during sex at the beach, and a knife attack on a business associate. Jardine's brother is also on Dara's list, but that murder happens off screen.

If this antihero jerk weren't so busy scolding his associates, he might spot the obvious killers in his midst. Assistant Kami reveals her treachery during the denouement, and Dara beats up her enemy while she taunts him about all the people she's killed. The choreography is amateurish, but the scene is interesting enough to include as an honourable mention.

Jardine takes out Kami by throwing her off a balcony, but Dara survives, and he ends up in prison plotting revenge. Hard to feel any sympathy for the guy, so her Pyrrhic victory is welcome.

Listen (1996) – Krista Barron (Sarah Buxton)

Only one lesbian psycho this time, though any 1990s movie buff will suspect Krista for that reason alone. She's the friend and on/off lover of Sarah Ross (Brooke Langton), a woman who enjoys listening to phone sex conversations via crossed telephone wires. Then she discovers one man she's been eavesdropping on lives in her apartment building, and local women are being murdered. The serial killer collects earrings from the victims and could be someone in Sarah's life.

Suspects include a sinister co-tenant named Randy Wilkes and her boyfriend, Jake Taft. Wilkes threatens Sarah after she shares her suspicions with the police, and Jake watches violent videos in a seedy screening room. He's *really* into female mutilation, and waves his hands like an orchestra conductor as classical music plays for added effect. There's also the weird apartment manager who has photos of women plastered over his bedroom wall... but he commits suicide after being falsely accused.

The finale is a double dose of fake suspect reveals and fatal shootings. Wilkes attacks Sarah and refuses to stop, even when the police show up. Then Jake acts all threatening, only for Krista to blow him away. This is part of the villainess' frame-up plot, and she plants evidence to incriminate the dead boyfriend. With the competition all deceased, Krista now how Sarah to herself.

Compulsion (2024) – Evie (Anna-Maria Sieklucka), Diana (Charlotte Kirk)

Two dangerous women in love, while a female psycho slices up male victims. Is there a connection? Set in sunny Malta and directed by Neil Marshall (*The Descent*), this steamy thriller has a poor reputation, but earns an extended honourable mention for its gory murders, stylish masked killer, and an insane action-packed finale.

The opening scene sets the tone. An intruder breaks into a luxury home by climbing a drainpipe and slashes a naked man taking a shower. Dubbed the "Maltese Phantom" (get it?), the leather-clad killer in a lace hood leaves no forensic traces.

Two female neighbours come under police suspicion. Evie despises her wealthy stepfather, but is happy to live in his house with hi-tech security systems and a collection of Japanese swords. Diana befriends her to get close while she plans a heist and double-cross with her boyfriend, Reese (Zach McGowan). The opening half is slow-going and dialogue-heavy, with awkward voyeurism and uninspired erotica. Then the Phantom stabs a taxi driver who sexually harassed Evie… through the mouth with a katana.

Desperate for money, Reese gets aggressive with Diana, who stabs him with scissors. Her girlfriend enters the fray with a kitchen knife, and they attack together. A chaotic scene unfolds over five minutes, with over thirty attacks on the unarmed but resilient male. It's almost comical as he crawls along the floor, refusing to die. When Reese *finally* goes down, Diana pauses for a smoke. Except he's not dead, so the blood-drenched women continue their frenzied assault.

To dispose of the evidence, the murderers burn their clothes, strip naked, and bathe. A crude excuse for lesbian sex, and the women don't seem worried by the brutal murder they committed. We get it: they're psychos.

A pool attendant sees the couple dump the body, so he blackmails them. A stupid idea, and the killer slits his throat in a nightclub toilet. We learn Diana is a copycat who killed the cabbie to get Evie arrested and lure the rich stepfather to the island. Then she finds a severed female head in her fall girl's luggage. Because Evie is the *real* Maltese Phantom, who wore a red wig at the club to *frame Diana*. Convoluted, but with two female assassins in leather, who's complaining?

In a frantic climax, the treacherous women fight each other. Black-garbed Evie is an agile killer, dodging gun and sword attacks. She doesn't hesitate to kill her stepfather, who chose this unfortunate moment to arrive. Diana needs his retina scan to unlock a hidden safe. Actually, she only needs his eyeball, which she cuts out. In the aftermath, crazy Evie ends up in hospital, while Diana sails off with the stolen money.

Rank #50

Signal One (1994)
Toni (Virginia Hey)

Movie

Also known as *Bullet Down Under*, this messy thriller caught my eye during research, but the DVD copy had dreadful sound quality. Thankfully, a more watchable HD widescreen restoration is available on streaming sites, and the dialogue is audible even if the plot remains incomprehensible.

Martin Bullet (Christopher Atkins) is a conveniently named American cop who's not as trigger-happy as his name might suggest. He has hated guns ever since he shot a kid during a bust gone wrong in the US. Now he's in Australia and partnered with the aggressive Jack Moran (Mark 'Jacko' Jackson). Like every buddy cop thriller, the two men have a frosty relationship to begin with but come to trust one another.

Jack is on a personal manhunt for a mysterious underworld assassin who put his old partner in hospital, so the last thing he needs is a traumatised foreigner to babysit. Martin has moral support from his wife, who's travelled with him to Sydney. She has no connection to the main plot, so it doesn't take an action movie buff to deduce she'll eventually wind up as a hostage.

The characters are mostly unsympathetic, especially the two brother criminals. One has serious mental health issues, and his supposedly smarter sibling is a nightclub owner who thinks it a good idea to play the cops off against gangsters. Scenes where they argue on the telephone are painful to watch, and it's a relief when the far more interesting assassin finishes them off. For a filler subplot, a punk rock band uses the same warehouse hideout, which leads to a bizarre and pointless confrontation.

The killer works for an Asian gangster who imports fake boomerangs (yes, really) when he's not dealing drugs. The boss shows up to issue orders a few times, only to disappear for the climax. Presumably he's too smart to get involved directly, or the filmmakers realised the leather-clad antagonist is the best thing about this shambolic story.

Villainess

The assassin is often seen at a distance, and her bandana disguise is effective enough that most viewers will assume the mystery figure dressed in black is male. Even though the billing implies a major role for Virginia Hey, the clever outfit choice sets up a great villainous reveal.

Knowing Bullet eventually teams up with Jack, it doesn't bode well for the aging partner in the prologue. Especially when the cops respond to a murder scene and tail a black car to a deserted warehouse. There's a dramatic chase, and the partner is badly injured. Then Jack does the hero thing and leaps onto the roof of the car. He doesn't get a good look at the assassin, and his only clue – before he's thrown into the ocean – is a T-shaped earring.

After that dramatic introduction, it's a while before the second appearance. Following boring legwork, the heroes encounter the villainess (still thinking she's a guy) at the crime lord's hideout. After a pursuit on foot – the first opportunity for the assassin to show her physical prowess – Bullet corners the killer at a pier. Memories of the kid's death haunt him so much he can't squeeze the trigger, much to Jack's disgust.

Bad luck catches up with the wannabe gangster brother, and the assassin crashes through a skylight. The shotgun-wielding target is outmatched, and she drowns him in a toilet. This badass certainly means business and wants the stolen drugs back, but a frantic search turns up nothing. The murderer likes theatrical death poses, and the "smart" brother discovers his sibling's body strung up in a junkyard. With his mouth covered in lipstick.

Jack learns the assassin's name – Tony – and goes to a gym, not realising it's a setup. He eyes many male customers, which makes the regulars suspicious. Then, a beautiful blonde introduces herself and suggests Jack come over to her place. Someone should tell him Toni can be spelt that way and that the deadliest assassins are female.

The club owner kidnaps Bullet's wife, leading to an apartment shootout. The secondary villain gets away, and Bullet focuses on saving his partner. Femme fatale Toni has her latest target alone and at her mercy. Jack is so infatuated with the naked woman that he never sees the knife in her hand. A violent mix of action and sex follows, but the picture is dark and grainy for the attack sequence.

The assassin badly wounds the cop and does her lipstick calling card thing, but first she gloats like all great female villains. The gangster confronts the assassin outside, but the strong woman tosses him onto a spiked railing fence. It's the lipstick and psychotic laughter combo for you, mate.

Bullet arrives in time to save Jack, though he's in no shape for police work. The setting for the finale is the warehouse, the docks, and finally a ship. Bullet pursues the villainess – who now has the drugs – and then it's another test of his mettle. The psycho woman taunts Bullet, but what she did to Jack helps him overcome his fears. This time, he doesn't hesitate to pull the trigger.

Honourable Mention: Masculine Names

Thrillkill (1984) – Adrian (Laura Robinson), Parrish (Colleen Embree)

Keeping with the tenuous theme of female villains with masculine names, the primary antagonist in this Canadian thriller is Adrian, a ruthless woman other people seem to trust. The movie is hard to find, but I sourced a DVD copy thanks to the Katrina's Nightmare Theater release. Some scenes are dark, and there are many flickering transitions and residual static that suggest a VHS scan. Still, this old favourite earns an extended mention.

Female computer hacker Carly pulls off a 1980s variant of an electronic bank heist. Somehow she succeeds despite a pre-Internet dial-up connection and code written in BASIC. But a criminal gang wants the money and is quite prepared to kill for it. Most of the gangsters are idiots who act tough but end up suspecting each other instead of the obvious traitor in their midst.

Adrian – more proactive than her associates – murders Carly in a truly inventive kill sequence. The villainess records a computer message that counts down the remaining seconds. When the timer expires, Adrian strangles Carly with a necklace and smashes her head through a glass table. However, it turns out Carly didn't trust her murderer since she left her own message… and no hint of where she stashed the stolen money.

Carly's sister Bobbie is left to piece together the clues. Together with a detective, she learns where Carly hid the secret: the title VR computer game. This involves laser gun battles, a space-age corridor setting, and cat-suited enemies.

Gangsters bite the dust as Adrian and her mystery partner take them out. Female villain Parrish makes the mistake of threatening Adrian with her switchblade, so no surprise she winds up dead. This murder occurs in a curtained photo booth, with only deposited image strips to suggest what transpired.

Adrian is a far more intimidating foe, and even when she doesn't speak, the smartly dressed woman projects a threat. It's revealed the detective is actually a villain, the first of three baddies to play the fake cop trick on Bobbie. Once the heroine cracks the computer code, it's time for a shootout in a convention centre. Good luck figuring out what happens with gloomy shots of people running down dark corridors.

The mystery villain, identifiable by his gold watch, is… some guy called Schofield, whom we've never seen before. After the generic baddie threatens Bobbie, the fake detective – who's now switched sides – guns him down. The couple get all romantic, forgetting about Adrian. After she eliminates the last remaining gangster, it's just her, Bobbie, the false cop, and an expendable security guard.

Adrian wounds her old partner but has to gloat instead of finishing him, which gives Bobbie the chance to grab the dead guard's gun. Those computer games were ideal shooting practice, and while the dying villainess flees up a downward-moving escalator, she doesn't make it far.

Rank #49

The Mummy Returns (2001)
Meela / Anck-Su-Namun (Patricia Velasquez)

Movie

The Brendan Fraser *Mummy* trilogy – which spans nine years of production and three decades in setting – delivers adventure, thrills, and humour. While the cast is mostly male, the women who feature are heavily involved in the action.

Returns takes place in 1933, nine years after *The Mummy* (1999). In the same vein and time period as *Indiana Jones*, the movie thankfully avoids including Nazis. Instead, the heroes battle mercenaries, Egyptian cultists, weird pygmy creatures with blowpipes, and an undead horde led by the Scorpion King (Dwayne Johnson, aka The Rock). And Arnold Vosloo as the title creature, Imhotep, reprising his role from the first film. Even with his immortal soul trapped in the underworld, this guy won't stay dead.

Franchise fans will already be familiar with Rick O'Connell (Fraser) and Evelyn (Rachel Weisz). Her oafish brother Jonathan (John Hannah) and the Egyptian Medjai (Oded Fehr) are back for another adventure too. Rick and Evelyn have married since we last saw them, and now have a son, Alex (Freddie Boath). It seems the hero's derring-do has rubbed off on his wife. Evelyn is no longer a timid librarian, but an action girl at ease with firearms and unnerved by danger.

The prologue introduces the Scorpion King and his pact with Anubis, who granted him an all-conquering army in exchange for his soul. The resurrected Imhotep and his reincarnated lover want dominion over the undead, and the heroes must save the world again. Alex becomes an unwitting pawn when he puts on the bracelet of Anubis, which reveals the way to a lost oasis but imposes a seven-day time limit. Not to worry – if anyone can handle the extra pressure, it's the O'Connells.

Villainess

The Pharoah's mistress was introduced in the first movie, but her only appearances were a flashback set in ancient Egypt – expanded upon in *Returns* – and the showdown in the City of the Dead. Later scenes had her wrapped in rags, and she looked decidedly unpleasant.

Villainess fans will be happy that Patricia Velasquez has a lot more screen time in the sequel. She plays a dual role: Anck-Su-Namun and Meela, a 1930s scholar with memories of her past life. Meela has inherited the treacherous Egyptian's evil traits and leads an expedition to dig up Imhotep's remains. When scarabs devour her workforce, she views them as expendable.

After her mercenaries fail to recover the Scorpion King's bracelet, Meela travels to London to handle the situation personally. There's a great villainous moment when she mistakes Jonathan for Rick and threatens him with a poisonous snake. Fortunately, the American hero saves the hapless Englishman. Undeterred, the villainess kidnaps Evelyn, leading to an action scene at the British Museum where the Mummy returns (get it?) from the dead yet again.

Meela is even nastier in Egypt when she threatens the

young Alex and tricks her mercenaries into opening a cursed chest. The evil Imhotep – now regenerated – restores his lover's soul. Reincarnation is a major plot theme, and we learn Evelyn was once Nefertiri, the Pharoah's daughter, in a past life. Cue another ancient Egyptian flashback and a melee combat duel between the two masked women.

The final battle takes place at an oasis sanctuary. With the henchmen wiped out by pygmies, it boils down to three concurrent battles: Rick vs. Imhotep (until a CGI Scorpion King joins the fray), Medjai vs. the undead, and Evelyn / Nefertiri vs. Anck-Su-Namun. The villainess kills the heroine before this, leaving Jonathan to fend off the more skilled princess. Fortunately, the Book of the Dead provides the means to restore Evelyn back to life. Then comes the rematch, when she fights her nemesis with twin sais and wins.

The ending is a tale of two romances. With the Scorpion King defeated, his lair collapses. Evelyn risks her life to save Rick, but Anck-Su-Namun abandons Imhotep to his fate. The anguished expression on his face is quite touching. Imhotep was mummified alive, all for misplaced love. The self-serving villainess doesn't last long, falling into a scorpion pit and earning a just reward for her betrayal.

Honourable Mentions: *The Mummy* Series / Reboot

The Mummy: Tomb of the Dragon Emperor **(2008) – Choi (Jessey Meng)**

Action shifts to China for the third entry, but many story elements remain. Once again, villains dig up a mummified evil-doer and resurrect him for their own ends. Jet Li is the title emperor, a merciless ancient commander with power over the elements and a cursed terracotta army.

Martial arts fans will find Li's contribution disappointing because, other than a few fights, it's all CGI, shape-shifting, and magic.

Now in the 1940s, Alex has grown up and Maria Bello replaces Rachel Weisz as Evelyn. There's an in-joke about her being "a completely different person," but the heroes lack chemistry. *Dragon Emperor* is a lacklustre effort, and the same could be said of its villains. A Chinese general named Yang wants to restore his nation's past glory, aided by his female lieutenant Choi. The scarred villainess mostly stands in the background, with the odd evil smile to remind us she's there.

Choi's best moment is when she confronts and subdues Evelyn at a museum in Shanghai. The villainess literally draws blood before the two women fight. Victory goes to the good girl, and Choi is then absent for most of the movie. No female villain for the street chase with literal fireworks, a shootout in a Himalayan monastery with Yeti, and a resurrection in Shangri-La. The final confrontation is at the Great Wall of China, with two undead armies in an epic battle.

Michelle Yeoh features in a supporting role, but she's wasted and her only action scene is a brief fight with the Emperor, which ends badly. Choi finally returns, but only to briefly fire a jeep-mounted machine gun before a bomb blast destroys the vehicle. Before the Emperor is laid to rest, Yang shows up. The heroes get the better of him, and a bloody-faced Choi – who survived the earlier explosion – dies while attempting to save her superior.

The Mummy (2017) – Ahmanet (Sofia Boutella)

It's rare that the first film in a planned series is a franchise killer. But this ill-advised reboot is the reason you've never heard of the *Dark Universe*.

Tom Cruise plays the hero (anti-hero?) Nick Morton, an uncharismatic military guy who moonlights as a tomb robber. After he unearths the sarcophagus of a mummified Egyptian princess, he envisions the beautiful woman calling to him. The villainess mind-controls Nick's comrade and flocks of birds to crash a cargo plane, leading to the only decent scene in the movie.

Ahmanet is a poor rip-off of Imhotep with none of his threat or interesting backstory. The modern-day London setting is dreary, and introducing Dr Jekyll / Mr Hyde (Russell Crowe) feels completely out of place. The female mummy resurrects Nick's dead buddy, vanquished foes, and crusader knights to fight beside her. She also has unnatural strength, but despite her godly powers, the encounters are boring. A sandstorm in Britain doesn't have the appeal of a desert backdrop.

Ahmanet's goal is to summon the Egyptian deity Set – a plan she failed to accomplish in ancient times – with Morton as the host. Eventually, he stabs himself with a sacred dagger to complete the ritual (!), uses his powers to defeat the villainess, and becomes... a mysterious creature. Nothing makes sense, and with the *Dark Universe* dead, this is the last we'll see of this unpleasant character. As for Ahmanet, she deserved a much better script.

A View to a Kill (1985)
May Day (Grace Jones)

Movie

My original draft included three James Bond films, with the rest covered as honourable mentions and discussions. On reflection, I added this entry from the Roger Moore era. Since he holds the record (seven) for official bond movies, there's plenty of material to discuss. May Day is an iconic villainess worthy of a mid-place ranking, even if she switches allegiance in the last act.

Many regard Moore's final outing as substandard, though I've always found it underrated. It's possible I'm biased by a masked villainess, the only true one in the series. Stacy Sutton (Tanya Roberts) is arguably a weak "Bond girl", but nowhere near as annoying as Mary Goodnight in *Golden Gun*. In the movie's defence, the story is okay, and the chief villain, Max Zorin, is great. What do you expect when he's played by Christopher Walken?

The plot is a retread of *Goldfinger*, except Zorin wants to corner the market on computer microchips instead of gold bullion. He plans to wipe out the competition – Silicon Valley, in this case – and Bond is the only person who can stop him. Zorin is an ex-KGB operative, but has severed ties with the Motherland. His former comrades aren't too happy about this, and send agent Pola Ivanova (Fiona Fullerton) to investigate. Pola is a fine female antagonist and deserved more screen time, but we get a decent wetsuit / espionage scene and reveal before her premature exit.

Moore had played Bond for 12 years by 1985, which shows in some action scenes with obvious stunt doubles. This might explain why May Day and the hero never have a true confrontation, as defeating a tough henchwoman in a straight-up fight would be unconvincing. If one villainess isn't enough, Zorin also has two female assistants in Jenny Flex and Pan Ho, though they are limited to support roles. Rumour has it that Jenny was the head of security in the original script, before she was ousted by the male Scarpine. A pity, but they didn't diminish the female role that really mattered.

Villainess

Like Fiona Volpe from *Thunderball*, May Day assassinates a man in front of Bond and later unmasks herself. Before that, she's introduced as Zorin's red-dressed right-hand woman and shows her strength by taming a wild horse. The muscular badass then pulls off an elaborate kill at the Eiffel Tower, using a fishing rod and poison-tipped artificial fly to murder a nosy detective. Was smuggling in a normal weapon too difficult? But the stage singer act and masked assistant provide perfect cover.

Unlike Fiona, Bond chases this assassin, but his quarry traps his ankles with fishing line to buy valuable time. The killer seems to run into a dead end as Bond chases them to the top of the Paris landmark. That's when she uses a parachute to escape, prompting a hasty descent and pursuit through the city streets. Bond destroys a lot of property – and the car he's stolen – and ruins a wedding. It's all for naught since May Day escapes with Zorin in a speedboat.

We then get the villainous reveal, complete with an insane laugh.

May Day is not the usual femme fatale, though she mounts Bond in a bizarre sexual encounter. A skilled martial artist, but the closest she gets to direct combat is subduing a clumsy Soviet agent on an offshore platform. And a late encounter where the villainess rips off Stacy's leggings.

Whenever people get too close to uncovering Zorin's plans, it's May Day's job to eliminate them. That's the fate of Sir Godfrey Tibbet (Patrick Macnee), an ally of Bond, who the henchwoman strangles at a carwash. Zorin attempts to eliminate 007 by knocking him out and sinking his car in a lake. His failed effort doesn't go down well with the KGB, and May Day shows her strength again by lifting a man. As Bond comments, she must take some vitamins.

The Russian survives, but Zorin's business associate isn't so lucky. When he refuses to go along with the psychotic villain's plan, he instructs May Day to "provide him with a drink." This is an instruction to the villainess to drop the man into the Pacific Ocean from a blimp.

Grace Jones looks the part and has a close encounter with Bond at Zorin's French estate before the action shifts to California. Stacy, introduced earlier, becomes Bond's companion in stopping the insane scheme. He receives help from a CIA colleague, but that man gets the "car back seat" assassin treatment. Compared to a formidable woman like May Day, Stacy is a much weaker female, and often the traditional screaming damsel in distress.

The finale takes place at a supposedly abandoned mine, where Zorin plans to trigger an unnatural flood disaster. As a geologist, Stacy provides exposition before she and Bond are discovered. Cut to a chase scene with May Day, Jenny Flex and Pan Ho pursuing the heroes through a maze of darkened tunnels. Too bad Zorin doesn't value their services enough to keep them around. He floods the mine without warning, and he and Scarpine finish the survivors with submachine guns.

This betrayal comes at a convenient moment for Bond, since the henchwoman had him within reach. She learns the hard way that Zorin never loved her. Jenny and Pan perish in the flood, but a tough cookie like May Day isn't so easily killed.

The repentant killer assists Bond by hoisting the booby-trapped bomb onto a mine cart. The handbrake is faulty, which gives May Day the perfect opportunity for redemption. Such a great henchwoman switching sides is annoying, but the look on Zorin's face as she scuppers his plans is priceless. Her final defiant stare makes this one of the best death scenes in the series.

Honourable Mentions / Discussions: Roger Moore Bond Movies

Live and Let Die (1973) – Rosie (Gloria Hendry)

Moore's first Bond film is best remembered for its occult and blaxploitation themes, and perhaps Clifton James as redneck sheriff J.W. Pepper. After three nondescript men are assassinated, we're still waiting to see the hero, but his introduction comes after the title song. Then we get a jokey mission briefing at Bond's London residence. The action livens up later, but some sequences are overlong, notably a speedboat chase in the Louisiana Bayou that lasts nearly fifteen minutes.

Female characters in the Moore era are antagonists with a heart or treacherous beauties. The tarot fortune teller Solitaire (Jane Seymour) is a mysterious and interesting character, narrating Bond's arrival in New York to investigate the recent murders. She follows a predictable path, falling in love with Bond – and losing her psychic powers as a consequence. For the showdown on the fictional island of San Monique, she's another girl in need of rescue.

Yaphet Kotto plays a dual role as a crooked diplomat and crime lord. The villain has a weird assortment of henchmen, including a hard-to-kill voodoo priest and the hook-armed Tee Hee. There's also a forgettable femme fatale in Rosie, a double agent who acts incompetent and scared to deceive Bond. Except it's not really an act because Rosie is as timid post-reveal. Bond susses her out after a cryptic tarot card hint, but she made so many mistakes her treachery was obvious. The baddies reward failure as you might expect, and eliminate Rosie after she ceases to be useful.

The Man with the Golden Gun (1974)

One of the weaker 007 entries, this starts with another Bond-less pre-credit sequence and doesn't get any better. The sole bright spot is Francisco Scaramanga, the title villain played by Christopher Lee. He's an assassin who charges one million dollars per hit, a lot of money in 1974.

Misplaced attempts at humour include an unwelcome return for J.W. Pepper from *Live and Let Die*. Watching a racist shout unpleasantries towards the Bangkok population is uncomfortable these days. The midget Nik Nak offers comic relief encounters instead of a genuine threat.

Mary Goodnight (Britt Ekland) is the most demeaning woman in the series. Allegedly, she's a secret agent, but goes through the entire movie doing nothing useful. She gets locked in a closet, stuck in a flying car, and spends the last act in a bikini. The bumbling bimbo even triggers a laser weapon when she presses a button with her backside (!).

Maud Adams, who'd later star in *Octopussy*, plays the assassin's mistress who hires Bond to kill him. Like many supporting females, she winds up dead halfway through.

The Spy Who Loved Me (1977) – Naomi (Caroline Munro)

Moore's third effort has an exciting teaser, which sets the bar for all that followed. The ski chase, stunt jump off a cliff, and Union Jack parachute are iconic, still impressive decades later. It's a brilliant setup, and we also get Sue Vanner as the unnamed "log cabin girl", a Soviet agent.

The titular spy is Major Anya Amasova (Barbara Bach), a refreshingly liberated woman for Bond to spar with. She is equally adept at opportune quips and gadgetry as 007, and the two form a reluctant alliance to investigate missing nuclear submarines. Their romance sours when Anya discovers Bond killed her lover on a previous mission, but she's eventually won over by his charm. The Russian is capable, but still needs to be rescued a few times, notably in the finale where she's held prisoner in a skimpy outfit.

The main villain, Karl Stromberg, is a madman bent on global nuclear destruction to create a new world beneath the sea. He has two elaborate aquatic lairs: a tanker and a submersible base, appropriately named Atlantis. The latter comes with a shark pool for disposing of suspected traitors. Besides a jumpsuit-clad army, he has a reliable henchman: the steel-toothed giant Jaws (Richard Kiel).

Regarded as one of the series' best, the film excels in "expected male is a female" reveals. The camera focuses on Anya's male lover before she's confirmed as the top Soviet agent. A sub commander is shocked the major is a woman, and she *almost* hides her gender from Stromberg's goons before they unmask her.

The best reveal goes to the villainess Naomi (Caroline

Munro) during a car chase in Sardinia. In her earlier scenes, she was eye candy with brief dialogue. Now she's a deadly henchwoman piloting a helicopter. She proves more elusive and dangerous than some female assassins, prompting Bond to drive his vehicle off a pier. Fortunately, the car is a Q-Branch special and converts into a submarine. It's also equipped with a surface-to-air missile for disposing of troublesome threats.

Moonraker (1979)

James Bond meets *Star Wars* to produce a climactic space laser battle that's far-fetched even for this franchise. There are some serious scenes on Earth beforehand, starting with a space shuttle hijack and the now mandatory pre-title action sequence. A femme fatale poses as a stewardess, only to reveal herself as a baddie after kissing the hero. She gets forgotten after a brief dialogue exchange, but the skydiving fight and stunt work make up for it.

The villainous Drax (Michael Lonsdale) and his henchmen try various methods to eliminate Bond. This includes sabotaging a takeoff simulator, a Venetian glassworks fight, and a bizarre canal chase. That ends with a gondola converting to a hovercraft while animals watch in amazement.

Females are well represented. Bond's ally is CIA agent Holly Goodhead, who fits the mysterious woman with her own agenda template. Drax is an equal opportunity employer with as many women as men among his yellow jump suited mooks. But since the villain's goal is to wipe out humanity and start over, it's advisable to have breeding capability.

Some white-dressed "perfect females" show their evil side when they lure Bond to a converted ancient temple and dump him in a pool with a huge python. Bond borrowed a poison pen from Holly earlier and kills the reptile, which upsets the sadistic onlookers.

All the major encounters are between men. But counting minor roles, *Moonraker* holds the record for the number of female villains in a Bond movie.

For Your Eyes Only (1981)

Follow-ups to an outlandish 007 movie are usually grounded in realism. So this is a serious entry with some cartoonish scenes, such as "Blofeld" (not officially him due to rights issues) being dropped down a chimney.

Villainesses are nonexistent in grittier films, with women not involved in the action. However, the movie has a tough leading lady in Melina Havelock, a Greek beauty who helps Bond to locate a sunken spy ship.

Not one to be sidelined, this crossbow-wielding woman is out to avenge her murdered parents. Melina gets a nice unmasking scene after she saves Bond from a pursuing henchman. In the hilltop monastery assault (the last action set piece), she's a silent and deadly killer. In another universe, Melina could have been a formidable foe, but after the Mary Goodnight travesty, we'll settle for a competent ally.

Octopussy (1983) – Magda (Kristina Wayborn)

Moore's penultimate film has the secret agent pursue a jewellery smuggling ring to India. The real action begins when he uncovers a plot by a rogue Soviet general to detonate a nuclear bomb on a NATO airbase. The chief villain is Kamal Khan (Louis Jordan), who's in partnership with an all-female crime organisation led by the title

Octopussy (Maud Adams).

Besides his tough bodyguard Gobinda, Kamal is also assisted by a duplicitous woman named Magda. She has more than one verbal joust with Bond, but her best moment is when she steals a Fabergé egg from a hotel room and escapes over his balcony using a long trailing dress as a makeshift rope. Of course, 007 anticipated this and planted a listening device.

The cat-and-mouse game between Bond and Magda goes on throughout the film, though she ends up fighting for the good guys in the end. She's a skilled martial artist during the climax when her circus troupe attacks Kamal's palace residence.

Octopussy has an interesting backstory, and Maud Adams survives the whole movie this time. Naturally, she gets captured by Kamal and Gobinda after they double-cross her and has to be rescued by the hero. Two interesting female roles, and Magda – because of her icy attitude when helping Kamal – just about qualifies as a redeemed villainess.

Rank #47

Half Past Dead (2002)
49er Six (Nia Peeples)

Movie

Steven Seagal movies aren't renowned for being high quality. After an impressive career launch in the early 1990s, the action star faded into direct-to-video obscurity. He insists on ludicrous one-sided fights, though the baddies in this movie get in the occasional hit – possibly because they're fighting a stunt double. Seagal sometimes makes a decent film, though, and this effort was good enough for a cinema release.

The plot is yet another *Die Hard* scenario, this time set in a high-security prison. Welcome to New Alcatraz, with San Francisco's famous "Rock" reopened to house hardened criminals played by rapper actors. The bizarre cast includes Ja Rule as Nick Frazier, Kurupt as the loud-mouthed Twitch, and Tony Plana as a tough Hispanic warden. The theme tune is loud and dumb, much like the movie as a whole.

New Alcatraz's death row inmates are offered the choice of five execution methods. A dubious policy, and first up is Lester McKenna, a train robber who stole two hundred million dollars' worth of gold bullion. Only he knows the location and plans to take the secret to his grave. The prize would tempt any criminal, so cue an airborne assault by a commando team dubbed the 49ers.

The good guy is Sasha Petrosevitch (Seagal), an FBI agent working undercover to bring down the crime boss who murdered his wife. After his sting operation went wrong, Sasha nearly died. Given his experience, Lester requests to talk with him before his own final journey. This conveniently puts Sasha in the right place to screw up the 49ers' plan.

For a film high on testosterone, many tough women feature. The authority figure on the outside is Agent Ellen Williams (Claudia Christian), and the 49ers' main bargaining chip is Judge Jane McPherson (Linda Thorson). In a potential hint at a futuristic setting, the priest overseeing Lester's execution is also female. Being a woman of God doesn't save her from the main villain, 49er One (Morris Chestnut), who's intent on acquiring the buried treasure at any cost.

Villainess

The henchwoman's number is a misnomer, since Six is second in command and the key operative for dealing with tricky situations. She's the first villain to show her face after the commandos parachute onto New Alcatraz. Before removing her helmet, she clears out a guard tower with an assault rifle and performs an acrobatic leap – all to pumping background music. How's that for an introduction?

Six spearheads the attack, descending on a rope to eliminate a guard with a thigh neck snap while she sprays a second man with bullets. Nobody could ever accuse her of being window dressing, though she looks stylish with her blue eyeshadow and long black cloak. The male prison population appreciates her entrance, though one steely look is enough to make them retreat into their cells.

Seagal hardly ever fights women (one of his "rules"), so

his first encounter with Six is at arm's length through a closed door. Sasha spins her weapon around, but that's the only physical interaction. The closest we get to a fight is a later meeting that involves a snappy dialogue exchange and a dramatic rope-swinging escape down a stairwell.

Nick – not restricted by chivalry – has a far lengthier encounter in the basement. He has the villainess at gunpoint, but can't resist her ironic suggestion to "do this like men". A fight follows, though it's more accurate to call it an ass-whooping by the woman in black. Fortunately for Nick, Sasha arrives to save him.

After a helicopter crash messes up the 49ers' escape plans, the villains switch to Plan B. That involves ransoming the judge for Lester (who's been rescued in a dramatic raid). The prison cells are opened, and there's a lot of shooting in the chaos that ensues. Six acts the tough girl quite a bit. She headbutts the warden, gives tense warning stares to the prisoners, and threatens the captive judge. The villainess also stands in for her boss when negotiating with the FBI.

The inmates arm themselves for an expected fight, which leads to a captive exchange in the cell block area. Naturally, the villains double-cross and switch out the judge for a female hostage, but the heroes have a plan of their own and armed felons for backup. Lester sacrifices himself and blows up the escape chopper, taking the big bad with him.

As for Six, she ends up on the receiving end of a beating by the warden. Rather than surrender, she tries to stab him, but Ellen and the FBI response team gun her down.

Honourable Mentions: Steven Seagal Movies

Under Siege 2: Dark Territory (1995) – Fatima (Afifi)

The sequel sees Seagal return as ex-Navy SEAL Casey Ryback for this *Die Hard* on a train adventure. Morris Chestnut (the villain from *Half Past Dead*) stars as a wimpy porter named Bobby, and he has the honour of dispatching the film's sole villainess. Before that, he receives a martial arts lesson from Ryback's niece, but he soon has bigger things to worry about when armed mercenaries raid the train.

The evil scheme involves a far-fetched earthquake-producing satellite, and it's hard to care given the uninspired action and mediocre villains. The female foe's limited screen time mostly comprises standing in the background, and she disappears for whole stretches of the movie. Her most impressive contributions are torturing two military officers for passcodes – with an eye-melting needle she's disappointed not to use – and wounding Ryback with a sniper rifle.

Drawing blood from a Seagal character (a rare feat) earns the villainess a mention. But it's Bobby who throws Fatima from a helicopter after a brief fight. The niece will be happy he put her earlier training to good use.

Maximum Conviction (2012) – Charlotte (Aliyah O'Brien)

Another Seagal film set in a prison, a low-tech black site that houses two important female prisoners. One is CIA courier Samantha (Steph Song) who has no combat training despite her dangerous profession. The second woman is Charlotte, a much tougher CIA operative in league with the villains. The bad guys are after a microchip surgically implanted in Samantha's body, but this plot device is given no explanation or thought. Really, it's just an excuse for gunfire and fistfights.

Michael Paré is the lead villain, and Seagal has another B-movie actor – Steve Austin – for backup. The males do the fighting early on, and the women don't play major roles until the second half. Then Charlotte comes into her own and introduces herself to Austin's character by beating him up. She also kidnaps Samantha and takes down a misogynistic heavyweight prisoner. This is a lady who likes to flex her muscles, and she isn't sidelined like most Seagal villainesses.

Ultimately, everyone gets into a shootout in the big finale. Disappointingly, it's Samantha who defeats Charlotte and not a main protagonist. It seems the courier can fire a handgun, at least.

Rank #46

The Rookie (1990)
Liesl (Sonia Braga)

Movie

Clint Eastwood transitioned from playing cowboys to cowboy cops in the 1970s when he starred as the iconic *Dirty Harry*. His five-movie stint as Inspector Callahan ended with *The Dead Pool* in 1988, but his character Nick Pulovski in *The Rookie* is identical in all but name. The title refers to his new partner, David Ackerman (Charlie Sheen), a suited, by the book detective who learns the ropes from his veteran colleague.

The buddy cop theme and Los Angeles setting are familiar, but instead of drug dealers or serial killers, the opposition is Strom (Raul Julia) and his exotic car theft ring. While the main villain is hammy, his tough-girl companion Liesl offers some welcome variety. Everything is standard to begin with: the murder of Nick's partner, an initially frosty relationship with Ackerman that softens over time, and a slew of wisecracks. The film overuses "repeat scenarios" where the rookie finds himself in the same situation as Nick and speaks the same dialogue. This is just humorous enough not to feel tiresome.

The plot takes an unusual diversion partway through when Strom captures Nick and holds him for ransom. Ackerman gets to play the hero cop while Nick is literally tied up at the villainess' mercy. During the third act, the badass rookie takes down a bar full of goons all by himself. His wife doesn't appreciate the change in personality until her motorcycle-riding husband saves her from a henchman.

There are attempts at character development around Ackerman: flashbacks to a childhood accident that killed his brother, and his wealthy father's lack of support. These are all secondary to the action, however. Memorable scenes include a trailer truck chase in the prologue, an unlikely escape by driving a car through a high window to escape an explosion, and a climactic shootout at an airport terminal. Braga's bad girl lasts the distance, so there's plenty for female villain fans to enjoy.

Villainess

Early on, Liesl is Strom's silent partner and apparently a minor character. Pulovski quips about her driving an expensive car, with no inkling she's part of the theft ring. She's often in the background while Strom conducts shady business, though her hardened features, muscular tattooed arms, and intense body language hint at what's coming.

After forty minutes, Liesl finally gets some action. By that point, Nick had used strong-arm tactics to persuade two lower-rung thugs to become snitches. That shortens their life expectancy quite a bit, and when Strom loses money, he soon identifies the mole. The villainess kickboxes the man into submission and puts a bullet in his head, though we only see her aim with the gunshot itself off-screen.

Strom and his crew raid a casino vault, desperate for cash. However, Nick and Ackerman are waiting thanks to the snitch's listening device. The arrest goes well until Liesl challenges Ackerman by walking towards him. Too honourable for his own good, the rookie cop refuses to shoot an unarmed woman. A scuffle follows before the villainess pulls out a backup weapon, calls Ackerman an amateur, and puts three slugs in him. The rookie is wearing a bulletproof vest, but that doesn't prevent his partner from being taken hostage.

While Ackerman is busy busting heads and following leads, Liesl shows her dominance by raping Nick. This is a full-on sexual assault that goes on for five minutes, and she threatens to cut off Nick's private parts with a razor blade. Then, she forces herself onto him and videotapes the whole thing as a memento. Nick looks decidedly uncomfortable, an experience likely shared by many viewers. Sonia Braga comes across as a nasty piece of work, and the only person enjoying herself.

Strom isn't happy to discover Liesl's side activities, but she's there for the climax. Ackerman has rescued Nick, and the two cops pursue their quarry to an airport. It's here Liesl goes trigger-happy with a submachine gun and the villains separate.

Nick goes after the main man and eventually kills him on a baggage carousel, while Ackerman gets the chance for revenge against Liesl. After a chase through the concourse, the hero confronts the villainess and surprises her from behind. People might expect a fight scene given Liesl and Ackerman are capable fighters, but the rookie calls her an amateur and pulls the trigger. Touche.

Honourable Mentions: *Dirty Harry* Movies

The Enforcer (1976) – Wanda (Samantha Doane)

By the third *Dirty Harry* movie, the audience knew what to expect: a tough-talking hero with a .44 Magnum and disregard for authority, shootouts with criminal scum, and partners with short life expectancies. That's worrying since Inspector Callahan has *two* partners this time, and both share their last moments with him. The second is a woman, Inspector Moore, played by Tyne Daly (one half of the TV cop duo *Cagney & Lacey*). Over the course of the film, their adversarial relationship matures into respect. That old chestnut, but this franchise is most effective when it sticks to the formula.

Striking further blows for gender equality, there are two female antagonists. Pity the villains are the weakest in the series, fake terrorists called the People's Revolutionary Strike Force (PRSF) on a campaign of violence. Villainess #1 is a blonde beauty who lures two men into a trap, only to vanish when the main baddie kills them. This female takes part in a raid on a munitions depot, only to get shot. Half an hour into a ninety-minute movie, her contribution is already over.

Wanda – a bandana-wearing brunette – survives a lot longer. She threatens a guard into raising a bridge (and murders him, but that bit is off-screen) and attempts to bump off Harry while disguised as a nun. Thankfully, Inspector Moore is on hand to save the hero's ass and gets to prove her capability in the Alcatraz-set climax that follows. That's before her name is added to the high body count.

Sudden Impact (1983) – Jennifer Spencer (Sondra Locke)

The main villainess is arguably an anti-heroine, given she targets the sadistic psychos who raped her and put her traumatised sister in a care home. By the film's climax, Harry sympathises with Jennifer and even sees the vigilante artist as a reflection of himself. San Francisco's mafia hoodlums and teen gang bangers are so ticked off with

Callahan they've gone on the offensive, so the brass send Harry to the small town of San Paulo to investigate a murder.

Things would never stay quiet with Harry around, so San Paulo becomes his new hunting ground as Jennifer's killing spree continues. Sondra Locke is the best series antagonist since Scorpio, the deranged sniper in the original. Jennifer is a woman with a cause who relentlessly executes those responsible by shooting them twice. Once in the genitals, then the head. She shows no mercy or remorse, but remains a sympathetic character since the men (and one lesbian) she murders are so unpleasant.

Harry's friend helps him in the investigation, but suffers the same fate as many other partners when a gang leader ambushes him. The villains try to kill Harry, but should have made sure he was dead before going after Jennifer.

The grand finale takes place at a carnival where the silhouetted hero arrives to save the girl and dispense his own brand of justice. Once the baddies are dealt with, Harry forgives Jennifer and covers for her crimes. Maybe they aren't so different.

Rank #45

***Masquerade* (2021)**
Rose (Bella Thorne), Woman (Skyler Samuels)

Movie

Many home invasion-themed thrillers feature female antagonists, but this recent release is a standout. There are two contrasting villainesses: a sympathetic burglar and a mysterious woman who may be a criminal mastermind. Both women dress all in black and wear fencing masks for a good portion of the film, and there's also a great (though confusing) plot twist to wrap things up.

The initial setup is simple and familiar. A young girl named Casey (Alyvia Alyn Lind) is at home with her babysitter Sofia when two masked intruders break in to steal precious paintings. The burglar in charge is male, and his nasty streak is established when he bludgeons Sofia to death while a terrified Casey watches from upstairs. The girl flees and proves a surprisingly elusive quarry to track. After a few tense moments – notably when Casey hides behind a standing mirror – the child takes refuge in the attic.

Where are Casey's parents while all this is going on? Art broker couple Daniel (Austin Nichols) and Olivia (Mercia Monroe) are on their way home from an influential society gathering. Masks are a common theme, so this was a masquerade event of some description. A waitress named Rose kindly offered the brokers a lift, but she seems in league with the art thieves.

Despite a slow first half and limited locations, things intensify when the brokers arrive home and Rose masks up to join the party. Casey is still in danger but gaining in confidence, and things are about to get bloody – and mind-boggling – before the end.

Villainesses

During the opening half-hour, the masked female thief searches for Casey. The woman is more sympathetic than her male counterpart, and she shows distaste at the brutal murder of Sofia. The thief plays a deadly game of hide and seek with Casey, making threatening comments that have little impact. After the girl falls through the attic roof and gives herself away, the burglars spend another ten minutes finding the access point. Then it's the masked woman's job to deal with Casey while the male intruder handles the parents.

To get close to the girl, the woman agrees to a request to remove her mask. Don't expect a great reveal here – this is a character we haven't seen before. In fact, the female thief is never referred to by name and is simply called "woman" in the credits. She comes across as concerned and is believable when she makes a promise not to harm Casey. However, those efforts are undone when Casey hears a commotion downstairs and jumps through the weak floor to relative safety.

Once again, Casey is effective at hiding and fixes a makeshift splint for her broken ankle. The male thief is angry at his female accomplice for removing her mask, and she has a mental breakdown in the last act. Eventually, Casey finds a revolver and confronts the man while he's stealing artwork. During the exchange that follows, the female is shot through the mask (and eye). The masked male then turns the gun on Casey and shoots her. Masquerade certainly isn't a film for anyone squeamish.

Before all this, Rose discusses artworks (and masks) with the brokers. She drops the facade when the couple arrive home, then dons a black outfit and fencing mask of her own. Rose surprises Olivia and ties her up before confronting Daniel. This is a brutal encounter involving torture and threats. By the time the leather-clad villainess has finished with her captive, he's a bloody wreck and capitulates to Rose's demands to provide the safe combination.

Then comes the big reveal, which culminates in the male thief taking off his mask to reveal... a younger Daniel. Meanwhile, Rose unmasks, and the older Daniel clearly recognises her. Yes, there are two separate home invasion plots going on, and Rose is actually a grown-up Casey-Rose. This twist is a cheat, since there's no overall framing device. Two narratives in different time periods unfold in parallel, and similar events (noises, parents attacked) happen in both timelines at just the point they need to.

In retrospect, there are clues such as the two thieves and Rose never meeting and the parents not being concerned about their daughter's safety. That's because their real little girl – not Casey, remember – is with a childminder who is Sofia's sister. Who is Rose's accomplice, and it was her she spoke with on the phone, not the art thieves.

Getting all this? If not, there's a convenient *Usual Suspects*-style montage that revisits key dialogue lines that now take on a whole new meaning. Plus some extra scenes, such as Rose tracking down the brokers, plotting her revenge, and doing surveillance. As for Daniel and Olivia, their fate is left ambiguous, and we're treated to a shot of Casey aging into Rose to clarify what the hell just happened.

Honourable Mention: Home Invasion Movies

Home Invasion (2016) – Victoria Knox (Kyra Zagorsky)

Take one guess what this movie is about. The unimaginative title doesn't generate high expectations, but production values are reasonable for a direct to video / streaming film. There's a decent cast to add some quality. Natasha Henstridge is Chloe, a woman trapped at home with her teenage son when three masked mercenaries come calling. Her best friend doesn't last long, though the "start the story in the middle" opening means the poor woman gets some pre-mortem dialogue later.

Victoria's mask is the worst of the bunch, barely covering her face. However, it's only a temporary measure while the mercs take out the security cameras. The obvious ones, anyway. Turns out the baddies have already killed Chloe's mysterious husband, but not before he converted the house into a private fortress with hidden surveillance. With the cops trapped across a sabotaged bridge, Chloe's only ally is an experienced security dispatcher (Jason Patric).

The primary villain is Heflin (martial arts star Scott Adkins), who disappointingly doesn't do much fighting. Since the main character is female, the job goes to his lieutenant, Victoria. Before the inevitable catfight with Chloe, the villainess strips down to a sleeveless leather top and patrols the rainy exterior. Victoria comes across as trigger-happy and gets the action she craves when she tosses a stun grenade to subdue the elusive Chloe. The mother / son team has a tough fight, but eventually takes Victoria down with a shovel. Being heroes, they only tie her up and don't kill her, which means she's not done yet.

What are these mercenaries after? An item the husband stole from Heflin and locked in a hidden safe. That's all we ever find out. When the robbers cannot breach the security, Victoria – now free from her restraints – threatens Chloe's son at knifepoint, hoping the wife knows the combination. That seems unlikely, but these guys aren't that smart.

The finale has Victoria chase the boy outside, only to be run over by the car he's driving. A bland death scene, and the main villain's isn't much better. Guess they weren't going for originality.

Rank #44

Crackerjack 2 (1997)
Jasmine (Katerina Brozova)

Movie

Sequels often feature better female villains than the original, and that's the case here. *Crackerjack* (1994) was basically *Die Hard* at a mountain ski resort, with Christopher Plummer doing a rather meek Hans Gruber impression as German baddie Ivan Getz. The villain and his trigger-happy mercenaries occupy an entire mountain just to get their hands on a repentant mob boss' diamonds. Surely there's an easier approach to getting rich.

The B-grade action movie is a complete rip-off of the 1988 classic and doesn't pretend otherwise. Jack Wild is a lone cop with family members among the hostages, and Getz shows no concern for human life, whether it be civilians or his own men. Sole female villain Alex (Dorothy Fehr) acts tough, crushes a nut and shoots some innocent guy, but her involvement is standing around while Getz does the talking. In the end, Alex gets a "blink and miss it" death when she's blown away without so much as a one-liner.

Thankfully, the villainess in *Crackerjack 2* is far superior. The film has a trashy, cookie-cutter plot, but at least there's something going for it. While the second film appears to be a train-set *Die Hard* clone (it was titled *Hostage Train* in the US), the action mostly takes place in a sealed-off tunnel. Convenient when you need nondescript concrete rooms to hide a low budget.

Thomas Ian Griffith must have been unavailable for the sequel as the main character is now played by Judge Reinhold. If you're wondering who that is, he was Eddie Murphy's sidekick in the *Beverly Hills Cop* films. One assumes B-movie action regulars turned the producers down, though Reinhold is passable in all fairness.

The setup is by the numbers. The terrorist Hans Becker (Karel Roden) murdered Wild's wife, and now plans to extort investors on the same train as Wild's fiancée Dana Townsend. She's played by Carol Alt – a former swimsuit model – so expect scantily clad scenes to keep the viewer's attention until the action kicks in. Once it does, it's revealed that Becker is not the main villain. That would be Michael Sarazzin as some guy called Smith (probably an alias, but never confirmed), who poses as an innocent passenger but abandons the ruse so soon it's pointless.

This is a generic cut-and-paste affair. Villains are way ahead of the incompetent authorities, and only Jack Wild can save the day. Special forces attempt an airborne assault only to get blown up along with a decoy train. The baddies have an escape plan, which involves killing the hostages. For comic relief, there's a model train enthusiast who exists solely to provide information. Just like the first *Crackerjack*, the plot reads like a *Die Hard* ripoff checklist, and without Jasmine, the movie would be unbearable.

Villainess

The prologue is the expected loud action sequence that introduces the feud between Wild and Becker, and also an incompetent boss who arrests the hero for obstruction of justice. Jasmine is absent for this, but shows up for the aftermath at the villain's hideout. The villainess claims a captured businessman was "no fun" moments before she garrotes him live on camera. The kill happens off screen, but this is already an improvement on the first *Crackerjack* film.

It's a little while before Wild discovers the hideout and the man's body (he was busy having sex with Dana and fighting off Becker's thugs). Turns out the dead guy was supposed to meet Dana on a train, except Becker takes his place and mails the snuff video to the authorities with a fake ransom demand. Wild – with the help of a helicopter pilot friend – gets on board and ends up trapped in the tunnel system with terrified hostages and terrorists. Does any of this sound familiar?

With her introduction over, Jasmine helps Smith interrogate the investor prisoners. She's one sadistic henchwoman who likes to pull out teeth with pliers. Plural, because Jasmine takes a tooth from the wrong side and is overjoyed at doing the whole thing again. Perhaps the investor should have taken the hint and provided his bank account details. This guy isn't smart, however. Not only does he insult his wife when she's threatened by Smith, but also threatens Jasmine after she drags him back to the cell. Does this idiot realise the villains don't need him anymore? A point the henchwoman is happy to clarify by shooting him in the back.

The next investor in the hot seat is reluctant to give up his details too. Jasmine's persuasion method this time is sexually assaulting the man's wife / girlfriend. The hostage squirms uncomfortably as Jasmine squeezes her legs, and eventually the investor caves in. Pity for the villain's tech guy, Krill – he was enjoying it.

Meanwhile, Wild finds his way into the hostage room, but nobody wants to escape. Perhaps they'd rather be tortured by Jasmine? Once Wild has annoyed Becker and taken out a few of his thugs, it's high time the two met. Wild sneaks up on Becker and has him at gunpoint. Does he shoot the man who murdered his wife? Of course not! Otherwise, the hero couldn't be captured and have a bomb taped to his chest.

Smith and Jasmine consider Becker and his thugs expendable, so they speed up the countdown and flood the tunnels with water from a reservoir. Just so Wild can obtain the disc with the investors' financial data, Krill is sent with one man for protection. The bodyguard goes down after one punch, and the techie puts up little resistance. Smith isn't too happy with Krill's failure, so Jasmine gets a second strangulation kill. She clearly gets all excited and sexually aroused, but the camera cuts away to shots of Wild struggling to escape. Another mostly off-screen murder, then.

After Jasmine takes Dana hostage to trade for the disk, the others decide it's a good time to leave. The final confrontation takes place in a shaft. Jasmine mouths off to Wild, but then it's her turn to get shot in the back. Smith really doesn't believe in sharing his ill-got gains.

The villainess' death is a disappointing end to what came before. Don't get hopes up for a good climax. Smith gets tossed down the shaft by Dana, who finally uses the self-defence training foreshadowed earlier. And the heroes survive an explosion with little more than blackened faces.

Honourable Mention: Prominent Henchwomen

Rush Hour 2 **(2001) – Hu Li (Zhang Ziyi)**

This action-comedy sequel pitted detective duo Lee and Carter (Jackie Chan and Chris Tucker) against Chinese triads in Hong Kong, though they were causing chaos in America by the end. Asian martial arts actors often get cast as villains in Hollywood productions, and Zhang Ziyi – of *Crouching Tiger, Hidden Dragon* fame – plays the enforcer to chief baddie Ricky Tan (John Lone).

Events play out with no major surprises. A female customs agent (Roselyn Sanchez) with questionable loyalty undresses while the cops stake out her Los Angeles apartment. Hu Li shoots Tan on his yacht and apparently kills him, but the old staged assassination ploy won't fool seasoned viewers. Why would they bother with a backstory about Tan and Lee's former partner?

Hu Li doesn't get any direct kills, despite having a fair chunk of screen time. Her major acts of villainy are setting off bombs in buildings, acting cold and mean, and knocking out the two heroes with high kicks. She also skewers an apple with a throwing knife, if you count that. All the encounters – mostly between Hu Li and Carter – finish with effortless victories for the villainess.

The main action set piece – where Hu Li finally does some serious fighting – is set in a Los Vegas casino. The villainess tapes a grenade in Lee's mouth while gloatingly holding a detonator, which leads to an inventive brawl with the hero desperately trying to remove the explosive. With Carter's help, Lee survives this messy situation and goes after the big boss while his partner takes on Hu Li. The fight is played for laughs, but Carter holds his own (mostly by accident) against a much more skilled opponent. Somehow the loud-mouthed cop wins, and Hu Li ends up impaled on a decorative spear.

If that "demise" was disappointing, then get ready for worse. Hu Li survives her injury to show up at the villain's penthouse holding a bomb. Why would an icy, composed woman suddenly become hysterical and suicidal? A stupid plot device to add in a gigantic explosion and one final stunt sequence.

Rank #43

See No Evil, Hear No Evil (1989)
Eve (Joan Severance)

Movie

One of several comedies starring Gene Wilder and Richard Pryor, this entertaining romp pitted the duo against a sexy and clever hitwoman in Joan Severance's Eve. Kevin Spacey plays the considerably less intelligent English henchman Kirgo.

Dave (Wilder) is the deaf owner of a New York news kiosk, and the blind Wally (Pryor) is his new assistant. The pair soon get into trouble – fistfights in a bar and arguments with pedestrians – but their problems get serious after Wally's bookmaker unloads a gold coin… shortly before he's bumped off by Eve. Wally hears the gunshot and smells the assassin's perfume as she makes her getaway. Dave sees the killer – and her legs – from behind. Naturally, the pair get arrested at the scene, but not before Wally unknowingly collects the coin.

With two disabled main characters, the jokes could easily have backfired, but everything is good-natured and the heroes overcome their handicaps to triumph. Besides the two killers and their mysterious employer Sutherland (Anthony Zerbe), Dave and Wally must also contend with the obsessed Captain Braddock (Alan North) who's convinced they are guilty. Fortunately, the duo has an ally in Wally's sister Adele (Kirsten Childs). No prizes for guessing the girl ends up captured, forcing the heroes to come up with a daring rescue plan.

See No Evil, Hear No Evil was one of several action comedies I considered for a top-half ranking slot. Ultimately, this movie triumphs over its competition because of the superior humour, stylish villainess, and inventive situations.

Villainess

From the moment Eve makes her first appearance, it's clear she's a dangerous woman. She may not be top of the villainous hierarchy, but she is the comedy duo's deadliest opponent. More competent than the hapless Kirgo and smarter than her employer gives her credit for. As the most interesting foe, it's no surprise the female assassin survives while her comrades bite the dust.

After failing to acquire the coin, Eve and Kirgo soon discover that the arrested Dave and Wally have their prize and so pose as lawyers. Tipped off by Eve's legs and perfume, the deaf / blind protagonists deduce their "attorneys" are there to kill them and make a dramatic escape. That part goes well – thanks to the inept NYPD – but the villains soon catch up.

Eve retrieves the coin and Dave persuades her to kiss him, but this villainess is not one for mercy and Kirgo is even less generous. With things looking gloomy, the duo combine their skills. Dave reads Eve's lips while she talks on a payphone, and Wally surprises Kirgo with a punch. The heroes then go on the run – or rather, a chaotic drive – through the streets of New York City.

This car chase goes on for several minutes with assassins and police in pursuit. Somehow Wally avoids a road accident, but crashes into a garbage-laden barge. Despite eluding Eve and Captain Braddock, the heroes realise the only way to clear their names is to get the coin back. This leads to a comical sequence at a rural hotel resort where the duo impersonate foreign doctors (rather hopelessly, it must be said). Adele distracts Kirgo while Dave searches Eve's room and Wally stands guard outside (until he's dragged into a medical conference).

After Dave retrieves the coin once more, a towel-wrapped Eve walks in after she finishes a shower. Dave uses – let's say unorthodox means – to improvise, and she raises her hands. He kisses the naked woman (who can blame him?) before leaving, but it doesn't take long for the assassins to realise Adele is working with the duo.

Sutherland's estate – the setting for the final showdown – is a mansion patrolled by a burly groundskeeper and ferocious guard dogs. Wally and Dave rescue Adele – after knocking out Eve – but they are captured. Kirgo brings Wally before Sutherland, who then reveals the "gold coin" is a room-temperature superconductor.

The foolish henchman renegotiates his cut, prompting Sutherland to switch off the lights and shoot him. It turns out the main villain is just as blind as Wally, leading to a standoff with the two men stalking each other around the room. This is a tense and original sequence, sadly cut short by Eve's arrival.

Sutherland's attempt to repeat the "lights out" trick ends with the henchwoman shooting him at point-blank range. Eve dashes to a waiting helicopter, but the heroes aren't about to let her escape. Dave and a reluctant Wally slide down a conveniently placed wire to get the drop on the villainess. Then Adele arrives with the cavalry.

Honourable Mention: Ruthless Robbers

Beverly Hills Cop II (1987) – Karla Fry (Brigitte Nielsen)

This comedy sequel made my original list, but on reflection there were better examples. Things get off to an explosive start as the statuesque blonde Karla leads a jewellery store heist in Beverly Hills. After she shoots up the place – overly dressed in a white coat, high heels, and sunglasses – the villainess leaves behind an envelope labelled with a capital A.

So begin the "alphabet bandit" crimes, and letter B is delivered after an attempted hit on police Captain Andrew Bogomil. That's Axel Foley's friend from the first movie, so the villains have his full attention. Up against Eddie Murphy as the con artist with a badge, they don't stand a chance.

Karla stands out because the other villains are uninteresting. Maxwell Dent (Jürgen Prochnow) is a shady businessman running an insurance scam and arms deals on the side, and Charles Cain (Dean Stockwell) is simply a fall guy. Among the jokes and various cons, which become tired and repetitive, there's an encounter with Karla at a gun club and not much else until the next big heist. The City Deposit is probably the best robbery, with the black-clad Karla masking up while Foley and his sidekicks race to stop them.

Karla plays policewoman and wears a gas mask for the final armed robbery at Dent's racetrack. It's here she gets her best moment, shooting Cain and another accomplice as part of a double-cross. Sadly, the finale at an oilfield is dull, with Karla only briefly seen and Dent too easily disposed of.

The villainess gets the drop on Foley, only to be shot by a secondary character. As anticlimactic as it sounds, unfortunately. Well, at least there's a (poor) joke at her expense and a trademark Eddie Murphy laugh.

Prey of the Chameleon (1992)
Elizabeth Burrows (Daphne Zuniga)

Movie

Serial killer movies are nothing new, but the premise of this made-for-cable thriller is a fresh concept. Alexandra Paul stars as small-town deputy sheriff Carrie, whose ex-boyfriend J.D. (James Wilder) is involved in her personal life and investigation. When the drifter picks up a stranded woman, he does not know she's the Chameleon: a mistress of disguise who assumes the identities of her victims.

As the police piece together the killer's MO, FBI agent Resnick (Don Harvey) provides some background information. The murderess is Elizabeth Burrows, a woman who recently escaped a mental institution by strangling a nurse. This murder is shown in the film's opening sequence, which begins with the topless victim having sex as Elizabeth fashions a wire coat hanger into a makeshift garrote. The strangulation is relatively lengthy and graphic, and Elizabeth smashes the nurse's head into a mirror as the title credits roll.

Carrie and J.D. had an unhappy previous relationship. Their bond doesn't improve after she discovers his involvement with Patricia Harper (the housewife Elizabeth has murdered and now become). When they're not discussing the case, Carrie and Resnick flirt, but this doesn't go anywhere. The FBI man is absent for the final sequence, where Carrie and J.D. put aside their differences to take down the psycho impersonator.

Villainess

After a steamy night in bed, things get weird when the blonde "Patricia" dyes her hair black and wears J.D.'s clothes. He smokes a cigarette, and so does she. This creeps him out, but not enough to ditch the brunette copycat – he's enjoying sex with her far too much.

On a drive through the desert, Elizabeth discovers J.D.'s revolver in the glove box, which he gladly shows off. Maybe he shouldn't have, because the psycho woman holds up a gas station and has the attendant drop his pants. No sexual attraction, but it gives Elizabeth the chance to get away. Carrie learns of the robbery soon after, and she and Resnick are already aware of J.D.'s involvement thanks to a bartender's eyewitness statement.

Things get worse for J.D. when Elizabeth disguises herself as a man, trims her hair, and tapes bandages around her chest to flatten her profile. Add sunglasses and a cowboy hat, and she's a decent (though not great) male impersonator. J.D. stumbles in on her and gets knocked out, but unlike her female victims, the murderess keeps this one alive. Elizabeth hides the unconscious man in a car trunk at a secluded junkyard. There is a guard dog, but the poor animal gets a bullet for barking too loudly.

Elizabeth graduates to armed robbery and murder when she rips off a bank and shoots two guards. Based on camera footage and body movements, Carrie and the FBI wrongly identify J.D. as the gunman. By now, Elizabeth has taken a female hostage, whom she seduces and kills off-screen. An FBI agent comes calling, but he hasn't been briefed on the Chameleon. He believes the woman's story about the bank robber being upstairs, which allows Elizabeth an easy backstab kill. To be fair, Zuniga is convincing in switching personalities.

J.D. escapes and returns to the small town where it all started. Carrie is already there and – not believing her boyfriend's wild tale – handcuffs him to a radiator. His story checks out in the end, but then Elizabeth arrives and targets another victim: Carrie. The women have an argument as the policewoman digs a grave at gunpoint, while J.D. desperately tries to free himself.

Elizabeth makes Carrie undress and somehow changes into her uniform (completely implausible given her victim is awake and unrestrained). The victim does the old "throw dirt in the face" trick, and a catfight follows. Carrie gains the advantage, and J.D. races to the rescue, only to attack the wrong woman just as she's about to shoot. Elizabeth knocks out the would-be hero, then we get a second struggle, which ends when Carrie turns the gun on the psycho.

Honourable Mentions: Mistresses of Disguise

Sofia (2012) (aka *Assassin's Bullet*) – **Vicky / Ursula / Sofia (Elika Portnoy)**

A female assassin targets Islamic extremists in this confusing action thriller. Unsurprisingly set in the Bulgarian city of Sofia, the opening kill sets up the black-clad antagonist as a mysterious – and efficient – hitwoman who leaves no witnesses. The execution draws the attention of the American ambassador (Donald Sutherland), who asks ex-FBI agent Robert Diggs (Christian Slater) to investigate.

What follows is a muddled mess, with several women involved. These include an English language teacher named

Vicky and the redhead belly dancer Ursula, who Diggs falls for. Vicky is a patient of Dr Aaron Kahn (Timothy Spall) who likes to draw sketches while he works. Corrupt police detectives sell a sniper rifle to an assassin and cover their tracks by erasing a videotape. Despite the suggestion that this might be important, they're never seen again.

Meanwhile, the leather chick receives kill orders from a mysterious coin-spinning controller. Since the director is Isaac Fiorentine, the assassinations are the best parts of the movie. Highlights include the female sniper lining up her shot and executing a praying man, a daring raid on a compound, and an inevitable chase scene. The killer confronts Diggs in an impressive fight.

Sadly, this is preceded by an obvious reveal that Vicky, Ursula, and the assassin are all the same woman with multiple personality disorder. Given their erratic behaviour and Vicky's recollection of a terrorist attack, this comes as no great shock. The ambassador is revealed to be the man behind the hits, but since he's the only person with the information, that's equally unsurprising. The movie ends with the assassin moving to Paris at the ambassador's request, as the obsessed Kahn shadows her. Little makes sense, but the stylish and rather bizarre antagonist earns a mention.

The Death of the Incredible Hulk (1990) – Jasmin (Elizabeth Gracen), Voshenko (Anna Katerina)

This movie features the final Bill Bixby / Lou Ferringo appearance as the Marvel comic character. As the title suggests, the hero dies at the end, but was slated to return. Sadly, Bixby passed away from cancer, and the project was shelved.

David Banner attempts to cure himself with the help of a

sympathetic scientist, but falls foul of Eastern European spies after top-secret genetic research. The villains blackmail a reluctant agent named Jasmin – an expert thief and mistress of disguise – by threatening her captive sister, Bella. Jasmin seduces a security guard and collects his fingerprints. Then, the deceptive spy swaps clothes and removes her earrings and wig. When she exits the restroom, she looks a totally different person.

Jasmin pulls off a similar trick to get a female guard's uniform, then later disguises herself as that same woman to access the lab. This interrupts the doctor's attempt to cure David, accidentally starts a fire, and triggers a transformation into the Hulk. Frustrated with Jasmin's failure, the villains decide she's outlived her usefulness. So, for the second half of the film, she works with David and uses her skills to claim revenge on the evil spy leader Voshenko. That would be Jasmin's sister who faked the kidnapping.

Voshenko isn't a great villainess. She spends her little screen time issuing orders to other people, and a henchman even points the boss' reluctance to get her hands dirty. A rushed finale has Voshenko escape on a plane, only for the Hulk to get on board and redirect her small arms fire. This results in an explosion, and – while sad music plays – the hero falls to his death on the runway below.

The Marine 6: Close Quarters (2018)
Maddy Hayes (Becky Lynch), Katrina (Anna Demetriou)

Movie

This WWE-produced franchise has a high inclusion rate for female villains. Six *Marine* films were made altogether, and four have a bad girl in the cast. For the last outing, we finally got a woman as the main antagonist. If Becky Lynch beating up men isn't enough, there's a second female who also gets a lengthy fight scene.

Fresh ideas are scarce, so why not use the obvious template for a lone action hero? You guessed it: *Die Hard.* Jake Carter (Mike "The Miz" Mizanin) is trapped in an abandoned brewery with a criminal gang holding the innocent Sarah (Louisa Connolly-Burnham) hostage. The villainess' father is on trial for – um, bad stuff that's not really explained in any detail – so Maddy threatens to kill Sarah unless her juror father rigs the verdict. Too bad Jake Carter is paying an old war veteran a visit when he hears screams from upstairs.

The villains lock the building down, so it's up to Jake and his former commanding officer Luke Trapper (WWE star Shawn Michaels) to protect Sarah. Cue the usual fisticuffs, shootouts and an air vent escape. The veteran provides assistance, but he obviously dies heroically, as minor characters do in these films. More shocking is the villainess killing Jake before the movie's done. Yes, the main character. Which grants Maddy a higher placing than would otherwise be the case.

Villainesses

The henchwoman Kat first seems to be a non-action role. She relays footage of Sarah to her father and attends court as a "friendly" reminder to comply. This proves an effective tactic, but it's in the second half of the film when things get more interesting. She returns to the brewery and leads a group of baddies on a hunt for the heroes. By now they've escaped the building and entered a tunnel system. An excellent setting for an ambush, and the gothic Kat looks creepy holding a chemical flare.

The hero party (down to Jake, Luke, and Sarah) openly displays distrust when Kat plays innocent, but foolishly follows her down the tunnel. Then she gets caught in a lie. While Jake fights a brute, Kat garrotes Luke with a wire cord she keeps handy for such occasions. The henchwoman is difficult to shake off, and instead of the expected quick fight, we get a drawn-out struggle. There are cutaway shots of Jake, but nothing too intrusive. Eventually, Luke uses his superior strength and slams Kat to the ground.

In the opening half, Maddy murders a civilian showing the ex-marines around, and one of her own men for failure (despite following her orders not to use weapons). The brutal knife executions establish Maddy's authority as the primary villain and her preference for close-quarters combat, perhaps an allusion to the title.

Maddy is an imposing authority figure with her fiery hair and leather jacket, and her mostly male crew is too intimidated to challenge her. When Jake is wounded during the tunnel shootout, the mooks know to leave the killing blow to the villainess. Maddy uses her knife to finish the hero, throwing it into his chest. This brings his heroic escapades to an end and leaves Luke with a death to avenge.

The new protagonist wastes no time tracking down Maddy and her thugs, who've kidnapped Sarah once more. The henchmen put up little resistance, leading to a confrontation on a boat. Maddy proves a much more challenging opponent, getting the better of the hero in the early rounds. After a couple of retorts about Jake, Luke uses a rope to ensnare Maddy and throw her overboard. The attached anchor weighs her down, and we get a lengthy shot of her drowning. Perhaps too brief a finale, but Maddy is a rare physical main villainess, and few women can claim to have killed a franchise hero.

Honourable Mentions: *The Marine* Series

The Marine (2006) – Angela (Abigail Bianca)

Long before female wrestlers were cast as series henchwomen, Angela was a more traditional femme fatale. The original *Marine* is essentially an 80s action movie brought into modern times with hero Sgt. John Triton (John Cena) is introduced on a Middle Eastern combat mission. This is a gung-ho sequence with loud explosions and nonsensical bravado – it's clear what tone the filmmakers were aiming for.

After psychotic jewel thief Rome (Robert Patrick) pulls off a heist, his crew encounters John and his wife Kate at a gas station. There's a psycho henchman who likes to shoot and blow up things without good reason, so Kate ends up kidnapped and John comes to her rescue. Perhaps the bad guys shouldn't have picked a fight with a former US Marine, as he wastes no time in hunting down those responsible.

Angela plays an innocent victim during the jewellery store job, but quickly shows her true colours. There's a sequence with gratuitous shots of her bare legs, and she's a willing – and equally crazy – partner to Rome. Angela wastes a couple of guys: a customer at the gas station and some poor trucker she flags down. Both kills are off screen and we only see the buildup, which means Angela is eye candy, mostly.

There's plenty of tension between Angela and Kate, which slowly builds over time, culminating in a catfight. That's the extent of any real action, and the only encounter with John is when he tosses Angela from a truck into an oncoming coach. Her demise is rather bizarre: lots of broken glass covered in blood, which suggests a mangled corpse we never see.

The Marine 4: Moving Target (2015) – Rachel Dawes (Summer Rae)

After a solo entry with Ted Diabase Jr., all the films had Jake Carter as the chief hero. The fourth movie started the trend of female wrestlers as baddies, and Summer Rae received top billing despite having little dialogue in the movie. Perhaps the producers realised sports stars with limited acting experience work better as the silent henchwoman type.

In this movie, Jake is working for a private security firm, only to get ambushed on his opening day. The target is corporate whistleblower Olivia Tanis (Melissa Roxburgh), and somebody doesn't want this lady talking. The movie is essentially one giant chase scene through a forest, with sections at a remote cabin safe house and police station to vary the scenery. Nowhere is safe from the mercenaries, and despite some initial distrust, Olivia realises Jake is her only hope of staying alive.

Rachel is a constant presence, shooting an assault rifle and operating a tracking device when the situation calls for it. She lasts for most of the movie and is the most prominent villain other than the main baddie, Simon Vogel, and traitor agent Ethan. The last encounter between Jake and Rachel is a brief fight, which ends with the knife-wielding villainess tossed to the ground. With a thug closing in, Jake uses her as a human shield to protect himself, and the series' first female WWE star ends up a bullet sponge.

The Marine 5: Battleground (2017) – Murphy (Naomi)

Jake obviously didn't like private security, since he's now working as a paramedic with Zoe (Anna Van Hooft). This doesn't stop him from getting into trouble, and when he rescues a wounded man in a sublevel parking garage, it's the beginning of a very long night. Turns out the man handled a hit on a biker gang leader, and his crew are out for blood.

The few women in this film all get seen off in brutal fashion. The prologue had Maryse Ouellet Mizanin (the Miz's real-life spouse) as a civilian trapped in a car. Despite a heroic rescue attempt, she dies on a gurney – essentially a glorified cameo. Zoe lasts approximately half the film and is reasonably helpful before the biker gang take her hostage and shoot her just for the hell of it. That's not a smart move with Jake Carter around, and he takes out the crew. Later on, the action shifts from the parking garage to an amusement park and the streets above.

The sole female biker is Murphy, the first main villain to die at Jake's hands. Like the other evil women in the series, she uses a knife. Murphy actually has two of them, switching to a second after Jake overpowers her. Despite less screen time, she gets a longer fight than Rachel. And a more satisfying end when Jake turns her own blade against her.

Legendary Tier (#40 to #11)

Black Widow (1987)
Catharine (Theresa Russell)

Movie

The top forty villainesses form the legendary tier because of their iconic status in movie history or great but lesser-known examples. First up is Theresa Russell's serial murderess from this 1980s thriller. Not to be confused with the Marvel Comics character, this black widow is a woman who kills her mates.

Don't expect a bloodbath. All the kills happen off screen, and the central theme is a psychological battle between the killer and US Justice Department agent Alex Barnes (Debra Winger). Films with two female main characters were rare in the eighties, and the rewarding dynamic makes up for the lack of action.

Alex is a work-obsessed loner with little interest in romance. But the workaholic takes an interest in the Black Widow killings when she discovers two wealthy men have died in suspicious circumstances. We don't really get acquainted with the victims. The first isn't shown, and we only witness the aftermath with the "grieving" widow disposing of the evidence.

Next on the kill list is Texas toy company owner Ben

Dumers (Dennis Hopper). A prominent actor, but he gets little more than a cameo. After a few scenes with his not so devoted wife, the murderess injects poison into a bottle of alcohol, leaves it for him to drink, and suddenly it's his funeral. Two murders in the opening fifteen minutes, but things slow down for the rest of the movie.

Villainess

The villainess is credited as Catharine, but that's one of four aliases. For each victim, the killer adopts a different name and appearance. Better to keep things simple, so I'll refer to Theresa's character as Catharine in this review.

As the murderer studies Native American artifacts to prepare for her next crime, Alex questions relatives of the previous victims and studies photos of her nemesis. The agent eventually tracks the killer to Seattle and poses as a newspaper reporter to question a museum curator – and next intended victim. So begins a deadly game of cat and mouse, with Alex hoping Catharine takes the bait and investigates *her* (she does).

The serial killer plans a trip to Hawaii, but only after she discovers the curator is allergic to penicillin. Catharine does her mate and kill thing, mixing some of the powdery drug into his toothpaste. This leads to a third off-screen death, and the Black Widow becoming even richer. Determined to catch her elusive prey, Alex pursues Catharine to Hawaii. From that point on, she's a lone wolf, though she enlists the help of shady private investigator Shin (James Hong).

Alex takes a leaf from the killer's book and uses a false name, while Catharine seduces her latest target: a hotel chain owner named Paul. The murderess learns Alex has followed her, and that she's a government agent. As the two women attempt to outsmart each other, they become acquainted. After an "accident" while scuba diving, Catharine confesses without being specific, carefully choosing words to taunt her foe.

Catharine suggests Paul date the investigator, but this is a setup. The villainess hires Shin to take photos of Alex with Paul, intending to frame her for the next murder. Catharine seduces Paul, so he dumps Alex to marry the killer. Then, Alex presents the villainess with a black widow brooch and promises to bring her to justice. This is an especially barbed exchange and typifies the dialogue-heavy nature of this movie.

After the wedding, Catharine poisons Paul and plants incriminating evidence in Alex's room. She then breaks into Shin's office, holds him at gunpoint, and stages a heroin overdose. Alex is arrested for the crime, and Catharine visits her at the courthouse.

The murderess gloats, thinking she's outsmarted her opponent. Then a relative of a previous victim walks in, followed by Paul, who'd been tipped off by Alex. She staged the arrest as a trap, and the overconfident killer fell for it.

Honourable Mention: Dangerous Relationships

Flirting with Danger (2006) – **Laura Clifford (Charisma Carpenter)**

Black Widow is a "template" movie, so the serial killer wife story is often copied by lesser productions. Such as cheap Lifetime thrillers. Among the many clones, this effort stands out because of the villainess' unique kill method. A psychopathic woman smears her victims with poisonous oil that's ingested through the skin when they take a bath or shower. That's a great excuse for a steamy intro where a mysterious naked beauty bumps off a topless male in a hot tub.

Things are quite dull after that, as Rafe Marino (James Thomas) digs into the mysterious circumstances of his friend's death. He and his police officer girlfriend, Gloria Moretti (Victoria Sanchez) discover other men have died recently. Seems they all received mysterious faxes, and femme fatale Laura Clifford might be the woman responsible. Other women are suspects because their Southern accents resemble the killer's voicemail message, but this won't fool experienced viewers.

After a slow buildup, Laura seduces Marino. This leads to a near-death experience after he gets oiled by the villainess and takes a shower. A weak confrontation follows as Gloria guns down the knife-wielding Laura with little fanfare. Nothing special, but worth a mention.

Rank #39

***Fallen Angel* (2000)**
Vicky Mayerson (Michelle Johnson)

Movie

Another direct-to-video movie with Alexandra Paul as a tough police officer, but while Daphne Zuniga in *Prey of the Chameleon* (1992) ranks just outside the top forty, Michelle Johnson's revenge-seeking psycho makes it into the upper tier. Vicky commits murder in disguise and stages elaborate crimes, so she's a more interesting foe than the average nutcase.

Detective Laura Underwood is unorthodox ("normal" cops don't exist in these movies). In the prologue, she sides with a woman holding her husband hostage and promises to kill the guy. In her defence, the "victim" is violent and abusive, but the cowgirl approach wouldn't be tolerated in real life. The villainess appears shortly after, and a duel of wits begins between the cop and the killer.

The murderess elicits a lot of sympathy, as her killing spree stems from an attack she suffered from a group of boys when she was a teenager. However, Vicky is crazy enough to be classified as a villain, and her victims become more sympathetic as we progress. It turns out Laura went to the same school as the dead guys, and there's an inconvenient past relationship with classmate Brian (Anthony Michael Hall). There just *had* to be an ex involved.

The other men in Laura's life are her father, Dan (Vlasta Vrana) – also a detective – and a charming rookie named Jimmy (Andrew Simms). He ends up as bait during a potentially deadly high school reunion. It's dangerous to know Laura.

Villainess

The villainess claims her first two victims within the opening twenty minutes. Not one to waste any time, is she? Vicky seduces the first man on a nightclub roof, acts daredevil by standing on a ledge, and then delivers her catchphrase: "Never trust a man after midnight". This links back to an assault on an elevated freeway years earlier that we're shown several times in flashback. Once she's spoken the line – which terrifies the man – Vicky pushes him off the roof.

It's hazardous to be in skyscrapers when Vicky is roaming around. For victim #2, she dresses as a maid and enters a hotel room. Pretty soon she has the sole male occupant at knifepoint and directs him to the balcony. Then comes the midnight phrase, and the panicked man protests his innocence. Vicky isn't big on remorse, so she slits his throat and pushes him over the edge. She casually wipes down the knife and leaves it behind, which puzzles the police.

It doesn't take long for Laura to realise she knew the victim at school, and they're dealing with a serial killer. After some scenes with Brian that thankfully don't slow the momentum, the killer calls the detective at the police station. The snappy dresser has changed into a bright outfit, cap and sunglasses to pose as a courier, and gives Laura a cryptic hint. This is clearly a woman with a vendetta who hasn't finished yet.

Vicky's third victim is the most unsympathetic: an aggressive male named Ron with no remorse or desire to co-operate with the police. The killer bluffs her way past the receptionist, takes him hostage at gunpoint and escorts him to... you guessed it – the roof. The police trace Vicky's call and arrive in time to save Ron. A tense chase scene through the deserted building ends with a brief shootout, and the killer escapes on a bicycle.

Things get more complicated after the police place Ron in protective custody, and Vicky phones Laura at her home. Brian listens in and, to Laura's frustration, speaks to the killer. It's clear they have a history, and he's a target. Ron is next up, though. Laura goes to warn him, only for the ungrateful man to point a gun in her face and force her to handcuff herself to a safe. Terrible decision on his part, because Vicky walks in and there's nobody to stop her this time.

Laura deciphers Vicky's cryptic hints and establishes that she dropped out of school (which is why she didn't recognise her earlier). There's a whole exposition segment where the police dig up a backstory and question a potential fourth target. Turns out Vicky is copying the MO of what happened to her and using similar props in her murders. Also, her catchphrase was spoken by one boy before the fall, which nearly killed her.

Unlike Ron, the next victim has the sense to co-operate, and Laura devises a plan for Jimmy to impersonate the target at a school reunion and lure the killer out. However, Vicky is too clever to fall for this, deceives the detective on guard duty and does her usual routine of staging a high fall. So much for police protection.

Vicky then turns her attention to Brian. We all saw this coming, right? The finale has Laura confront the murderer on the roof and repeat the prologue "offer to shoot the hostage" trick (which actually works!). Unfortunately, Brian falls for it too, which gives Laura's plan away, and Vicky pulls out a second weapon. Brian does the hero thing and takes a bullet for his girlfriend. With the police closing in, Vicky commits suicide by jumping off the roof and becomes the Fallen Angel of the title.

Honourable Mentions: Sympathetic Killers / Michelle Johnson

Time of Death (2013) – Megan Welles (Sarah Power)

Another film with a sympathetic killer, this time avenging the rape / murder of her sister. This is a thriller from Canadian producer Incendo, who made a slate of female-driven TV movies before switching genres to romance. As usual, a notable actress plays the lead. Kathleen Robertson is FBI agent Jordan Price, who gets assigned to Baltimore to assist with the murder investigation.

The title refers to the killer's unusual MO, where victims are killed at exactly 10:44 PM. The first victim is CEO Robert Loring, who gets bumped off in his office with no forced entry. Naturally, the early suspects are his fellow executives and son. But then the assailant kills them at exactly the same time, and Jordan realises someone else is behind the deaths. And that person appears to be an expert climber.

There's an awkward romance subplot that comes from nowhere, where Jordan hooks up with rookie detective and reluctant partner Elliot Larken (Gianpaolo Venuta). This side angle is utterly pointless and feels tacked on to fill time between the murders. When they get back to work, the duo discover the connection between the victims and a historic case, and that the killer is an ex-Marine named Megan.

The villainess' background leads to some interesting kill sequences, especially in the finale where she snipes a target and bodyguards with tranquilliser darts. Jordan then confronts Megan at the same waterfall location where her sister was killed. The murderess has her target at gunpoint and threatens to commit suicide by dragging him over the edge. Jordan shoots her dead first, which angered many reviewers. They realise Megan is a cold-blooded killer, and the arrested guy will still be brought to justice, right?

The Donor (1995) - Dr Lucy Flynn (Michelle Johnson)

Jeff Wincott headlines this thriller as stuntman Billy Castle, whose life falls apart after black marketeers steal his kidney. That's after he sleeps with a beautiful woman who sedates him, but she's too minor a character to qualify as a villainess.

No loss, because the doctor Billy romances (didn't he already make that mistake?) is the mastermind behind the illegal organ transplant ring. She plays innocent and supportive, but frames a colleague when her lover gets too close. Positioning the patsy as someone the hero trusts implies *he* will be the surprise villain, but would they bother introducing Billy's ex-girlfriend if Lucy was innocent?

An interesting (and surprisingly deep) subplot has the stuntman refuse to accept he's a victim until he attends a mostly female group of violent crime survivors. The movie reverts to standard thriller fare when Lucy kills off a few loose ends and reveals herself as the evil doctor. For the climax, there's an above-average chase where the villainess pursues Billy in a car. Then he uses stunt work to fake his death and pull the treacherous woman over a cliff edge.

Maleficent (2014)
Maleficent (Angelina Jolie)

Movie

Ranking this villainess protagonist as legendary is a debatable decision because she's an innocent girl for the prologue and the heroine for the entire last act. However, this live-action adaptation of Disney's 1959 animated classic *Sleeping Beauty* is ultra-stylish, and its central character is too iconic to omit. For the villainous portion, Angelina Jolie has such a powerful screen presence that she – literally at times – lights up the somewhat basic redemption story.

In the old animated tale, Maleficent was a straight-up villainess, but here the chief baddie is Stefan (Sharlto Copley), a thief who befriends the titular fairy as a child. When humans invade the Moors (fairy territory), Maleficent and her magical army fight off the offensive. In desperation, the mortally wounded king offers his crown to anyone who slays the winged fairy who bested him. Stefan uses his past relationship to get close, but cannot kill his former lover, so he clips her wings as a trophy.

This sets Maleficent on her dark path, and soon she's crafted a staff and developed a wicked green aura. To symbolise the transformation, the moors grow dark and gnarled tree branches create an impenetrable barrier between the fairy and human kingdoms. Now the villain of the story, Maleficent magically changes a raven into a man and gains a faithful servant in Diaval (Sam Riley).

Many elements from *Sleeping Beauty* feature: three bickering fairies, a handsome prince, and the beautiful and sweet Aurora (Elle Fanning). The fairytale landscape is captivating, with sprawling fields, towered castles and a variety of weird and wonderful creatures. But viewers expecting the story to unfold like the animated original will be surprised by key changes.

Villainess

The birth of Aurora brings out the worst in Maleficent. During a celebration party, the black fairy visits the castle and bestows a gift. Actually, it's a curse that Aurora shall prick her finger on a spinning wheel needle and then fall into an everlasting sleep. Heard of that one? The villainess gives a dramatic speech as green fire bursts from her. Stefan begs for mercy, so Maleficent decrees the curse won't take effect until Aurora is sixteen. It *can* be broken… but only by true love's kiss.

Stefan – obviously unaware that curses always happen – orders every spinning wheel in the kingdom burned and sends his army to assault the Moors. Fire has no effect on the wall of branches, and Maleficent's magic wards off the lowly footsoldiers. For extra security, Stefan tasks the three fairies to guard Aurora and keep her away from the castle. Over sixteen years, the threesome morph into adults, but they are more interested in playing games and arguing than childcare.

Maleficent and Diaval have a change of heart and keep the princess safe. Over time, the protagonist becomes fond of the girl, and the child regards Maleficent as her fairy godmother. The softened villainess is shocked at the notion, but Aurora's sweetness and innocence inspire the curse's creator to revoke it. Unfortunately, Maleficent's own words – that the curse will last for all time – come back to haunt her.

When Aurora learns the truth, she flees to the castle. Then the inevitable happens: a spindle reassembles, the girl pricks her finger, and drops into a magical sleep. Before all this, she met a prince, so Maleficent brings him to the castle hoping his kiss will break the curse. Unlike the animated tale, this doesn't work as there's no love between them. That's when Maleficent visits the sleeping beauty seeking redemption and kisses her. Anyone care to guess what happens next? Yes, in this version, it's Maleficent who truly loves Aurora, and the curse is duly lifted.

With the females united, Stefan's troops drop a metal net over the anti-heroine. Since iron burns fairies, that's not good, but before she falls unconscious, Maleficent transforms Diaval into a dragon. This leads to an epic clash of steel and magic, with armoured troops fighting the beast. While the guards are busy, Aurora smashes a display case to release Maleficent's wings. They fly back to their owner, turning the tide of the battle. Maleficent shows the deposed king the mercy he deserves – none – and he falls from the castle parapet.

And everyone lives happily ever after… until the sequel, at least. That aspect of the fairytale was never going to change.

Honourable Mentions: Sleeping Beauty

Sleeping Beauty (1959) – Maleficent (Eleanor Audley – Voice)

I've focused on live-action movies, but it's only fitting to grant an honourable mention to one of Walt Disney's best animated features. The classic tale is strictly good versus evil, so don't expect any character development or grey moral areas.

Stefan is a noble king. Maleficent is a villain just because the story requires one, and there are many musical overtures. And comical moments as the three good fairies fight over the teen princess Aurora. Some key plot details are common with the live-action version, notably when Stefan orders every spinning wheel burned. And of course, Maleficent casts her diabolical curse on the infant.

As children's entertainment, it's not overlong at seventy-five minutes. Simplistic by today's standards, but the animation is top-notch for the era. The highlights are Aurora being deceived into pricking her finger, and the duel between Prince Phillip and Maleficent. Or rather, the dragon she's shapeshifted into. In the end, the dashing hero vanquishes the evil fairy, wakes his love with a kiss, and marries her. Of course, everyone lives happily ever after.

Maleficent: Mistress of Evil (2019) – Queen Ingrith (Michelle Pfeiffer)

The sequel picks up five years later, and many characters return for another epic adventure. Newcomers include the prince's parents: a peace-seeking king and a scheming queen mother.

Ingrith is so intent on conquering the Moors she frames Maleficent for cursing her husband. This instigates a bitter war between humans and fairies. Michelle Pfeiffer's villainess has no moral ambiguity, but her backstory is not as interesting as Maleficent's. A few tyrannical speeches on being a "strong" queen are all we get for motivation.

Ingrith and her gnome assistant harvest anti-fairy powder and stockpile iron weapons for their diabolical plot.

The final battle – when we get there – is spectacular. A female guard captain shoots Maleficent with a crossbow contraption, but is then sidelined into shouting announcements and playing an organ. Admittedly, the pipes double as a powder-launching device, and the music accompanies the slaughter of fairies. But soldiers should be fighting.

A swarm of winged fairies joins Maleficent to assault Ingrith's castle, only to be annihilated by the defences. The marriage of Aurora and the prince is a side story, and there's some poor exposition about Maleficent being the last living descendant of a phoenix. That's an excuse to resurrect her from the ashes and shield Aurora from the evil queen. You didn't expect the central character to die so easily?

Despite the increased stakes, this instalment is a weaker effort. As a humorous touch, Maleficent transforms the defeated villainess into a goat, but that can't disguise the inferior story.

Rank #37

The Perfect Bride (1991)
Stephanie (Sammi Davis)

Movie

A routine psycho-woman thriller, but the inventive kill sequences and high body count – plus an over the top bad girl – earn this film a legendary rank. That's probably why the movie airs on Lifetime despite being over thirty years old. Few modern productions have such longevity. Whenever you need a reliable made for TV effort, the 1990s is the decade to choose.

The title character is a woman with high standards for any future husband. Any sign of infidelity or even a hint of imperfection, and you can expect a lethal injection. That also goes for anyone who dares to get in her way, and plenty of minor characters have "unfortunate" heart attacks. One wonders whether the police in this town know about forensics and autopsies. But the plot requires only the heroine, Laura (Kelly Preston) to see the truth about Stephanie, so the deaths are written off as natural causes.

Laura has a stubborn family, which is a problem when her brother's bride-to-be is a homicidal lunatic. Who spouts "bad girl" lines (in a posh English accent) whenever she eliminates an obstacle. Besides the besotted groom Ted (Linden Ashby), Stephanie also charms Laura's unsupportive mother, her senile grandfather, and a policeman friend. So it's down to Laura to be the snoopy investigator and save Ted from the psycho's needle.

Villainess

Like all good TV movie villainesses, Stephanie claims her first victim early. A groom looks forward to premarital sex on the eve of the wedding, only to discover the hard way his bride is a psycho. She is *not* pleased about his visiting his ex-girlfriend. After literally making her point with a syringe, Stephanie smiles at her own reflection in the bathroom mirror. It's clear this woman is crazy, but that moment should erase any lingering doubts.

With that dealt with, it's time for Stephanie to enter Ted and Laura's lives. Initial impressions are good, but Laura becomes suspicious when Stephanie reacts coldly to a receptionist and snaps at a dress fitter over a trivial mistake. Purchasing a cheap tablecloth and claiming it's a family heirloom is a ruse Laura soon sees through, and now she's really worried about her brother. Nobody listens to Laura (that would be too easy) and Stephanie always has an excuse ready for any odd behaviour.

To keep things moving, Stephanie bumps off two more victims. First up is a caterer who recognises her from a previous wedding. That's a threat, so the killer bride comes calling with her hypodermic needle. Surprisingly, the woman puts up a good struggle, considering she's a minor character and they're usually killed with little fanfare. After a lengthy scrap in the kitchen, Stephanie flees, but the caterer is stupid and checks out the basement. A fatal error in judgement, but in a cruel twist of fate, Laura's mother decides not to employ her services.

Laura asks a priest to give Ted and Stephanie marriage counselling, so no surprise he's next on the kill list. The murderess has flashbacks to her childhood when her mother committed suicide and warned her about men. Quite an impression on a distraught young girl, which explains the obsession with finding Mister Perfect. After one insane rant, the priest postpones the big day. That's the villainess' cue to induce a heart attack.

The desperate Laura digs deeper into Stephanie's past and tracks down a woman who knew the previous groom. Unfortunately, Stephanie listens in on the phone call and puts on a clever disguise – and an American accent – to lure the witness into a trap. There's a funny moment when Stephanie narrowly avoids a road accident, which causes her to yell "Bloody hell!" and give herself away. The witness escapes, only to be knocked down by an oncoming car.

Stephanie learns the woman survived from a news report, so she visits the hospital disguised as a nurse to finish the job. It's never a good thing to be unconscious or badly injured in one of these films. Once the killer has asphyxiated her victim, she returns home. Laura's grandfather sees Stephanie in a nurse's uniform, but he's a doddering old guy nobody believes. After gloating over Laura's dead lead, Stephanie turns her attention back to Ted.

With such ludicrously high standards, the groom was always going to disappoint the bride. The snapping point is when Stephanie sees Ted with the receptionist (remember her?) at a bachelor party. So she dons her wedding gown and readies her needle. Laura comes racing to the rescue and saves a disbelieving Ted, but he changes his tune once Stephanie stabs him with a kitchen knife. There's a short, semi-decent stalk/chase scene and a brief catfight that ends with Laura hiding in the attic. She arms herself with a baseball bat and sends the psycho on a fatal tumble downstairs.

Honourable Mention: *The Perfect...*

The Perfect Marriage (2006) – Marianne Danforth (Jamie Luner)

The Perfect prefix usually designates a TV movie aimed at Lifetime audiences, and this is indeed another of those films. Marianne is a scheming woman quite prepared to murder her husbands for their money. She killed her previous spouse with a lethal injection, a crime she planned with her lover Brent (James Wilder). After he used the large payout to settle his debts, Marianne dumped him.

A few years later, she's happily married to a wealthy businessman's son. Then Brent re-enters her life, and soon they have eyes on the family fortune. The villainess delays killing the father until he seals a company deal, then it's time for an induced heart attack. When a nosy assistant gets too close to the truth and carelessly gets seen snooping, Brent murders her.

A female associate named Tia picks up the trail and becomes the protagonist for the last act. As the net closes in, Marianne decides Brent is expendable, so he gets the lethal injection treatment. Perhaps he shouldn't have provided potassium chloride to a scorned woman.

In the finale, Marianne tries to silence Tia. This leads to a longer than usual chase scene with the villainess hunting her prey in a parking garage. Eventually, after a scuffle and stalking scene, a random motorist runs over Marianne. A disappointing end to a decent thriller.

Double Impact (1991)
Kara (Cory Everson)

Movie

When I put together my list, Cory Everson's muscular henchwoman Kara – one of two "enforcer" roles she played in her career – was an obvious choice. On reflection, Kara dropped down the rankings quite a bit, but still does enough to be legendary. Amazingly, Kara barely features until the latter half of the movie, but then comes into her own with three impressive scenes to savour.

Before that, there's the setup with two loving parents murdered by Chinese criminals in Hong Kong. That leaves their bodyguard / security man Frank (Geoffrey Lewis) to look after their twin infant sons Chad and Alex. Actually, he only rescues Chad, and the family maid takes care of the other boy. She gives up on the idea, though, and drops Alex off at the local orphanage.

Chad grows up in relative luxury in California, and twenty-five years later works as a fitness instructor. Since Jean-Claude Van Damme plays both grown-up brothers, this is an excuse to show off his trademark leg split. Frank persuades Chad to go to Hong Kong, and they soon run into Alex, who's not too friendly, especially after he catches his twin with girlfriend Danielle (Alonna Shaw).

There's simmering friction between the brothers that's continually brought up, but eventually they work together. Van Damme times two? The villains really should have killed these boys when they were babies.

Alex – now a criminal smuggler – gets into a shootout on his boat following a deal gone bad. Chad, who gets mistaken for Alex, has a run-in with the gang leader who killed his parents. That would be Zhang (Philip Chan), who has a brutal bodyguard named Moon (bad guy regular Bolo Yeung). Moon gets the better of Chad in a very one-sided fight, but Zhang leaves the hero alive (yes, that mistake again) so inevitably there will be a rematch later on.

Meanwhile, Danielle searches her office for clues, because it just so happens she works for the other main villain, Nigel Griffith (Alan Scarfe). Both the actor and the character are British, naturally. This is where Danielle has her first encounter with Kara (finally!), who handles security for Griffith. Only a few seconds long, but it's their second office scene that viewers remember.

Villainess

The action intensifies after the brothers raid a drug shipment (thanks to information Zhang gave Chad earlier!) and cause a lot of damage. This is typical action hero stuff with lots of gunfire and near-death moments, and since there are two heroes – plus Frank as backup – it's no surprise the place goes up in literal smoke.

Griffith isn't too happy with his employees for screwing up, and that's Kara's cue to stick a knife in some poor guy's chest. She flexes her muscles, and the skimpy outfit means we get to see her powerful legs as she kneels over her terrified victim. Anyone who thought this woman was there for show should think again. No wonder the men at the meeting look scared as Kara returns to Griffith with her bloody knife.

The brothers crash the party and are seen together for the first time. Zhang and Griffith know they're up against a double dose of the Muscles from Brussels, and they need to up their game. So Kara gets the job – and the satisfaction – of frisking Danielle in the office. This is more than a customary pat-down and closer to sexual assault. A leather-clad strong woman gropes a terrified assistant – the imagery is pretty clear, and Kara clearly enjoys it. Danielle does the expected thing afterward and calls Alex while the villains and their henchwoman listen in.

Kara is strictly the enforcer from that point. The action shifts from a restaurant (and secret back room) to the streets of Hong Kong and moored sampans. Kara's action is limited to kicking a civilian and long-distance shots of her in pursuit of Chad. After that, she takes to the skies in a helicopter to search for him and Danielle, and follows their boat back to the island hideout. Don't expect her to be involved in the raid, though. That's left to Zhang and his henchmen.

Alex and Chad fall out over… what else? Danielle. Alex imagines her having sex with his brother, though they never did in reality (an excuse to show Alonna Shaw naked). The twins put aside their quarrel to rescue Frank and Danielle from a cargo ship. This final sequence is a long string of fight scenes. Alex and Chad waste the goons pretty easily, then come the bigger battles against a spur-heeled killer and Moon. The last one ends with an obvious death by electrocution (the junction box was in shot for a good half minute beforehand).

Eventually, both Zhang and Griffith are defeated. Not much fighting compared to what came earlier, but their ends are suitably brutal considering the pain they've inflicted. From a villainess' perspective, the highlight is Alex against Kara. The muscle woman has changed into an all-black outfit and leather gloves now, and enjoys steaming Frank and threatening Danielle at Griffith's request.

Knowing one hero is coming for her, Kara leaves Danielle alone with a henchman who molests her. His reward is a headbutt from Alex, but then the enforcer gets the drop on him, trapping his neck between her thighs. Somehow he gets out of that, leading Kara to draw her blade in anger. She cuts Alex – while Danielle watches helplessly – and grabs her opponent by the crotch. Does she want to inflict pain, or feel like groping Alex's private parts? We'll never know.

Alex punches her in the face. Kara loses her cool and kicks out in anger, damaging a steam pipe. It's then a straight test of strength, but no female – even an Amazon like Kara – is a match for Van Damme. She briefly gains the advantage thanks to support fire from Zhang, but Alex turns Kara's own knife against her and finishes the villainess with a belly stab. Overall, the fight is about a minute and a half long. Not great, but better than many other efforts.

Honourable Mention: Cory Everson

Ballistic (1995) (aka *Fist of Justice*) – Claudia (Cory Everson)

This review is a Cory tribute, as her other notable film gets an honourable mention. Her climactic fight scene in this direct-to-video action flick is better, but Kara is the strongest overall villainess. I previously owned a terrible VHS copy with poor quality, low-resolution footage. A DVD was released in Germany weeks before I wrote this review, and had an English language soundtrack, which was unexpected.

Good thing Cory stars, because the movie is bland otherwise. Detective Jesse Gavin (Marjean Holden), the statuesque martial arts heroine, is out to prove corrupt cops framed her father (Richard Roundtree). There's a lot of dirt in the department, from the rookies to the captain. Gavin's only allies are another female called Lynn and her boyfriend (who's a handy fighter himself).

The villain is Braden (Sam J. Jones) who deals in drugs and illegal weapons, and arranges rigged fights for money. All the generic bad guy motives rolled into one, which makes the story feel tired. There's also a witness who gets silenced while Gavin is protecting him, and a busty assistant for Braden to have sex with. Michael Jai White plays a henchman named Quint, but his fights aren't really that impressive. So it's left to Cory to save the show, which she does admirably.

Besides being the silent, glaring type whenever Jesse shows up, Claudia is the villain's chief henchwoman for eliminating problems. She bests a corrupt cop who knows too much, and knees the guy in the groin just to show her superiority. Then Claudia tosses the guy around his apartment and breaks his neck, leaving a dead body for Jesse to explain. The charges don't stick, though she is suspended.

This all leads to a climax at Braden's warehouse hideout. Once again, the main villains are easily beaten – albeit with a big explosion – and it's Claudia who provides Jesse's only real test. Holden and Everson get a rewarding and lengthy fight scene, with Claudia in red spandex and Jesse in black. It's an even contest with the women trading blows and insults. Boxes are used as makeshift weapons, and Jesse's exonerated father shows up with a gun. Fortunately, he stays out of it.

Jesse gets her opponent in a chokehold, then Claudia regains the advantage with an overhead kick. The overconfident villainess puts her arm around Jesse's neck, ready to snap it, but lets her guard down and allows the heroine to turn the tables. After a struggle, Jesse inverts the hold and snaps Claudia's neck. Few impressive scenes in the movie, but this makes up for it.

One Flew Over the Cuckoo's Nest (1975)
Nurse Ratched (Louise Fletcher)

Movie

Perhaps a controversially low rank, given many female villain lists rate the tyrannical nurse highly, but I consider all the top forty choices to be legendary. The film is undoubtedly a classic, one of only three (to date) to win all five "big" Academy Awards. A lot of time is devoted to patient bonding, and the antagonist is the corrupt US mental health system, even if Nurse Ratched makes a terrifying figurehead.

The biggest threat to her authority comes from Randle McMurphy (Jack Nicholson), a recent transfer suspected of faking mental illness to lessen his sentence for statutory rape. This guy is hardly hero material, but he comes across as likeable because the head nurse is a sadistic control freak and his charisma has a positive influence on the other patients.

From the outset, it's obvious a rule-breaker like McMurphy won't approve of Ratched's tight-ship approach. Early on, he's a quiet participant in group therapy, while the nurse and her passive assistant watch in silence. But then Randle encourages his fellow patients to disregard the rules and forms a bond with the giant deaf-mute Bromden, also known as "The Chief". This relationship matures into friendship, leading to eventual triumph in a bad-tempered basketball game against the hospital orderlies.

The pacing is much slower than in modern movies. A few scenes feel stretched out, notably where the patients play cards for cigarettes, the therapy sessions, and a long section where McMurphy leads an unauthorised fishing expedition. These parts could have been trimmed without losing substance, but the ensemble cast – which includes a young Danny DeVito, and film debuts from Christopher Lloyd and Brad Dourif – all give terrific performances.

Despite the positivity from McMurphy, this is a dark tale and would never end happily. Not a film to watch when you're feeling depressed and want to finish on a cheery note.

Villainess

Early confrontations between McMurphy and Ratched are over trivial matters. First, he wants her to turn down the music on the ward. She refuses, showing an intent to control every little thing. Next on the agenda is the more serious matter of the baseball World Series, which McMurphy wants to watch on television. This goes to a vote, but few patients support the motion, and Nurse Ratched responds with a gloating smile.

McMurphy isn't one to quit, and after a bit of unorthodox hydrotherapy where he drowns two men and a Monopoly board, he's got the other men thinking about free will and escaping. For the second vote on the World Series issue, the group votes unanimously in favour. Nurse Ratched, remaining super calm, points out there are nine other men on the ward (the crazy and delusional patients), and McMurphy doesn't have a majority.

He runs around searching for the one supporter he

needs, showing real leadership, but his rallying attempt seems doomed to fail until the Chief raises his hand. Ratched argues the session was closed before the final vote, so it doesn't count. Do you get the impression she decided the result beforehand?

After McMurphy's disorganised fishing trip, the head doctor suggests sending him to the work farm, but Ratched insists on helping him. Or so she claims, but her joyful smile when Randle finds out there's no time limit on his hospital stay suggests she wants to regain control. The previously calm nurse gets angry when the patients act defiantly. One man demands she return his cigarettes, and Ratched shifts blame to McMurphy over gambling to turn the others against him.

Following a ward fight, the staff subject McMurphy to electrotherapy, but this only stiffens his resolve. The Chief – previously thought to be mute – reveals he's been faking it the whole time, and McMurphy throws a Christmas party. He bribes a staff member to let booze and women onto the premises, and things predictably get out of hand. Another strict nurse almost discovers the patients out of their beds, but this is a delaying tactic until Ratched returns the following morning.

Then the nurse shows her truly evil side. She'd always been a controlling sadist, but could have been misguided. Until she drives a patient to suicide by threatening to tell his mother he'd slept with a woman. This prompts McMurphy to attack Ratched and – tellingly – nobody helps her. Eventually, the staff subdue the anti-hero, and it's later revealed the nurse had ordered him lobotomised. Talk about extreme measures.

The Chief kills the comatose McMurphy out of pity and uses a hydrotherapy fountain – as Randle suggested earlier – to break out. Nurse Ratched survives with only a neck injury, and she's back in charge of her patients. This is one villainess victory nobody will want to root for.

Honourable Mention: Controlling Women

The Devil Wears Prada (2006) – Miranda Priestly (Meryl Streep)

To show I'm considering villainesses from all sources, I'm delving into an area I'm hardly an expert in: women's fashion. It's debatable whether Meryl Streep's "Dragon Lady" boss is actually a villain. She'd make a fine presenter of *The Apprentice*, but her acts are more ruthless than outright evil. The tough businesswoman even comes to respect the main character, Andrea Sachs (Anne Hathaway).

It doesn't start out that way. Andrea is a fresh college graduate who shows up unprepared for a job interview with no knowledge of fashion. Hardly good credentials for an assistant role, but her defiant moral speech gets Miranda's attention, and she takes a chance. That's the only break she gives Andrea, though, since this boss is akin to a slave driver. Employees run around the New York office to meet her endless list of demands.

Andrea isn't popular given her unfashionable dress sense, and her relationship with fellow assistant Emily (Emily Blunt) is frosty. After a few mishaps, the newcomer has a wardrobe change and attends high society events, which leads to friction with her unsupportive friends. Andrea is uneasy with Miranda's ruthless streak, especially when she promises a job to her assistant Nigel but gives it to a rival to save her own skin. That's as villainous as it gets with Miranda. Welcome to the cutthroat business world.

The movie ends with Andrea quitting her job, but Miranda is pleased for her and gives her a positive reference.

So maybe a tough experience was exactly what this young lady needed to further her career. If you're after a lighter take on female authority figures, this movie is worth a look.

X-Men: Dark Phoenix (2019)
Jean Grey (Sophie Turner), Vuk (Jessica Chastain)

Movie

The *X-Men* film series kick-started the 21st-century comic book adaptation craze. An original trilogy, a prequel quadrilogy, and spinoffs that usually featured Logan / Wolverine. With a large cast of mutants, it's no shock the series featured some powerful female foes, but *Dark Phoenix* is the only entry with a woman as the big bad. Throw in the ultra-powerful Jean Grey as an out-of-control antagonist, and the result is an entertaining spectacle.

After a prologue set in 1975, where a young Jean cannot control her telekinetic powers and accidentally kills her mother in a car accident, the rest of the movie takes place in 1992. This continues the trend of setting each reboot film in a new decade. By now the X-Men – and women, as Raven (Jennifer Lawrence) bluntly points out – are international heroes, and Charles Xavier (James McAvoy) has a hotline to the US President. Every team member wears a stylised jumpsuit, and the school HQ building is pristine and modern.

When a space shuttle gets stranded near an odd flare-like phenomenon, the heroes come to the rescue. The team saves the crew, but Jean is trapped after going back for the commander at Xavier's insistence. She absorbs the energy and somehow survives, though she's a lot thirstier and um... flirtier. Jean wastes no time in kissing her lover Scott / Cyclops (Tye Sheridan). Anyone familiar with the story (or who's seen *Last Stand*) will know what happens next. Jean loses control over her powers, becoming a vengeful and dangerous woman able to match any mutant in combat.

Xavier and his team put their differences aside to counter this new threat, whose destructive rampage threatens to destroy the fragile peace between humans and mutants. To complicate matters, an alien race plans to use Jean to remake the world. Dark Phoenix and aliens? Talk about upping the ante.

Villainesses

The newly empowered Jean Grey closes her mind to Xavier (yes, she can do that) and goes searching for answers. She starts at her childhood home and confronts her father, who still blames Jean for the car accident. Their meeting ends rather amicably (all things considered) with Jean rendering her pop unconscious. Upon leaving, she discovers the entire X-Men team waiting. Guess they figured this mission needed a full squad.

Jean is bitter that Xavier sealed away her memories, and her fury erupts after the police arrive. The quiet suburban street turns into a war zone as the mutants confront their former teammate. Jean's powers are so great she shrugs off their attacks, whether that be a bolt of lightning from Storm, the teleporting Nightcrawler (who she traps mid-shift) or the time-slowing Quicksilver.

Xavier freezes the cops by mind control to give Raven a chance to talk to Jean. This goes badly wrong when she kills Raven in anger by impaling her on a fence. The young woman is clearly distraught, and flies off, leaving the X-Men to nurse their wounds and mourn. Raven's death causes rifts among the team, and Hank / Beast (Nicholas Hoult) argues Xavier is partly responsible.

Jean seeks the help of Magneto (Michael Fassbender), now a mutant community leader on a secluded island. She wisely doesn't mention who she killed, but a military attack prompts another angry outburst. It's magnetism versus telekinesis as Magneto battles Jean for control of a helicopter. He just about wins the titanic struggle and demands she leave the island. But when rogue X-Man Hank delivers the news of Raven's death, Magneto dons his trademark helmet, ready to kill once more.

Meanwhile, the alien Vuk kills an American woman, assumes her identity, and wipes out her family with a literal touch of death. Turns out she and the other aliens were tracking the glowing space dust and are interested in Jean. Her father gives up information after some "persuasion", and Vuk tracks her quarry to a bar. Jean's mental powers make humans think she's a harmless old man, but this ability doesn't work on aliens. Vuk takes Jean to a house in New York and shows her images of planets and stars. It's all pretty and awe-inspiring, designed to deceive Jean into helping her. By now the mutant is such a lost soul that she falls under Vuk's evil influence.

This all leads to… where X-Men films always seem to end up: Xavier and Magneto battling it out over their differences. Mutants go at each other in the street, causing all kinds of carnage and destruction while bystanders watch helplessly. The two opposing forces are evenly matched. Storm fights a guy with whip-like braids, Hank and Cyclops duke it out on crashed vehicles, while Xavier and a telepathic female have their own mental battle.

To show his superiority, Magneto lifts a subway train above ground and blocks off the entrance to Vuk's residence.

His powers are no match for Jean, and his attempt to skewer her with a staircase rail is easily thwarted. Jean crushes and shatters Magneto's helmet and tosses him out the window. It's then Xavier's turn to convince Jean. At first, she refuses to listen and has the cripple walk awkwardly upstairs. The telepath is powerless to stop her, but gets through by showing images of the past.

Vuk absorbs Jean's energy, granting her the same all-conquering powers, and it's only through Xavier and Cyclops intervening that she's saved before being drained of life. Vuk survives an energy blast, but is now a truly dangerous foe. Before the X-Men can pursue her, they're captured by special forces armed with anti-mutant weapons.

The captured mutants reconcile on a prisoner transport train, but there's no time for further talk since Vuk leads a raid to recapture Jean. Eventually – after failed persuasion efforts and many casualties – a guard releases the mutants. Then it's humans, X-Men and Magneto's outcasts against aliens for one last battle. These creatures are hard to kill and resistant to small arms fire. Thankfully, mutant powers are far more effective at dealing with the threat, although some minor characters get killed in the fight.

Vuk joins the fray personally. What follows is like Jean earlier, but even more one-sided. The powerful alien defeats Storm and Nightcrawler with little trouble, then it's Magneto and every weapon on board. Assault rifles and handguns have no effect, and Vuk soaks up damage like a literal bullet sponge. She tosses Magneto aside, but Jean chooses that moment to break free, crash the train, and create telekinetic bubbles to shield the mutants. She didn't lose all her powers.

After Jean disposes of the surviving aliens by ripping them into dust, Vuk comes to claim her prize. The redeemed heroine gives her the remaining energy – enough to cause an explosion – after she ascends into space to avoid collateral damage. Think we all knew a heroic sacrifice was on the cards.

Honourable Mentions:

X-Men (2000) – Mystique (Rebecca Romijn-Stamos)

First films are usually origin stories, so expect background for the main characters. Meet a power-sucking girl named Rogue (Anna Paquin), the adamantium-clawed Wolverine (Hugh Jackman), and the two opposing mutant leaders, Professor Charles Xavier (Patrick Stewart) and Magneto (Ian McKellen).

The villain plans to transform prominent humans into mutants, and his henchmen are the whip-tongued Toad (Ray Park), dumb muscle Sabretooth (Tyler Mane) and Mystique. She's as acrobatic as Toad and can change her appearance at will. This includes copying Wolverine's claws for an epic fight, but Mystique remains in her natural blue-skinned form where possible. Her best scene is where she reveals herself to an anti-mutant senator and gives him a good kicking. Not one for diplomacy when defending her kind.

Battles between the X-Men and Magneto's mutants are an ongoing franchise theme. In this outing, it's mainly Wolverine with help from weather woman Storm (Halle Berry), laser-eyed Cyclops (James Marsden) and telepath Jean Grey (Famke Janssen). The last battle is at the Statue of Liberty, where Wolverine takes down Mystique – but not before they've had a good fight. Toad and Sabretooth are one-time villains, but Mystique gets the honour of appearing in every main *X-Men* movie.

X2 (2003) – Mystique (Rebecca Romijn-Stamos), Deathstrike (Kelly Hu)

With the introductions over, there's a lot more action. The principal antagonist is Colonel Stryker, a madman planning to wipe out all mutants. But he's happy to employ their services provided they've been brainwashed or controlled through technology. Stryker created Wolverine, so their personal feud is a major subplot.

Mystique is back, and her infiltration of Stryker's base turns up more than expected when she discovers plans to convert Cerebro – Xavier's mutant-locating machine – into a weapon. Mystique poses as a beautiful blonde to seduce a security guard and inject him with liquid iron. Not good for his health, especially since he's guarding Magneto's plastic prison. Unwittingly smuggling metal into his cell is a surefire way to get killed.

The X-Men team up with Magneto and Mystique to stop Stryker after he raids Xavier's school and kidnaps the professor. With their combined skills, the mutants gain the upper hand, though Magneto has devised a nefarious scheme of his own. What else is new? This leads to a dam bursting, and Jean Grey perishes holding back the flood. Anyone familiar with *X-Men* lore will know what comes next, but her Phoenix story is deferred until the third instalment.

For newcomer mutants, we have Iceman and Pyro. They have opposite powers, and will finish on opposite sides. More important from a villainess fan's perspective is Deathstrike. She's the female equivalent of Wolverine, which makes her ideal for bodyguard duty. Early on, she does little except crack her knuckles and follow Stryker around. To show her prowess, Deathstrike takes down Cyclops in

Magneto's prison, a contest she wins easily.

The standout scene is the inevitable fight between Deathstrike and Wolverine. She has claws on her fingers and the same accelerated healing powers he does. Thus, she can survive attacks that would kill any normal human. Wolverine took down scores of opponents beforehand, but Deathstrike is not so easily killed. Eventually, the hero drops his nemesis into a chemical vat, which ends the threat. Then Deathstrike springs back into action, and to ensure she stays dead, Wolverine injects her body with liquid adamantium.

X-Men: The Last Stand (2006) – Jean Grey (Famke Janssen)

Like the prequel / reboot stories, the original trilogy closed with Jean Grey transforming into the unstable and powerful Phoenix. This was tired and forgettable stuff focused around an anti-mutant drug and the politics of its use. The climax involves a battle between the military and a mutant army led by Magneto, and a showdown on Alcatraz Island with the X-Men caught in the middle.

Mystique returns, but don't expect much from her. After some playtime with her captors, she snaps a guard's neck, only to be injected with the cure while saving Magneto. He turns his back on her, and Mystique is forgotten after that. Other females join the fight, notably the tattooed Callisto and a woman who generates shockwaves, but none of their scenes are memorable.

Jean is by far the biggest disappointment, though. She disintegrates her lover Cyclops, but most of that occurs off-screen. Even Xavier is no match for Phoenix, and is obliterated when he attempts to reason with her. After being established as such a powerful adversary, Jean becomes a silent observer. She stands back and watches as Magneto repositions the Golden Gate Bridge and leads an all-out assault.

When Jean gets involved, she turns humans and mutants alike into dust in an outburst of rage. It takes Wolverine – the only one able to withstand Jean's powers – to convince her to stop. Jean begs him to kill her, and he duly obliges. Apparently, the producers didn't like this ending either, because they rebooted the franchise.

X-Men: First Class (2011) – Emma Frost (January Jones), Angel Salvadore (Zoë Kravitz)

This movie is set before the original trilogy, mostly in 1962 at the height of the Cuban Missile Crisis. We see Charles Xavier, Erik Lansherr and Raven before the characters become Professor X, Magneto and Mystique. Prototype tech includes a primitive Cerebro, the X-Men jet, and fashionable jumpsuits. The titular first class members are inexperienced mutant teenagers who eventually prove their worth.

The main villains are the Hellfire Club, led by Sebastian Shaw (Kevin Bacon), a mutant who can absorb and release energy. His plan is to start World War III so that mutants will thrive in the radioactive wasteland. Villains aren't known for sanity. Lansherr has a vendetta against Shaw for murdering his mother, which leads to a difference of opinion with Xavier.

The main female antagonist – to begin with – is Emma Frost, a telepath able to change into diamond form. A mix of physical and mental, she shows off these abilities several times. Highlights include beating up Lansherr, blocking Xavier's mind control, and seducing a Soviet general by implanting sexual experiences. Unfortunately, she's defeated far too easily when Lansherr traps her against a bed and cracks her diamond shell with twisted metal tubes. So much for the hardest substance in nature.

The injured Frost has no defence against Xavier's mental powers and spends the rest of the movie off-screen in a secure cell. Actually, it's not that secure as she cuts through the glass divider and speaks to the agents on the other side.

Shaw gets a replacement villainess in the winged Angel, a woman who spits acid. Seems this young lady didn't enjoy being a recruit as she betrays her classmates. There's a long aerial battle between her and Banshee, a boy who uses projected sound waves to fly. Until a blast from Alex Summers / Havoc clips Angel's wings.

The last scene has Magneto – now in a more familiar outfit – recruit Emma Frost, but viewers shouldn't get their hopes up. She never featured in the franchise again.

X-Men: Days of Future Past (2014) – Raven (Jennifer Lawrence)

In the only main series entry without a standout female villain, Mystique (Raven) features again, but she's more misguided than evil. If *First Class* was a prequel with retroactive continuity, this movie ends with a straight-up reset. The adversaries are Sentinels, machines that can adapt to any mutant power. In a dystopian future, these creations hunt mutants, so the solution is – you guessed it – time travel.

Wolverine is the designated hero when another mutant transfers his consciousness back to his younger self in 1973. The original trilogy and prequel series casts unites, giving us two versions of key characters, though it's never explained how Xavier is still alive. Past Wolverine convinces other mutants to join forces against Dr Bolivar Trask (Peter Dinklage), the scientist responsible for creating the Sentinels. The X-Men must prevent Raven from assassinating him and setting the dark future events in motion.

Things don't go according to plan (do they ever?), and Magneto betrays his fellow mutants to fight against humans. The set-piece finale in Washington, DC has Magneto moving an entire stadium and turning the Sentinels against their creator. In the end, Raven is the heroine, and the future – the entire original trilogy – no longer happens.

X-Men: Apocalypse (2016) – Horseman – Death (Monique Ganderton), Psylocke (Olivia Munn), Storm (Alexandra Shipp)

Following the trend of moving forward a decade, this movie is set in the 1980s, though we get a prologue in ancient Egypt that introduces the villain En Sabah Nur. He's a mutant able to transfer his consciousness to another's body and absorb their power, so this blue-skinned baddie has many abilities. Handy when your goal is to enslave humanity.

The resistance entombs him mid-transfer, but not before they're wiped out by the Four Horsemen of the Apocalypse. Monique Ganderton plays their leader and gets a few kills before she sacrifices herself to protect her master. Too bad, because she made a better impression than the main female villains.

Those two women would be young Storm and Psylocke, recruited by the resurrected En Sabah Nur to be his new lieutenants. Also joining him are Angel and – drum roll – Magneto. His anger, combined with enhanced abilities, makes him even more dangerous. Xavier and the X-Men do their best to contain the threat, but the villain's almost godly powers make him the most dangerous foe they've ever faced. The ancient mutant is intent on restoring his rule and creates a giant pyramid through sheer will alone.

Storm and Psylocke get shiny matching armour sets, but their battles with the heroes are sadly nothing special. Storm has a change of heart when she witnesses Raven (her hero) stand up to En Sabah Nur. Psylocke uses purple energy weapons – swords and whips – and puts up a struggle, but her screen time is still short and she's often on the wrong end of a beatdown. The henchwoman's best moment is riding with Angel to attack the X-Men jet, but the heroes simply teleport away and Psylocke makes a narrow escape.

Magneto redeems himself, but even with his help the ancient mutant is strong enough to survive a combined onslaught from all the X-Men. So, Xavier instructs Jean Grey to unleash her true power. Even En Sabah Nur can't survive the Phoenix, and turns to dust. Her talent for utter destruction provides a glimpse of what's coming in the next film.

Rank #33

Fatal Attraction (1987)
Alex Forrest (Glenn Close)

Movie

A must-include on any movie villainess list to be taken seriously, Alex is the ultimate deterrent against infidelity. The movie has a straightforward plot and would be nothing special but for Glenn Close's performance. Don't expect a murder spree. This is a psychological thriller, with no human fatalities until the frantic climax.

Dan Gallagher (Michael Douglas) appears to be happily married to Beth (Anne Archer) and has a young daughter named Ellen (Ellen Hamilton Latzen). So Dan's motive for having an affair with Alex is a mystery. The protagonist is unlikeable, but Alex's increasingly dangerous responses to his rejection gain him sympathy. Signs of obsession are already there when Dan meets Alex at a work social and later in the office. It's clear she's interested in sex, and that's where the relationship goes, and they even make out in a seedy apartment elevator.

Over time, it becomes clear Alex is unstable. She's not thrilled when Dan feigns a heart attack, as it brings up a childhood memory of her father's death. When Dan doesn't return his girlfriend's affection and regards their fling as a one-off, she tries to commit suicide. Dan cares for Alex, but turns down an offer to go out with her a second time. The repentant protagonist has fun with his family and friends while the psycho woman sits alone in the dark. This is clearly *not* over yet.

As Dan tries to forget what happened, Alex won't let him, constantly calling him at the office and at home. Perhaps this man should have been more faithful to his wife and child, and the rest of the movie is about him trying to resolve the mess he's partly responsible for.

Villainess

If telephone calls in the night weren't enough, Dan *really* panics when Alex insists on a meeting and tells him she's pregnant. Viewers will think she's lying, though it's confirmed as the truth after Dan discovers medical test kits in her apartment. Alex wants the baby, regardless of whether her ex-lover agrees. In desperation, Dan asks his best friend for legal advice, and the tactful reply could be summarised as "You're screwed."

After Alex shows up at Dan's apartment pretending to be an interested buyer, he finally snaps and goes over to her place. That's when Close delivers her famous line of dialogue: "I'm not going to be ignored, Dan!" (as if she needed to tell us that). The best part of the movie has Alex in full stalker mode. She wrecks Dan's vehicle by tampering with the radiator, then tails him to his new home in upstate New York. To keep him occupied en route, Alex leaves him an audio cassette (remember those?), full of pre-recorded ramblings about their relationship.

Dan goes to the local police and explains the situation, though he claims the victim is a client and not himself. This gets him nowhere, and Alex watches the house dressed in black, angry that Dan wants to be with Beth and not her. When Dan purchases a rabbit for his daughter, it's clear that will be significant as it's continually mentioned / shown. This leads to the well-known bunny-boiling scene where Alex leaves a nasty surprise for Beth in the kitchen.

Dan, realising just how crazy Alex is, tells his wife everything. They're hardly on happy terms from that point, and he spends time away from the house. After Alex abducts Ellen and takes her to the funfair – and the panicked Beth has a road accident – the Gallaghers reconcile. Dan goes to Alex's apartment and attacks her, but realises what he's doing and breaks off. She responds by lunging at him with a kitchen knife, and he narrowly avoids injury. With the movie in slasher mode, Dan tells the police the full truth, and they bring Alex in for questioning.

Obviously, Dan doesn't watch horror films, as takes him time locking the house doors. Alex breaks in and attacks Beth while Dan is brewing up. After he hears the commotion, Dan rushes to the rescue. This time he shows no restraint and drowns Alex in the bathtub. Like any respectable slasher villainess, Alex comes back for a final scare, but it's only a brief one since Beth – much more savvy – is ready with a revolver.

Honourable Mentions: Obsessed Women

Disclosure (1994) – Meredith Johnson (Demi Moore)

Michael Douglas gets into another ill-advised relationship, though in fairness it's non-consensual with the female guilty of sexual harassment. This scenario being harder to prove is a central theme of the movie. The setting is a tech company, and Meredith is a new vice president who uses her attractiveness as a weapon, especially against her ex-boyfriend Tom Sanders (Douglas).

Meredith is out to get Tom from the beginning, but it's a

late evening meeting where things heat up. The aggressive woman assaults and practically rapes Tom despite him rejecting her advances. Of course, nobody believes she was the offender, and Meredith threatens or bribes all the witnesses. It's only through sheer luck – and a mis-dialled phone call – that Tom produces an audio recording to force a settlement.

The harassment case becomes a subplot, part of a conspiracy to oust Tom. Since the boss, Bob Garvin, is played by Donald Sutherland, no prizes for guessing he's involved. Get ready for technical jargon and laughable virtual reality scenes. Tom enters a digital vault, Meredith's avatar deletes files with a laser (!), and a mystery "friend" warns Tom by e-mail. After a few red herrings, he turns out to be a guy we've never seen before.

In the end, Tom gives Meredith her comeuppance by making her look foolish at a presentation. This leads to a satisfying resolution where Garvin replaces her as VP, but aside from the interesting gender reversal – which just about merits an honourable mention – there's little to praise.

Play Misty for Me (1971) – Evelyn Draper (Jessica Walter)

Clint Eastwood plays Dave Garver, a disc jockey who becomes the target of a crazed female stalker. This film is often brought up as a precursor to *Fatal Attraction*, and was also Eastwood's debut as a director. He mostly does a solid job, though there's an overlong jazz concert scene with Evelyn out of the picture in a mental institute. A tension-free fifteen minutes is never desirable in a thriller.

The story is overly familiar today, making the plot feel basic, but psycho females were relatively fresh in 1971. There's the usual harmless introduction where Evelyn calls

Dave's show and then meets him in a bar. Obsession surfaces as the woman ruins a business deal through her hysterics, though it's a slow burn for the first half. Then, Evelyn attacks a cleaner, and Dave realises just how dangerous she is.

After Evelyn's release, she targets Tobie Williams (Donna Mills), the other woman in Dave's life. Tobie's character was reportedly added late in the production cycle, which may explain why the romance feels underdeveloped. In the finale has Dave solves a cryptic clue from the villainess and saves Tobie. But he arrives too late to prevent Evelyn killing the (obvious victim-in-waiting) detective. Don't fret - the hero punches the psycho woman over a balcony after a well-staged stalk and slash scene in the dark.

Rank #32

Final Score (2018)
Tatiana (Alexandra Dinu)

Movie

It had to happen eventually. Ever since *Die Hard* in 1988, the formula of a lone hero against armed villains has been used in every conceivable scenario. Now the action has come to a football stadium. Americans might call it a soccer stadium, but doing that in East London is likely to get you a punch in the face (as Agent Cho learns the hard way).

Michael Knox (Dave Bautista) is a former soldier whose brother died following a questionable order. Now Mike wants to make amends with his niece Danii (Lara Peake). What better way to do that than to take her to a football match? Especially when that game is a high-profile European semi-final and West Ham United's last match at the Boleyn Ground (or Upton Park). The team has now moved to London's former Olympic Stadium, so producers could set off an explosion and do serious damage in the dramatic climax.

The villains are mercenaries led by Arkady (Ray Stevenson), a ruthless general who wants to find his supposedly dead brother, Dimitri (Pierce Brosnan). So badly he's prepared to threaten the lives of thirty thousand people. The siblings were once leaders of a revolution in Sakovia (a fictional Soviet bloc country) and now Arkady wants to lead a second revolt. For once, the motive isn't nuclear weapons or money. Everything else is formulaic, including the villains planting C4 explosives to mask their escape and Knox throwing a dead guy off the stadium roof to convince authorities the threat is real.

West Ham fans are so shocked at reaching a European semi-final they don't notice the chaotic events happening around them. Gun-wielding baddies swarm the concourse, mobile phones go dead, the stadium is locked down. Even a bike chase and crazy stunt jump go ignored. To keep the crowd occupied, West Ham score two goals at convenient times.

It's only when the hero runs onto the pitch to avert a disaster that anyone pays attention. Knox's only allies are Steed, a police commander on the outside (competent for a change) and Faisal Kahn, a timid steward who provides comic relief. There's some dark humour as Faisal acts the Middle Eastern terrorist to clear out hostile spectators.

Don't think too hard unless you want the plot holes to cause a headache. Predictable, but that's not necessarily a bad thing, as the movie delivers what action genre fans expect from a *Die Hard* clone. A gung-ho hero, nasty villains, fights in claustrophobic locations, and an unexpectedly great bad girl who leaves a lasting impression.

Villainess

After a long series of disappointing henchwomen, it's high time we had a female version of Karl from *Die Hard*, and that essentially sums up Tatiana. Arkady's lieutenant doesn't care about being attractive – this is a tattooed warrior with a cornrow haircut and acts every bit as mean as she looks. All that's missing is a last woman standing scene, since Tatiana dies before the grand finale. At least she goes down fighting and has several run-ins with the hero and his niece. That's enough to earn Tatiana legendary status.

This movie is the UK's answer to *Sudden Death*, with a lot of similar themes. Tatiana takes a leading role in the stadium takeover, infiltrating the ground as a paramedic (like in the Van Damme film, the terrorists disguise themselves as employees). Upon arrival, she guns down a security guard and innocent civilians in the police control room to quash any notion of resistance.

After Knox takes out a terrorist in an elevator (or should that be lift?), he gets a big fight in the kitchen. No killer penguin (she featured at #92), but the brute Vlad proves tough to take down. Eventually, Knox finishes the big guy off by dunking his head in boiling fat. This really ticks off Tatiana, since she and Vlad were lovers. In an explosion of rage, she smashes random items and demands to be the one who kills Knox. Getting Karl vibes yet?

By now, Knox has tipped off the police and offers to rescue Dimitri before the villains find him. Time is of the essence since the stadium is rigged to explode when the match ends, so Knox grabs a motorcycle to speed things up. There are plenty of other bikes (indoors!), which is an excuse to have an action scene. Tatiana and her goons pursue Knox while stunned spectators wonder what's going on. When her handgun proves ineffective, Tatiana swaps it for a submachine gun. Knox reaches the roof with her not far behind, though her aiming is predictably terrible. Much too early to have the crowd flee in panic, so how about a goal so people don't notice the motorcycle jump overhead?

After Knox makes it to Dimitri, the villains up the ante by kidnapping Danii to use as a bargaining chip. Tatiana takes great pleasure in knocking out Faisal and torturing the hostage girl. Things are personal as far as she's concerned.

Knox agrees to trade Dimitri for Danii, leading to a prisoner exchange scene on the stadium roof. The villains plan to double-cross the heroes and detonate the explosives anyway (did you expect anything else?). But Knox chose the location wisely, as blinding floodlights hide his own deception: to take Dimitri's place.

Knox takes down several mooks with the help of special forces. Then it's the hero against Arkady, with Knox attempting to retrieve the "kill switch" to deactivate the bombs. This is when Tatiana joins the fight and gives him a good beating. He holds the villainess off, but the kill switch rolls off the roof. That's a convenient time for Knox to grab a banner and do a swinging stunt. He reaches the device, but the henchwoman isn't finished yet.

Tatiana's final fight is rather brief (and somewhat disappointing), but still delivers excitement while it lasts. The knife-wielding villainess attacks Knox, but the hero gets the better of her, and they fall over the roof edge. The villainess is impaled on a metal bar, but gloats that the kill switch is fake before she dies. Of course, the hero saves the day, but Tatiana went out believing she'd won.

Honourable Mention: *Die Hard* Scenario

Velocity Trap (1999) – Pallas (Jorja Fox)

Yes, they've done *Die Hard* in space, too. One of the better futuristic variants, with Olivier Gruner as Stokes, a security officer framed by corrupt colleagues after an assassination. A female killer is involved in that plot, but after she detonates an explosive, we never see her again.

The first half of the film is mostly a stretched-out setup. Stokes is too honest to be bought off, and killing him would attract too much attention, so the conspirators assign their patsy to guard duty on a transport ship carrying 40 billion US dollars. That's the intergalactic currency, and paper money is still apparently in use in the space age.

Before this subplot, we're introduced to the main villains: Simmons (Ken Olandt) and his thrill-seeking wife, Pallas. Before she played Sara Sidle on *CSI*, Fox was a crazy henchwoman in this B-movie. Pallas likes to live dangerously, leaving it to the last second to escape an asteroid explosion. The purpose of the sabotage becomes clear later, when the transporter drops out of light speed. The "accident" is part of a plan to heist the money and destroy the evidence. Stokes – with the help of navigator Beth Sheffield (Alicia Coppola) – is the proverbial "fly in the ointment."

The hijackers are light on manpower, probably because they expected no resistance. Besides the psycho husband/wife team, there's a tough guy named Fallout, a tech whiz who gets no action, and a treacherous engineer who disabled the sentry guns. Fallout gets the honour of a major fight with Stokes before he's incinerated by Sheffield. All the villains wear stylish body armour, and Pallas sports a feminine version that makes her "assets" stand out.

After a few onboard encounters, the heroes must take a shuttle ride in space. Pallas – *really* annoyed by now – comes after them in her own fighter craft. There's an above-average chase with Pallas proving a worthy opponent. It's disappointingly a vehicle confrontation, but the villainess evades the sentry guns (no small feat) and damages the heroes' ship. Then she loses control and crashes into a support strut, which also takes out the engineer. A decent demise, better than the anticlimax that follows.

Lethal Tender (1996) - Sparky (Karyn Dwyer)

Die Hard in a water treatment plant, with Jeff Fahey as macho cop David Chase. Villains led by Montesi (Kim Coates) follow the standard playbook, taking hostages as a distraction while they steal bearer bonds. A scenario copied wholesale from the 1988 classic, but the above-average casting offsets the dull location.

Gary Busey is Turner – the same charismatic, dangerous bad guy he always plays. He double-crosses *everyone* and kills more criminals than the good guys. For added effect, Turner provides an unreliable narrator opening voice-over. Melissa (Carrie-Anne Moss from *The Matrix* series) is the love interest, but don't expect a Trinity-level badass. She gets some action, but her role is mostly to provide technical information and get rescued by David.

The one female villain limit applies, but Sparky is a fiery redhead in a sleeveless leather jacket who doesn't mind getting physical. The demolition specialist objects when Turner kills two unarmed civilians, but has no qualms slaughtering a special forces team with an assault rifle. When David is injured, Melissa fights Sparky and lands a few punches. Then the enraged villainess pulls a knife, and the hero shoots her in the back.

No Contest II (1996) (aka *Face the Evil*) - Lisette (Fiona Highet)

Shannon Tweed returns as martial arts actress Sharon Bell for this sequel that replaces a beauty contest with a museum for the *Die Hard* scenario. Criminals want a deadly Nazi nerve toxin hidden in a statue, and while Lance Henriksen does an innocent bystander act, it's so obvious he's the main villain that the reveal comes within the opening thirty minutes.

Production values are above average, and the 5'10" Tweed is convincing as an action heroine. This time, she has support from her sister, Bobbi (Jayne Heitmeyer). Everyone else is expendable, starting with the least important / likeable characters.

Lisette is the sole female baddie who dons surgical gloves to prepare the chemicals. Once Sharon becomes a threat, there's a decent chase through the war-themed exhibit halls. Inventive props – barbed wire fences and hanging bamboo – provide background flavour to the gun-fu and kickboxing. Lisette is skilled enough to fight back and twirl a snapped-off wooden pole, but Sharon kicks her off-balance opponent onto the sharp object.

Another early exit (Lisette dies halfway through), but an honourable mention for a decent encounter with a semi-competent foe.

Rank #31

Eve of Destruction (1991)
Eve VIII (Renée Soutendijk)

Movie

A moderate-budget sci-fi actioner from the golden age of B-movies, with lead actress Renée Soutendijk in a dual role as Dr Eve Simmons and her android lookalike Eve VIII. She performs admirably as human and machine, and the characters are so different it's easy to forget they're played by the same actress. To avoid confusion, I'll refer to Simmons by her surname and the android as Eve for the rest of the review.

Eve is intended for battlefield use, and Simmons' flagship prototype for a funding review. A routine test run in San Francisco goes well until two masked men commit a bank robbery with Eve on the premises. The android's programming didn't include armed criminal etiquette, so she ignores their demands to hit the floor. Eve's handler intervenes and kills one criminal, but gets shot by the other. The robber loses patience with Eve and blasts her with his shotgun, which barely slows her down. She treats the robber as a threat and sends the shocked man flying through a window.

With the machine now locked in battle mode, she collects a dropped Uzi, then purchases ammo and a stylish red leather jacket. Hoping to keep a low profile (yeah, right), the authorities call in anti-terrorist expert Colonel Jim McQuade (Gregory Hines). We get the usual chalk and cheese relationship between science and the military, with Simmons and Jim at each other's throats from the start.

As Eve goes on a murderous rampage through the city, Simmons and Jim work together to stop the killing machine. The android's defences and near invulnerability to conventional weapons make her a tough opponent. Mixing 1990s images with future tech always looks silly, but the key takeaway from the briefing is to aim for the eyes. Jim questions why Eve doesn't have an off switch, but things are never that simple.

Villainess

Eve has been programmed with the thoughts and feelings of her creator, but no longer has restraint. This leads to an interesting character dynamic where Eve acts out Simmons' fantasies, doing things the doctor contemplated in the past but never went through with.

First on the agenda is a visit to a seedy motel where she seduces a misogynistic man and takes him to her room. Things get messy when this conflicts with Eve's self-defence priorities. When the guy calls her a bitch, she bites off... an important piece of anatomy. The guy's friends – who had been listening at the door – burst in looking for payback, but engaging a killing machine in hand to hand combat ends badly.

The police outside – who've traced Eve's rental vehicle – are no match for the android. Several Uzi bursts later, there are five dead officers for the sheriff to deal with and an enemy who shows no sign of stopping. Eve's only concern is the single bullet hole in her expensive jacket, and that was the first taste of destruction. Simmons witnessed her alcoholic father abuse her mother, which ultimately led to a fatal road accident, and now Eve is out for revenge.

Things get worse when she encounters a motorist who acts aggressively (and calls her a naughty B word). Eve takes road rage to the extreme and rams his car into the dirt. When the guy thinks it's all over, the killer android psychs herself up and drives into the stranded vehicle. The physical and emotional shock triggers a device in Eve's spine. McQuade learns that the nuclear bomb inside Eve is now active and set to explode in twenty-four hours. And he's not too impressed the military kept him out of the loop.

Jim and Simmons trace her father's address, which leads to a showdown between the special forces man and the android. McQuade tells his men to wait outside, but Simmons isn't good at following instructions. After a verbal exchange over the radio gets her nowhere, she enters to witness Eve snap her dad's neck. Being Eve's creator doesn't grant Simmons any special status, and Eve opens fire. The doctor escapes without harm, but some of Jim's men aren't so lucky.

Simmons predicts Eve will travel to New York to visit her son, who's staying with her ex-husband. While the guess is accurate, covert surveillance by government agents doesn't prevent Eve from reaching her target. Simmons warns a surprised ex that the "woman" he's with is an android, but it's too late. Jim waits in the apartment building lobby, weapon at the ready, but Eve uses the elevator distraction / takes the stairs trick. This android sure is a quick learner.

Eve's path of destruction moves to the streets, with the leather-clad walking time bomb gunning down agents and narrowly missing Jim, and then to a subway station. If you're in this movie, you're potential cannon fodder, and Eve murders a bystander who makes the mistake of calling her a bitch. Everyone else wisely flees, and it's Jim against Eve in a darkened tunnel. He's wounded by gunfire after he breaks his own rule and loses concentration. Simmons convinces Eve to toss her the child by triggering a memory, and Jim puts a bullet through the android's eye.

Anyone familiar with killer robot films won't be surprised that Eve is still functional. She attacks Simmons and Jim – without a clean shot – slides his weapon to the cornered doctor. Bullets don't stop Eve, but a name-calling bluff from Jim distracts her. Simmons rams the pistol into her empty eye socket, and that kill shot is an effective "off switch".

Honourable Mention: Synthetic Women

Steel and Lace (1990) – Gaily Morton (Clare Wren)

A year earlier, we had another B-movie sci-fi thriller with the same concept. Gaily Morton commits suicide after a powerful businessman is acquitted in a rape trial, thanks to false alibis from his four male accomplices. The men escape justice for many years, but the victim's brother, Albert (Bruce Davison) is an expert in artificial intelligence. Time to send his creation – a robotic replica of Gaily – to exact revenge.

The targets – particularly the rapist Daniel Emerson (Michael Cerveris) – are unrepentant scum, and Albert's desire for vengeance leads to innocent victims too. Being a machine, Gaily is arguably not a true villainess, but stylish kills gain her an honourable mention. Albert satisfies his bloodlust by watching recordings of the murders, which are graphic thanks to the android's weapons. She has a talent for blending in and uses latex masks to pose as other women. Her best moment, though, is impersonating a man by holographic technology (an unexpected narrative feint).

A former court artist named Alison (Stacy Haiduk) assists the police investigation, though Daniel is the prime suspect until they realise what's going on. The movie ends with Albert and his creation jumping off a tall building. By then, all five targets are dead, and the android says, "Pretty. Very Pretty," to reference the rape.

Fans of gory deaths will be satisfied with the killing methods. These include drilling a hole through a man's chest, decapitation with her bare hands, and draining blood. The later murders – chopping her target's head in two with a helicopter blade and incineration by lightning bolt (a rather cheap effect) – are almost a letdown.

Rank #30

The Wizard of Oz (1939)
Wicked Witch of the West (Margaret Hamilton)

Movie

The oldest movie on my list was difficult to place, as I'm not a huge fan of musicals, but the Wicked Witch belongs among the legends. Special effects were basic in this era, and the whole feel – simple costumes and painted backgrounds – is akin to a stage production. For a film made in the late 1930s, this was way ahead of its time and an amazing technical accomplishment.

The prologue looks black and white, but filmmakers shot it with a sepia tint. We're introduced to Dorothy Gale (Judy Garland), a teenage girl who lives on a Kansas farm with her aunt and uncle. There are three farmhands, a mysterious fortune-telling professor, and the nasty Miss Gulch, who wants to put down Dorothy's dog Toto.

Dorothy longs for adventure and sings the iconic "Somewhere Over the Rainbow." But she gets more than she bargained for when a tornado sweeps up her house and deposits it (and her) in a strange land. The grand reveal that follows, with a switch from sepia to full colour as Dorothy steps into Oz, is startling even to modern viewers. It must have seemed a technical marvel in the mid-twentieth century.

The residents – a dwarven race known as Munchkins – and the Good Witch of the North aren't unhappy to see a stranger. Quite the opposite, since Dorothy's house landed on the Wicked Witch of the East. Nobody seems regretful, so one assumes she must have been a horrible person. In fact, the Munchkins burst into song and treat Dorothy and her dog as practical royalty.

The Good Witch is so indebted that she offers to help Dorothy get home. This involves a long journey along the Yellow Brick Road to the Emerald City, meeting three companions on the way: the Scarecrow, the Tin Man, and the Cowardly Lion. On arrival, they receive an audience with the Wonderful Wizard of Oz. He's not an all-powerful man as first seems, but a charlatan operating machinery from behind a curtain. The fraudster can provide assistance, but demands that the heroes perform a dangerous task. With no magic, Dorothy has to rely on wits, Toto, and her new friends.

Villainess

Like any grand quest, there are obstacles to overcome. Turns out the dead witch has a sister even more evil than she. This woman is straight out of a Halloween party with green skin, a black outfit, a shoddy broomstick, and a pointy hat. It's likely the Wicked Witch was the inspiration for party costumes, such is her cinematic legacy. From the moment she appears in a puff of red smoke, she is a screen presence to be reckoned with and a terrifying sight to young viewers.

Luckily, the Good Witch of the North is around to teleport the ruby slippers from the deceased Witch of the East onto the heroine's feet and shield her from the Wicked Witch of the West. So many compass directions it could get confusing, but the other two are minor characters. The villainess will be called the Wicked Witch for brevity.

Dorothy's quest along the Yellow Brick Road brings her into contact with the Scarecrow, Tin Man, and Cowardly Lion. They join Dorothy in search of a brain, heart, and courage, respectively. The supporting cast play multiple roles, distinct characters on Earth and in the fantasy world of Oz, which raises the question whether Dorothy's experience is just a dream.

In this fairly repetitive section, the Wicked Witch is absent from the proceedings, except for a brief appearance when Dorothy encounters the Tin Man. No epic confrontation, just some threats and a fireball which narrowly misses Scarecrow. There's only one human antagonist, though she has an army of monkey creatures to do her bidding.

With Dorothy and her three companions (four counting Toto) almost at the Emerald City, the Wicked Witch casts an evil spell. After gazing into a crystal ball, she cackles and creates a poisonous atmosphere. This puts Dorothy and the Lion to sleep, while the Tin Man and Scarecrow are less than helpful. Only the Good Witch's intervention saves them, but the villainess won't be stopped so easily. She takes off from her castle lair, riding her broomstick to the Emerald City. Then she flies around and leaves a message in smoke: SURRENDER DOROTHY.

If the heroes are hoping for help from the Wizard of Oz, none comes. He demands that Dorothy bring him the Wicked Witch's broomstick. Talk about a steep price! The residents of the Emerald City are accommodating and give the heroes all kinds of comforts. But it's a dangerous mission, especially once the villainess captures Dorothy and her companions must save her.

There's a lengthy confrontation where the Wicked

Witch torments Dorothy and threatens to kill Toto, but she's thwarted by the magic of the ruby slippers. The shoes won't come off while Dorothy is alive, so the Wicked Witch unveils a giant hourglass and proclaims her foe will perish when the sands run out. A good thing Toto escapes and brings the rescue party, though the Wicked Witch and her monkeys prevent the heroes from escaping.

After a pantomime chase scene through the castle with the usual chandelier-dropping antics, the Wicked Witch confronts Dorothy and threatens to set the Scarecrow aflame. Dorothy puts out the fire with a bucket of water and inadvertently drenches the villainess. The splash is deadly to witches, and the antagonist melts away, screaming insults as she turns to steam.

Honourable Mentions: Witches

The Witches (1990) – Grand High Witch (Anjelica Huston)

This adaptation of Roald Dahl's novel is better regarded than the 2020 version, even if the unfaithful happy ending doesn't fit the dark comic tale. The scene is set early on when an old woman tells her grandson, Luke, all about witches. These evil women have no toes, glowing purple eyes, and masks to conceal their true appearance. Witches hate children and do nasty things like trap them in paintings until they grow old and die. No wonder the tale scares the youngster.

After Luke's parents die in a car accident, the grandmother Helga becomes his legal guardian, and they move to England. A witch tries to lure Luke from a treehouse with chocolate, but Helga's knowledge – and the witch's pet snake – means Luke is not deceived. However, the real danger comes when the family goes on a South

Coast holiday. They picked the wrong hotel because every witch in England is there to attend a national convention.

With literally dozens of female villains, it's disappointing that many are extras. The women cackle while their leader – the Grand High Witch – announces her scheme to turn all British children into mice. Ironically, they masquerade as members of the Royal Society for the Protection of Children. Yeah, right. Luke overhears their plan from a hiding place and watches them test the potion on another child. But the witches discover Luke, capture the boy, and transform him into a mouse!

Luke and his new friend Bruno spend the rest of the movie in animal form, but get the potion into a soup bowl so the witches drink it. There are some comic antics where Bruno's disbelieving parents almost drink the soup and Rowan Atkinson runs around as an easily panicked hotel manager. But it's Angelica Huston's character who steals the show with her disfigured face and insane rants about children.

There's a sequel hook with Luke transformed back into a boy and finding a list of American witches, but this is a one-off movie. The villainess gets a suitable demise, though. Being evil, the witches change into nasty-looking mice, which gives the holidaymakers a fright. The Grand High Witch seems immune to her potion, but eventually succumbs to the spell and the manager chops her up.

Harry Potter and the Order of the Phoenix (2007) – Delores Umbridge (Imelda Staunton)

Bellatrix Lestrange (Helena Bonham Carter) is the main villainess in the evil magician hierarchy, but her contribution is disappointing for someone who had four movies (*Order of the Phoenix* onward) to make an impact. She kills two characters, but this doesn't carry the emotional weight it should because we don't know the victims well enough. Bellatrix is defeated too easily, with no major confrontation against any of the three central characters.

In the fifth movie, the Dark Lord Voldemort is still regaining his powers after his resurrection, and the main plot at Hogwarts is the Ministry of Magic attempting to quash rumours of his return. Conveniently, the Defence Against the Dark Arts teacher slot is free (isn't it always?), so they plant a sadistic woman to "educate" young witches and wizards. Delores' methods are strict and demeaning, and she clearly has no love for children.

Harry resists Delores' influence and gets detention for his trouble. The villainess has the hero write lines in blood, which carves the same message in his own flesh. This woman is on a power trip and gets the headmaster Dumbledore fired so she can take over the school. Up go notices to remind students who's in charge, and the House of Slytherin pupils are happy to be Umbridge's bullying prefects.

When the nasty Dolores is attacked by Centaurs, she begs Harry to tell her captors she's a nice person. The hero simply responds with the line Delores forced him to write: "I must not tell lies". Touché, Harry.

Delores Umbridge receives an extended cameo in *Harry Potter and the Deathly Hallows: Part One* (2010), but she's not that threatening outside of Hogwarts. With the main villain now in the ascendancy, Dolores is a minor antagonist. While her return is certainly welcome, since female villains are poorly represented in the series, there's little to comment on.

Rank #29

***Who Dares Wins* (1982)**
Frankie Leith (Judy Davis), Helga (Ingrid Pitt)

Movie

This British action / spy movie is best known for its action-packed finale, which could be summed up as brutally short and effective. Don't expect typical Hollywood clichés. There are no extended fight scenes or one-liners, and the main villains are killed as easily as the unnamed terrorists. The title is the motto of the British Special Air Service (SAS), and the story was inspired by the real-life operation that ended the 1980 Iranian Embassy siege in London. Known as *The Final Option* in the US, presumably because the elite unit is not as familiar to American audiences.

The villains are anti-nuclear extremists with no qualms about resorting to violence. When they discover a secret agent among them, they use a peace demonstration as cover to kill him with a crossbow sniper. That forces the British authorities to implement Plan B (or Plan A again) and send a second man undercover. The chosen hero is Peter Skellen (Lewis Collins), a charming SAS captain who deliberately gets kicked out of his unit by roughing up two foreign officers. That leaves him free to infiltrate and "advise" the terrorists while working against them from within.

The cloak and dagger stuff is rather amateurish, and it's no surprise the villains soon become suspicious of Skellen.

The main villainess, Frankie, is more trusting because she's willing to risk success for SAS inside information. Her introduction is a bizarre nightclub scene where she plays a rocket on stage while people dance around her in weird costumes. Skellen goes for a direct seduction approach, which is surprisingly effective, but Frankie is the crazy, thrill-seeking type.

The first hour is devoted to training exercises and talk, with little action. There's an especially long part with a rock concert in a church, where a sympathetic bishop preaches to the audience. Frankie and her crew incite violence and paint the campaigners in a bad light. That's about as exciting as it gets, and the henchwoman Helga is far more threatening during the buildup. The tension rises when Skellen gives himself away by visiting his wife. Evidently he's better at SAS antics than spy craft, and his foolish actions put his family in danger.

Skellen is not exactly discreet about meeting his SAS contact either. While he eludes a male motorcyclist at Westminster Pier, Helga observes the two men together. Frankie is now more suspicious, but wants Skellen around. Helga isn't one to give up, though. The villains pull off the obvious tail / discreet tail trick again, and Helga uses poison disguised as perfume to eliminate the contact on a bus. With no way to pass on information, it's up to the lone hero to foil the villains' scheme.

Who Dares Wins isn't a *Die Hard* scenario plot since Skellen infiltrates the terrorist group deliberately. But Frankie and Helga achieve legendary status as the main villainess (relatively rare in this genre) and a nasty henchwoman who poses a threat throughout.

Villainesses

Seventy minutes into the two-hour movie, Frankie and her gang execute their plan. The terrorists pose as a military band after they stage a road accident and abduct the real performers. The US ambassador's remote countryside residence is the setting for an overnight siege. Frankie kills a hostage during the attack – this is a woman willing to get her hands dirty. Skellen is still embedded with the group, but Frankie orders Helga to hold his family at gunpoint to ensure his loyalty.

Not long after the takeover, Frankie issues demands to Commander Powell (Edward Woodward) who's taken up position outside the estate. The terrorist leader demands that the British government launch a nuclear missile at a Scottish submarine base. In the name of peace, apparently. When questioned by the US Secretary of State, Frankie rants about a nuclear holocaust while blaming politicians. The Secretary sums it up nicely when he says Frankie is a lunatic.

Powell doesn't even engage in discussion and gives no pretence that the government will comply. A US general present at the dinner grabs a gun from a terrorist and gets shot and killed. This convinces Powell to call in the SAS. Fortunately, Skellen provides a mix of truth and misinformation to Frankie and signals the authorities from a bathroom window. The oft-used toilet excuse and a mirror to reflect the moonlight do the trick.

The authorities put Skellen's house under watch after the contact was eliminated, so have already set up a staging post in the building next door. The SAS joins the police and makes a mess of the neighbour's wall. If drilling a hole for a camera wasn't enough, special forces blow their way into the Skellen household. Just in time, since Helga had turned nasty. In a matter of seconds, the SAS breach the wall and eliminate Helga and her accomplice with headshots. These guys don't mess around.

It's back to the main siege, with the SAS given the go-ahead by the Prime Minister. Skellen reveals his true allegiance after a power cut and frees the dining room hostages in a dramatic shootout. Frankie panics as her plan falls apart, and the SAS executes a perfect raid with no special forces casualties or collateral damage.

Efficient and ruthless, they use the element of surprise to take down the terrorists before they can react. We get a very effective POV through one soldier's gas mask as the unit wipes out the opposition. Some villains still think Skellen is on their side until he guns them down, links up with his SAS squad, and leads the final charge.

Frankie is the last one standing (what else did you expect?), but Skellen hesitates to shoot her. Perhaps he genuinely feels something, and the undercover work dulled his killer instinct. To the SAS soldiers, Frankie's just another terrorist, so they kill her without a second thought.

Honourable Mention: Special Forces

SAS: Red Notice (2021) – Grace Lewis (Ruby Rose), Zada (Jing Lusi)

A more traditional action film, closer to the *Die Hard* mould. While there's more fighting and shooting in this one, the SAS tactics are far less realistic. Trained soldiers stand in the open, waiting to get shot by the villains, in this case a militant group led by Grace Lewis, aka The Black Swan. Her mercenaries – who've run covert black ops for the British government, only to become expendable – hijack a train in the Channel Tunnel and ransom the hostages.

By pure coincidence, one passenger is Tom Buckingham (Sam Heughan), an SAS officer as upper-class as he sounds. He was taking his girlfriend, Sophie Hart (Hannah John-Kamen) to Paris when the terrorists took over the train. The rest of the movie is routine, with Tom doing the solo hero thing and taking out the villains one by one. The SAS has a traitor in its ranks, and it's no great surprise the mole ends up being Tom's best mate Declan Smith (Tom Hopper).

Grace employs female mercenaries, including the henchwoman Zada. She's not that memorable in truth, with action limited to shooting innocent civilians when the villains torch a village. And she threatens Sophie, who predictably becomes a bargaining chip. Zada goes out tamely, falling to a sniper shot when the terrorists pose as hostages as part of their escape strategy.

Grace gets more satisfying bad girl moments and comes across as a dangerous psychopath. She doesn't hesitate to kill, which includes putting a bullet in the SAS commander's head to establish her authority. The finale on the French coast has Tom rescue Sophie from Grace, then engage the villainess in close-quarters combat. This is a lengthy fight, with Grace proving a deadly foe with a blade. After that, there's a conversation where the wounded woman claims she and Tom are not so different. He agrees and slices her throat.

Rank #28

***Total Recall* (2012)**
Lori (Kate Beckinsale)

Movie

This remake of the Arnold Schwarzenegger film is widely regarded as inferior and falls short in key areas. The Earth setting doesn't capture the sci-fi feel of Mars, and Jessica Biel is bland as resistance fighter Melina. But Kate Beckinsale's version of Lori – an all-action, tough as nails operative – is a notable improvement on Sharon Stone's great but under-used femme fatale.

Anyone who's seen the 1990 movie will mostly know what to expect, though the update throws in a few variations. Douglas Quaid (Colin Farrell) is a factory worker from The Colony (22nd century Australia) and employed in the United Federation of Britain (UFB for short). In this post-apocalyptic future, most of the planet is uninhabitable, and commuters travel through the Earth using a gravity elevator known as The Fall.

Doug dreams he's a secret agent on a mystery mission with a beautiful woman. Fleeing UFB troops in black armour is more exciting than his day job, so it's no wonder Doug wants more. Against the advice of his friend, he goes to a company called Rekall, which implants memories. The tech wizards have a safety policy that nothing in the simulation can be true in real life, but it's only a dream...

right? It turns out Doug really is a spy (with a heavy dose of amnesia), and the UFB is *very* interested in finding him.

Whatever Rekall did activates Doug, and he bests a dozen UFB troops with martial arts and inventive use of grenades. Not sure what to do, he goes home to his devoted wife, Lori. Except she suddenly develops a British accent and reveals herself as a UFB operative who's only known Doug for six weeks. He gets her at gunpoint for some brief questions, but Lori is far more skilled than regular troops and quickly regains the upper hand. Doug flees with Lori hot on his tail, which leads to a chase across the enormous Colony shantytown and its Oriental-style tiered levels.

After eluding his false wife, Doug gets a call from a phone implanted in his hand and a message from a former colleague. The man advises the fugitive to get rid of the phone – also a tracking device – and directs him to a safe deposit box. Happy for the assist, Doug cuts out the phone with broken glass and gives it to a homeless guy, who soon receives an unfriendly visit from Lori. That's a woman you don't want to be on the wrong side of.

Lori asks her boss for information about Doug's identity and isn't happy with his reply. In fact, she orders the UFB soldiers to shoot on sight. In the safe deposit box, Doug finds recorded video instructions from himself before the memory wipe. And high-tech spy equipment, which may come in handy for figuring out who the hell he is.

Villainess

The villainess becomes Doug's main foe over the course of the movie. Despite working for the ruthless UFB dictator Chancellor Cohaagen, she's the antagonist with the most screen time. Action ramps up several notches when Doug travels into enemy territory, escapes the authorities, and jumps onto a highway. Good thing the woman of his dreams arrives to rescue him. Melina is a member of the resistance and a skilled hovercar driver. Apparently, she and Doug were lovers, which adds romantic spice to the high-speed chase that follows.

Lori (who else?) leads the pursuers. Besides regular troops, the UFB has a droid army at its disposal. This leads to a CGI-heavy action sequence with all kinds of crazy stunts. Melina gets in a few jibes about Lori before she pulls off a dramatic swerve and shoot manoeuvre. Lori is not that involved in truth. Mostly it's shots of her looking frustrated, and Quaid eludes the UFB by disabling the hovercar's magnetic system and dropping to the streets of London. Down there, vehicles still have wheels, including the traditional red buses.

Doug finds another message from his former self, which reveals he previously looked very different and was called Hauser. The former UFB agent apparently had a change of heart and wants to aid the resistance by providing information stored in his brain. Not long after this revelation, Doug's friend from work (remember the mundane factory job) turns up and claims it's all a dream. His arguments aren't at all convincing, such as wearing a bulletproof vest because Doug "put it" on him. He speaks in an unfamiliar accent to reinforce the fantasy, and it takes Melina sweating to stop Doug shooting her and turn his weapon on his "friend" instead.

After that dialogue-heavy ruse, Lori ditches her concerned wife act and resumes her role as the badass agent. The ensuing chase – with a relentless Lori and her droids hunting Doug and Melina through the transporter shafts – is the movie's most exciting scene. The villainess is actively involved, whether she vents insults at Doug or uses her robots for mobile cover while advancing on the trapped heroes. Lori thinks she's victorious after she bests Melina in a catfight and plants an explosive charge, but the fugitives prove equally resourceful and jump to another platform to escape the blast.

We're then treated to bleak landscapes as the heroes enter contaminated territory. However, Doug's joy at contacting the resistance proves short-lived when it's revealed the "information" in his brain is really a virus. The entire sequence of events has been a clever charade by Cohaagen to locate the rebel leader. Hauser never switched sides and volunteered to have his mind wiped. Lori gloats as the UFB take Melina prisoner and strap Quaid to a memory-implanting machine. Fortunately, the villains don't stick around, and a resistance trooper frees Doug before the procedure.

Cohaagen launches a droid invasion of The Colony to gain the most valuable resource in this dark future: living space. Lori's not as involved in the big action set piece that follows. She chases the heroes around a Fall transporter and is ordered not to intervene directly, while Quaid plants explosives to sabotage the operation. Cohaagen shows up in person to fight the hero and has numbers on his side until Melina pilots a gunship to even the odds. With the villain foiled, the heroes escape the explosion, and Lori is seemingly killed in the blast.

Quaid wakes up in an ambulance with Melina by his bedside. A tough villainess killed off-screen – that can't be right, surely? Lori's holographic disguise might have worked if the real Melina hadn't wounded her hand. Quaid fights Lori – briefly – then finishes her with an electric paddle stun and a gunshot.

Honourable Mention: *Total Recall*

Total Recall (1990) – Lori (Sharon Stone)

To avoid repetition, this extended honourable mention is light on story details. Douglas Quaid is played by Arnold Schwarzenegger, Melina by Rachel Ticotin, and Cohaagen by Ronny Cox. Other than that, it's the same tale of an ordinary worker discovering he's a secret agent and that plenty of people want him dead. The second half is on Mars, with a subplot about an alien device that generates oxygen from ice. The primary henchman is Richter (Michael Ironside), and Lori is relegated to a supporting role.

Despite this, Sharon Stone makes an impression that leaves the viewer wanting more, though what we get is very good. Lori's reveal is better handled, with a shadowy figure attacking Quaid after he returns home from Rekall. After a brief shootout, the "intruder" is revealed as Lori, and Doug discovers his wife has martial arts skills. She plays the innocent woman to buy time, but Doug is too smart to fall for it.

After flying to Mars, Melina becomes the female lead while Richter pursues the hero. There's an annoying taxi driver who's obviously a mole, so the reveal is unsurprising even to a first-time viewer. The false wife doesn't show herself until the villains try to convince Doug he's experiencing a false memory. After he sees through their lies, Lori stops pretending to be nice and kicks the hero in some rather sensitive places.

Lori's best scene is her last. She gets into an extended fight with Melina after the heroine arrives to rescue Quaid. This is a drawn-out tussle – one of the better female v female examples – and it's Lori who comes out on top. Just when the villainess is about to kill Melina with her own knife,

Doug shoots the weapon from her hand. Lori pleads for mercy, but Quaid shows her none and gets a trademark Arnie one-liner: "Consider this a divorce".

First Target (2000)
Nina Stahl (Ona Grauer)

Movie

In a familiar setup, an assassin targets the US President and must outwit an elite Secret Service agent. The narrative twist: both major players are female. This is the second part of a trilogy, set between *First Daughter* (1999) and *First Shot* (2002). For this outing, Daryl Hannah – not Mariel Hemingway – plays Alex McGregor.

A cabal of powerful businessmen is unhappy with policy decisions, so they hire a nasty and deadly woman to eliminate the problem. There's a secondary plot about an extremist sending video threats – a stereotype weirdo in a log cabin. Add traitors in the Secret Service working against Alex, a rookie agent eager to prove herself, and an obvious late reveal that the Vice President is involved. The result is a mostly predictable story. However, this TV movie has decent production values, and Ona Grauer's ruthless hitwoman is a memorable villainess.

Nina's introduction is a scene any bad girl fan will relish. Off the Seattle coast, a blonde woman in a bikini seduces a guy on a yacht. Then, she mixes drugs into his margarita and kicks him overboard. Nina could take this man without the advantage, as she's a competent fighter, but she enjoys besting her opponents. Her confidence almost undoes the plan as the mark proves resilient. He refuses to drown easily, but Nina finishes the job before escaping on a speedboat with her brother, Evan.

With the stage set, the assassin reports to her client, Hunter (Tom Butler). He's a typical shady money man who lives on a luxury estate and throws lavish parties. His interest in Nina goes beyond professional – watching her shower – and she regards her sexiness as a tool to manipulate and control. Evan is not pleased with Hunter's attitude, but Nina is twisted enough to torment her sibling.

This is all foreplay before a weapons test, where Nina practices her sharpshooting skills. Hunter isn't the type to leave things to chance, so Evan builds a custom-made weapon. This classy rifle takes special explosive bullets designed to detonate at a specific range. In theory, a miss will be a kill shot. Nina shows off by destroying a boat, and the satisfied smirk tells us she's looking forward to blowing up the President.

Villainess

Alex's first encounter with the assassin comes while scouting out a national park the President is due to attend. Nina deliberately bumps into the heroine and gives her a smile. It's the audacity that elevates the villainess to legendary status.

This woman enjoys living dangerously. The technician flirting with Nina doesn't know he's given a deadly assassin access to the park's sky tram system. As Evan overrides the security, Nina plays the seductress with her brother and toys with his emotions. To her, manipulation is second nature.

Alex is up against it, especially with the crazed militiaman threat to deal with and a traitor on her team.

The man Nina killed on the yacht took photos without her knowledge, but the inside man replaced the incriminating picture to throw Alex off the trail. When the President gives his speech in the park, Nina takes position on a rooftop and prepares her rifle. The killer has a clear shot at the target area, and the sky tram is under Evan's control. So, the President is an easy target once he's on board and isolated from his Secret Service detail.

Fortunately, Alex remembers Nina from earlier and identifies her as the shooter. The heroine has help from her boyfriend Grant (Doug Savant), who's spent most of the movie planning to propose to Alex. Now he gets to play the hero. While Alex and the rookie agent deal with the male villains, it's Grant's job to take on Nina. His surprise attack knocks off her aim, which results in a harmless mid-air explosion and one *really* pissed-off female assassin.

The dramatic fight that follows appears to be formulaic, with Grant given a hard lesson in kickboxing by Nina. In most movies, he'd emerge the unlikely victor, but the confident Nina remains in full control. She counters every move and finishes with a spinning kick. A fantastic slow-motion takedown ends with Grant falling off the roof, much to Nina's delight. He survives, but won't be involved in the action any further.

Alex is the only person who can stop Nina from completing her contract. The assassin swaps out her rifle for a conventional submachine gun, but Alex gets the President to safety. After a three-way tussle between the heroine, the President and the traitor, Nina has a free shot at her target. That's when the rookie proves her worth (of course) and guns down the assassin. Martial arts aren't much protection against bullets.

Honourable Mention: Sniper Assassins

Sniper: Assassin's End (2020) – Lady Death (Sayaka Akimoto)

Another movie with a sniper / martial artist villainess. This entry in the long-running *Sniper* series has Brandon Beckett (Chad Michael Collins) team up with his veteran father, Thomas (Tom Berenger) to uncover a corporate conspiracy.

The pre-title sequence establishes Lady Death as a mysterious and lethally efficient killer. In a stylish scene, she assassinates a South American politician from a hotel miles away. Before firing, the female sniper plants hair and saliva to frame Brandon as the shooter. The secondary plan is to stage his suicide, but the authorities arrest him before Lady Death gets there.

The assassin's employer is annoyed, so he hires mercenaries to attack the prisoner convoy. Lady Death is backup and proves far more effective at killing the security personnel. Even with her fire support, the villains still mess up and Brandon escapes. Lady Death is an exceptional operative who avoids loose ends, so why did the head villain waste his money on incompetent thugs?

Beckett gets help from a mysterious government agent known as Zero (Ryan Robbins) and a female analyst. They don't believe the obvious story and uncover a plot to make money from a trade deal. The story and lead villain are dull, leaving Lady Death to inject some welcome action and excitement.

The highlight is a sniper duel in the forest. Government operatives are little more than cannon fodder, but the father and son team is a match for the former Yakuza assassin. After a standoff in the woods with the snipers scoping their targets, shots are exchanged and Brandon gets the drop on the villainess.

She dumps her camouflage for more practical clothing (a tight-fitting black outfit) and fights the hero with martial arts and blades on ropes. It's a lengthy contest, much better than the usual half-minute affair. It takes the father aiming a sniper rifle at Lady Death's head to force her to surrender.

That's about it for major scenes. Now in custody, Lady Death cooperates with Zero and the Becketts to bring down the main villain. She pretends to capture the hero, but the bad guy doesn't fall for it, and the redeemed sniper gets shot for her betrayal. Thankfully, Lady Death survives, and the last scene has Zero recruit her for a special ops unit.

Rank #26

Double Indemnity (1944)
Phyllis Dietrichson (Barbara Stanwyck)

Movie

My original list didn't include films made before the 1960s, mainly because of personal preference. Plus, the black and white era is more dialogue-heavy. However, when said dialogue is well written it becomes timeless, and Barbara Stanwyck's scheming femme fatale – perhaps *the* classic film noir villainess – more than merits her place among the legends.

Double Indemnity was produced during World War II, but set in 1930s Los Angeles. The main character is insurance salesman Walter Neff (Fred MacMurray). The story is told in flashback, and since we see a wounded Neff record a confession on a dictaphone (no tape recorders back then), we know it won't end well. Some advice: getting involved with a beautiful woman who plans to murder her husband is a bad idea.

From the moment Phyllis Dietrichson appears on her upstairs landing, it's obvious she's trouble personified. Seduction was family-friendly in this era, long before nudity and steamy sex became the norm. Instead, we get suggestive comments about Phyllis' anklet and sizzling dialogue laden with double entendres. Friendly conversation, but it's not long before Neff returns and the woman enquires about accident insurance. He quickly deduces what Phyllis has in mind, but it's her way of testing his intelligence. After he thinks it over, he's on board with the deadly scheme.

Neff has the husband sign a policy document without his knowledge, by deceiving him into thinking he's buying automobile insurance. The policy comes with a double indemnity clause – an increased payout for more unlikely accidents – so Neff and Phyllis arrange for their victim to travel by train. As an insider, Neff is careful to create suitable alibis and witnesses and avoid obvious traps. The scheming duo meet in a convenience store to discuss their plans, and the setup seems perfect after the husband injures his leg.

The chief obstacle to the culprits getting away with the murder is Barton Keyes (Edward G. Robinson), a dogged claims investigator who verifies every detail. Long before Columbo found little things wrong with "perfect" schemes, there was this man. By the time Neff learns Phyllis may have also killed her previous husband, it's already too late. He's about to learn the hard way that a beautiful woman means trouble.

Villainess

With the groundwork laid, Neff hides in the back seat of Dietrichson's car while she drives her husband to the train station. After Phyllis beeps the horn – a pre-arranged signal – Neff does the dirty deed. The murder occurs off-screen with only an anguished cry to hint at what takes place, but this is beneficial as we see Phyllis in close-up. Watching her smirk in silence is far more chilling than any 1940s cinema death could be.

The next ten minutes are devoted to Neff staging an

accident. Many things go wrong with the plan, notably a witness on the rear carriage platform. Neff gets rid of the man by asking for a cigarette, whilst concealing his face from view. With the coast clear, he jumps and meets up with Phyllis. They place the body and his crutches on the tracks and get away after *another* scare where the car engine won't start.

The scheme and convincing act fool Keyes, and the company is prepared to pay out after suicide is dismissed as a possibility. Then the investigator finds the key flaw: that the injured Dietrichson didn't claim for the accident where he broke his leg. Keyes discusses this with a worried Neff, which leads to a tense moment as Phyllis hides behind the apartment door. Keyes soon locates the witness who testifies that the man on the train was much younger than the husband. That's when the lies unravel.

Neff learns some disturbing information from Dietrichson's daughter, and her boyfriend is the perfect fall guy. Phyllis makes it clear she'll drag Neff down with her, and there's no option for him to back out. Now the villainess shows her true evil – a woman without remorse who'll do anything to escape justice.

Neff foolishly confronts Phyllis at her house. This leads to a scene where she switches off the lights and lights a cigarette in the dark. Even though, or perhaps because, the film is black and white, this creates the perfect ambiance for a double cross. It's obvious Phyllis will shoot Neff because we know he ends up injured. Neither the gunshot nor the wound is shown, and the question of what happens to Phyllis is resolved when Neff fatally wounds her with the same gun.

Soon after that, Keyes arrives to hear the end of Neff's confession. Walter tries to escape, but dies before he reaches the office elevator. One last victim of the conniving femme fatale.

Honourable Mention: Femme Fatales

Body Heat (1981) – Matty Walker (Kathleen Turner)

Supposedly inspired by *Double Indemnity*, this is a steamy 1980s thriller with added sex and nudity. It's a triumph of style over substance, with clever camera angles but a rather basic story. Turner makes a great femme fatale in her film debut, alongside William Hurt as South Florida lawyer Ned Racine.

Heat is a prominent theme, and the sweltering conditions are a good excuse to have the two leading stars naked. When Ned meets Matty in a supposedly chance encounter (genre-savvy viewers will know it isn't), they quickly get involved. After a few sweaty nights in bed and cooling off with ice in a bathtub, the lovers plot to murder Matty's husband, Edmund (Richard Crenna). A name actor, but it's a cameo role before Ned whacks him over the head and sets up a staged arson gone wrong.

We're halfway into the film, but the post-murder section is where the double-crossing Matty shows her devious and deadly nature. Racine is incompetent, so the villainess forges a will in his name with a deliberate legal mistake that means the spouse gets the entire inheritance. Matty's greed tips off Ned's colleague and detective friend, and they dig into the supposed accidental death.

Matty concocts a crafty scheme where she assumes the identity of a high school classmate, stages her own death, and lets Ned take the fall. By 1981, it was acceptable for a femme fatale to get away with murder, and this villainess was always going to outsmart her dumb patsy. A solid film overall, but no standout moments.

Rank #25

Betrayal (2003)
Jayne Ferré (Julie du Page)

Movie

Director Mark L. Lester's contribution to female villainy is outstanding. Two movies and their respective antagonists make the legendary tier. As a bonus, the third film gets an honourable mention. For plot, the three movies are totally generic, but the female villains don't disappoint and all have at least one great kill scene. *Betrayal* is also known as *Lady Jayne Killer*, a much better title. When you have a fantastic villainess, why not make her your selling point?

Jayne is a mob hitwoman who doesn't believe in loose ends. This becomes clear early on when she kills an undercover FBI agent and a mafia man because he betrayed her boss. Jayne's calling card is to stuff luxury women's underwear into her victims' mouths. A unique MO, but contract killing pays well, and given her kill count, she can afford the expense.

Other characters are nowhere near as interesting. A generic mob boss, a corrupt police officer (there has to be one), a bland undercover agent, and a single mother and teenage son who get caught up in things. The kid Kerry (Jer Adrianne Lelliott) deals cocaine to help his mother Emily (Erika Eleniak) pay her bills. A bad idea, since a rival gang steals the drugs and their house gets shot up in retaliation.

This is an excuse for Emily and Kerry to go on a road trip. Unfortunately, they offer a certain female assassin in a leopard-skin top a ride, not knowing she has stolen a suitcase of mob money. Jayne has dropped two more bodies by this point. The first is another signature kill: a naked man tied up in a hotel room, gagged with panties, and shot in the head with a silenced pistol. The second murder is far less elaborate, where she stabs a thug to evade capture at a train station.

With the mafia in pursuit, things are sure to get hot again, though there's a lengthy "cooling off" period with little action. This makes the middle third of the movie a chore to sit through. The ending is a lot livelier, even if Emily turns into an unlikely heroine who can best a trained killer in combat.

Villainess

The deceptive villainess claims to be an actress, but that falls apart under Kerry's questioning. So Jayne tells the truth – she's a hitwoman with over twenty kills – while making it sound implausible. Emily and her son laugh this off, but when Jayne confronts another motorist and smashes his side window with her bare hand, it really should be obvious this woman is psycho. There's also a trucker she threatens to ramp up the tension while we're waiting for the mafia's arrival.

When the hitwoman isn't scaring people, she practices seduction on Kerry. At a diner, Jayne speaks openly about fondling breasts while Emily has stepped away. The mother returns in time to stop the conversation and save Kerry's blushes. That doesn't stop him fantasising about sex with the beautiful assassin in a shower, but he's brought back to the real world when he discovers the money in Jayne's motel room.

Realising he's in danger yet has the answer to Emily's financial problems, Kerry makes off with the briefcase. Jayne is really ticked off and drops the innocent traveller act. Emily barely has time to react to the assassin holding her at gunpoint before the mafia show up at the motel. In the shootout, Jayne easily outsmarts her opponents, playing dead to gain the advantage and using cover effectively. One guy takes Emily as a human shield, but she escapes, leaving Jayne a free kill shot.

The villainess abducts Emily (she's used to it by now) and uses her as leverage to recover the stolen money. Emily grabs the wheel of Jayne's car and escapes, helped by the fact that she's too valuable to kill. This doesn't bother the hitwoman. Jayne simply gloats about murdering Kerry now that she knows where he and Emily live.

Kerry hides the case in the laundry room and calls the authorities. Naturally, the man he speaks to is the corrupt cop on the mob boss' payroll. Meanwhile, Emily is picked up by Jayne's contact. Putting aside all the coincidences, it's time all the key players met. The detective and mafia head visit Kerry's house, but he sees through their lies. Soon after that, Jayne arrives and finishes the men easily. Being a major character in this film just means you last longer than usual.

It's Kerry's turn to be the bargaining chip, and Jayne demands Emily bring her the money for her son's life. Pity the assassin didn't search the house, eh? The final showdown is a letdown, though better than *White Rush* (below). Emily – with the mystery man at gunpoint – brings the briefcase to a secluded industrial site. Here, the guy reveals he really *is* an undercover FBI agent, then throws the money in Jayne's face and pulls a gun.

There's a somewhat chaotic scuffle where everyone

teams up on the assassin. This leads into a catfight where Emily proves resilient and breaks free of a chokehold with a headbutt. Then she shoots Jayne, who falls back onto a convenient sharp piece of metal.

Honourable Mention: Criminal Hitwomen

White Rush (2003) – Solange (Sandra Vidal)

A movie directed by Mark L. Lester, released in 2003, that features a sexy hitwoman as the antagonist. Plus Tom Wright as a detective and Louis Mandylor as a bad guy. There must be a script template for B-grade action films, because *White Rush* is *very* similar to *Betrayal*. Sadly, the assassin lacks Jayne's style. While she has her moments – notably a brilliant seduction kill in a hot tub – the ending is mediocre.

A group of friends out camping stumble across a drug deal gone bad. That's when they get greedy and decide to make money selling narcotics. The leader is a corrupt cop who lives the high life, threatens people, and does side deals with criminal gangs. Everybody except the sensible Eva (Tricia Helfer of *Battlestar Galactica* fame) goes along with the dangerous scheme. Smart move on her part, as the Cartel boss sends in the beautiful and deadly Solange, who is a sicario (an example-setter).

Most of what follows is tired, and the victims' stupidity and selfishness will have the audience rooting for Solange. To prove how sadistic she is, the assassin kills a minor character even after he helps her. The first main kill is the best, with Solange using her feminine attributes to get close to a guy, lure him to a secluded location, and slit his throat. This outstanding sequence gives new meaning to the word bloodbath, but the standard drops afterward.

Cue panic among the drug dealer wannabes as the lethal assassin thins their ranks. She threatens an undercover cop, who's smart enough to bargain for his life. The next victim is a woman who surprises Solange with a knockdown, but stupidly traps herself in a room. Walls don't stop bullets, love. This all leads to a showdown at a refinery, where Solange arms herself with a sniper rifle. However, the expected shootout never materialises, and the hitwoman is defeated all too easily.

Rank #24

Gone Girl (2014)
Amy Dunne (Rosamund Pike)

Movie

Spoiler alert, though including Amy on my list already gave it away. A film best known for its plot twist, the reveal is unusual because it comes at the midpoint. Savvy viewers – especially those familiar with the unreliable narrator trick – will guess the twist before it happens, but what follows is unpredictable and gripping. The screenwriter Gillian Flynn wrote the novel on which the film is based, so we get the same two-part structure: a mystery for the first half and a suspense thriller for the second.

The story revolves around the disappearance of Amy Dunne, wife of Nick (Ben Affleck). On finding signs of a disturbance at his Missouri home, the concerned husband calls the cops. But when the evidence suggests a staged crime scene, he finds himself suspected of murder. His wife set up an anniversary treasure hunt, and following the clues leads to more incriminating finds.

Amy was the inspiration for the children's book character "Amazing Amy", so the case garners widespread media attention and puts Nick in the spotlight. He's heavily in debt (though he doesn't seem to know about this), which gives him a motive. With the police suspicious, Nick's only ally is his twin sister Margo (Carrie Coon).

As the story unfolds, Amy recites passages from her diary in flashbacks. These cover her first meeting with Nick, their marriage, and the happy early years. After Nick's mother is diagnosed with terminal cancer and the couple moves away from New York, Amy's story takes a dark turn. A victim of physical domestic abuse, she fears for her life. When the police discover the partially burned diary in a basement furnace, the case against Nick is even more compelling.

At a vigil for the missing Amy, her friend drops the bombshell that the missing woman is pregnant, and the media frenzy intensifies. The film is a commentary on television and celebrity obsession, with news reports appearing prominently throughout the story. Ultimately, we find out Amy is a scheming liar who staged her own murder to gain revenge on Nick for having an affair. That part is true, so Nick is no saint, even if he married a twisted psycho and a sizeable portion of what Amy wrote is pure fiction.

Villainess

When Amy narrates her wicked scheme, and the clock rewinds to the day of her disappearance, it's a five minute long mixture of confession and hatred. The villainess talks about her plan as if it's commonplace to frame someone for murder and get them the death penalty. Amy discusses faking her pregnancy, leaving washed blood at the house to implicate her husband, and preparing to kill herself when it's over. The whole setup could be described as a "how-to" book for budding psychopaths.

When Nick realises how dire the situation is, he hires high-profile defence attorney Tanner Bolt (Tyler Perry) and works with his sister to expose Amy. Nick visits other men in her life, including one guy she framed for rape and another who still loves her. His mistake will come back to haunt him soon enough. It seems setting people up is second nature to Amy, and nobody knows where she is.

By now, the villainess has changed her appearance and gone into hiding in a rural area. She has plenty of cash, but like all cocky killers, she makes a mistake and reveals her money bag to a couple of local drifters. The two criminals rob Amy, and she's forced to amend her carefully planned scheme. Time to woo old lover Desi (Neil Patrick Harris) and convince him to be her partner.

The guy should have listened to Nick, because Amy frames him too. After the persecuted husband appeals to his wife on TV, she decides Desi is a liability. So, Amy fakes rope marks on her wrists and puts on a feigned horror show for the CCTV cameras. With the stage set, she seduces Desi and slits his throat with a box cutter. Sorry, pal – you're just the latest sucker.

Things look bad for Nick when police discover the "murder" weapon and charge him with the crime. He's barely out on bail when the blood-smeared Amy returns home and falls into his less than welcome arms. She recites a sob story about Desi kidnapping her and blames the cops for arresting her husband. The authorities are happy to believe her version of events, if only to close the case and put an end to media scrutiny. As for Nick, Tanner abandons him and leaves the couple to their own devices. It's a fake marriage that breaks Margo's heart, but the lawyer calls it right: Nick and Amy deserve each other.

Honourable Mention: Treacherous Wives

Shattered (1991) – Judith Merrick (Greta Scacchi)

Another film with a treacherous wife (spoiler alert!), this 1990s thriller mixes a standard amnesia plot with enough twists to keep the story original and compelling. Dan Merrick (Tom Berenger) wakes up after a car accident and lengthy coma, but can only remember general details and nothing personal. Following extensive plastic surgery to reconstruct his damaged face, he returns home to his loving wife Judith.

However, a mix of troubling flashbacks and information from his business partner, Jeb (Corbin Bernsen), leads Dan to suspect something is amiss. After he discovers Judith was having an affair with a man named Stanton, who hired private investigator Gus Klein (Bob Hoskins), it appears the car accident may have been attempted murder.

Things get even more mysterious when Dan and Gus observe Judith meet Stanton at a remote hotel, only to get shot at and nearly have a fatal road accident themselves. Then "Stanton" shows up at Dan's house, and it's revealed "he" is Judith in disguise. The villainess tells her husband that he's a murderer. They hid Stanton's body in a shipwreck, and she's been covering for him ever since.

Someone fatally stabs Jeb's wife, Jenny (who *Dan* was having an affair with) when she gets too close to the truth. Keeping up with this? The biggest twist comes when Dan examines the body – preserved in formaldehyde – and finds it's actually... well, himself.

Dan is really Stanton, and Judith killed the real Merrick. The wife goes psycho, shoots Gus and takes Dan... er, Stanton on a car ride. Judith disappoints as a villainess since the first murder was self-defence, but she's still a lunatic responsible for killing Jenny. The murderer gets all crazy and suicidal, and Stanton bails just before she drives over a cliff. Another car accident, only this time it's Judith who goes up in flames.

Rank #23

Misery (1990)
Annie Wilkes (Kathy Bates)

Movie

This adaptation of Stephen King's novel earned Kathy Bates an Academy Award for her portrayal, which took obsessed fandom to a new level. It's essentially a "can he escape?" story with the main character trapped in a remote house with the villainess. The movie captures the claustrophobic feel, with limited locations and camera angles from the captive's point of view.

As the film begins, Paul Sheldon (James Caan), author of the popular *Misery* romance series, finishes an untitled manuscript and travels from Colorado to New York. Perhaps he should have waited for the blizzard to pass. Instead, he winds up in an accident and loses consciousness.

When Paul comes to, he has serious leg injuries and is under the care of Annie Wilkes, a former nurse who lives alone on a farm. Paul is grateful for Annie's help, but things become tense when his rescuer shows a deeply religious attitude towards profanity. She's also named her pig after the *Misery* character – think she might be crazy? Paul figures as much, and since Annie reads the unpublished work, maybe he ought to be worried he's killed off the fictional hero she adores so much.

Yeah, Annie doesn't take that well at all. In fact, she screams abuse at Paul – in a brilliantly insane and scary way – and revels in her deception that she never phoned for help. The victim tries to escape, but can only crawl a short distance, and the locked door is a seemingly impassable obstacle. To ensure Paul stays focused (at God's behest, apparently), Annie has him burn his manuscript on a portable barbecue.

Paul's agent (Lauren Bacall) is now concerned and asks the local sheriff to search for the missing writer. His investigation becomes a subplot that unfolds in parallel. After initial questions turn up no leads, the authorities locate the car wreckage and assume the worst, but the sheriff doesn't believe Paul is dead. Still trapped with the deranged Annie, help from the outside world may be his only hope of survival.

Villainess

Annie brings Paul a second-hand typewriter, sets up a writing studio, and demands he resurrect Misery in a reworked novel. Understandably, he doesn't share her enthusiasm, but he notices a hairpin on the floor. To get Annie out of the house, Paul tells a convincing lie: he needs special writing paper to avoid smudging. She gives him a piece (or several pieces) of her mind before leaving for town, but once she's gone, Paul fashions a makeshift lock pick.

The daring escape plan works, but he's still trapped in the house. In a wheelchair, Paul's movement is limited, but he discovers a *Misery* shrine with the novels lined up behind a picture of himself. Too bad the phone is a useless prop with the mechanism removed. Yes, the kidnapper really is nuts, and there's no way to call for help. Realising he's alone, Paul finds Annie's stockpile of sleeping pills, secretes a packet, and returns to his room.

Paul uses the few tools available, and plans to turn the tables on Annie during an evening meal. Having emptied the pills into a paper sachet, he proposes a toast and insists on drinking wine by candlelight. Paul drugs Annie's drink, but she spills it and foils the plan. With no other viable strategy, he works on the novel and waits for another opportunity.

When Annie leaves the house again, Paul looks around. He arms himself with a kitchen knife and finds a scrapbook of news clippings about his captor's past. Seems she was a nurse whose infant patients died, and she was put on trial (as if we needed any evidence of psychosis). Paul stows the knife and returns to his room, now ready for violence. Eventually he drifts off, only to find Annie standing over the bed with a syringe of morphine when he wakes.

She knew of Paul's escape because he accidentally knocked over a ceramic penguin and put it back the wrong way. The fussy woman noticed and discovered Paul's hairpin and knife (and likely spilled the wine on purpose). To dissuade any further breakouts, Annie hobbles Paul. Tat translates as breaking both his ankles with a sledgehammer in a graphic scene that often makes "top scary movie moments" lists.

Away from the torture, the sheriff reviews news archives and connects a quote to something Annie said at her trial. He follows up with a visit to the Wilkes farm, but Annie sedates Paul and dumps him in the basement, while spinning a convincing yarn that she's a harmless devotee. The sheriff thinks he made a mistake until he hears Paul's muffled cries for help. Annie kills the nosy sheriff with a shotgun blast to the back and informs her despondent prisoner that she's loaded a revolver with two bullets. The intent is clear.

Paul – realising he will only get one more chance – finishes the manuscript and demands his customary cigarette and champagne. When Annie leaves, he douses the pages in lighter fluid (which he found in the basement) and sets them alight. This enrages the villainess, and Paul strikes the distracted woman's head with the typewriter. That's not enough to kill her, so we get a drag-out fight – during which the gun goes off and wounds Paul – that ends with Annie banging her head.

Just when Paul thinks it's over, the villainess launches a surprise attack. After a struggle, Paul grabs an ornament and bludgeons Annie, finishing her for good. Upon his return to New York, Paul has lunch with his agent. He sees the psycho wheel a serving tray towards him, but this turns out to be a hallucination. Of a waitress who tells Paul she's his number one fan.

Honourable Mention: Stephen King

Carrie (1976) – Margaret White (Piper Laurie), Chris Hargensen (Nancy Allen)

This is the adaptation that started it all, based on King's first published novel. Now considered a classic, *Carrie* has spawned a sequel and several remakes, but the original is the most loved and acclaimed. It features several prominent stars in early appearances, notably Nancy Allen, John Travolta, and a breakout role for Sissy Spacek.

The title character is a schoolgirl tormented by her classmates, a group of mean girls led by the sadistic Chris Hargensen. Carrie is an oddball who doesn't fit in because of a tyrannical upbringing by her religious mother. Margaret beats her daughter, forces her to recite passages from the Bible, and locks her in a prayer closet to atone for her sins (anything she can think of, basically).

Carrie smashes an ashtray – the first sign of telekinetic powers. Eager to find out more, she reads up on the phenomenon and learns to amplify and control her abilities. Most of the movie is a slow burner as Chris plots revenge for a detention she blames Carrie for, and a repentant student convinces her boyfriend to invite the outcast to the school prom. That's the big event the film is known for, which makes the final twenty minutes worth the wait.

Thanks to a pretty homemade dress and a rigged contest, Carrie gets voted prom queen and receives applause from those present. However, it's a prank planned by Chris, who drops a bucket of pig blood on Carrie while she celebrates on stage. Terrible mistake, because now this girl is *really* upset.

A powered-up Carrie slams the doors, sprays the crowd with water, and electrocutes them. Nobody escapes her wrath, not even the sympathetic gym teacher, who was genuinely happy and supportive. Many kills are off screen, but the carnage is clear from the burning school Carrie leaves behind.

With the main cast almost wiped out, Chris and her boyfriend – lucky to escape – attempt to run Carrie over. A stupid move against a psychic, who flips the car over by concentrating. Margaret White – convinced her daughter is a witch – stabs her, only to be impaled by flying objects and crucified. Despite the prom bloodbath, it's easy to feel sympathy for Carrie as the house collapses. Margaret and Chris are the true villains in this story.

The Hand That Rocks the Cradle (1992)
Peyton / Mrs. Mott (Rebecca De Mornay)

Movie

A story recycled dozens of times: a nanny with ulterior motives worms her way into an overly trusting suburban family. This will surely sound familiar, but a strong actress can elevate a film above the mediocre competition, and Rebecca De Mornay delivers the goods as the scheming Peyton Flanders.

Before she employs the nanny from hell, Claire Bartel (Annabella Sciorra) reports a sexual assault during a medical examination. More allegations by other women follow, and the not so good Dr Mott commits suicide to avoid facing justice. Why is this important? Because the nanny is Mrs Mott, a revenge-seeking widow out to ruin the lives of Claire, her husband Michael (Matt McCoy), and her daughter Emma (Madeline Zima). And since Mott had a miscarriage, she sees herself as the true mother of baby Joey.

Like many movie families, Claire and Michael don't do a background check, though Peyton – as she now calls herself – is charmingly sweet. One person the villainess doesn't fool is Solomon (Ernie Hudson), a mentally ill handyman whose curiosity might shorten his life expectancy.

The first two acts are slow going, with the psychotic

nanny undermining family relationships and playing people against each other. Peyton wanders the house at night and breast-feeds Joey, which leads to odd behaviour that Claire can't understand. The villainess develops a false friendship with Emma, lets her watch horror movies in secret, and uses their alone time to manipulate the young girl.

Peyton threatens a child who bullies Emma, scaring him witless. The villainess also steals a document from Claire's handbag to undermine Michael's standing with his employer. Rather than simply throwing the paperwork away, she rips it up and smashes a toilet cubicle with a plunger. The rage is building, ready to be unleashed, and this is one film where the climax is *not* disappointing.

Villainess

The villainess is more effective than most copycats. There are no suspicious deaths until late on, and few reasons for the Martels to be wary. Peyton is a conniving woman who twists facts and plants seeds of doubt. She tells Emma to keep their movie watching secret and convinces Claire that her daughter is hiding something more sinister. The villainess arranges a surprise party and meets Michael at unusual times and locations. Then she plants evidence to insinuate an affair with family friend Marlene (Julianne Moore).

Peyton's plan unravels when Solomon sees her breast feed while cleaning an upstairs window. She threatens him into silence and mocks his mental condition just to remind us she's evil. This is a tactic to buy time while she figures out a more permanent solution. Surprisingly, this doesn't involve murder. Peyton plants Emma's underwear in Solomon's cart and tells Claire he's been acting strangely, which is enough to frame him for child molestation.

Alone with the family, Peyton overhears Claire suggest a holiday to smooth things over with Michael. The villainess sets a trap in the garden greenhouse so that entering will cause the swinging glass roof panels to shatter. Her deadly setup is intended for Claire, but Marlene discovers the wind chimes are from Mrs Mott's former house. The stupid friend confronts the nanny and dies by raining glass shards.

Expecting Claire to have an asthma attack when she discovers the body, the villainess sabotages every inhaler in the house and takes the baby out for a stroll. The plan almost works, but paramedics arrive in time. After a lengthy stay in hospital, the suspicious heroine follows up a note from Marlene, a clue that leads her to the old Mott residence. When she realises the decor matches her baby's room, Claire deduces the nanny's true identity, and finding a breast pump confirms it.

Michael and Claire fire Peyton, but no psycho villainess of merit is dealt with so easily. The crazed widow returns and attacks Michael, ruling him out of the chase that follows. Emma outsmarts the killer and protects Joey by using the baby monitor as a distraction, which leads to an attic confrontation. Fortunately, Solomon has been watching Emma and is on site to help the family.

Before the poker-wielding Peyton can snatch Joey, Claire comes upstairs armed with a kitchen knife. It's a makeshift weapon duel, and soon the asthmatic is on the floor and out of breath. Peyton taunts her, but Claire – who faked the attack – surprises the psycho when she turns to deal with Solomon. The rush attack sends the villainess flying through the window... onto a picket fence below.

Honourable Mentions: Psycho Nannies

The Sitter (2007) – Abigail Reed (Mariana Klaveno)

One of many psycho-nanny clones, this formulaic thriller has a couple of plus points. The director is Russell Mulcahy, whose credits include *Highlander* (1986) and *The Real McCoy* (1993), so the action scenes are well shot with stunt sequences superior to most TV movies. And the performance by Mariana Klaveno brings a threatening presence. Just as well, because the story is strictly by the numbers.

A nanny with a traumatic past is hired by Carter and Meghan Eastman (William R. Moses and Gail O'Grady). Except she plans to dispose of the wife to have the man all to herself. Her motive is a mystery until the end, but ultimately it's lacklustre. Abigail fell in love with Carter when he worked as an attorney on her abusive mother's trial. Hardly riveting, so it's left to Klaveno to stare insanely and act over the top to maintain the tension.

Standout psycho moments include Abby threatening a school bully and a striptease to seduce the neighbour's teenage son. Just for the hell of it. Victims are obvious the moment they walk on screen. Carter's business partner gets a shovel in the neck after he flirts with Abby at a house party. The nosy neighbour gets a late-night visit and a stereo in her bathtub, and the best friend exists for one last kill before Abby reveals her true intentions.

That murder is well done for the genre. The psycho suffocates her victim with a plastic bag and snaps her neck. After that, the viewer expects a showdown and perhaps a catfight, but Abby is killed easily with a pair of scissors. Restrictions on TV movie runtime may have resulted in a rushed and unsatisfying wrap-up. Abby returns from near death, only to get stabbed again and collapse on the stairs. Then the credits roll and… that's it.

Devious Nanny (2018) (aka *The Nanny Betrayal*) – Elise (Michelle Borth)

A brief honourable mention for this twisty variation on a tired theme, the story starts out on a familiar path when a loving couple hire a nanny called Amber (Olesya Rulin), who turns out to have a mysterious past. But that's a red herring because the wife, Elise, is the woman responsible for the recent murder spree.

Sourcing Lifetime movies in the UK can be difficult, and those that are shown on afternoon TV are usually edited for content. Fortunately, there's always Marvista Entertainment whose spoiler-heavy trailers often sum up the entire movie, reducing 90 minutes to 90 seconds. The official trailer is no longer available on the official site, but can be found on YouTube or video archives.

Everything is included: the setup, characters, key plot developments, and yes… even the final act plot twist that reveals the true murderess and her bizarre motive. Killing people is justified to keep a family together, apparently.

Rank #21

The Ex (1997)
Deidre Kenyon (Yancy Butler)

Movie

The second film directed by Mark L. Lester to rank in the legendary tier, this movie shows a great villainess can overcome the burdens of a simple plot. Especially since Yancy Butler's psychotic Diedre gets as much – if not more – screen time than the protagonist David Kenyon (Nick Mancuso). He's another guy who made the mistake of marrying (and later divorcing) a murderous lunatic.

From the opening scene where Deidre stalks David's wife Molly (Suzy Amis) and child Michael (Hamish Tildesley), it's clear where the story is going. The villainess gives us a cold-eyed stare as she watches her prey drive away. These generic psycho moments happen a lot, as do montages of Deidre working out with weights. This is a woman who likes to show off her strength when she murders minor characters.

Deidre still has feelings for David and turns up at his workplace one day. As expected, he's not happy to see his psycho ex-wife, but goes out for a meal. Deidre grips his hand tightly and makes a big deal of him turning around for one last look as he leaves. Still, this counts as rejection, so when another married guy comes onto Deidre, she has sex and drowns him in a bathtub. There's only one man this villainess wants – everyone else is expendable.

It's no surprise a woman with these issues has a psychiatrist, and Deidre impersonates Dr Lillian Jonas (Babs Chula) to get close to Molly. After small talk at the local gym, the psycho accompanies the unsuspecting woman and her son on a riverboat trip. Deidre contemplates throwing the boy into a waterwheel until his mother returns, forcing a warm and friendly act. Time to "introduce" herself to David, who goes along with the cover story and pretends he doesn't know his ex.

If the villainess' plan is to push David over the edge, it works because he shows up at her hotel and threatens her. Being a psycho, Deidre enjoys this and even stands in an open window daring her ex to push her. To add extra spice, the villainess claims she killed her sister, whom the younger David was in love with. David doesn't believe it, but flashbacks of the murderess drowning the girl tell us otherwise.

David becomes increasingly stressed and shows his dark side by getting rough with Molly in bed – to the point she's truly scared. Deidre is out for revenge, and she's just getting started.

Villainess

Determined to destroy David's life, the villainess makes a false rape allegation to Molly. Deidre backs up her claim by describing a birthmark, but the husband comes clean and reconciles with his wife. The ex has other ideas and murders an unfortunate female tenant with a crowbar. She follows the kill with a cheesy postmortem line about a lease being terminated. This gives her access to an apartment across the street from her target's place, and a perfect vantage point.

Dr Jonas confronts Deidre about her sister's suspicious death. Talking to a suspected murderer alone is a surefire way to get yourself iced, but the doc evidently hasn't watched too many made for cable thrillers. This intervention gives the villainess the excuse to drown a second minor character in a bathtub. And say another psycho one-liner. This is becoming a habit.

David asks his attorney for help, but Deidre turns the tables by showing the lawyer an old video of rough sex to make her ex appear the aggressor. The psycho makes sexual advances to David when he visits her new apartment and allows herself to be seen by Molly. Not content with destroying a marriage, Deidre visits a rough part of town in disguise and pays a guy to beat her up. This frames David for domestic violence, a story the cops are ready to believe.

With him out of the picture, Deidre breaks into his apartment (she copied the key earlier) and tracks Molly and Michael to a cabin. Just the spot for a finale, where the villainess knocks out Molly with a fire poker. David – released on bail – shows up to confront his psycho ex, and only love for his new family prevents him from killing Deidre. The villainess attacks again, and is so busy taunting David for letting her live she doesn't notice Michael step up behind her with a flaming log.

Yes, the kid gets to be the surprise hero, and we're treated to a lengthy scene of the psychotic Deidre ablaze. The log cabin burns down as the survivors watch from a safe distance.

Honourable Mentions: Yancy Butler / Drowning Kills

The Last Letter (2004) – Ms. Toney / Alicia Cromwell (Yancy Butler)

A thriller centred on a jury deliberating a verdict, with the twist that things aren't as they first seem. Jack Hamilton is on trial for murdering fourteen people, and there are flashbacks of nearly every killing. This ought to be a treat for villainess fans, given that the serial killer is female, but historic events have a sickly yellow tint and a second twist that puts everything in doubt.

Jury members don't seem to have been selected for their mental stability, which is at odds with the instruction that the verdict be impartial. For diversity, there's a racist, homophobic bigot who abuses the others, an ill man who can barely speak, and shy people afraid to speak up. Ms Toney offers little to the discussion but becomes more vocal when the foreman (William Forsythe) presents the evidence.

The methodical killer wears a wetsuit and cloth mask to avoid spreading their DNA. Thanks to the foreman's summary and crime scene photos, we learn the murderer is brazen enough to kill people in their own homes. They also slay an advertising executive at her office and a police detective. Other than a fire and two accidental deaths, the MO is to drain the victim's blood and paint a letter on their forehead. The foreman writes these on a whiteboard in a certain order, which gradually spells out a cryptic message.

After Hamilton commits suicide, Toney rants at the foreman, but mentions one victim was deaf. A mistake, as this information was never made public. The other jurors then reveal the truth. They are all police officers, and the entire trial – plus the arrest and suicide – was staged to trap the murderess, Ms Toney aka Alicia Cromwell. The foreman is Dr Markley, a criminal psychologist hired as a consultant. This explains his obsession with profiling the killer and the stereotyped jury.

Cromwell murdered four people in London, which gives sixteen alphabet letters. Markley speculates the last letter is Y, and the message is KILLER WAS ME O TONEY. However, the villainess grabs an officer's gun, scratches the letter G on her head, and blows her brains out. After the jurors leave, Markley discovers Toney has no scars on her body, which contradicts his theory of a struggle.

The doctor deduces the true anagram solution – ONE GAME TWO KILLERS – before an unknown person attacks him. With one of those annoying cliffhanger endings that will never be resolved, we're left wondering who the villainess actually killed.

Eisfieber (2010) – Daisy Mac (Anneke Kim Sarnau)

This honourable mention is covered here since its villainess also gets a memorable drowning scene. A two-part miniseries released as a movie, this thriller is set in Scotland at Christmas, a good excuse to feature medieval locations with a snowy backdrop.

My source is a German DVD release, but the familiar plot doesn't require translation. Scientists have developed a deadly virus in a "secure" lab, and terrorists devise a plan to steal it. One of them is a hacker who's overconfident until the blonde henchwoman Daisy teaches him a lesson in humility. She's not that tall or muscular, but still dunks the guy in a swimming pool and holds him underwater. Normally, that would herald a premature demise, but the hacker is essential to the heist. He emerges from the ordeal alive, though drenched and far more afraid.

The first part of *Eisfieber* is mainly padding, focusing on a family get-together where the hacker is also a guest. That gives him access to a scientist's keycard, so he works his techno magic and disables the lab security. Daisy wears a brunette wig for the raid, but is mostly a silent player while the villains disguise themselves as maintenance crew. This woman enjoys violence and takes out a security guard with a baton. A well-executed plan, until a road accident forces the terrorists to improvise and find shelter in the local mansion.

As the snowstorm intensifies, lead scientist Toni Gallo (Isabella Ferrari) tracks down the villains and teams up with two family members who escape. Toni gets to be the heroine, and the hacker swaps sides when things look bad for him. With the blizzard raging, no outside help is coming. The tech guy rejoins the villains (!) after a big scuffle with Daisy and everyone else in an all-out brawl. More hostages get away, leading to a shootout and frustration from the henchwoman.

Toni confronts the main villain and isn't afraid to use a gun. After Daisy has a disappointing non-confrontation with the escapees, they run the henchwoman over and leave her bleeding and cursing in the snow. The villain also ignores Daisy's cries and rides off with the hacker and the stolen virus. He should have followed the bad guy rulebook and executed her for failure, because the vengeful woman uses her last action to shoot the boss through the rear windscreen.

Rank #20

Basic Instinct (1992)
Catherine Tramell (Sharon Stone)

Movie

A familiar story: Michael Douglas gets involved with a dangerous woman. He ought to know better by now. His character this time is Nick Curran, a San Francisco detective with a dark side. *Basic Instinct* is a modern film noir, with sets designed for stylish camera angles and composition rather than authenticity. The 1990s were a golden age for erotic thrillers, so expect nudity, mystery, and plot twists.

The movie opens with – what else? – sex and murder, when a rock star is stabbed repeatedly by a naked blonde wielding an ice pick. Before the kill, the mysterious beauty ties his wrists to the bedposts with a silk scarf. If this sounds like fiction, that's because the MO is based on a novel by Catherine Tramell. As she was also the victim's boyfriend, the police have a prime suspect, and the key question is "Did she do it?"

The killer is clearly a woman, and other suspects include Roxy (Leilani Sarelle) – in a lesbian relationship with Catherine – and Dr Beth Garner (Jeanne Tripplehorn). She enjoys passionate sex and argues with Curran in her spare time. Against the constant backdrop of dangerous romance, Stone's character is the most mysterious. From her first appearance, where she rides with Curran and his partner Gus (George Dzundza), she toys with the police.

Next up is the infamous interview scene where Tramell crosses her legs in front of an all-male team of detectives. Are suspects allowed to smoke? It adds to the ambiance, anyway. The femme fatale passes a lie detector test, but she invents stories for a living. By this point, Curran is in deep and at odds with his fellow officers, someone whom Catherine can easily manipulate.

Villainess

Catherine researches Curran's background, allegedly to research her latest novel, where a detective dies at the end. When Curran learns Dr Garner gave his file to an internal affairs cop, an assault follows. Not long after that, the guy turns up with a bullet hole in his head. Then it's the detective in the hot seat being interviewed by his unsympathetic colleagues, with earlier dialogue repeated. Yes, Catherine has got well and truly under Curran's skin.

The relationship with Beth – if there was one – falls apart as the suspended detective gets dangerously close to the suspect. If conversations about an ice pick weren't provocative, the two have steamy sex and Catherine re-enacts the murder (minus the actual killing). Tension builds when someone tries to run Curran over. After a high-speed chase through the streets of San Francisco and a fatal crash, it's revealed to be Roxy behind the wheel. No surprise, given their earlier encounters, when she claimed Catherine was *her* girl.

The novelist grieves, though this is forgotten when she has more sex with her latest lover. Catherine rejects his suggestion that the fictional detective in her novel should live, saying someone has to die. Curran should probably take the hint (and Gus' advice) and get the hell away from this woman, but of course he doesn't. When it's revealed that Catherine spends time with convicted murderers and Beth is a former college acquaintance who changed her name, Curran has a new angle.

With Roxy dead, there are only two plausible suspects. When Curran and Gus meet an informant in a deserted office building, things are inevitably going to end badly. This murder occurs on screen, as a cloaked psycho armed with an ice pick attacks Gus. Curran races to the rescue, but arrives too late to save his partner. Beth shows up and reaches for something in her pocket. Not wise when a tense cop has a weapon trained on her, and he opens fire after Beth ignores his warnings.

Police find all the clues: an SFPD jacket, a blonde wig, an ice pick, the gun used to murder the internal affairs cop, and research on Catherine. The deceased Beth looks guilty, but she was nowhere near manipulative enough to be the true killer. Savvy viewers will expect a last-minute reveal, which comes with Curran and Catherine in bed. She reaches for an ice pick but doesn't use it. Is there something between them? Or is the murderess planning to frame someone else?

Honourable Mentions: Sharon Stone

Calendar Girl Murders (1984) – Cassie Bascomb (Sharon Stone)

Sharon Stone played a female villain early in her career, though this TV movie role had her billed behind Tom Skerritt as Lieutenant Dan Stoner. As the title suggests, calendar girl models are getting bumped off, and Stoner must identify the killer. Suspects include a crazy stalker, an ex-lover with gambling debts, and a shady magazine editor. Naturally, none of them did it, and the old principle of "the least suspicious major character is guilty" applies.

The DVD transfer of this 1980s thriller isn't great, with many dark scenes, including the first murder where Miss January is thrown from a balcony. Soon after that, Miss February (Claudia Christian in her movie debut) is stabbed in a kitchen, and the police are after a serial killer. The deaths are blood-free with no nudity, but the setting is an excuse to feature glamorous women in skimpy outfits.

The highlight is a water volleyball game at a luxury estate, where the killer arranges a blackout and almost drowns Miss March in the swimming pool. That's the most inventive part of this pedestrian affair, with little action in the second half. To keep the audience awake, there's a vehicle chase, and a witness ends up in hospital only for the black-gloved killer to see him off. Then it's a bad-tempered interview with the red-herring lover before the true culprit is revealed.

Cassie Bascomb is a former model and daughter of the editor, and revenge provides a flimsy motive for murder. She and Stoner have a romantic fling, a filler subplot that's a precursor to *Basic Instinct* without the raciness. In a slow-motion sequence that lasts a full minute, a sexy model in red spandex swings a fire axe on a garage movie set.

As for the anticlimax, Stoner's wife is a photographer who develops incriminating photos of the murderer. The detective interrupts Cassie before she kills the wife in a fake arson attack, and the suddenly repentant murderess breaks down in tears. It's impossible to make this sound any more exciting because it isn't.

Basic Instinct 2 (2006) – Catherine Tramell (Sharon Stone)

San Francisco is swapped for London in this sequel, where Catherine Tramell is again suspected of killing a celebrity lover. Instead of a detective, the femme fatale ensnares psychologist Dr Michael Glass (David Morrissey) in a game of cat and mouse.

Glass suspects Tramell but still ends up in a relationship, including a provocative scene where Catherine splits her legs while sitting on a chair. This time, the backrest hides the explicit parts of Sharon Stone's anatomy. Pretty soon, people in Glass' life die, including an inquisitive journalist and his ex-wife Denise. Catherine's latest novel is about a shrink, with the characters and events mirroring real life. Talk about recycling a plot.

As a result, everything feels tired, and while Stone does her best (and succeeds to some extent), the film is underwhelming. The resolution has Tramell manipulate Glass into shooting a police officer, and the trauma lands him in a mental institution. We're shown flashbacks of him committing the murders, but it's not clear whether he did or these are more lies spun by Catherine. Her smirk suggests she's a villainess, but this is another example where the original is better.

Rank #19

Hangman (2001)
Grace Mitchell (Mädchen Amick)

Movie

The underlying theme – a sadistic killer using the children's game to taunt the police – has been used many times. The guess the word puzzle is almost as common as chess, and nearly every movie that features it is called *Hangman*. To remove ambiguity, this film stars Lou Diamond Phillips as Lieutenant Nick Roos.

He caught the "Hangman Killer" several years back, leading to a rookie cop's death and an internal investigation. Still traumatised by those events, the lieutenant has another psycho to deal with after a man's body is found with HYPOCRITE written across his shoe soles. That's the word Nick failed to guess when someone challenged him to an online game. Like all serial murder cases, this is just the beginning.

Grace Mitchell lived with the victim, is on antidepressant medication, and claims she heard nothing. With no other leads, the police question her about the dead man and place her under police protection in a hotel. A mystery man stalks Grace, hacks into computers, and uses a climbing rope to access his room. To avoid the officer on guard duty, he calls a masseuse up and gags her with duct tape. Think this guy might be the killer?

The following morning, the familiar Hangman game appears on a police computer with a video showing the masseuse's neck in the noose. The psycho insists Grace play, but after inputting the vowels, she's all a wreck and doesn't come close to solving the puzzle. Nick does his best to console her, but the police receive a recorded message that leads them to the hotel. A second victim, and the word HIPPOCRATES is written on the topless woman's back.

Nick's troubled history gets dropped fairly quickly, and the choice of MO appears to be coincidental. The clues refer to the Hippocratic Oath taken by all doctors, and it's revealed Grace knew both victims. She used to be a psychiatrist but was forced to resign because of ethics charges, and the murdered woman was Lynn Farmer, wife of a former patient. These incidents led to tension between Grace and her father, Henry. Since our mystery guy – Paul Jarvis – works at the hospital, it appears he is specifically targeting Grace and humiliating the cops.

After she identifies him as a potential suspect, the police find evidence in his office. Confident he's got the killer, Nick grills Jarvis, shows him crime scene photos, and theorises he's obsessed with Grace. Then, a smarmy lawyer presents a witness who places Jarvis at the hospital when the first victim was killed. While the movie seemed to have revealed the culprit in the first twenty minutes, it's clear someone else is involved.

Villainess

Roos is determined to solve the case, and even makes a crossword with the answers. A woman named Natalie Walsh, who works with Henry, provides an audio recording and reveals she is Grace's stepmother. Another angle, but Nick spends time with the beautiful suspect and explores her luxury property.

Although tailing Jarvis produces no results, Nick and his partner arrest him again for assault. Knowing he's not acting alone, his aggressive attitude and eagerness to be detained suggest another round of Hangman is coming Nick's way. This time the victim is Natalie – who Jarvis kidnapped before his arrest – and once more the killer demands Grace play. She correctly guesses the Latin phrase PRIMUM NON NOCERE (Do no harm), but exceeds the time limit.

The murderer gloats, and the cops face further embarrassment when they trace the call to their own precinct. Despite a frantic search, they're too late to save Walsh from the hangman's noose. With Nick's captain demanding results and another visit from Jarvis' sleazy attorney, a detective provides a welcome lead. Both Henry and Walsh are listed owners of Grace's land, so the inheritance provides a motive and implicates the father.

Even with Grave under police protection, Jarvis breaks into her home and attacks her. It's then revealed she is his partner and lover, and they planned the entire thing to frame Henry. The accomplice improvised some details – which Grace isn't pleased about – but that doesn't stop her from having sex with him. The villainess says Henry's fingerprints are on a laptop used in the last murder, but this is contradicted when Nick reports the computer was wiped clean. Looks like Grace is setting you up too, lover boy.

The police suspect her because of the slip-ups she's made and do trial runs to time the distance from the station's entrance to the basement crime scene. Meanwhile, Grace stages her latest crime kill: Henry in her barn. She uses dry ice to support a stepladder, which explains how Jarvis could (in theory) commit the murders alone. A convincing cover story, and the killer enjoys watching her hanging father squirm at gunpoint. Grace wants revenge against those involved in her lover's death and is the mastermind behind a double frame-up.

The killer stages an attack, makes a fake video recording, and sets off an alarm clock to wake the police officers outside. Grace screams and hangs herself to set up a last-minute rescue by Nick. The exonerated woman murders Jarvis at a motel and fakes a suicide, giving the police a neat closed case. Everyone is satisfied except for Nick, who tries to get a confession from Grace. However, his bluff about her eyelash being found on the laptop is unsuccessful. Clever enough to plan a twisted scheme and escape justice, this relatively unknown villainess earns a place in the legendary tier.

Honourable Mention: Mädchen Amick

I'm Dangerous Tonight **(1990) – Gloria (Daisy Hall), Wanda (Dee Wallace Stone)**

Mädchen Amick is the heroine of this made for cable horror, though she gets to be the bad girl in a few scenes. That's because the real antagonist is an ancient Aztec cloak that brings out the wearer's evil side. Hence, normal people act out their vicious fantasies and become cold-blooded killers.

After college student Amy O'Neill (Amick) acquires an old chest, she fashions the cloak stored inside into a bright red evening dress. A pity she doesn't know the cloak's history, or that the historian who found it went completely nuts and killed his team. Anthony Perkins – better known for *Psycho* (1960) – shows up as a professor who's too interested in the cloak's legend, but he's really there to provide exposition.

Amy is mean to her cousin Gloria and seduces her football player boyfriend at a social event. This causes a rift between the two women, though the bully reverts to her normal shy persona on removing the cloak. After the ancient curse causes Amy's grandmother to fall to her death in a struggle, the student hangs the dress in a closet. However, Gloria finds the outfit and wears it on a date with her boyfriend.

Gloria – lacking Amy's moral compass – is fully under the spell, so when her hunk shows more interest in the NFL, it's time for revenge. In the standout moment, Gloria tears strangles her victim in the shower with a curtain rope, laughing like a maniac as she chokes him to death. Not finished yet, the bewitched Gloria attempts to ram Amy's car off the road, only to crash and perish in the explosion.

That's not the end, for the next dress wearer is a morgue attendant named Wanda. She goes on a killing spree, executing several low lives and drug dealers. This includes slitting a dealer's throat to satisfy her cocaine habit. The police believe Amy is behind the killings, so she must face the red-dressed psycho alone. This leads to a showdown and a hectic knife attack climax that somehow ends with the heroine back in the dress.

Because of her good nature, Amy resists the curse and her boyfriend's wishes, and she disposes of the dress by tossing it into a shredder. Amy dumps the torn fabric in Gloria's grave and watches the scraps get buried with the coffin. The final – typical horror movie – scene has Perkins' insane professor recover what's left of the cloak, though it's in no condition to be worn.

Rank #18

Urban Legend (1998)
Brenda (Rebecca Gayheart)

Movie

One of the wave of slasher flicks released after the success of *Scream* (1996), this is a formulaic yet stylish horror outing. The villainess makes the legendary tier thanks to some inventive kill sequences – themed on urban legends – and a great post-reveal overdose of insanity.

The movie begins with a woman driving at night. When her vehicle runs low on fuel, it's inevitable she'll be the only person who pulls into a gas station. I could stop right there, as being the opening female in a slasher is invariably a death sentence.

To fill in the details, Brad Dourift plays the weirdo attendant in a cameo. So when he asks the woman to come inside and answer a phone call (cell phones were rare in the 1990s), she doesn't hesitate to use her mace spray when things get creepy. After a daring escape, the real threat is revealed: someone hiding in the back seat. A bloody axe shatters the side window, and we have our first victim.

The action switches to the Pendleton University campus, which is full of attractive young students for the unknown psycho to kill off. Among them are the main character, Natalie (Alicia Witt) and her best friend, Brenda.

For potential victims and psychos, we have reporter Paul (Jared Leto), sexy radio host Sasha (Tara Reid), urban legend guru Parker (Michael Rosenbaum) and joker Damon (Joshua Jackson). Stereotypes are in force, but the film feels fresh thanks to the theme.

To set the eerie tone – and explain the urban legend concept – meet Professor Wexler, played by Robert Englund of *Nightmare on Elm Street* fame. This gives Damon the opportunity to fake a death scene after swallowing Pop Rocks and soda. Legend says he will explode, but this is too early in the story for a public murder. False alarms are common, with many characters surprised in dark locations and/or when they're alone. Jump scares and loud music will keep viewers on their toes, but it's obvious when an actual kill is on the cards.

When Damon drives Natalie out into the woods, he's surprised she rejects him. Perhaps choosing a more suitable location for a date would have helped? Damon has a lot more to worry about when the gloved killer surprises him and scares Natalie by jumping on the car. This makes her drive off without realising the murderer has hung Damon from a tree and tied the rope to the vehicle. How a lone female pulls off this physical feat isn't explained, though Brenda is a strong swimmer. Must be psycho-killer adrenaline.

Naturally, the body has disappeared by the time Natalie brings security guard Reese to investigate. This woman is the typical unbelieving authority figure, played by Loretta Devine in a comedic homage to Pam Grier. Everyone thinks it's another Damon prank, but Natalie is on edge and also knew the first victim, Michelle Mancini. If her reaction to news reports didn't confirm it, looking in an old school yearbook does.

Natalie researches urban legends at the library and

finds a sketch that matches Damon's murder scene. Another image foreshadows the next: a girl murdered while her roommate sleeps. We've already been introduced to Tosh (Danielle Harris), an aggressive goth girl who has sex in the dark. Since she's a minor character and the main cast needs to remain suspects, she's next to die. The unwitting victim sets up an online date, only to realise she's been messaging a psycho. Natalie returns and conveniently doesn't turn on the light as the killer strangles Tosh.

When Natalie wakes up, she finds her roommate's body with the wrists slashed and a message in blood. Reese has a body this time, so the Dean gets involved. Somehow Tosh's death gets written off as suicide, but this is horror movie reality where every creepy person (and female swimmer!) has a parka coat like the murderer. And clueless teens party hard while dead bodies drop over campus.

Villainess

Moving into the second half, it's time for another minor character to get killed. The dean checks his back seat, but guesses the wrong urban legend. The killer – hiding under the vehicle – slashes the man's ankles and releases the brakes so the car presses the latest victim against tire spikes. Nasty way to go, but Parker has it worse when the psycho phones him (using a voice disguiser) and explodes his dog in a microwave oven. Alone in the toilets, he's easy prey for the killer, who force-feeds him Pop Rocks and drain cleaner.

That's the same legend Wexler brought up at the lecture, so when Natalie and Paul find a parka coat (another one!) and an axe in the professor's office, he becomes their number one suspect. He looks even guiltier when he vanishes during the last act.

The best stalk and slash scene is when the murderer attacks Sasha during a radio show. She's wearing her microphone, so the terrified screams are broadcast all over campus. Nobody takes her cries for help seriously, leaving the axe-wielding psycho free to chase her around the radio station. Sasha narrowly escapes a fall, but this merely prolongs her fate. Natalie arrives to watch the killer add another student to the death list and wave from an upstairs window.

Time to – you guessed it – eliminate another suspect. The weird janitor (there *had* to be one) ends up in a fatal accident when the killer re-enacts a gang initiation legend. For non-experts, this involves a car with its headlights switched off at night. This is familiar to Natalie, as she and Michelle caused the death of a man with the same deadly prank. Genre-savvy viewers will guess this backstory is important, but there are some red herrings to dispose of before the villainess' reveal.

Wexler is ruled out when Natalie and Brenda discover his body in the trunk of Paul's car. Thinking he's guilty, Natalie flees into a deserted building. There was a massacre at the site many years ago, and the killer leaves a series of dead bodies for the heroine to find. This ends with Brenda's "corpse" on a bed, but it's a trick and the murderess knocks her surprised friend out cold.

Natalie wakes up to find herself tied up and at the villainess' mercy. Motive rants are the norm in these movies, but this bad girl prepares a full presentation. She even sets up a slide projector just because the images splashed across her face look sinister. It turns out the guy who died was Brenda's boyfriend, and she didn't take it well. The actress plays a full-on psycho brilliantly, and it remains a wonderful villainess reveal decades after the film's release.

After Brenda finishes explaining, she prepares Natalie for the kidney heist – as gruesome an urban legend as it sounds. The murderess hasn't killed everyone, and both Reese and Paul arrive to confront her in the finale. There's a drawn-out confrontation with crazy words exchanged and Reese slashed. Paul has a lengthy struggle with the killer before she grabs the handgun and prepares to shoot Natalie. Reese reveals she has a second firearm, and the rescued victim blasts Brenda through a window.

Paul reminds us to expect a twist, and we finish with two. Brenda – like any horror film villain – is not so easily killed and surprises the survivors in a car. She's out of urban legends by now, so recycles the axe murderer in the back seat. During a claustrophobic struggle with the enraged Brenda, Paul crashes the vehicle and sends the villainess flying off a bridge into the river below.

But that's not the end of the story! Still alive, Brenda returns for the epilogue set at a different university campus with students who appear to be crew member extras. She recounts her version of events, now an urban legend.

Discussions: *Urban Legend* Series

Urban Legends: Final Cut (2000)

The premise remains the same: a psycho killer kills university students with murders themed on urban legends. The victims are budding filmmakers competing for a prestigious prize, which is really an excuse to have bizarre backdrops for gory deaths. When murders are shown, they're usually more disgusting than frightening, and the sequel has none of the original's style.

Amy Mayfield (Jennifer Morrison) teams up with the twin brother of a suicide victim to prove the death was actually murder. But somebody in a fencing mask and black overcoat will kill to protect their secret. The murderer switches things up with "disguises" such as a scarecrow mannequin and a Halloween mask that looks downright stupid. In the best scene, Amy is attacked in a sound studio and pursued across the deserted campus, but the overall movie is derivative even by slasher movie standards.

The urban legend killer is a male professor (Hart Bochner) who wants to massacre a film crew to pass their work off as his own. There's a welcome return by Loretta Devine as the security guard Reese, who gets some genuinely funny moments. And female villain fans who make it to the end will be rewarded by a spoiler cameo from Rebecca Gayheart. However, it's a case of too little, too late.

Urban Legends: Bloody Mary (2005)

The third film ditches the slasher theme in favour of supernatural horror, though its title villainess is a sympathetic character and the chief antagonist is actually a corrupt politician. Many decades ago, Mary Banner was killed during a high school prank gone wrong, and the boy responsible hid her body in a trunk to cover up the murder.

In the present, Samantha (Kate Mara) and her friends are victims of a similar incident, and Mary's ghost returns to exact revenge. There's no connection to the first two movies except for a brief mention of the serial killers in a newspaper clipping and a few urban legends. Deaths involve an invisible foe, mostly. One victim is roasted in a tanning bed, and a second girl is attacked by spiders that hatch inside her body.

Considering Mary is the title character, we see very little of her. Her main on-screen attack comes when she crawls out from under a bed to stab a guy with a broken bottle. Samantha teams up with a voodoo priestess to recover the girl's body and return it to the grave, thus ending the curse. There's an easy to solve murder mystery where a figure in black kills Samantha's brother, and a scheming politician is the culprit.

The finale has Mary literally return from the grave to save Samantha, with cheap CGI effects to end this unrewarding tale. No honourable mention, but there's always the legendary villainess in the original.

GoldenEye (1995)
Xenia Onatopp (Famke Janssen)

Movie

Pierce Brosnan's four Bond movies were escapist material, which allowed for outlandish characters like a Georgian assassin who crushes men between her thighs. Xenia is the first villainess from the Brosnan era to make the top twenty. This was *the* golden age of evil Bond girls.

The change of leading man comes with a new supporting cast. There's now a woman in charge of the 00 section, with Judi Dench in her first appearance as M. Samantha Bond is Moneypenny, and Q (Desmond Llewelyn) is a mainstay. Bond one-liners and crazy gadgets are included, and director Martin Campbell – helming his first franchise reboot – brings style to the frantic set pieces. Massive explosions, dramatic escapes, and impossible stunts are packed into two hours of entertainment.

By this point, filmmakers were experimenting with the tried and tested formula. Two surprise bad guys are thrown into the mix, though savvy viewers will guess both twists before they happen. A secret lair and army are standard for a Bond villain, but controlling a Russian satellite weapon requires technical genius. The female lead is Natalya Simonova (Izabella Scorupco). If we discount her, that leaves only the egotistical Boris Grishenko (Alan Cumming) as the insider.

Besides introducing a new lead actor – with ambiguous camera angles before his grand reveal – the prologue assault on a Soviet chemical weapons lab gives us Sean Bean as 006 Alec Trevelyan. He is supposedly executed after the mission goes wrong, setting up a vendetta between 007 and Colonel Ourumov (Gottfried John). However, Bean is second on the credits and always plays bad guys, so it's no shock he survives to become the main villain.

Xenia is the most physical female opponent Bond has ever faced. That covers sexual activity (not advisable with her) and getting beaten up by the hero. She can take a lot of punishment (and enjoys it) given her background as a Soviet fighter pilot.

The villainess knows how to exploit male weaknesses. Her first appearance comes early when a female operative tests Bond's driving skills. That goes how any fan would expect, with Bond flouting the rules and racing a mysterious brunette in a Ferrari. She's an excellent driver herself, able to pull off swerving manoeuvres at high speed. There were several close calls before Bond wisely broke off the contest. And takes the safer option to romance his passenger.

Bond catches up with Xenia at a Monte Carlo casino. She's enjoying good luck at the baccarat table until the tuxedoed charmer shows up to change her fortune. The typical Bond introduction then follows, with names exchanged in classic style. Xenia has a date with an admiral, but Bond suspects something is amiss, so he has Moneypenny run a background check.

Not spending the night with Xenia turns out to be a smart move, since the assassin murders the admiral in bed with her signature thigh-crushing routine. When Bond discovers the body the next morning, it appears he died in ecstasy.

Xenia and her male accomplice use the officer's stolen ID to board a French warship. The villainess murders two pilots to steal their flight jackets (and dark-tinted visor helmets), all to hijack a prototype helicopter. Bond arrives too late to stop them, and the detained hero can only watch as they escape.

Villainess

Three murders in the opening half hour tell us Xenia is not a woman to trifle with. Ourumov – now a general – runs a weapons test at a remote Siberian facility, a ruse to steal the arming keys for a satellite-based electromagnetic pulse (EMP) weapon. Xenia slaughters the civilian staff with a submachine gun once they've outlived their usefulness, and even Ourumov looks uneasy at her enthusiasm for mass murder. The only survivor is computer programmer Natalya, who escapes the massacre through luck and ingenuity. As Bond women go, she's at the more competent end of the spectrum.

We're shown how devastating the stolen GoldenEye is when the villains fry the computers and cover their escape. Back in London, Bond watches the attack unfold on monitors, and Natalya is the only person who can identify the thieves. Of course, the person she contacts is the traitor, Boris. Natalya is already nervous when she arrives at an eerie church, and things get worse when she discovers her confidant is in league with Xenia.

Bond's investigation takes him to St. Petersburg, where he receives help from CIA agent Jack Wade. Joe Don Baker is one actor to play multiple roles in the series, in a non-villainous role this time. The hero also forms an uneasy alliance with Russian mob boss Valentin Zukovsky (Robbie Coltrane).

Bond asks too many questions, a pet peeve of villains. So it's time to send Xenia for a (literal) steamy encounter in the hotel sauna. This meeting is more intimate – a bizarre mix of verbal exchanges and rough sex. Xenia attempts to thigh-crush Bond, but he frees himself. The hero has had quite enough of the foreplay and demands to meet the boss.

Another gloomy meeting spot: a statue graveyard, where Bond knocks Xenia out and discovers the missing helicopter. The hero is surprised to see his old partner Alec alive, but soon realises he's walked into a trap. But does Trevelyan kill Bond? No, he locks him and Natalya in the helicopter and sets off radar-guided missiles to destroy the evidence and the pesky secret agent. A stupid move that allows the heroes to escape the blast with an ejector seat.

The hero barely has time to argue his case to Natalya before the Russians show up. In the interrogation, she fingers Ourumov, but the villain frames Bond for the defence minister's murder. Xenia is absent from the action that follows: a chase through an archive building where Natalya is recaptured. After a dramatic escape, Bond steals a tank to pursue the bad guys. A one-sided chase with Bond even more indestructible than usual.

After wrecking half of St. Petersburg, the hero tracks the villains to an old Soviet missile train. The armoured vehicle survives a cannon blast, but not a head-on collision with the tank. Bond has the upper hand against Trevelyan, but his foe knows his weaknesses and has Ourumov bring Natalya in as a bargaining chip. Now that the true villain has shown his face, the accomplice is expendable.

Trevelyan repeats his mistake by locking Bond in with Natalya and setting off an explosion. Didn't he learn the first time? After *another* narrow escape and a loud bang, the heroes swap dreary Russia for sunny Cuba. We get romance on the beach and a more human Bond, but that's only a brief interlude. The final confrontation takes place at a secret control facility hidden underwater. Everything is formulaic: gadgets, a resourceful female ally, close-quarters fights. But it's worked for thirty years, so why change things?

Bond's last encounter with Xenia occurs in the jungle after his plane is shot down by a missile. With the hero dazed from the crash, the henchwoman descends on a rope from a helicopter and overpowers him. She's armed, but wants to humiliate Bond, and squeezes him between her thighs. Natalya intervenes, but gets head-butted (if you're watching the uncut version). After a quick struggle, Bond uses Xenia's rifle to shoot the helicopter, and the villainess – still hooked to the rope – is crushed between two tree branches. A Bond one-liner to cap things off, but Xenia deserved a longer fight scene.

Honourable Mentions / Discussions: Timothy Dalton / Pierce Brosnan Bond Movies

The Living Daylights (1987)

Timothy Dalton plays a more serious Bond, but the fantastical plot elements remain. Locations are still exotic, the gadgets hi-tech, and the women beautiful, but villain ambitions are toned down somewhat. The grittier 007 films tend not to feature female foes, and even the leading lady – Maryam D'Abo as the cellist Kara Milovy – is incompetent and present for romance only.

Kara gets an intriguing introduction, going from an innocent concert performer to a sniper whom Bond is reluctant to kill. This is later revealed to be a setup to fake a defection, and Kara is no weapons expert. When Bond asks Q to research female assassins, one muscular woman's MO is strangulation by thighs. Foreshadowing for *GoldenEye*?

Other than Kara, the key players in this Cold War thriller are male, and the villains are some of the weakest in the series. The CIA uses Bond's sexism against him by employing two beautiful agents, but besides trapping the hero, they are given little to do.

Licence to Kill (1989)

Dalton's second and final entry dispensed with the humour and gave us a violent revenge thriller. James Bond goes rogue and seeks payback when drug dealer Franz Sanchez (Robert Davi) leaves Felix Leiter a hospitalised widower. The plot is not so outlandish, even if Sanchez runs a drug factory disguised as a temple. The trademark action and stunts are present, with a ten-minute tanker truck chase (as explosive as you might expect) to finish.

No henchwomen on show, but the female characters are stronger than expected. Pam Bouvier (Carey Lowell) is a competent lead who can handle herself in a fight. Absent for the first half, she makes a powerful impression in the second as an operative equal to 007. Most of the plot revolves around their infiltrating Sanchez's organisation and turning the villains against each other. There's an extended role for Q as an unlikely field agent, but ultimately this comes down to Bond versus the drug dealer.

Talisa Soto as the villain's mistress Lupe is a more traditional Bond girl, but she proves a valuable ally. We get an unmasking scene after two Asian "ninja" narcotics agents – one female – capture Bond on a rooftop. Their interference messes up his plan to kill Sanchez, and the woman dies in a hail of bullets soon after.

Tomorrow Never Dies (1997)

An insane villain plans to start a war between two

nuclear powers. Sound familiar? This time it's the UK against China, and the bad guy is Elliot Carver, a media mogul who thinks global conflict will improve his ratings. After the era of fake news, this techno-thriller doesn't seem so implausible. And there's enough action, including a spectacular motorcycle chase in Saigon, to make this a watchable, if routine, adventure.

As the only Brosnan movie without a female villain, the enemies are fairly generic. Jonathan Pryce is a hammy foe who reveals his scheme too soon. For henchmen, he has a tough guy to do the fighting and a computer hacker for the technical stuff. Fortunately, the women are more interesting. Teri Hatcher is Carver's wife, who had a previous relationship with Bond, and that suggests her life will end tragically.

China sends an agent of its own – Wai Lin – to investigate Carver's network. She's played by Hong Kong action star Michelle Yeoh, so does all the fighting and stunts you would expect. Other than a couple of moments of idiocy, she's an effective secret agent. Her one-woman ninja army is a highlight during the otherwise weak climax on a stealth boat. She gets captured during the finale, and the romance feels awkward, but Wai Lin is among the best female leads.

Die Another Day (2002) – **Miranda Frost (Rosamund Pike)**

Michelle Yeoh was slated to return for Brosnan's final Bond outing, but she dodged the proverbial bullet by not appearing. The end product is a mess, with a watchable – though far-fetched – first half followed by a truly awful second half. The villain is a North Korean colonel obsessed with conquering the South by any means necessary. After his supposed death, he takes on the identity of British entrepreneur Gustav Graves (Toby Stephens) to complete his evil scheme.

The ability to replace human DNA and completely change one's appearance seems believable compared to other elements. Such as an invisible car, a solar-powered ray satellite operated by a wrist computer, and electrified armour. Other than the fencing match between Bond and Graves that turns into a brutal sword fight, the film is overblown and ridiculous, even for 007.

Halle Berry is NSA agent Jinx, who becomes the main protagonist for some parts. This includes daring solo action and spouting awful puns. When she converses with Bond, it's truly painful. A female Korean interrogator stings her prisoners with scorpion venom, but she only features in the prologue.

The main villainess is Miranda Frost, an MI6 operative working undercover as Graves' publicist. In fact, she's a double agent who betrayed Bond to the North Koreans. Frost is introduced as an Olympic champion fencer (complete with an unmasking scene). But when Bond confronts Grave in his ice palace (more silliness), he discovers his fellow agent is untrustworthy.

After Bond escapes and rescues Jinx (no surprises there), the two agents go after the villains. The climax takes place on a military aircraft with Bond battling Graves and his electric suit, while Jinx and Miranda have a sword duel. The skimpy outfits make the fight seem ludicrous, and Jinx completes Bond's revenge mission. When he arrives to see Miranda already dead, he doesn't look too happy.

Note: The "missing" third Brosnan film will be covered as a ranked villainess entry later

Final Contract: Death on Delivery (2006)
Lara / Lorca (Alison King)

Movie

This fast-paced action flick is a throwback to the days of real stunts, unlikely heroes, and tough women with ponytails dressed in black. The villainess Lorca answers to a sleazy criminal paymaster, but be in no doubt. The primary threat (and selling point) is the ruthless assassin with the crossbow. Too bad the police finger an innocent patsy and spend the movie chasing him.

David (Drew Fuller) is an American motorcycle courier working for his uncle in Berlin, and he has a blossoming romance with fellow employee Jenny (Tanja Wenzel). David has teenage love issues and a few speeding tickets, but nothing serious. That changes when a beautiful woman jumps into his car.

The brunette claims to be a cop hunting a contract killer who's just murdered a key witness. Bad guys are after her, leading to the first of many chase scenes where David shows off his driving skills. The passenger Lara is handy with a sidearm, and after a high-speed shootout – and traffic chaos – she shows her appreciation with a kiss.

David realises Lara has left her bag behind, so he follows her into a hotel. She warns him that the lobby is under surveillance, so David agrees to check in at reception and enquire about a contact. Lara later joins David in the room, now scantily dressed and in full-on seduction mode. The young man lets his guard down and stands up Jenny (something she's clearly not happy about) in favour of Lara. Pity it's a setup and the woman David spent the evening with is actually Lorca. That would be the assassin who murdered a second witness while he slept.

David wakes up to find the hotel swarming with police. Hillman (Ken Bones) is the man in charge and has a personal vendetta against the killer. So he's awfully pleased when his response team corners David on the roof and takes the "assassin" into custody. The courier's act of kindness was a trap, since Lorca stowed a crossbow inside to implicate him.

Two dumb cops take a detour and beat up David for crimes he didn't commit. They're enjoying their brutality until the real assassin shows up. Now dressed in black leather and looking far more villainous, Lorca executes the two men with a spinning kick and headshots. She contemplates killing David too, but spares his life. Seems the patsy is still important to her plan, if only as a distraction for the cops to chase while she targets the third and final witness.

Villainess

With the entire Berlin police force after him, David is a stranger in a foreign land with few allies to call on. His frustrated uncle refuses to help, and Jenny is reluctant, given recent events. Lorca has vanished, but David has enough problems with the cops. There are multiple car chase scenes and lots of property damage, but David evades the authorities thanks to help from a shady mechanic. Jenny isn't pleased with the danger she's now in, and since the romantic tension is over, it's time for the villainess' return.

The third witness is well guarded, so Lorca beats up David and kidnaps Jenny to force him to co-operate. The hero has a clever idea to use the vehicle's GPS tracker, but the villainess expects this, and the trail ends at an abandoned warehouse. Meanwhile, Jenny frees herself by cutting her bonds on a conveniently sharp object. A bold escape attempt, but one that ends quickly after Lorca recaptures her. The crossbow-wielding killer is pissed off with her heroism, so she tortures Jenny with electric shock therapy to show David who's in charge.

The assassin has David wear special camera glasses, so she can watch everything on her hi-tech monitor screens. She instructs him to attend the courthouse, where she's already stashed a gun for her patsy. David is out of options and can only watch as a young girl is brought in. The witness is a child, and if David refuses to eliminate her, Lorca will kill Jenny. To make matters worse, Hillman and the police are on site.

The prosecutor questions the girl and asks her to point out the offender. Lorca demands David shoot her and gets increasingly angry. Seeing no response as the witness identifies her client, the villainess grabs her trusty crossbow and threatens to shoot Jenny. After a tense exchange, David – who tracked the villainess using a clue Jenny provided – shoots the assassin. As Lorca struggles to comprehend the turn of events, it's revealed David's uncle is wearing the glasses at the courthouse.

Lorca isn't finished and attacks David while his girlfriend watches in terror. Being a trained assassin, she has the advantage. After receiving a few blows, David takes advantage of a rare opening and throws the villainess over a guardrail. Seeing her plan fall apart, she uses a speedboat to make her getaway. David is determined to prove he's innocent, and chases after the assassin on a motorcycle.

The final action scene follows, with a police helicopter following David. Snipers attempt to shoot the hero, despite Jenny (who's now a suspect) doing her best to inform Hillman the woman in black is the assassin. After a lengthy pursuit that includes some narrow escapes, David rides up a ramp and performs an improbable jump to Lorca's boat.

The villainess fights David and gets the better of her weaker opponent, but then readies her crossbow. That tips off Hillman who the real assassin is, and he finally realises his mistake. Now exonerated, it's still up to David to best Lorca and send the speedboat crashing onto dry land. This takes the assassin out of the equation, and an apologetic Hillman has Lorca arrested while the heroes kiss and make up.

Honourable Mentions: Crossbows / Assassins

Hard Target 2 (2016) – Sofia (Rhona Mitra)

This sequel to the 1993 movie doesn't involve Jean-Claude Van Damme or John Woo, but we get the leather-clad villainess Sofia. Yes, Rhona Mitra is another badass female, alongside Scott Adkins as a martial artist seeking redemption and Robert Knepper as a psychotic criminal fond of big speeches. Exactly the casting – or should that be typecasting? – we expect in the direct-to-video action market.

After MMA fighter Wes Baylor accidentally kills his friend and competitor, he winds up on a much less prestigious underground circuit in the Far East. When a sinister man named Aldrich offers Baylor a half-million payday, he accepts the offer. Except the proposed fight in Myanmar never was, and Baylor is the latest player in a sadistic game of hunt and kill. Aldrich's crew includes generic rough types plus tough girl Sofia, who has a serious chip on her shoulder and loves crossbows.

Standard stuff, so don't expect any surprises. As the hunting party tracks Baylor through the jungle, he teams up with a local named Tha (Ann Truong). She's the resourceful type who gets into the occasional fight when Baylor is occupied, but is mainly there so the hero can confess his sins and pray to Buddha. Aldrich gets super annoyed with his target's survival skills, so he orders out weaponised motorcycles to give the villains an unfair advantage.

One of the best action scenes has Sofia and two thugs chasing Baylor. The other hunters go down easily, leaving Sofia to fire her vehicle's weapons and corner her prey in a deserted village. Baylor steals a bike of his own and fires a net to dismount the villainess. Not finished yet, she draws two mini crossbows and advances while scenery explodes behind her. After a thankfully brief bad-girl speech, Sofia fights Baylor with a baton and puts up a decent struggle before he sends her flying through a wall.

Baylor does the heroic thing and leaves Sofia alive, and inevitably it's the two women who confront each other in the final battle. Sofia – armed with a big crossbow now – fights Tha, but prefers to show off her unarmed combat skills. This is a disappointing finale on a rusty old train, with the action interrupted by those cutaway moments directors seem so fond of. For an experienced killer, Sofia is beaten too easily and never looks like winning before she's impaled on a spike.

Ballistica (2009) – Alexa (C.B. Spenser), Fang (Lauren Mary Kim)

No crossbow this time, just secret agents able to dodge

bullets at close range. The title refers to the ludicrous concept of – as the villainess puts it – kung fu with guns. Besides the bizarre fight scenes, there's a training montage of the hero Damian (Paul Sloan) working out with dual pistols. And a shadowy CIA department, minor female agents as eye candy, and a treacherous blonde who seduces the main character before she reveals her true motives. Derivative stuff.

Several B-movie stars feature. Robert Davi is the agency boss who might be corrupt, Martin Kove is a dependable ally, and Andrew Divoff's Russian baddie is the chief antagonist for acts one and two. Special effects are atrocious, and the fight scenes are poorly done with no physical contact, but there's fun to be had if you can forget the laws of reality.

The plot involves a nasty bomb terrorists want to acquire. Lauren Mary Kim – known for stunt work, with the occasional acting role whenever a female Asian badass is required – plays the minor villainess Fang. She's a nondescript… um, Asian badass who beats up the captured hero and throws a prototype weapon his way. Too bad she forgot to lock the door, and Damian tosses the bomb back. A stupid death scene to end a far too brief role.

Alexa is convincing as an innocent scientist who wants to help. She receives martial arts training, talks with Damian about his tragic past, and even gets to make love in a pool. This seems to be the standard sidekick trajectory until Damian kills his nemesis with half an hour left. Then Alexa reveals herself to be adept at ballistica and wipes out an entire SWAT team with acrobatic gunfire. Damian arrives to discover she has activated the bomb before the villainess puts a bullet in his chest.

Good thing Damian was wearing a pendant – yes, that shot-stopping trick we've seen countless times. While politics unfold back at base, Damian chases after Alexa in a car, bringing the bomb along for the ride. There's a lengthy pursuit through the streets of Los Angeles with green screen backdrops. Then, the villainess crashes, and the confrontation continues on foot.

Alexa gives a speech when cornered by the hero. The usual nonsense about committing a terrorist act to secure funding, then a ballistica duel. Alexa is Damian's equal in agility and style, but somehow the two elite agents can't hit a target at arm's length. Finally, the villainess gets Damian in her sights, but he loads a spare bullet mid-twist and finishes her.

Kill Bill Vol. 1 (2003)
O-Ren Ishii (Lucy Liu), Vernita Green (Vivica A. Fox), Gogo Yubari (Chiaki Kuriyama)

Movie

In Quentin Tarantino's two-volume revenge saga, the men do the talking while women fight to the death. Often violent and bloody, but what do you expect when the protagonist is a deadly assassin and her former cohort are the targets? Uma Thurman's Bride is left for dead at a wedding rehearsal, but the Deadly Viper Assassination Squad should have finished her when they had the chance.

Ten chapters are split across two films, presented out of order. The first target we see is actually the Bride's second: Vernita Green, aka Copperhead (Vivica A. Fox). She's enjoying retirement in suburban America, but that doesn't earn her any sympathy. She and the Bride fight each other and wreck the furniture in an even contest before Vernita's little girl shows up, and the killers put their feud on hold. A brief pause before Copperhead draws a concealed gun. It's a bad idea to miss the target, especially a woman armed with a throwing knife.

Moving back in time, Texas cops investigate the wedding chapel aftermath and the supposedly dead Bride, who turns out to be alive. Elle Driver (Daryl Hannah) is a psycho assassin, so she's not pleased when Bill (David

Carradine, though we don't see his face) says it's not chivalrous to kill a woman in a coma. Skip forward four years, and the Bride wakes up with a metal plate in her skull and a vendetta against the hit squad who killed her fiancé.

The four-hour saga (counting both films) is overlong with lots of dialogue. The Bride has a samurai sword made by a Japanese master smith, but did we need five minutes where she pretends to be an innocent Yankee tourist? He survives and should consider himself lucky. Most men (and women) are treated as expendable, often with fancy camera angles and tinted palettes to add variety to their demises. A handful of characters put up a worthy fight, but most last fewer than ten seconds.

While the solo female antagonists might just scrape legendary status, the ensemble trio of villainesses are worthy of a top fifteen ranking. And the Bride is a one-woman army, firmly in antihero territory.

Villainess

As the final boss of Volume 1 – using a video game analogy – O-Ren Ishii gets a badass introduction. Actually, three of them. First is an animated backstory that shows revenge against the Yakuza boss who murdered her parents, her rise as an assassin, and the wedding attack that made her the first target. The cartoon is as violent as the live-action segments. For those eager for "real" action, that comes soon enough when O-Ren decapitates a crime lord who refuses to fall in line. That ends all dissent and establishes the villainess as truly ruthless.

In Tokyo, there's a montage of the Bride wearing a yellow jumpsuit on a motorcycle while O-Ren rides in a limousine flanked by her biker enforcers. A voice-over narration introduces the key lieutenants. These are the domino-masked leader of the Crazy 88 gang, timid assistant Sofie Fatale, and the far more deadly and sadistic Gogo. For O-Ren's third introduction (we get she's a badass), she enters her club with her minions close behind as epic music plays.

The final chapter of Volume 1 is a half hour long action sequence where the Bride takes on all comers. Like any crime boss, O-Ren has a horde of disposable goons. After the Bride chops off Sofie's arm, one poor guy is sent in alone and routinely dispatched as the villainess watches from the balcony. Then come a few more guys, none of them any good. There's a female in their ranks, but she doesn't last much longer.

It's not until Gogo steps forward that the Bride has any competition. As the only henchwoman with an introductory flashback, it's obvious the ball and chain wielding psycho will be more difficult to defeat. After a lengthy opening attack where Gogo demolishes the club decor, she disarms the Bride and gets her in a chain chokehold. The Bride is equal to the challenge and improvises with a block of wood (and sharp protruding nails) to kill her opponent.

There's a humorous interlude where O-Ren gloats it won't be that easy before more masked thugs arrive. Most of the Bride's carnage is shot in black and white, but the violence isn't toned down. Plenty of people lose arms and legs, but don't land a single blow against their well-trained adversary. Even the leader dies quickly, knocked from the upper balcony after the Bride slices off his leg. O-Ren walks away mid-fight, almost as if she expects her foe to kill her underlings. The villainess even admits this when the bloody victor steps into a snowy exterior landscape to confront the boss lady.

After all the buildup, don't expect a great battle. It's stylish enough – with the two swordswomen circling about each other as the tempo raises – but few blows are traded. O-Ren is a worthy match and slashes the Bride in the back. After a few more moves, it's the crime boss' turn to get cut, only this swipe cleaves off her scalp. O-Ren has just enough time to acknowledge the victory before she collapses dead in the snow.

My prevailing thought: "Is that it?" I suspect many other villainess fans will feel the same. So brilliant up to the last encounter, but ultimately a letdown.

Honourable Mentions: *Kill Bill* / Stylish Assassins

Kill Bill Vol. 2 **(2004) – Elle Driver (Daryl Hannah)**

While the first volume had 50% action, there's barely 5% in the second half. The Bride has three targets remaining. Budd (Michael Madsen) is a washed-out hitman living in a trailer, and Bill has become a family man fond of lengthy conversations. Once more, it's the females that deliver the excitement. If this summary seems brief, there's not much to discuss despite the movie being over two hours long. Even a minor character – an Asian assassin whom the Bride talks down by revealing she's pregnant – gets more action than Bill, who's killed by a death touch.

Yes, the final boss fight never materialises. The movie subverts expectations, and skilled assassins achieve victory over superior opponents by cheating. The Bride – decked out in ninja garb – confronts Budd, only to get shot and buried alive in the desert. It's a good thing she listened to her brutal sensei and can bust her way out of a wooden box.

The treacherous Elle murders Budd – who she could easily kill in a fair fight – by planting a snake in a bag of money. There's a chilling scene where the assassin lists the symptoms of the poisonous venom, then the Bride returns and the proper fight begins. Elle has the sword and the advantage, but the Bride is a tough woman to take down. Like most locations where female assassins battle it out, the trailer ends up destroyed.

Telling a vengeful killer you murdered her old mentor is not the smartest play, and the Bride responds to Elle's confession by plucking out her remaining eye. The anti-heroine leaves the blind woman alone with her pet snake, but the villainess' fate is left to the imagination.

Guns, Girls and Gambling (2012) – The Blonde (Helena Mattson)

Not a Tarantino film, even though it pretends to be. Weird characters populate this "man caught in a gang war" tale, all introduced with title cards so we know who they are. Cowboys and Indians is a prominent theme (two assassins even go by those names), and there's a modern western feel. Two bosses – The Chief (Gordon Tootoosis) and The Rancher (Powers Boothe) – fight over a tribal warrior mask stolen by a gang of Elvis impersonators. Yes, this movie is just as crazy as it sounds.

The man in the middle is John Smith (Christian Slater), and there are also appearances by Jeff Fahey as the double revolver-toting Cowboy, Gary Oldman as the ringleader Elvis Elvis, and Megan Park as the sweet Girl Next Door. Except she's faking it, naturally. Plenty of people die before the final showdown is done, with minor characters biting the dust before the more important players.

The deadliest assassin is the unnamed Blonde, who recites Edgar Allan Poe before blowing her victims away. This woman – dressed in black and the subject of frequent sexy rear shots – is the coolest character, skilled in acrobatics and firearms. She emerges unscathed from her bloody encounters, escapes double-crosses, and rides off into the sunset with her prostitute accomplice and a suitcase full of money. Everyone else is on the losing side, except for John Smith, who played everyone from the start.

The Blonde's standout moments are assassinating a man in a toilet cubicle (!) and besting the Indian who brings a tomahawk to a gunfight. In a movie full of corpses, this female assassin has the highest body count. So John Smith wisely lets the Blonde and her leather-clad lover keep their share.

Batman Returns (1992)
Selina Kyle / Catwoman (Michelle Pfeiffer)

Movie

This sequel to the 1989 blockbuster had Michael Keaton reprise his role as the brooding caped crusader and Tim Burton return to the director's chair. No iconic Joker, but a villainous duo with Danny DeVito as the evil Penguin and Michelle Pfeiffer as the devious and sexually charged Catwoman. The tone is akin to *The Nightmare Before Christmas* (1993), with Gotham City in peril over the festive season and henchmen dressed in bizarre costumes.

The first half-hour gives us origin stories for the two antagonists. Backgrounds aren't faithful to the source material, with Oswald Cobblepot (aka The Penguin) disfigured at birth and abandoned by his uncaring wealthy parents. That means locked in a cage and tossed into an icy river. Two decades later, the grown-up villain makes his grand entrance. A surprise Christmas present bursts open and unleashes a goon squad to cause havoc. Batman responds and has a chance encounter with a woman named Selina Kyle. Sound familiar?

Instead of a jewel thief, she's an accident-prone secretary tossed through a window after she discovers her boss' dark secret. That boss is Max Shreck, played by Christopher Walken. He's a minor villain, even if he likes to pretend otherwise. Selina survives the fall after she's resuscitated by cats (!). Upon returning home, she gulps down a carton of milk. More importantly, she fashions a costume with a shiny black PVC dress and a sewing kit.

To begin with, the black-clad villainess is shown at a distance through her apartment window, and it's only when she saves a woman from a mugger that we see Catwoman up close. How Selina developed acrobatic abilities with no training is a mystery, but she easily dispatches – and scratches – the criminal, then gives the victim a lecture on feminism.

Michelle Pfeiffer often tops polls of the (many) actresses to play Catwoman in film and TV. Her weird origin gives her character a dangerous edge, and she's closer to a villain than previous incarnations. This version also has the best double life / romantic subplot with Bruce Wayne, actually wears a cat-eared cowl, and wields the iconic whip. Catwoman doesn't get top billing, but is the foe people remember most. If only for her stitched, tight-fitting catsuit.

Villainess

The Penguin sells himself as a hero by rescuing a baby kidnapped by his own henchmen. He blackmails Shreck into helping him gain revenge on Gotham's wealthy families. While chaos rages on the streets and Batman fights to maintain control, a certain woman in black unleashes her own destruction. And what better target than her former boss' store?

Catwoman beheads several mannequins with her whip, showing skill that should take years of practice. She then vandalises and loots a display case. The writers remembered Selina is supposed to be a thief, but this is her only robbery. Two bumbling security guards try to stop her, but are quickly disarmed and sent packing. Then it's time to crash the party with a burst gas pipe, aerosols left in a microwave as a makeshift timer, and a single word to herald the resulting explosion. Meow.

Penguin leaves Batman to handle the newcomer, and the hero manages okay until he strikes Catwoman in the face and she plays the female card. This gives her the opportunity to strike back when the noble Batman lowers his guard, but from that point on he treats Catwoman like any other opponent. After a sexual ploy to get close, she claws the hero's chest – an attack thwarted by his body armour. Batman throws Catwoman from the roof into a truck of kitty litter. One life down, but she has eight remaining.

Shreck works with the Penguin and devises a scheme to elect him the mayor of Gotham City. This is merely a sideline, and while he happily schmoozes with female assistants, even those fall out of favour when the cat drops in. Seduction is an effective weapon, but Catwoman is hostile to her sleazy host's sexual advances. This is an uneasy alliance destined to collapse later, but for now the villains have a common enemy.

An emboldened Selina Kyle returns to Shreck's office and after some... cat and mouse antics, the young woman romances Bruce Wayne. There's soul-searching and close comfort in Wayne Manor before The Penguin wreaks more havoc. His latest scheme involves luring Batman into a trap and framing him for the murder of a buxom celebrity. Catwoman is the accomplice, and she and Batman have another fight. No chivalry or feigning injury this time, and the hero pulls no punches.

The villainess escapes with the hostage, and thanks to a combination of the Penguin (and his trick umbrellas) and the police, Batman lands on his back. A perfect (or should that be purrfect?) opportunity for sexual assault. The hero doesn't resist and is somewhat lost for words. Catwoman ruins any chance of reconciliation when she stabs Batman, breaking off a clawed nail on his body armour.

Batman disappears into the night, only to find his Batmobile sabotaged and under the Penguin's control. After causing a lot of property damage, the hero foils the plot and records the villain's gloating transmission. As he recovers from Catwoman's attack in the Batcave, Bruce uploads the audio file during a mayoral campaign speech. With Penguin's credibility in tatters, he dumps Shreck and launches the final phase of his evil scheme.

Catwoman – who treads the line between anti-heroine and villainess – isn't pleased that Penguin killed an innocent woman. And he's not happy that she complains, so he hooks Catwoman to a helicopter umbrella that whisks her into the air. A daring escape – and glass-shattering fall – later, Catwoman emerges unscathed.

Time to dress up as Selina Kyle and romance Bruce Wayne at a ball, but their double lives collide when they repeat dialogue from the earlier roof encounter. That's when they realise their opposite's nocturnal identity. No time for debate, because the Penguin's thugs arrive to kidnap Shreck.

The finale is a disappointing mess, as the deranged villain orders penguins armed with rockets to attack Gotham, only to be foiled by a signal jammer. The Penguin is a better schemer than a fighter, and no umbrella tricks can save him. After a few unimpressive brawls, he falls over in the snow and dies. Shreck and Catwoman get a more interesting climax, as the wild, out-of-control woman desires revenge and an unmasked Bruce attempts to talk her out of it.

The hero appears to get through to Selina before she knocks him down with a claw swipe. The villainess advances on Shreck, shrugs off several gunshots to the chest (more multiple lives nonsense) and dies in an electrical explosion. Apparently, because while Bruce finds Shreck's body, there's no sign of Selina. Just before the end credits roll, Catwoman (with a repaired cowl) reappears in silhouette form, but the hinted return never happened.

Honourable Mentions: Catwoman

Batman (1966) – The Catwoman / Kitka (Lee Merriwether)

The 1960s *Batman* was a campy TV series with Adam West and Burt Ward as the dynamic duo, and a feature-length movie between the first and second seasons. Four principal adversaries – Penguin, Joker, Riddler, and Catwoman – team up to take over the world. The result is as colourful and silly as you would expect.

Julie Newmar – who played Catwoman in the series – was injured before filming began, so Lee Merriwether took on the role. Actually, it's a dual role because Bruce Wayne and Dick Grayson aren't the only characters with alter egos. When unmasked, Catwoman is Kitka, a Russian journalist as fake as they come. The Penguin puts on a flimsy disguise that Batman sees through, but Kitka's feminine charms have him completely fooled.

After half an hour of hokum, Catwoman suits up in her black outfit and announces the evil scheme: to abduct the Security Council (think the United Nations). The sole villainess is a conniving femme fatale who poses sexily while the men do the muscle work. Catwoman throws in an evil smirk and mimes claw swipes, but that's about it.

The big fight at the end has the superimposed comic-style text that this campy production is known for. As the duo fight on Penguin's submarine, Catwoman gets the drop on the heroes and dunks them in the ocean. No hard physical contact in this era, so she trips and falls. Her mask comes off in the lame defeat, revealing her dual identity to a stunned Batman.

The Dark Knight Rises (2012) – Selina Kyle (Anne Hathaway), Talia al Ghul (Marion Cotillard)

A more serious take, the conclusion to Christopher Nolan's Dark Knight trilogy had Christian Bale as Batman go up against Bane (Tom Hardy). Grounded in reality – as far as caped crusaders go – so the villain is a huge imposing guy in a mask without the venom backpack. Bane is bent on bringing chaos to Gotham's streets. The twist is he's supposedly the son of Ra's al Ghul (Liam Neeson), the antagonist of *Batman Begins*.

Selina Kyle is a thief closer to the source material, but is never referred to as Catwoman, though several headlines mention a cat burglar at large. This devious woman is introduced as a maid in Wayne Manor who encounters the reclusive hero. Against a retired cripple, she easily escapes with an acrobatic window leap. Besides stealing pearls from a safe, Selina absconds with Bruce's fingerprints. Her shady employer attempts to betray her, only to find she's smarter and can easily defeat his goons in combat.

After Bane's violent campaign convinces Batman to return, we see Selina in a catsuit. Her all-black outfit has cat-ear goggles and razor-sharp heels useful for threatening bad guys. Unlike other movies, Batman recognises Selina through her domino mask, and they defeat an army of thugs with little trouble. Selina even does a stealthy disappearing act when Batman turns around on a roof.

The hero is unwise to trust a criminal, because she rats him out to Bane. Selina can only watch as the brute beats

Batman senseless and breaks his back. A paralysed Bruce finds himself in a hellhole prison and learns the only person who ever climbed the well-like entrance to escape is a child. As Bane takes over Gotham City, two prisoners heal Bruce as he hallucinates about Ra's al Ghul. After several failed attempts, the hero makes the climb and returns home.

Selina Kyle, uncomfortable with the new Gotham, joins Batman on his mission to stop a nuclear bomb. Batman has a flying vehicle after his trademark Batmobile was destroyed in *The Dark Knight* (2008), and the reluctant heroine gets to ride the Batcycle. She's a natural at the hero thing and takes out armoured vehicles. Selina even finishes Bane with the cycle's rocket launcher. Overkill, maybe, but it needed something powerful to take down this foe.

In the climax, it's revealed that Bane is not the true mastermind. That would be Talia, the daughter of Ra's al Ghul, who's been posing as a civilian named Miranda Tate. She gained Bruce's trust, and they even had a brief romantic fling. But anyone familiar with the comics knows about the female heir, and Miranda drops several hints. The surprise works because of the late reveal, but by the time Talia stabs Batman in the back, there's only twenty minutes to go.

For a trained assassin who escaped a hellish prison as a young girl, Talia's contribution post-reveal is very limited. She issues kill orders and climbs into a moving truck, but it only takes a few missiles to crash her vehicle. That's it for any action. The dying Talia gloats Batman will never disarm her bomb in time, but a female assassin without a fight scene is a waste of potential.

The Batman (2022) – Selina Kyle (Zoë Kravitz)

Ten years since the previous incarnation, it's time for another reboot. Robert Pattinson is a raw and violent vigilante, and Gotham is so dark that even the Burton and Nolan movies seem bright. There's less focus on Bruce Wayne and more on detective work, with Batman chasing a psycho who wants to bring chaos to the streets. The Riddler is a masked villain reminiscent of the Zodiac Killer, leaving cryptic messages for the police.

Selina Kyle – not referred to as Catwoman – is a prototype who wears a leather outfit and a makeshift balaclava. The motorcyclist anti-heroine has a mission of her own, and she's adept at thievery, disguise, and beating up criminal scum. Her acrobatic kickboxing skills are less effective against body armour, and Batman defeats her with ease. After that, it's flirty romance and the occasional partnership.

Selina is a subplot in an overlong, three-hour movie. Long fingernails are a natural weapon dangerous enough to claw the face of a mob boss. A length of chain stands in for a whip during a nighttime assault, and her mask already has distinctive cat ears. Overall, a faithful version of the comic character. Zoë Kravitz will apparently return for the sequel, so let's hope for an iconic outfit and more involvement.

Rank #13

Les Nuits Rouges du Bourreau de Jade (2010)
Carrie Chan (Carrie Ng)

Movie

Also known as *Red Nights*, this joint French / Hong Kong production has extensive nudity and bloody violence throughout. The antagonist, Carrie, is arguably the main character. She sells perfume by day, but is a truly evil and sadistic serial killer by night. When the cast keeps their clothes on, there are erotic sculptures, brutal murders, and sexualised camera angles of women to remind us this movie is intended for an adult audience.

The opening scene introduces a beautiful, long-haired Asian girl named Tulip, whom Carrie blindfolds and drives back to her place. The villainess has a secret lair with a vac bed centre stage in a spherical construction. And the innocent Tulip ought to be more concerned about the gloved male assistant. Instead, the naive girl strips naked, lies down on the bed, and Carrie encases her body in latex. The sweat-drenched Tulip stretches her body after the session, but that's just the warmup before the main event.

Carrie tapes over the breathing holes, then – while the victim squirms and suffocates under the latex – puts on her trademark jade claws, one for each finger and thumb of her right hand. This villainess likes to inflict maximum pain, but not before twisted fun. Once she's done running her claws over the trapped Tulip, she kneels on the bed in a sexual pose and stabs the girl in the stomach. That's the pre-credits sequence over, and the tone set.

For viewers wanting a longer prologue – albeit tame in comparison – the US DVD release includes a fifteen-minute short titled *Betrayal*. In the minimal plot, a foolish gangster captures Carrie and goes back on a deal. She gets her revenge, using her belt to gag the man and a hairpin to stab him. This happens off screen, followed by a long scene where the high-heeled murderess stalks a woman who betrayed her through dark streets. After dealing with that problem, Carrie poses on a Hong Kong balcony wearing her jade claws.

Les Nuits Rouges is full of evil schemers, all interested in an ancient Chinese box and prepared to kill to get it. Carrie is the most ruthless, and since the prize is an ancient poison that heightens a person's senses (including any pain), the villainess *really* wants it. The protagonist Catherine (Frédérique Bel) is a cold-blooded contract killer who murders her lover accomplice to sell the vial on the black market, but she's out of her league. Carrie is unmatched in intelligence and villainy.

Villainess

With the brutal introduction out of the way, it's time to get down to business. Catherine – now a wanted woman – brings the stolen box to a broker contact. The killer practices with her weapon beforehand and brings it to the meeting, but doesn't factor in that her contact is also a ruthless bitch. She's already made a deal with Carrie and shoots first, using a weapon hidden under the table. The nervous woman is an amateur at this betrayal thing, as the gun jams and she has trouble firing the second shot.

The broker doesn't suspect that Carrie is even more murderous, and gets slammed teeth-first into a table before she can go through with the double cross. Like in *Betrayal*, Carrie uses her belt as a makeshift weapon. We see the murder in full, except for a few cutaway shots to the wounded Catherine, but this choking death – despite being graphic – is mild compared with the two torture death scenes to come.

Catherine tracks Carrie by identifying a woman with the distinctive high heel shoes she saw at the dojo meeting place. There's a standoff in the street as the two killers stare each other down, but Catherine is reluctant to pull the trigger with cops around. Carrie takes advantage of this – and her enemy's wounded shoulder – to flee the scene. The foreign woman has connections in the Hong Kong underworld, but no longer has the precious box to bargain with. So she settles for a risky IOU.

Perhaps cutting her losses would be wise, but Catherine kidnaps Carrie's associate Sandrine (Carole Brana) and reveals herself to the villainess. Mimicking a gunshot in a public place is hardly discreet, but this is a setup. Catherine has already spotted a vacant apartment across the street from her safe house, so she handcuffs Sandrine to a loose pipe and pulls the old "let her think she escaped" trick. Sandrine is oblivious to the ploy, and once Carrie realises she's in Catherine's sights, the sadist is a cool and fearless customer.

The assassin aims to wound as she still needs the box, so it's a shot in the shoulder for the villainess. Before Catherine can do any more damage, the henchman switches off the lights. That doesn't stop Carrie from taunting her foe before the narrow escape, though.

The villainess has already shown a sexual interest in Sandrine at her nightclub, and this presents the perfect opportunity to try out the poison on the woman who failed her. The victim soon realises her evil employer has paralysed her and watches in terror as she's strapped into a harness and raised into the air. Once again, Carrie has a naked woman at her jade-clawed fingertips, and the torture begins in earnest.

The gruesome scene lasts several minutes, beginning with psychological groping before the villainess cuts deep into Sandrine's bare foot. The victim is clearly in pain but unable to scream. Next up is a swipe that causes several cuts at once, and Carrie pauses occasionally to walk around the suspended Sandrine. Unlike the murder of Tulip, which cut to the opening titles, most violence happens on screen. One gruesome moment has Carrie slice out and remove a butterfly tattooed piece of skin as a trophy.

The killer pauses mid-torture to open a case full of surgical instruments and blades. Sandrine fears even worse is to come, but Carrie stirs a glass of martini with a sharp fork. The evil woman stands beside Sandrine and sips her drink, then pours the rest onto her bloody victim. Carrie phones Catherine and has her listen in to the muffled agony, which is so disturbing that even the cold-blooded hitwoman is unnerved. Then, the villainess stabs Sandrine in the chest to end her suffering.

The local gangsters have no use for a wounded woman, so they shoot Catherine on a beach. Yes, the protagonist doesn't even make it to the end, but at least she gets a quick death. Far worse awaits the criminals after they poison Carrie's lover at a deserted estate. He makes it to the roof and dies in her arms, and a stormy night is the setting for the revenge of the jade-clawed killer.

The criminals have guns, but that doesn't help them. Carrie knows the building layout and uses a mirror reflection trick to surprise one guard and gut him. Another henchman gets a swipe to the face and goes down instantly. Carrie stalks the final villain through the dark halls, running her jade fingers across the wall as a scare tactic. She punches through a weak panel to stab the guy in the back.

With the last victim barely alive, Carrie pours the poison down his throat and tortures him. The camera pans up to the sky as he screams, and another villainess earns legendary status.

Honourable Mention: Asian Killers

Sharp Guns (2001) – Rain (Anya)

This Hong Kong actioner is mundane and formulaic, except for the ruthless female assassin among the mercenary protagonists. Tricky On (Alex Fong) is hired to find and rescue a kidnapped teenage girl, but shouldn't have trusted his old friend, especially since that guy is untrustworthy and has no problem executing his own men.

Tricky recruits a sharpshooter (the only character with a moral compass), another man for hired muscle, and a doctor who has no issues with violence. The standout – of course – is the sadistic Rain, who specialises in torturing people and is also skilled with close-combat weapons. She seems more interested in money than loyalty, which foreshadows a betrayal later in the film. However, this is all a ruse, as Rain helps Tricky gain revenge on the man who betrayed him.

An ice-cold killer, Rain isn't someone you want to piss off. Her best moment comes after she gets herself arrested to gain access to a police station. By this point, a corrupt and misogynistic cop has added himself to Rain's hit list by sexually groping her. Too bad the police missed the plastic lock pick and piano wire the assassin concealed in her clothes.

While the action rages, Rain surprises the cop and brutally strangles him in front of a terrified female prisoner. Her repulsion doesn't stop the sadistic woman from enjoying her kill, though. Rain may be on the less evil side, but she's not exactly good.

Rank #12

The Return of the Musketeers (1989)
Justine de Winter (Kim Cattrall)

Movie

The third part of an unofficial trilogy, this movie follows on from the 1970s Musketeers films and has the director and most original cast members reunite. The production was overshadowed by the tragic death of Roy Kinnear, who plays hapless servant Planchet, during filming, hence the awkward rear shots of his stand-in and dubbed voice. A pity this entry gets overlooked, since its female villain is terrific.

Justine de Winter is the daughter of Milady and Rochefort, and their offspring is a mistress of deception, complemented by her expertise in swordplay. Add two unmasking scenes and many encounters with her victorious, and the result is a legendary villainess.

Twenty years after the events of *The Four Musketeers* (covered below), the heroes are washed out. The devious Cardinal Mazarin hires D'Artagnan, the only one still in active service, to reunite his former comrades. He finds them reluctant to join and is at odds with his old friends after an important prisoner escapes. There's a plot to work with English rebels, and Justine has no qualms about executing royal targets.

Politics is a subplot to her personal vendetta, and despite Rochefort returning from apparent death, there's no doubt who the main adversary is. By the end, the heroes put aside their differences, travel to England and back, and save the King of France.

Villainess

It takes a while for Justine to make an appearance. Disguised as a priest, she sets a trap for the headsman and confronts him with his own axe. Anyone who noticed Kim Cattrall in the credits will see through the deep voice and cloaked figure, but it's reasonably effective.

Athos' son Raoul (C. Thomas Howell) has a chance encounter with the assassin and chases them into the forest. He clashes blades with the fake priest and fences well until he knocks off the killer's hat to reveal a beautiful blonde woman. Faced with a female adversary, he's disarmed by her. Justine is after the musketeers who executed her mother and sees an opportunity after she learns who Raoul's father is.

It isn't too long before Justine confronts the heroes in a red cloak. Like her mother, this female assassin has a fondness for glass weapons, though she uses crossbow bolts instead of daggers. The musketeers are reluctant to fight a woman, but ditch their chivalry when they realise she can take all four at once without even any support. The villainess uses scaffolding to escape and nearly gets shot in the back until Raoul gets all noble and saves her. What happens next is on you, hero.

Distracted enough to fail, the musketeers are employed by the Queen to save King Charles I of England. Historians will know how that turns out, though probably not that the musketeers almost saved him by sidelining the headsman.

Almost since the masked Justine takes over as the king slayer. An action that leaves Raoul and Rochefort shocked, but one the villainess acts casual about.

The musketeers track Justine to her hideout, which is full of traps she uses to turn the tables. A slapstick combat sequence typical of the series, with the hopeless heroes beaten many times by the agile and clever opponent. Justine escapes on a ship heading back to France. The musketeers get wise and use indirect methods to blow up the vessel and defeat Rochefort. His daughter has main villain immunity and comes away relatively unscathed.

Justine uses guile and beauty to kidnap the young King of France. The last fight takes place in a castle, with the musketeers launching a rescue attempt by balloon. This fools the inept guards, but Justine realises the threat and dons her leathers for the grand finale. In the chaotic climax, the villainess is a worthy match for D'Artagnan and his companions, though their actions force Justine to take the King hostage.

The musketeers save the boy, but Justine escapes by leaping down to a moat. Having had enough of her for one lifetime, the heroes let her ride off into the sunset.

Honourable Mentions: Three Musketeers

The classic Alexandre Dumas novel has been adapted for film many times, with various actresses starring as the villainous Milady de Winter. As one of the most rebooted tales in cinema history, there are far too many to discuss, and honourable mentions are restricted to the 1970s onwards.

The Three Musketeers (1973) – Milady de Winter (Faye Dunaway)

The first two films in the Richard Lester trilogy were shot back-to-back, with the novel adaptation split into two parts. Most humour is slapstick, and might become tiresome depending on taste. The swordplay is light enough on violence to receive a universal rating in the UK.

Milady is mostly absent from this half, and only becomes important when the dastardly cardinal hires her to seduce an English duke and steal diamonds. This is a plot to undermine the King of France, and Milady takes a back seat to Richelieu and Rochefort in the villain stakes. Once the usual story elements – such as D'Artagnan fulfilling his dream to join the Musketeers – have played out, the bumbling heroes confront their enemies.

There's time for a comical fight between Milady and the Queen's dressmaker Constance, but don't get too excited. The two women chase around furniture and use whatever items are available, while the men do the real fighting elsewhere.

The Four Musketeers (1974) – Milady de Winter (Faye Dunaway)

Faye Dunaway returns in a larger role, out for revenge against the heroes for foiling her scheme. There's a subplot about French rebels besieging La Rochelle and Richelieu using the conflict for his own ends, but the main story is the four musketeers dealing with the villainess and her lover.

Milady's romance with Athos comes into play, revealing her murderous past. When her initial plan to seduce D'Artagnan fails – after he overhears her wicked scheme – she attacks him. The assassin is a capable sword fighter despite the hindrance of her long dress, and her poisoned glass daggers are deadly. D'Artagnan escapes, but we get a welcome action scene for the female villain.

Richelieu sends Milady to murder the English Duke, but she is captured by savages before she completes her mission. Imprisoned in the Tower of London, she charms a dim-witted sentry into releasing her and even convinces him to kill the Duke. Constance escapes a bumbling male assassin. But it's all for nothing, since Milady disguises herself as a nun, infiltrates a convent, and strangles Constance with a rosary.

The murder enrages D'Artagnan enough that he agrees to a unanimous vote to behead the killer. Though seen at a distance, the ending is dark in tone. With the villainess dead, the stage is set for her daughter's revenge twenty years later.

The Three Musketeers (1993) – Milady de Winter (Rebecca De Mornay)

Receiving the "and" credit usually means a brief role, and we pass the half-hour mark before the villainess makes an appearance. This is light-hearted family fare, but more serious than the Lester version. Plenty of adventure and sword fights, and Tim Curry hams it up as Cardinal Richelieu, the chief baddie plotting to assassinate the King.

Milady is a spy, and a beautiful and dangerous seductress, though sadly underused. Besides threatening Richelieu with a dagger and confronting Athos about their past, Milady plays no part in the evil scheme. The master spy is intercepted before she leaves France after a tame encounter. After that, she repents and commits suicide. Dreadful stuff for such a key character.

The Three Musketeers (2011) – Milady de Winter (Milla Jovovich)

Adapted for the video game era, the title heroes are now secret agents with multi-bladed daggers, and Milady is a double-crossing acrobatic beauty. The opening sequence plays out like an *Assassin's Creed* mission, as the hooded Aramis breaks into Leonardo da Vinci's vault to steal plans for a war machine.

Except for basic plot elements, the steampunk story bears no resemblance to the source material. This is a loud action tale, with one against many fights, giant explosions and ridiculous set pieces. Picture a raid on the Tower of London and a sky battle between two airships. That means sea vessels on balloons, by the way.

Milady is a physical foe, capable of duelling armed guards in a 17th-century dress. Besides the usual seduction and villainy, she imitates Indiana Jones by sliding through a trapped hallway. This sequence has Jovovich do her *Resident Evil* thing. After dealing with the rooftop sentries, the thief descends on a harness to the Queen's private quarters. Then she somersaults through a string-based security system. They didn't have laser beams back then, but who cares?

After such a badass setup, one hopes for an epic fight with the musketeers. That never comes, and Milady is captured and defeated too easily. She also commits suicide. Or so it seems, because she survives a long drop to the ocean and returns for the last scene to set up a nonexistent sequel.

Rank #11

Bounty Tracker (1993)
Jewels (Cyndi Pass)

Movie

The top ten ranks are reserved for main villains, so Cyndi Pass' lethal mercenary has the honour of being the highest-ranked legendary henchwoman. A constant presence throughout, Jewels is always involved. Not content to be a background character, she happily guns down innocent civilians. She also provides technical support, acts as an intermediary between Erik Gauss (Matthias Hues) and his mafia paymaster, and looks badass whenever there's a lull in the action.

B-movie martial artist Lorenzo Lamas (known for the TV series *Renegade*) is Paul Damone, a bounty hunter who gets the typical establishing scene when he beats up a gang of thugs. With that out of the way, it's time to move on to the main plot. An accountant and his partner plan to give financial data to the police that incriminates a mob boss. He might think he's safe in his office, but Gauss and his hit squad have other ideas.

Jewels – wearing smart clothes and shades – leads the assault. An innocent secretary barely has time to ask a question before the assassin blasts her with a machine pistol. The first of many killing sprees then follows, with nobody safe from gunfire. One man takes cover in an office, but Jewels shoots him through the wall. Gauss wipes data from computers and kills the accountant, but his partner escapes. Matthias Hues is often cast in muscle roles, so we must have a scene where two cops attempt to arrest Gauss, only to get a brutal response.

When it's revealed the man who escaped is Damone's brother, and the bounty tracker is in Los Angeles, any action fan knows what's coming. The witness has police protection, but the officers are no match for Gauss' team. Jewels takes up a sniper position overlooking the house, coolly kills a sentry, and announces the coast is clear. Fifteen minutes in, and the villainess has racked up several kills.

Damone and his brother were enjoying a family get-together. That's until Gauss raids the house. The hero puts up some resistance and takes out two minor henchmen. Jewels isn't about to die this early, so she pins Damone down with bursts of gunfire. The villainess doesn't care an innocent female relative is caught in the crossfire – she's simply another witness to eliminate.

Without Damone to protect him, the brother is easy prey for Gauss. The police give the hero the lowdown on the suspect, and it's a routine revenge thriller from this point on. Gauss and Jewels make fine adversaries, and there are plenty of criminals for Damone to get through first.

Villainess

Mercenary work is expensive, so Gauss sends Jewels – posing as a smartly dressed attorney – to visit the imprisoned mafia boss. She arranges payment in diamonds, but the man unwisely romances the deadly assassin. Her response is cold, and even in this dialogue-heavy sequence, the henchwoman finds time to slam another prisoner into the cell bars.

Damone's investigation takes him on a montage trek through the city streets, and he gets a lead from a crippled veteran. The clue is a martial arts school staffed with men loyal to Gauss, which is an excuse to have a mass brawl. When unarmed attacks prove ineffective, the tougher thugs arm themselves with melee weapons, but the hero is unfazed.

Gauss – being the meticulous sort – sends Jewels after Damone as backup, and when the martial artists fail, she follows the hero back to his hotel. A maid becomes her latest innocent victim, then the assassin bursts into Damone's room. In the resulting shootout, he escapes (killing heroes is never that easy) by jumping down into a garbage bin. Time for Jewels to report back to Gauss and promise not to fail again.

One witness remains at large, but the assassin tracks a police detective to the isolated safe house. The cops are again outgunned by the mercenaries, who come equipped with silenced weapons and tear gas. The black-clad Jewels and Gauss wear gas masks to eliminate their targets. Sadly, this is a murky scene, but the henchwoman body count keeps on rising.

After Gauss murders the cripple, Damone teams up with the gang members the victim was helping rehabilitate, and the unlikely heroes locate Gauss' base of operations. The trailer is empty, but Damone makes the mob boss connection after he sees a television news report. Planning to follow the money trail, a gang banger hides in a car trunk and provides directions to the bounty tracker, who follows in a van.

The mafia men are smart enough to pay Gauss with genuine diamonds, but after a radio call from Damone reveals the stowaway, the mob is expendable. Jewels shoots a slow to react henchman and easily hunts down the escapee. Eventually, there's the expected big fight with Gauss that goes on for several minutes, with the villain taken out by a conveniently protruding nail and a spectacular kick from Damone.

Before that, there's a certain henchwoman to deal with. Jewels gets a couple of shootouts and an unexpected fight with Damone. Her martial arts skills are rather weak, so the hero defeats her quickly. The hero is daft enough to leave Jewels alive, but her next attack ends with a fatal gunshot. A somewhat bland ending, but this leather-clad henchwoman might have the highest female kill count in movie history.

Honourable Mention: Cyndi Pass

Mission of Justice (1992) – Rachel Larkin (Brigitte Nielsen), Erin Miller (Cyndi Pass)

Both Matthias Hues and Cyndi Pass are in this one too, but instead of Lamas it's Jeff Wincott as hero ex-cop Kurt Harris. His establishing scene is an old favourite: a store hold-up. That's before a combination of red tape and a domestic violence victim convince him to quit the force. It's not long before his boxer friend Cedric meets a sticky end, and Harris is on the case as a civilian investigator.

The hero's partner and contact on the force is Lynn Steele, a woman as tough as she sounds. Played by martial artist Karen Sheperd, she takes down her fair share of bad guys. Harris' off-book detective work leads him to mayoral candidate Dr Rachel Larkin (Brigitte Nielsen). The actress is attractive in a blonde wig and has a private army of vigilantes to clean up the streets. That's the cover story, because Larkin's true agenda is to gain money and power.

The villainess ditches the wig when she visits Cedric to persuade him to support her. The boxer puts up a fight against her brutal brother Titus (Hues), but has no hope of winning. Once Titus has done the roughing up, Larkin finishes the job with twin daggers, but the kill scene is brief. Most of the movie has Harris infiltrating the Peacemakers and doing some nocturnal detective work. Surprisingly, there are no corrupt cops on Larkin's payroll, though Titus kills a bureaucratic sergeant to frame Harris for the murder.

The Peacemakers are an all-male group except for Erin Miller, who's there as a female opponent for Steele during the climax. Miller is Larkin's secretary and just as evil as her boss. The henchwoman enjoys torturing people for information and helps murder an elderly woman for her inheritance. A wonderful villainess duo, but Miller doesn't put her martial arts training to use until the last encounter.

In fairness, she puts up a better fight against the heroine than most of the men. It's a rough catfight in the office that results in a lot of destruction, but Steele wins comfortably. Miller comes back for another try, but it's maybe ninety seconds of action in total.

After Harris defeats Titus, he confronts Larkin during a press conference. Thanks to a recording of her involved in torture and a murder confession, the hero is exonerated. The villainess refuses to go quietly and comes at Harris with her twin daggers, but the last hurrah is over within seconds. Worth a watch, if only to see Cyndi Pass as a henchwoman before her role in the superior *Bounty Tracker*.

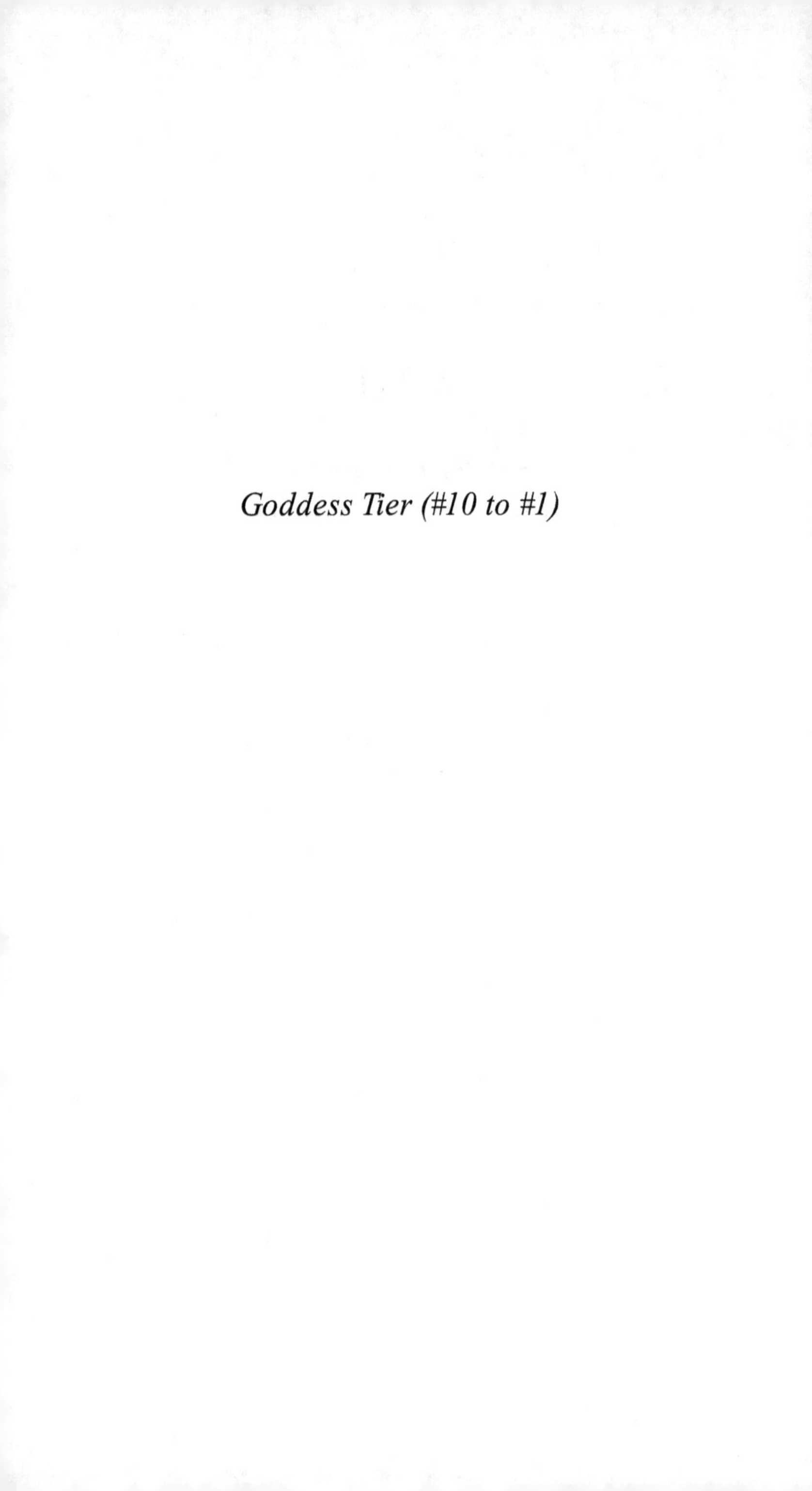

Goddess Tier (#10 to #1)

Rank #10

Single White Female **(1992)**
Hedra Carlson (Jennifer Jason Leigh)

Movie

1992 was the year of the psycho-template thriller. Besides *The Hand That Rocks the Cradle* and *Basic Instinct*, moviegoers were treated to a brilliant performance by Jennifer Jason Leigh as a crazy bitch determined to take over her roommate's life. The opening phase is slow-burning, but once the villainess has finished with creepy behaviour and nocturnal stalking, she goes on a murderous rampage for the last half hour.

Allison Jones (Allie for short) is a software designer who specialises in fashion products. When her boyfriend Sam cheats on her and a sleazy businessman reneges on a contract, Allie puts out a newspaper ad seeking a single white female. Several candidates apply for the tenancy, and most are weirdos who don't impress. Allie instantly takes a liking to Hedra – nicknaming her Hedy – and things seem to be on the up. But thriller fans will know that the "nice" people are often the most dangerous.

The eerie New York apartment building has an incinerator in the basement, a creaky old elevator with a screwdriver stored nearby to fix the door, and vents with

no soundproofing. Allie provides exposition when she gives Hedy a welcome tour, and these details all come into play later. The women start off on good terms. They socialise, eat out, and discuss their romantic problems. Best enjoy the calm, Allie, because it's all downhill from here.

The warning signs start when Hedy purchases a puppy and pretends it was given away, only to kick the dog (literally) and snap when Allie leaves her alone one night. Psycho episodes continue as Hedy imitates Allie's behaviour and interferes with her life. The roommate dates Sam, purchases matching clothes, and even dyes her hair and styles it to match. Identity theft, crazy style.

Villainess

It's never made clear why Hedy is so obsessed with becoming Allie. The heroine finds a shoebox of old letters and news clippings about Hedy's sister drowning in an accident, so childhood trauma is the vague explanation. That doesn't matter much since we get a chilling performance from Jennifer Jason Leigh. Even in the action-lite first two acts, she's a constant threat.

Finally, realising Hedy is dangerous, Allie discusses her concerns with a tenant on the floor below. Unfortunately, their voices carry through the vents, and Hedy listens in on the entire conversation. After Allie leaves, the gloved psycho sneaks in and knocks the tenant out with a pole. That's one problem dealt with.

Next, Hedy has sex with Sam, posing as Allie until he sees through her deception. After an angry rejection, the loony snaps and throws a high heel at him. That one hits the door, but her second shoe becomes a bizarre murder weapon when she swings its pointed end into Sam's eye.

Allie learns of the tragedy after it's reported on

television and then discovers Hedy's blood-smeared high heel in the bathroom. Of course, that's when the villainess returns to the apartment, and Allie is a poor liar, so gives herself away. The killer puts on her black gloves and pulls a gun on her roommate, but Allie can only cower in terror.

Done playing games, Hedy reverts to being a brunette, takes her hostage to the flat downstairs, and binds her prisoner to a chair with duct tape. Allie sees an opportunity after Hedy leaves, so turns up the volume on the television to attract attention, but it would never be that simple. The psycho returns just as the staff are about to force entry. Of course she does! The heroine attempts to send an e-mail message when Hedy has her book some plane tickets, but the villainess expects that move.

Earlier in the film, dodgy businessman Myerson attempted to assault Allie, and she broke off dealings with him. He's past due on paying an invoice, so his computer records are automatically wiped. Heading over to Allie's place to confront her, he instead finds Hedy. She feigns ignorance, but that lie is exposed when Myerson notices a suitcase with Allie's name tag. After forcing his way into the room, he finds the tied-up occupant. A struggle follows with Hedy apparently taken care of, but the still conscious villainess finishes Myerson with a gunshot and the old cushion muffling trick. His unlikely redemption arc didn't last long.

Hedy forces Allie to fake a suicide note and take pills, but the heroine smashes a glass into her captor's face and breaks free. That's when the (still alive!) tenant makes a dramatic reappearance, does his hero thing, and buys Allie precious time. The heroine drags Hedy out into the hallway, which leads to a prolonged fight in the elevator where the villainess seemingly strangles her roommate to death.

Hedy prepares to incinerate the "body", but finds Allie

gone when she returns. Arming herself with a sharp hook, the killer searches the basement for her quarry. There's a tense sequence where she bangs on furniture and smashes things up. But after hiding on a pipe, Allie surprises Hedy and stabs the crazy woman with the screwdriver (remember that?). The tough to kill woman clings on for a little while – enough to give Allie a scare – before she succumbs to her wound.

Rank #9

Centurion (2010)
Etain (Olga Kurylenko)

Movie

Ever wish for a physical female antagonist in a historical adventure? Look no further. Set in the second century, when Britain was the uncivilised wild north of the Roman Empire, this movie has a serviceable plot and epic battle scenes. The opposition are the Picts to the north of Hadrian's Wall, who believe in equal opportunity recruitment.

Quintus Dias (Michael Fassbender) is captured during an assault on a fortified garrison. After the Picts slaughter the other Romans, their leader spares the prisoner because he speaks their language. General Titus Virilus (Dominic West) and a legion of men are sent north to retaliate. For support, the ambitious governor also recruits Etain, a mute female scout, who shows off her combat skills in her introductory scene.

Dispatching a slave assassin "proves" Etain's loyalty, but the tense, silent woman sends out alarm signals constantly. If she's not sharpening her blade at camp, she stares coldly at the Romans and always seems on edge. So, it's no surprise when she betrays the legion after an ambush in a misty forest. Dias escapes and joins up with the survivors, and with the general taken prisoner, the

centurion assumes command.

The journey south is fraught with danger. A traitor sacrifices a fellow soldier to wolves to save himself, and later plots to murder the centurion to cover his tracks. The governor views the legion's defeat as a disaster, and orders assassins to silence Dias. This includes a beautiful woman who fetches poisoned wine after Dias makes it to presumed safety. Several women are in the Pict army, notably an archer named Aeron (Axelle Carolyn) who dispatches her foes with lethal accuracy.

The bow woman serves as a "mini-boss" in the final battle and gets her own one-on-one fight scene. But Etain steals the show as a silent, ever-present threat. The male Pict leader has historical immunity, so the female becomes Dias' nemesis, the final warrior that stands between him and his goal.

Villainess

For a woman who doesn't speak and relies on gestures to imply threat, Etain is a frightening foe. It's debatable whether she's a true villain given her hellish backstory. When she was a child, Romans slaughtered her village and cut out her tongue. So it's reasonable to hate their guts, and it's a stupid move by the governor to trust his men's safety to this vengeful woman.

Etain still ranks in the Goddess tier because it's rare for a female warrior antagonist to get much action. This movie bucks the trend, and she's a relentless opponent that makes the other dangers seem minor in comparison.

Every great villainess needs a fantastic kill or establishing scene. Etain gets her moment when the Pict leader releases the captured general, offers him a sword, and pits him against the spear-wielding warrior. Virilus puts

up a good fight against Etain, but his period in captivity has left him weak. As the Pict crowd jeer, he falls to her superior combat prowess and stamina. The victorious Etain walks off with no emotion – it was just another kill to her.

Olga Kurylenko is an action veteran, but this is a different role, which she handles admirably. After Etain paints her face and sets off on horseback, the film becomes a hunt and kill saga. The Romans regard their pursuer as unnatural, and an attempt to outsmart her ends badly. Etain is a skilled tracker, and her Pict warrior group finds the tired legion easy pickings. North of the border is a cold, unforgiving place when you have a huntress on your tail.

Dias and his men find respite with Arianne, an exiled Pict woman who's mistrustful at first. Good thing the centurion speaks her language, and the Romans find temporary comfort in her home. Eventually Etain tracks her quarry down, and a tense hide and seek scene follows as the huntress searches the property. Arianne has her own reasons for hating Etain, so she doesn't betray the Romans. Fed and rested, they will need their strength for the battle ahead.

The few remaining men reach the "safety" of a garrison, but it's deserted, and the army has retreated behind Hadrian's Wall. Tired of running from Etain – and realising a fight is inevitable – the survivors fortify their position. When the huntress arrives with her brutal Pict army, the stage is set for an epic battle that doesn't disappoint.

Like any feared leader, Etain has underlings to do her bidding, so she sends them in first to soften the Romans. The lesser warriors don't last long, and ultimately it's the surviving Romans against the two chief lieutenants: a tough axeman brute and the female archer Aeron. It takes a lot of fighting – and heroic sacrifice – to bring down the more competent Picts. A decent melee fighter, Aeron gets a gory

death when a Roman stabs an arrow into her eye.

With the battle going poorly, Etain rides in for the inevitable duel with Dias. The warrior woman is a good match for him, able to fight unarmed and with a sword now she's used her favourite spear. Multiple fights occur at once, but the cutaway shots to other Romans and Picts are short. For once, the villainess has a fantastic last encounter before the centurion's scripted victory.

Rank #8

Set It Off **(1996)**
**Stony (Jada Pinkett), Cleo (Queen Latifah), Frankie (Vivica
A. Fox), Tisean (Kimberly Elise)**

Movie

Female cat burglars were covered much earlier in the
rankings list, and now it's the turn of an all-female heist
crew. This 1990s movie centres on four women from inner-
city Los Angeles who rob banks to get back at the system
that failed them. This leads to three action-packed,
increasingly frantic heists, though it finishes in tragedy, as
violent crime sprees often do.

Other than Cleo, who's essentially a gangster, the
characters have sympathetic backstories. Frankie loses her
job as a bank teller after she panics during a robbery. Stony
does everything to support her brother, only for him to be
gunned down by police after they mistake him for a
criminal. Tisean loses custody of her child because she can't
afford to pay for care. None of these women are evil, but
despite the origin stories, they are criminals. With
exceptional performances all around, the charismatic team
earns a place in the Goddess tier.

While Stony and Tisean are reluctant to become career
offenders, Cleo and Frankie are eager to rob banks. These
"ringleaders" are on personal power trips and enjoy their
addictive new life of crime, which leads to tense arguments.

The film benefits from the unusual situation where the women begin as amateurs with weak disguises, but finish as an organised, masked-up professional crew.

The detective hunting the four women is the same man who mistakenly shot Stony's brother. He's onto them from the first heist, leading to personal standoffs and a nighttime gun battle on the streets of L.A. Don't expect a happy ending – it's not that kind of film.

Villainesses

The women pull off their first job at a bank they haven't cased, wearing wigs and sunglasses. Hectic, panicky stuff from the newbie robbers, and Tisean gets nervous and backs out. There are no major complications, and the gang escapes with the money. That's cause for celebration, with Frankie gleeful and Cleo dancing in celebration, though whether Tisean deserves her cut becomes a heated discussion point.

The argument boils over after Cleo spends her money on her girlfriend and booze. For Stony and Tisean, the robbery was a one-time deal, but the others are desperate for more money. A second heist follows, with a much better planned robbery where Tisean plays an innocent customer and disarms a would-be hero. The heist almost goes to pieces when a pedestrian outside causes a commotion and the police show up. Then Cleo rams a stolen vehicle through the window, and the women make a dramatic getaway.

Away from the action, Stony romances an account manager she met while staking out a target bank. The relationship blossoms, and Stony's boyfriend buys her an evening dress. After her taste of high society, she's reluctant to continue her criminal career. But as the main character, it's inevitable she will join her team for a big heist. The

women see themselves as gangsters and even do jokey mafioso impersonations at a boardroom table. With classical music playing in the background.

Things go smoothly when the women take advantage of their day (actually night) job to stash the stolen money in a tower block vent shaft. This turns out to be a mistake when their shady employer, Luther, discovers the money and absconds with it. He's not a smart man, so the women track him down. Cleo is angry and armed, so viewers will expect her to get trigger-happy. Instead, a nervous Tisean shoots Luther fatally in the back.

The police suspect Cleo (she is the obvious choice) and bring her in to take part in a lineup. The suspect intimidates a witness into silence through cold, psycho stares – enough to frighten anyone – and tapping her pocket where she stowed the woman's ID. Scare tactics work, and the police are forced to release Cleo. Now wanted women with no money, it's time for a big payday.

Naturally, the bank is the same one where Stony's lover works, but she lures him out of the building beforehand. This time the heisters move smoothly, dressed in true armed robber gear: blue overalls, braided haircuts and face masks. Someone trips a silent alarm, leading to a standoff between the police and the thieves. The women remove their masks when they realise the game is up and are on the verge of surrender when a nervy security guard guns down Tisean.

The aftermath is as bloody as you'd expect, with Stony and Cleo shooting cops and guards in retaliation. Cleo has a submachine gun she empties into any target available. Time for a *Heat*-style car chase and shootout on the streets. It's satisfying to see an all-female team engage in such carnage, but it's a losing battle since every local cop is after them and roadblocks are everywhere. There's time to grieve Tisean as

she bleeds out, before the women abandon her to go on the run.

Eventually, the police trap the robbers in a tunnel, and Cleo goes out in a blaze of glory to buy time for Stony and Frankie to escape. Frankie gets cornered and is confronted by the detective, but she refuses to give herself up. Stony can only watch from a bus to Mexico as the cops shoot her friend, and she's left to reminisce and count her hard-earned money south of the border.

It's Cleo – who else? – that gets the best death scene, surviving a hail of bullets that wreck her car as she rides a police gauntlet. As epic music plays, she steps out for one last confrontation. But even this tough cookie isn't invincible, and a small army of cops put her down.

Rank #7

Terminator 3: Rise of the Machines (2003)
T-X (Kristanna Loken)

Movie

Few would argue that this movie is weaker than *The Terminator* (1984) and *Terminator 2: Judgement Day* (1991). But this "conclusion" has a shockingly dark ending, a welcome cameo from the traumatised Dr Silberman (Earl Boen), and a cyborg enemy with a default female form. This fitting finale should have been the last act, but a popular franchise demands unwanted reboots. And so came messy follow-ups that completely contradicted the narrative that came before.

Future resistance leader John Connor (Nick Stahl) is now an adult living off the grid. Being hunted as a child leaves mental scars, and John has nightmares of the apocalyptic future he supposedly prevented. He's wise to be sceptical, because the artificial intelligence Skynet remains a threat and is about to be activated by naïve military commanders. Judgment Day – global nuclear destruction and the end of the world – is coming, and machines will rise against their creators.

To ensure victory, Skynet sends a cyborg through time. Previously, we'd had Arnold Schwarzenegger's T-800 target John's mother, Sarah, in the 1980s, and Robert Patrick's liquid metal T-1000 come after the man himself in the 90s. The latest model is Kristanna Loken's T-X, a solid metal

skeleton installed with advanced weaponry and covered in a liquid metal exterior. The "terminatrix" has the shapeshifting abilities of the T-1000, plus a plasma cannon and the frightening power to take over other machines.

Skynet is determined to win the coming war before it begins, and the T-X arrives in the early twenty-first century with a deadly mission. After the trademark nude arrival scene – in a Beverly Hills fashion store window (!) – the female cyborg hijacks a vehicle from a passing motorist. With John Connor in hiding, Plan B is to eliminate the men and women who will become his key lieutenants. The T-X goes on a murder spree through Los Angeles, taking out minor players with the usual efficiency.

The familiar storyline – a retread of the first two films – has a protector sent back in time. It's another less advanced T-800 series model (actually a T-850) that arrives naked in the desert. The scene that follows is a humorous variant on the "acquire clothes" objective, with Arnold's cyborg gatecrashing a strip club to widespread female applause. Pretty soon he has the classic leather outfit and an inappropriate pair of funky glasses, which he replaces with more traditional dark shades.

Until the end, the movie plays out as expected, with the human heroes and the "obsolete" terminator proving a match for the more technologically advanced opponent. Other characters – even named ones – are cannon fodder as Los Angeles again becomes a battleground for the fate of humanity.

Villainess

After eliminating two targets, the T-X goes after Katherine Brewster (Claire Danes), a woman destined to be Connor's wife and second in command. By chance – or fate,

according to the narrative – a wounded John breaks into the animal surgery where Kate works, only to get captured when she responds to an early morning emergency. There's barely time for conversation before the T-X arrives and guns down an innocent woman, believing her to be Kate. Then the cyborg tests (actually tastes) a bloody bandage and learns her primary target, John, is nearby.

Kate flees the scene, but the T-X corners her in a parking lot. The cyborg asks about John's whereabouts before she's interrupted by the reprogrammed T-850. Kate witnesses the destruction that follows as a vehicle crashes into the T-X, resulting in a huge explosion. The rescuer is more interested in keeping her away from harm than freeing her, so secures her in a van.

John escapes as the T-X – buried in rubble – reforms, and encounters Arnold's leather-clad protector. Time for the villainess to get serious, so she shrugs off conventional weaponry, reveals her plasma arm cannon, and blasts the old Terminator model into a storage shed. In the middle of all this, John drives off with Kate still in the vehicle. We then get a demonstration of the T-X's machine control power when she takes over the autopilots of emergency vehicles and sends them in pursuit.

The lengthy chase scene – with the T-X driving a Champion crane truck down a highway after her much flimsier target vehicle – is one of the best action scenes in the franchise. Besides remote-controlled cop cars, John must outrun a seemingly unstoppable truck that smashes its way through traffic. And the T-X uses her plasma cannon to devastating effect.

Eventually, the T-850 reactivates and commandeers a motorcycle. Arnold comes to the rescue by jumping on the crane – with destruction raining around him – and gets on board despite his foe's best efforts. Other drivers watch on

as the two cyborgs battle amidst carnage and explosions. It takes dropping the crane hook down a manhole to stop the T-X. She emerges from the wreckage unscathed, a determined opponent that will not be bested so easily.

After that chaos, it's time for some less action-packed story segments. John explains the situation to a sceptical Kate, and the T-850 takes the heroes to a cemetery. There John finds his late mother's resting place, except the coffin is really a weapons cache. Alerted by a witness, the police arrive in force. In response to the recent chaos, they bring a full S.W.A.T. team to stop the T-850. That goes as poorly as expected, though the reprogrammed cyborg avoids human casualties.

Before all the shooting started, we were introduced to Kate's boyfriend, Scott. Being a relative of a main character is normally fatal in these movies, and Scott soon has a deadly encounter with the terminatrix. The T-X impersonates Scott to deceive two detectives, who take "him" to the cemetery. The two cops become expendable once the cyborg locates John, leading to a not so happy "reunion" with Kate in a graveyard.

Kate witnesses the cyborg morph into her natural form and prepare to fire. Frozen in shock, she's fortunate that the T-850 arrives to save her in a bullet-riddled hearse. An RPG stops the T-X, but she reforms and comes after the vehicle, sprinting at high speed. After another chase – shorter and less chaotic than the city pursuit – a passing truck provides the T-850 an opportunity to slice the hearse in two and remove the threat. The T-X's cannon is damaged beyond repair, but the villainess has many secondary weapons at her disposal.

Kate learns her future self sent the T-850 back in time, her own father is the man in charge of Skynet, and the nuclear war is only hours away. After those shocking

revelations, she and John join their cyborg protector and head for the military facility. As the general ponders whether to activate Skynet, the T-X is already on site, disguised as female military personnel. The villainess uses her machine control function to take over T-model prototypes, which include advanced drones and minigun-armed tanks.

Kate and company arrive, but they're too late. The T-X impersonates the heroine and guns down the general in the control room. One more future lieutenant disposed of, but the T-850 buys precious time by shooting the T-X and knocking her down a vent shaft. As the rogue machines massacre the civilian staff, the dying general tells his daughter about a secret bunker within flying distance.

Now battle-hardened, Kate shows her strength by grabbing a rifle and destroying a machine to save John. The T-850 rips a minigun from one tank and destroys another. But it's the inevitable one-on-one battle between the terminators that's the standout scene. The two cyborgs destroy a corridor and bathroom, reducing concrete walls to rubble. Against a superior opponent, the T-850 uses makeshift weapons, including a gas tank and a urinal (!). But the T-X wins the lengthy fight, decapitates the T-850, and takes control of it. We all knew that plot development was coming.

John comes up with a clever strategy to defeat the T-X by powering up an accelerator, which creates a magnetic field. That's ideal for dealing with a cyborg armed with a flamethrower, and with the liquid metal spread over the pipe, Kate gets her first badass quote when she tells the "bitch" to die. Anyone familiar with the earlier movies knows that initial attempts to defeat ruthless Terminators don't work. And history repeats as the T-X escapes the trap by cutting the pipeline with a circular saw.

After a confrontation with the corrupted T-850 – that nearly ends with the out-of-control machine snapping John's neck – the heroes fly to the remote bunker. On arrival, they find an old nuclear fallout facility, not the system core they were told to expect. This leads into the bleak finale where nuclear missiles launch, nearly wiping out humanity, and the dark future comes to pass. With the VIPs likely dead, John and Kate are now in charge of the survivors, and the fightback against the machines begins.

Before this, the T-X arrives at the bunker to eliminate the future threat. A submachine gun barely impacts the liquid metal, so it's good the T-850 has fought off the corruption. John and Kate almost escape through the closing bunker door, but the T-X makes one last attempt to crawl through before the T-850 pulls her damaged skeleton away. In an earlier scene, we were shown the T-850 was powered by two energy cells that cause massive explosions when ruptured. A convenient explosive to ram into the T-X's mouth and terminate her for good.

Rank #6

Double Edge (1992)
Carmen (Susan Lucci)

Movie

This female assassin thriller took the unusual step of casting Susan Lucci in a dual role as the villainess Carmen and FBI agent Maggie. She's less effective as the heroine, but her ruthless and intelligent hitwoman is Goddess tier material. This movie doesn't skimp on body count, with eight people dead – ranging from unnamed extras to lead roles – by the denouement.

After the introductory credits sequence shows Carmen and Maggie getting dressed for business, the two women meet in a hotel lobby. Maggie attends a function, but Carmen has a far more deadly purpose. The assassin uses her seductive charm to get close to Hector Barrado, a key witness in a trial. And then murders him with a needle weapon disguised as a hairpin. Carmen's first on-screen kill occurs within five minutes, the opening move of a deadly cat-and-mouse contest.

Maggie – already researching the assassin – builds a profile and realises it's the same woman she met at the hotel. Typical of this kind of film, the female agent has someone she doesn't like for a partner. That would be her ex-husband Carter (Robert Urich), whom she blames for her child's death. The relationship subplot is formulaic. Cold to

begin with, their affection gradually warms, and most viewers will guess where this is going.

Carmen also has a lover: her assistant Paul, who stands in as a masseuse when not negotiating his boss' contracts. True romance isn't reciprocated, since she views him as a source of information and not an equal. The assassin's latest contract is personal since she's after the man who killed her father, but that doesn't stop her demanding a higher fee.

Carmen disguises herself as maintenance staff and attempts to snipe her target from a van in an underground parking garage. That ends in failure when she's disturbed, leading to frustration with Paul. Do you suspect he'll become a loose end later? Meanwhile, Maggie hunts the elusive killer.

Villainess

Forced to up her game, Carmen builds a homemade jamming device that disperses iron filings. Just the thing to hook up to a ventilation system and blind a CCTV system. Dressed all in black leather with white surgical gloves, the assassin infiltrates the upper-floor offices while the guards are distracted. Then, she accesses her target's computer to view his itinerary. And this is just the *preparation work* for a cleverly planned hit.

Carmen takes too long because the cameras come back online before she's made her escape. A guard spots something on the monitor, but the assassin evades him by taking the staircase down instead of the elevator. Another man asks for identification, but he's about to learn the hard way Carmen is no ordinary criminal. The assassin plays the role of a clumsy employee and drops her purse to distract him. When he takes the bait and kneels down, the killer stabs him.

Maggie follows the money trail to a church and learns her quarry's name is Carmen Moore. Given the close resemblance, the FBI woman pretends to be a loving sister and discovers that the hitwoman's donations support a mentally ill father. Maggie leaves her contact details with the mother superior, causing further friction with Carter. A dangerous move intended to panic Carmen, but she learns of Maggie's visit, and the huntress and prey roles switch.

Deciding to repay Maggie's curiosity, Carmen watches the agent's house and breaks in after she leaves. The assassin finds a photo and takes an interest in a porcelain figure because of a personal connection before the housekeeper, Rose, arrives to clean the rooms. After the maid hears a disturbance, she encounters Carmen in her leather outfit. Initially, Rose mistakes the woman for Maggie, but her hostile intent soon becomes clear. Before Rose can call for help, Carmen pushes her over the balcony.

To gear up, Carmen visits a shady arms dealer – who works in a store basement – and tests out several firearms before asking for a sniper rifle. The dealer thinks double-crossing an assassin and ratting her out to a corrupt cop is a wise move. Except Carmen is suspicious and follows the guy to the meet. Betrayal is a surefire way to get killed, and the execution scene is darkly comical. The dealer calls out to his dog, Shotgun, only for the leather-clad assassin to greet him with the same phrase. Before she blows the idiot away with a laser-sighted… yep, shotgun.

With a family acquaintance dead, Maggie feels the pressure. Carmen piles on the misery by leaving a telephone message and a broken ornament in Maggie's bed. No wonder the FBI has assigned its agent a protective detail, but that doesn't prevent a hit-and-run attempt. That almost succeeds, and a bodyguard becomes the latest victim of an assassin's bullet. All this excitement causes Maggie to hook

up with Carter, and the former spouses put their ill feelings for one another aside to focus on the problem at hand.

Carmen isn't pleased the dealer Paul referred her was crooked, so she concludes her "boyfriend" is no longer useful. The assassin gives him a dressing-down speech as she relaxes in an outdoor pool before she pulls out a gun. That body count keeps rising - they sure knew how to keep thrillers exciting in the 1990s. With the loose ends taken care of, it's time for the assassination we've been building up to for the whole movie.

Since the two women look alike, it's no surprise that Carmen impersonates Maggie to gain access to a private estate. A large-scale event gives the assassin the cover she needs to hide out in a storeroom and assemble a sniper rifle. Tipped off by security, Maggie prevents the hit, but Carter sacrifices himself by taking a bullet. Viewers who thought the lead would hook up with her partner just got a nasty surprise, because there's no Kevlar vest or plot device to save him.

In the final showdown between the Susan Lucci characters, Carmen – still disguised as Maggie – shows up at the church to support her father. Maggie finds it difficult to shoot (!) and the assassin gains the advantage. That's when her old man realises how evil his daughter has become and shoots her in the back. A bittersweet ending to finish things.

Exception to the Rule (1997)
Carla Rainer (Kim Cattrall)

Movie

The title and one-line plot synopsis – a man blackmailed over diamonds – promise little. But show any villainess fan the opening scene, where a woman in black leather bumps off a South African diamond trader, and the excitement should build. For once, the events that follow don't disappoint, and this movie is an easy selection for the goddess tier.

The killer's face is not shown, but the long blonde hair and voice are a giveaway. Carla features prominently on the poster and is played by Kim Cattrall, so no prizes for guessing who the antagonist is. The villainess shoots the trader above the heart to paralyse him, then moves closer for a headshot execution. A killing style that establishes Carla as someone who likes her victims to suffer in their last moments.

Carla doesn't get the diamonds, as the victim passed them on just before she arrived. So now it's time to devise a new plan, which involves Tim Bayer (Eric McCormack). He's an American who's unhappily married to the pregnant Angela (Sean Young). The woman is also the daughter of Tim's boss and firm owner Larry Kellerman (William Devane), which is sure to cause friction. Tim has marriage counselling from psychiatrist Dr Beeson and support from his friend Ron Lansing, but neither man is trustworthy.

Carla works her way into Tim's life by pulling the broken-down vehicle trick, which convinces the good Samaritan to offer the beautiful woman a ride home. Soon after that, she poses naked in her apartment, though we only see rear shots of a body double. Still, the seduction tricks are effective, and Carla visits Tim at the office to tempt him further.

The broker is sent to San Francisco to close a deal with the shady Mr Ferguson, whose next visitor is a black-gloved assassin with a syringe full of snake venom. Her screaming victim takes a fatal plunge from a skyscraper, then Carla "accidentally" encounters Tim in a bookstore. The villainess seduces her mark, leading to wine sipping and passionate sex. Once again there's a body double, though we see Carla's face this time around. Getting involved with a femme fatale will only end badly, Tim.

Villainess

Shortly after Tim returns home and spends time with Angela, he receives a videotape of his one-night stand. Carla set up a camera, and when Tim revisits the apartment, it's the usual story of the blackmailer using a false address. Dr Beeson isn't much help, so Tim hires Burt Ramsey, a loan shark who moonlights as a private detective. Ron is in debt to Burt – who sends two goons round as an unfriendly reminder – and the gambling problems are a hint that the best friend can't be trusted.

Time for Carla to up the ante, so she shows up unannounced during an evening out to join Tim, Larry, and Angela. This leads to an awkward conversation where the others don't know the woman posing as Susan Bradshaw has evil intent. This is all designed to make Tim nervous, and to increase the pressure even more, Carla goes with Angela to the women's restroom. There, the villainess shows off a heart and snake tattoo on her thigh, and tells Angela that her lover has the other half.

With Tim on edge, Carla meets him at a remote location to make her demands, looking sinister in black leather and dark glasses. She wants Tim to bring her the shipment of diamonds that she's failed to steal so far and uses the videotape and threats of violence as leverage. Carla fondles Tim's groin just because she can, while Burt watches from a distance. The villainess spots her tail quickly, and there's a rather short car chase before she loses him.

Not too happy with Tim hiring a PI, the leather-clad Carla confronts him in a parking garage. They trade threats before the killer warns Tim that she "does the fucking". A line *intended* to have a double meaning. Angela is unaware of what's going on and attends a gallery event with her husband. She works on metal sculptures in her private workshop, and her latest effort is Blind Justice, a statue of a woman with raised hands pressed together. The sculpture appears in several scenes, so it will become important later.

Carla decides the nosy Burt has become a problem, so drives to a cliff edge and exits her car. Being rather stupid – and not considering that the suspect is dressed in black – he joins Carla and questions her while drinking booze. The deranged woman gives an obviously fake story about being in love with Tim, then injects Burt with sea snake venom. While he's paralysed, the villainess pours alcohol over him, sets his vehicle on fire, and watches with smiling glee as he's knocked over the cliff by the flaming car. A brilliant death scene, and Carla enjoyed every second.

A detective named Garcia shows up at Tim's office to question him about Burt's death. Tim provides a false reason for hiring the PI, but the cop doesn't buy it. After a run-in with Garcia while visiting Burt's nightclub, Carla raises the stakes by attempting to run Angela over in broad daylight. This leaves Tim's wife very shaken, and he contemplates giving the psycho what she wants.

Tim appears to cave in to her demands and meets at yet another secluded spot. After Carla leaves with the diamonds, Tim follows her to a motel and learns she's involved with Dr Beeson. It's quickly revealed the stones are fake, so Tim contacted the police and Larry about the scheme and went there wired up. Carla looks like she might kill the doctor, but leaves him alive. A show of mercy? Or maybe she didn't have her silenced pistol or syringe handy.

Beeson reconsiders and telephones Tim, but is cut off when a masked assailant barges into the hotel. The latest murder victim is a weak opponent, whom the mysterious male attacker drowns in a bathtub. Given the lack of suspects, it's obvious who Carla's accomplice is, but it takes several minutes for an official reveal during the finale at Angela's house.

Tim has moved out, so his wife is alone and easy prey for the villainess. It's already been established that Angela doesn't like snakes, while Carla is fond of them. The killer even has a distinctive metal pattern on her gloves. Naturally, the villainess leaves a live snake in the bed as a nasty surprise and interrupts to issue demands when the terrified Angela calls Tim. At gunpoint, the resilient woman grabs a golf club while Carla taunts her and uses it to knock away the gun. Inexplicably, Carla can't shoot accurately at a fleeing pregnant woman.

Ron, who shows up outside, advises Angela to hide. Once inside, it's revealed (to no great surprise) that Ron is romantically involved with Carla and working with her. The accomplice roughs himself up to convince Angela he's dealt with the villainess, but tearing open his shirt reveals the other tattoo half that tips his would-be victim off. After she locks herself in the workshop, Carla surmises Ron is expendable, rediscovers her pistol skills, and does her double-shot execution trick.

Angela takes cover in her workshop as the leather-clad villainess shoots her way in. Time for some obligatory taunts as she searches the building. It doesn't take long to find Angela's rather obvious hiding place. That's when Tim arrives, leading to a brief scuffle that ends with Carla victorious. With Angela still recovering from a knockdown, the killer shoots Tim in the chest and lines up her trademark headshot. Then it's the wife to the rescue with a blowtorch.

Angela keeps Carla at bay with the flaming weapon, but has spent too much time welding because the gas supply runs out. The smirking villainess senses victory, but Angela surprises her by using the torch as a makeshift club. The blow sends Carla crashing through a guardrail, and the conveniently placed sculpture interrupts her fall. That sharp hand is an effective spike that skewers the villainess, and while her fingers twitch, there's no sudden resurrection.

Murphy's Law (1986)
Joan Freeman (Carrie Snodgress)

Movie

Charles Bronson movies are typical gusto hero stuff, but this offering adds an excellent psycho villainess to ramp up the enjoyment factor. Tough cop Jack Murphy prefers to shoot bad guys instead of reasoning with them, but meets his match when a recently paroled killer sets him up for murder. There are many lesser goons to deal with, ranging from a mafia boss to a rural gang operation. These mini-battles usually end messily with gunfire, dead bodies, and explosions. Fortunately, Snodgress' kill scenes are so excellent that the distractions don't dilute her contribution.

Kathleen Wilhoite makes her feature debut as Arabella McGee, a punk with a loud mouth and a creative vocabulary. Every other word she utters is an insult, which adds humour amidst the violence. Arabella makes the mistake of stealing Murphy's car during the title credits, but he soon catches up to her after some wild driving and a spectacular crash. The female thief is much better at kneeing a guy in the balls and escaping. Murphy is better prepared for a later encounter in a women's restroom, leading to a tirade of expletives as he restrains her.

What else is happening in Los Angeles? A mob boss' brother becomes a murder suspect after physical evidence is found at the crime scene, but refuses to go quietly. Confronted at an airport, the bad guy takes a hostage and kills her once she becomes a burden. Enough justification for Murphy to shoot him dead. With the mafia boss out for blood and a separated wife filing for divorce, it's no wonder Murphy is a depressed alcoholic.

Things are about to get even worse when Joan Freeman arrives in town. The paroled murderess meets with a private investigator to get information on her targets: various men in the police force and legal system who put her away. Joan shows how psychotic she is when the PI negotiates for more money. Perhaps he shouldn't have followed her from the public park to a secluded underpass. The villainess points a gun at the man, demands he open his mouth wide, and blows his brains out. Face covered in blood, Joan is a terrifying killer about to screw with Jack Murphy's life.

Villainess

Murphy's spouse is a strip club dancer, an excuse for gratuitous nudity before Murphy tries to smooth things over. The cop follows the wife to watch her romance another guy, but Joan is also watching and plotting her next move. Late one night, she knocks out Murphy in his car and uses his weapon to blow away the couple while the hero sleeps it off. The framed cop is puzzled about how he got home, but finds out soon enough when his colleagues show up to arrest him.

Murphy curses his luck when he's locked in a cell with Arabella, but doesn't endure her insults for long. He stages a fight and makes a run for it... with the handcuffed loudmouth in tow. Murphy reaches the police station roof and makes a dramatic helicopter escape. Unfortunately, the chopper is low on fuel, forcing him to crash into a drug farm. Just a few more punks to deal with, then.

Murphy is injured during the gun battle but makes it to a remote cabin where a crippled ex-cop offers to help. Arabella is in way over her head and not happy about it, and the old man offers the hero some friendly advice. They seem to like each other, but any savvy viewer knows that spells certain doom, especially since Joan has the friend in her personal scrapbook of targets. After Murphy leaves with Arabella, the leather-clad Joan pays the cripple a visit. She takes one of his many shotguns, knocks him to the ground, and says nothing as she pulls the trigger.

Joan's next target is a prominent judge, so the villainess puts on a redhead wig, dolls herself up, and acts the seductress in a restaurant. After the other customers leave, the judge flirts with Joan, despite feeling her face looks familiar. He should have trusted his instincts because the insane woman reveals her evil side and drowns the man in a bathtub. Easy to make it appear like an accident when there's a lamp on a balcony above to drop into the water.

Murphy suspects the mob boss is behind the murders, so he and Arabella trick their way into a private suite. The hero confronts the man – a scared wreck without his henchmen – and demands he confess at gunpoint. Eventually, the hero realises the boss is innocent (of these killings, at least) and asks a police contact to research other leads. That's when Murphy learns who his true enemy is.

Joan's next victim is her psychiatrist, who's too inquisitive for her own good. The psycho strangles her with a power cable after pumping weights. Murphy and Arabella arrive too late, but find Joan's scrapbook, which leads them to a remote property. Too bad the occupant is already dead, suffocated with a plastic bag. The murderess surprises Arabella and sedates her with chloroform, then leaves a message in lipstick to set up the denouement.

That showdown takes place in the Bradbury Building, which makes a great location with its winding dark staircase and antique elevator. Joan gags and restrains Arabella, and has a loaded crossbow with many bolts to fire in Murphy's direction. The mafia interrupts proceedings, and the psycho is happy to hide and eliminate the gangsters while Murphy has a shootout with them. After taking out the boss' henchmen through a combination of heroism and luck, the rogue cop confronts and finishes the boss with a one-liner.

It's Murphy against Joan, with the hero dodging bolts as the murderess proves an expert markswoman. Disarmed by the villainess' sharpshooting, Murphy races downstairs to save Arabella from being crushed under the descending elevator. Joan shoots the woman (non-fatally) to lure Murphy back upstairs. Out of bolts, the lunatic grabs a fire axe and attacks, slicing Murphy's chest.

With the villainess off balance, Murphy takes advantage and knocks her over a railing. She clings in desperation to the axe (trapped in the rails) and pleas for her life. Murphy isn't a man for noble actions, so he watches Joan lose her grip and retorts to her "Go to hell" comment with the catchy "Ladies first".

The World Is Not Enough (1999)
Elektra King (Sophie Marceau), Cigar Girl (Maria Grazia Cucinotta)

Movie

My *GoldenEye* discussion omitted one of the Brosnan films. That's because the only female main villain in the Bond series deserves a goddess tier spot. As a bonus, we get the greatest pre-credits villainess, which *almost* makes up for the female baddie wilderness in the Daniel Craig era. In classic 007 fashion, the Cigar Girl assassin gets her own dedicated section. And it's a logical review structure since Elektra doesn't appear until after the title song.

Brosnan films are relatively fun and escapist compared to what followed, but this entry has a more serious tone. Valentin Zukovsky (Robbie Coltrane) makes a welcome return as Bond's reluctant ally, and the MI6 series regulars are also present. Sadly, this was Desmond Llewelyn's last appearance as Q, but he passes the torch on to R (John Cleese) and delivers comic antics and gadget-testing chaos.

Action sequences are hit and miss, and the major set pieces – attacks by para-hawks and saw-blade helicopters, a gun battle in a missile silo, and the climax on a doomed submarine – fall flat compared to the spectacular opening. Still, this is a must-watch movie for any villainess fan, and the twist of having a Bond girl be the main baddie is a refreshing take. There's also a good female: Denise Richards as nuclear physicist Christmas Jones. An excuse for bad jokes, but this is an entertaining outing.

Pre-Title Villainess

This epic opening gambit – and the longest before *No Time to Die* – begins in Bilbao, Spain, with Bond mincing words with a sleazy banker. A beautiful woman offers him a cigar (hence her nickname) and even gets a double entendre quip. Then it's down to business with 007 demanding answers about a murdered MI6 agent. Things predictably turn nasty, and Bond makes quick work of some armed thugs. Too bad he forgets about the Cigar Girl, who eliminates the banker with a throwing knife.

Trapped and unable to pursue the assassin, Bond makes a dramatic getaway with a suitcase of money with the help of a mystery sniper. This ensures 007 makes it safely back to London, where he's introduced to Sir Robert King, an oil tycoon who won't be with us much longer. The money is laced with explosives, and King's lapel pin is a proximity trigger. With MI6 under attack, a familiar female foe returns, and this time it's Bond in her laser sight.

The big chase along the River Thames has Bond in a gadget-equipped boat pursuing the Cigar Girl past famous landmarks, including the Houses of Parliament and the Millennium Dome. The elusive assassin is as skilled at piloting a boat as at murder. More than once she evades Bond by making sudden turns or cutting under a descending bridge. Bond submerges the boat to bypass the obstacle and straightens his tie. Remember when these movies were pure fun?

The Cigar Girl uses a machine gun, which is ineffective against the armoured Q-Boat, so she switches to a grenade launcher. Plenty of collateral damage and explosions, but Bond is never easy to get rid of. The villainess wrecks another boat and cuts 007 off, or so she thinks. Like all vehicle chases in Bond films, the hero finds a detour – a land ride through a street market, narrow alley, restaurant – back to the Thames.

Bond launches torpedoes at the Cigar Girl, but she makes her own dramatic escape like any good pre-credits villain. Then she hijacks a hot-air balloon, and Bond leaps onto the mooring rope. Realising there's no way out – and rejecting Bond's offer of protection – the henchwoman blows up a gas tank. Bond drops to safety and the Millennium Dome does something useful by breaking his fall. This hitwoman and sequence could push for a ranking all by herself, but there's plenty more female villainy to come.

Main Villainess

Straight after the title song, Elektra attends her father's funeral. The first half of the movie sets her up as a traditional Bond girl whom the hero must protect. The main villain is implied to be Renard (Robert Carlyle), an anarchist who previously kidnapped Elektra and now appears to be targeting her again. King's daughter has taken over his oil company and oversees a pipeline construction in Azerbaijan. Not the safest part of the world, and after Elektra and Bond are attacked by para-hawks while skiing in the mountains, the two become dangerously close.

Surprisingly, Bond *doesn't* make love, and instead shows genuine concern when Elektra invites him to her luxurious Baku residence. There are plenty of dodgy-looking males around, including a tough henchman and the head of security, so no shortage of insider suspects. It turns out they are *all* working with Renard, but the mystery element works well. As a villain before the more serious Craig films, there's a gimmick, in this case a bullet lodged in Renard's brain which suppresses pain.

Determined to identify his attackers, Bond visits Valentin at a Russian mob casino. Everyone present, from the high rollers to the attractive female employees, is armed. Elektra shows up and acts recklessly, losing a million dollars on a high-card draw game. The first sign this woman may not be as innocent as she pretends, but Bond still beds her. That moral compunction didn't last long, eh?

Bond's investigation leads him to the pipeline construction site where the treacherous head of security learns the British spy has a licence to kill. A long plane ride later, Bond discovers a plot to steal a nuclear bomb from a missile silo. This is where we meet Christmas Jones, an improbable scientist who becomes an unlikely ally once Renard's men open fire. She's the reliable, non-screaming Bond girl who's happy to help, even if bullets and explosions are not a usual day at the office.

Despite Bond's efforts, Renard escapes, and it's revealed he plans to detonate a nuclear device in Elektra's pipeline. With a second woman involved, it's inevitable (in this era) that one girl will be bad. When Bond and Christmas discover only half the plutonium core is in the bomb, 007 makes a calculated choice to let the device explode. Believing her nemesis to be dead, Elektra reveals her true intent to M – present at the villainess' request – by having the MI6 bodyguards killed. And we finally have a female main villain to celebrate.

Now we know Elektra is behind her father's murder, it's time to reveal the endgame. Bond questions Valentin and learns that the villainess and Renard have purchased an old nuclear submarine. Their plan: to create a meltdown, destroy Istanbul, and contaminate the surrounding sea. And Elektra's pipeline will become the only viable oil supply in the region.

With so much wealth and power, no wonder this woman has a hold over Renard. The two have a sinister sex scene where she runs ice over her body and clearly enjoys inflicting psychological torture. Meanwhile, M is locked in a cell in Maiden's Tower, but broadcasts a signal using a missile locator card (which Bond gave her earlier) and a clock battery.

After an amusing scene where the heroes interrogate Valentin as he drowns in caviar, a gold-toothed henchman sells them out. Time for physical torture, and the villainess uses an antique chair and neck restraint to secure Bond. Perfect for strangling a man during a villainous motive rant, and an opportunity to drop the title, which is Bond's family motto. The sadistic Elektra rapes Bond while he's at her mercy and is enjoying her triumph until Valentin crashes the party.

If Bond was expecting a rescue, he shouldn't have been so optimistic. Elektra shoots Valentin, and the Russian mobster – despite having a gun in his cane – targets a wrist restraint instead of the female villain. Perhaps a reference to their history, as the Russian acknowledges Bond in his dying moment. That's enough for the hero to escape and chase Elektra up Maiden's Tower.

Disappointingly, she's not the last villain to die, as there's a lengthy sequence where Bond stops Renard melting down the submarine reactor. And then it's the usual scenario of rescuing the Bond girl, who actually proves useful, and an old-style ending with a poor joke and M surprised by her top agent's womanising.

Before the anticlimactic finale, Bond faces off with Elektra. She gets one of the best villain deaths: taunting the spy as he pursues her, before boasting he can't kill a woman in cold blood. Turns out Bond has no problems with cold-blooded murder with evil women, though he shows regret afterward.

Honourable Mention / Discussions: Daniel Craig Bond Movies

Casino Royale (2006) – Valenka (Ivana Miličević)

The sole honourable mention for this review goes to a mostly silent, sexy henchwoman who looks the part but doesn't do much. And that faint praise sums up the lack of female villains in the Daniel Craig era.

The second Martin Campbell-directed reboot (after *GoldenEye*) is an origin story with a black and white prologue and a reckless 007. A long way from Connery's suave secret agent. A back to basics approach, but there are action scenes aplenty, notably a free-run sequence across a construction site. The bad guy is Le Chiffre, a banker funding terrorists whom Bond must outwit in a high-stakes poker game at the titular Casino Royale. Judi Dench remains M, but with no Moneypenny or Q, Bond relies on actual spy work and resilience to complete his mission.

The main female character is Vesper Lynd, a treasury agent with the usual pun introduction, who later becomes a genuine love interest. Eva Green delivers a standout performance in the franchise, with real chemistry between her and Craig's 007. Bond's weakness for women makes him blind, and he doesn't know Vesper is working with the shadowy organisation behind Le Chiffre. It's eventually revealed that he had her boyfriend kidnapped to coerce her, so she's a tragic character and not a true villain. But her death in the Venice finale is the most downbeat outcome since *On Her Majesty's Secret Service*.

As for Valenka, she gets a sexy introduction and is present for Le Chiffre's business dealings. Despite being attacked by a machete-wielding thug, she remains loyal and isn't too bothered by violence when she's not the target. Her best moment is poisoning Bond's drink at Casino Royale, but she vanishes near the end. A scream implies Valenka is killed when Le Chiffre's employers decide he's no longer valuable. Get used to disappointment with this Bond – it only gets worse from here.

Quantum of Solace (2008)

The story is hard to follow in this weak outing, and the jump-cut action sequences are more likely to induce headaches than thrill. Add unnecessary, arty title cards whenever events shift to a new location, poor direction during exposition scenes, and a truly pathetic henchman, and the result is dire. A woman named Strawberry Fields (yes, really) gets coated in oil for her death scene as homage to the superior *Goldfinger*. Painful stuff.

Olga Kurylenko is Camille, a former Bolivian agent who allies with Bond. She handles herself well in the action scenes, notably a parachute escape from a crashing plane. Pity her vendetta is even less interesting than Bond's quest to avenge Vesper. The climax in a desert hotel is messy, and the only plus point is brevity. Clocking in at 106 minutes, *Quantum* is the shortest Bond movie to date.

Skyfall (2012)

Craig's third movie breaks with tradition by not giving us a true Bond girl. Judi Dench is M for the last time, with a more prominent role in the story and a great sendoff. Naomie Harris' MI6 operative does more harm than good.

More importantly, her name is Eve Moneypenny, an entirely different origin for the world's most famous secretary. Q makes a comeback in the guise of a young boffin, though gadgets are limited to a palm reader, gun and radio.

The closest fit to the traditional female role is Séverine (Bérénice Lim Marlohe), a former sex slave who is now a trophy girl and accomplice to the main villain Silva (Javier Bardem). He's a former agent out for revenge against M, and the story is mainly set in the UK. Séverine looks beautiful, matching the exotic locations of Shanghai and Macau. But like many ill-fated women in 007 movies, she romances the British spy before the villain disposes of her in theatrical fashion.

Skyfall is one of the better Bonds overall, perhaps because it doesn't follow the established formula. The terrorist attacks on the London Underground and parliamentary hearing are well staged. The grand finale is a MacGyver-style final confrontation in Scotland as Bond dusts off a familiar Aston Martin. However, female antagonists are notably absent.

Spectre (2015)

The return of Ernst Stavro Blofeld (Christoph Waltz) and his evil organisation promised much, but delivered little. Mexico City during the Day of the Dead is a spectacular backdrop for an action-packed opening sequence, a helicopter stunt, and thousands of extras. Unfortunately, that's the sole highlight. A shadowy Spectre conference, a car chase through Rome, and a train fight with a tough henchman should be exciting. They are not.

No female villains (again), and the leading lady Madeleine Swann (Léa Seydoux) has no chemistry with 007. Monica Bellucci appears – briefly – as the suicidal widow of a Spectre agent Bond killed in the teaser. He saves her life and seduces her for information, which ends with the most uncomfortable fling in the series.

Best not to mention the unnecessary twist about Bond's guardian being Blofeld's father, revealed in a painful exposition scene. Add a tedious plot about intelligence control, a flat finale in the ruined MI6 building, and the hostage girlfriend ploy, and there's little to get excited about. Need to cure insomnia? *Spectre* is the solution.

No Time to Die (2021)

The producers remembered what the series is about: thrilling action and sensational women. Despite a family subplot and a weak villain scheme that bogs down the last act, it's a fitting sendoff for Craig. In this one, nobody is safe. Major characters, including the dependable CIA ally Felix Leiter and Blofeld, are killed off, foreshadowing the controversial end when Bond dies in a missile strike. The rulebook has been well and truly torn up.

The longest pre-credits sequence to date begins with a flashback to Madeleine as a child before we shift to the present and Spectre agents come after Bond in Italy. A dejected Bond retires from MI6, and an agent named Nomi (Lashana Lynch) becomes the replacement 007. On a rogue CIA mission to recover a traitor scientist, Bond receives help from Paloma (Ana de Armas), a rookie operative who is surprisingly proficient. The best action woman in Craig's tenure only appears for ten minutes, but Paloma isn't a disappointment.

Nomi gets some badass moments too, but is overshadowed by Bond. Madeleine shoots some bad guys during a chase in Norway, but the story is about saving her – and Bond's – child Mathilde. Safin (Rami Malek) is a decent enough foe, but is defeated too easily. Three major female characters, and no villainess. Let's hope the next Bond actor gets to face some bad girls.

Rank #2

***The Punisher* (1989)**
**Lady Tanaka (Kim Miyori), Tanaka's Daughter (Zoshka
Mizak)**

Movie

The Punisher is classic 1980s action nonsense that pits
the tough title character (Dolph Lundgren) against a horde
of mafia and Yakuza goons. And the two female villains
have remained etched in my memory ever since I first saw
them.

The historical body count – before the movie even
begins – is over a hundred, and many more die before the
end credits. For the opening setup, we have a perfect tone-
setter as the leather-clad antihero breaks into a house. Then
he eliminates some hapless bodyguards and closes in on a
mobster who foolishly thought himself invincible. A big
explosion (there had to be one) and the introduction is over.

With the opening cannon fodder disposed of, it's time to
introduce more challenging opponents. First to fly into town
is Franco (Jeroen Krabbé), a pragmatic godfather who unites
the warring mafia families. The Punisher gets a lead on a
drug shipment from a drunk English thespian who speaks
in rhymes, but the Yakuza have already set up an ambush.
Lady Tanaka, a truly evil woman who makes Franco seem
small time, is the main antagonist. And her mute adopted
daughter is far more important – and deadly – than she first

seems.

As a subplot, Lieutenant Jake Berkowitz (Louis Gossett Jr.) believes his old partner Frank Castle is the Punisher, and teams up with Detective Sam Leary (Nancy Everhard). Their investigation in the sewer tunnels is a sideline to the carnage, where the cops provide useful backstory while we wait for the next action set piece.

Comic book fans criticise the hero for not wearing the iconic skull emblem, but villainess lovers won't feel shortchanged with this action classic. Picture 1980s glory with two female villains – a boss lady and a skilled henchwoman – who are *not* wasted. That's why Tanaka and her daughter rank so high on my list. They only come second because a solo villainess deserves the top slot, but this is the greatest ever female baddie pairing.

Villainesses

With two female villains, I'd normally split the summaries up, but Tanaka rarely goes anywhere without her daughter for protection. So it seems fitting to cover them both in one large section.

An early action scene has the Punisher intercepting a drug shipment, only to find an army of ninjas with other plans. The stealthy attackers take out the sentries, while a scuba team hijacks the incoming vessel. The wetsuit ninjas are well trained, and a false Coast Guard distraction gives them cover to eliminate the mafia crew. After two males use dart guns and spiked balls, the female leader shows off her martial arts skills. Two leg swipes chop a guy's hand off and slit his throat. How does she manage that? With a sharp blade attached to the side of her foot, one of many weapons in her arsenal.

One great thing about this enforcer is she never conceals

she's female, and it's only a question of whose face is behind the dark scuba goggles. That will be answered soon, but first it's the Punisher against the ninjas who mark him as a threat. The antihero kills quite a few men and crashes an escaping van into the ocean by taking out the driver. The female is a more worthy foe and throws a knife into the Punisher's chest from a long distance. Once again we see a close-up of the villainess' dark visor, and are left to relish the next female ninja encounter.

The samurai sword and ninja outfits are not-so-subtle clues that the Japanese are behind the assault, but Franco grants Lady Tanaka an audience. She plays hardball and demands a controlling interest in Franco's organisation. This is a smart and ruthless woman who knows he would never agree to such terms, even if she torments an objector with her jewelled finger blade.

Tanaka tells Franco she's taken steps to ensure his cooperation. Yakuza speak for abducting the mafia family heads' children, including Franco's son Tommy. The Punisher is happy to let the gangsters wipe each other out until the drunk informant mentions the children are innocent. And because Frank Castle (yes, Berkowitz is right) lost his own family in an underworld hit, he dishes out his own justice. This involves crashing through the roof of a Yakuza casino and unloading entire clips of ammo into roulette tables and slot machines.

Franco shares Lady Tanaka's history, and we learn she killed her own brother as a test of loyalty. And we're shown her fake affection for the kidnapped children she plans to sell into slavery. She would never take the casino attack lightly, so she does what any evil villain would and sets a trap.

Lured to a deserted funfair by false information, the Punisher takes the bait. Instead of the children, an army of ninjas awaits. Despite the advantage of sheer numbers and surprise, not to mention the bizarre sliding entrance, the Punisher kills a fair few masked mooks with his shotgun. He makes it to his trusty motorcycle and would be home free were it not for a certain female ninja. Once again, the woman is more competent that her underlings and disables the bike with a thrown ball and chain.

Dazed by the fall and unable to mount a defence, the Punisher suffers quite a beating before the female takes her turn. After a few swivel kicks, the villainess unmasks herself, and it's no surprise she's Tanaka's daughter. However, the reveal has an epic quality since it's all about her victory. Two matchups so far, and she's won them both.

When the hero wakes up, he's literally on the rack and Tanaka wants payback for the casino raid. What does a trapped man do in this situation? Come out with wisecracks, of course. Tanaka runs her finger blade over the Punisher's bare chest and uses the classic technique of threatening a friend (in this case, the drunk informant). This being a dark tale, the tough guy looks away and lets the Englishman endure. Not through with them yet, Tanaka leaves her goons in charge while she attends another meeting. A perfect opportunity to escape, put a Yakuza thug on the rack, and find out where the children are.

Tanaka's meeting is with the mob heads after they pay the ransom. Franco is a notable absentee since he didn't trust the crime lord to keep her end of the bargain. A wise decision, as the other customers are Yakuza plants who wipe out the mafia bodyguards. One guy voices his disgust, only to learn the daughter has yet another concealed weapon: earrings that double as throwing daggers. The henchwoman's aim is implausibly perfect and pins the man's wrists to the wall.

The mafia bosses don't last long, since Tanaka poisoned their champagne glasses. All she has to do is gloat as they clutch their throats and die. The man against the wall didn't drink because of a medical condition, so the villainess blows his brains out. Preamble to establish the women as badass before the final showdown, but it works.

Tanaka and her daughter disappear for twenty minutes of downtime while the Punisher rescues the children (except for Tommy) from a Yakuza hideout. The hero hijacks a bus, which doubles as a getaway vehicle until they run into a police roadblock. Berkowitz and Leary get some alone time with Castle, but he's not the best conversationalist. The police don't keep their man long since Franco stages a dramatic rescue. An alliance as fragile as they come, but the mafia boss has Berkowitz as a bargaining chip, so the Punisher reluctantly agrees.

The Punisher and Franco infiltrate the Yakuza base – concealed in a downtown skyscraper – and wipe out an entire room of thugs. After the usual air vent sneaking about, the drunk sidekick blows the lights, which turns the interior an emergency red colour. That hides the blood nicely, and Berkowitz – who's escaped from the mafia – cannot interfere from the outside.

Two samurai henchmen challenge the hero in Tanaka's inner sanctum, but he defeats them. That leaves only the Yakuza boss and her daughter to contend with. The dragon lady lures Franco into a trap using his son as bait, and the henchwoman drops behind him, ready for a deadly stealth attack. Then the Punisher crashes through an Oriental wall panel and knocks the daughter aside.

The last fight between her and the Punisher is extended as she uses martial arts and every concealed weapon in her arsenal. After a brief scuffle, the villainess plays dead, only to throw a knife into him. The daughter pulls another hidden blade, which the Punisher knocks away. He gets her in a necklock, but she uses the earrings to cut his wrists and escape. There's time for the shoe blade and deft kicks before the muscular male snaps the woman's neck.

No surprise Franco turns against the Punisher, leading to a rather tame shooting compared to what came before. Fortunately, the villainess gets a better demise. Franco catches up with her as power is restored, and she proposes he kill himself to save his son. Of course, there's no guarantee Tanaka will keep her word (she probably wouldn't). So it's good for Franco that the Punisher comes crashing through a window and throws a knife – possibly the weapon the daughter used – into the villainess' head.

Rank #1

Tuno Negro (2001)
Alex Alonso (Silke)

Movie

Also known as *Black Serenade*, this Spanish slasher has all the elements you expect from teen horror. An attractive lead, gory murders, minor characters as suspects. Plus practical jokes, and the inevitable false scares where other students dress like the killer. *Tuno Negro* benefits from its European setting, with Spanish buildings as an eerie backdrop for the murders. It's an appreciable change from the usual American university, and a killer targeting students who fail exams is an interesting angle.

The prologue in Alcala sets up the plot, with a young woman contacted by someone calling themselves the Dark Minstrel. With a creepy name like that, she should log off and call it a night. But like all introductory females, she does the stupid thing and continues chatting until the Minstrel reveals that they know everything about her. Through a remote camera, the terrified girl is shown a green-tinted view of her residence – time delayed by a couple of minutes – that ramps up the tension.

After some aggressive verbal exchanges, the Minstrel sneaks into the student's room and attacks. Thanks to a disturbance outside, the victim escapes. The corridors are deserted, leading to a chase through dark rooms. Everyone is at a graduation event with traditional Spanish music, so nobody hears the young woman flee to the chapel. The Dark Minstrel sneaks up on her, and we get our first look at the creepy rough-skin mask before the victim pulls it away. The attacker's face isn't seen by viewers, but the woman clearly recognises them. A scream brings everyone running, ending with a false scare where two students have sex. Then the victim's roommate spots the body suspended above.

The action shifts to Salamanca, another town with historic buildings galore. The first time we see the protagonist, Alejandra (Alex for short) she arrives at a deserted student dorm in a thunderstorm. An ideal time for a practical joker to fake a minstrel attack. Like other surprise villainess reviews, this comes with a spoiler alert, so readers already know Alex is the killer. However, the film does a great job with deception, setting her up as the main character viewers will expect to be the final girl. Even this early on, there are clues this woman is cold and calculating, with little patience for student pranks.

Plenty of men are potential suspects. These include criminology student Fonseca, who's obsessed with the dark minstrel case, an urban legend nobody believes is real. The womanising Edu sees women as trophies, a lecturer obsessed with history is also dean of the creepy cathedral, and a police detective has a dark side. These are red herrings, but Alex casts suspicion on them while appearing an innocent heroine. She even set up a computer chat that reacts to her voice. This makes her the conduit to the killer, to throw everyone off the trail, and her amateur sleuthing diverts attention to others.

A clever murderess, and knowing the eventual outcome doesn't affect enjoyment on repeat viewings. Since it's great to watch the villainess set everything – and everyone – up.

Villainess

Once the character introductions are done, it's time for a murder to liven things up. This comes at a wedding celebration where students perform a classic song while the murderer offs a woman in the restroom. Nowhere is safe from the Dark Minstrel, and we see the masked killer in close-up bashing the victim's head with a mandolin. Some mischievous students sneak into the women's bathroom and record the murder without realising it. What they think are sexual groans are really whimpers as the killer repeatedly stabs the victim to death.

Get used to gory knife kills, as there are plenty more. After committing the foul deed, the killer paints a symbol in blood on the wall that represents the word "Victor", a tradition from the 1400s that suggests an obsession with historic minstrels. Alex visits the cathedral chapel and convinces the dean to let her write a thesis on the topic. Stone sculptures show a secret society of masked men burned alive by the Spanish Inquisition, but the dean hints at a secret hidden in the artwork. The film spans an academic year, so when Alex isn't murdering people or planting false leads, there's ample time to solve a mystery.

Alex as the killer protagonist is one of those rare twists that makes perfect sense and seems obvious in hindsight. Many clues are presented, from Alex looking unhappy at other students cheating, her keen interest in minstrels, and a woman always at the centre of events. And a reveal partway through when another student attacks Alex, only to get beaten up by a skilled martial artist. Cut to a kickboxing ring where she trains, and even spars with the investigating cop. The femme fatale flirts with students and manipulates them into thinking they're using her when it's the other way around.

Kill scenes often have the dark minstrel slash underperforming students – and anyone who gets in the way – with a long serrated blade. Unimaginative mostly, but the minstrel's all-black outfit befits a slasher and conceals the murderer's gender. While one can never be sure, it appears the actual actress – or at least a convincing stunt double – plays the killer.

There's an impressive sequence in a morgue when a student cheats in a medical exam by reading instructions off a corpse. She gets surprised by pranksters, only for the actual killer to attack them. Numbers are no advantage against a trained opponent with a weapon. Sadly, the three murders take place off-screen – with only the aftermath shown – but we see the murderer kill a nosy doctor. Another victory symbol, but the surviving students are happy to stick around for final exams.

Next on the minstrel's list is the perennial failure nicknamed Scorpion, who prefers to deal drugs than study. After taking some hallucinogenic concoction, the minstrel pays a visit to his shadowy den. There's terrible CGI as Scorpion's bloody arm morphs into a snake while the killer stands over him. Then more imaginary reptiles burst from his chest during the fatal stabbing that follows.

With the suspect list dwindling, it's time for final semester exams. Alex spots other students cheating, and no doubt compiles a list of potential targets. The lecturers are canny and notice a woman named Michelle reading answers from a folded paper up her leg. Edu tries to switch his exam paper, but the dean catches him out by trimming the real test papers short. And Fonesca hands in a blank sheet, a deliberate fail as he hopes to ensnare the killer.

The murderer "contacts" Alex (or so the others think) via the chat page and shows images of stalking Michelle through the city. A perfect setup to create an alibi as a fellow student watches events unfold. Alex follows the phantom minstrel through Salamanca and the busy evening crowds, arriving at a courtyard where Michelle is tied up inquisition-style. Alex – alone with her victim – watches as fire trails spread and ignite the funeral pyre.

Edu inadvertently helps Alex solve the cathedral mystery, and she discovers that the historic minstrels escaped their punishment. After passing the dean's challenge, Alex hands him a gift to open later. All this leads into the finale after the police discover the images transmitted during Michelle's murder were pre-recorded. The cop is convinced there are multiple killers because it seems impossible for one person to pull this off. Thankfully, this is another red herring, and the murderer – the woman nobody suspects – is intelligent enough to operate alone.

With the men suspecting each other, the masked killer wipes out the weak students in the creepy cathedral. Fonseca and Edu are at each other's throats until they hear Alex scream. They get separated, and Fonseca discovers a hanging woman. However, it's not Alex but her assistant Sandra who's the victim. Turns out hiring a lookalike and giving her similar work clothes was a ploy to create a decoy.

The killer pours gasoline over Fonseca and jumps down acrobatically from above. The terrified man demands to know who the minstrel is, and she promptly unmasks herself. His earlier claim that females couldn't be psychopaths is debunked, and he screams in frustration. At Alex's mercy, she takes pleasure in setting him aflame and watching him burn. Alex replaces her mask to escape the watching Edu and uses the scream trick again to lure him into a fatal encounter. Edu doesn't notice the now unmasked Alex is dressed like the dark minstrel, and is truly surprised when she stabs him. Ignorance kills, indeed.

The police are also on the scene and still believe there is

more than one culprit. The chief investigator's partner is so terrified by now he guns down everyone dressed like a dark minstrel. This results in a bloodbath as the main cop confronts the masked killer. Already established as a superior martial artist, she easily betters him. After a lengthy fight, the masked Alex lets the guy live, presumably because he's impressed her. Lucky him! The cathedral's secret passage proves handy for a getaway, though Alex unmasks herself one last time to prevent the cop shooting her.

It's revealed that the real Alejandra is dead and the fake Alex adopted her persona, so the killer's true identity remains a mystery. The dean's gift is a recorded video message from the minstrel who's changed her appearance. Her stated motive is simply to wipe out weak students, which she sees as her calling. No revenge or childhood trauma, so a refreshingly unique background for the female psycho.

There are ten criteria I think make a great villainess. Intriguing backstory and setting, a spectacular entrance, memorable outfit, physical prowess, high intelligence, kill scenes, acting and dialogue, reveal / twist, exciting climax, and a victorious conclusion. While individual female villains may beat "Alex" in some categories, she's the greatest overall villain I've ever seen. And a deserved top ranking.

ORIGINAL THRILLER SERIES

Available from your favourite retailer

ABOUT THE AUTHOR AND PUBLISHER

Andy Phillips was born in Oldham, England. He holds a PhD in Applied Mathematics and a BSc Joint Honours Maths/Physics degree. In a varied career, he has worked as a scientific researcher in the USA, a police intelligence analyst, a data analyst, and a higher education teacher.

From a very young age, he became fascinated with strong female characters — whether good, evil, or somewhere in between — that appeared in action, science fiction, and thriller movies. His favourite era is 1990s direct-to-video, back when VHS tapes and rental stores were still a thing. Determined to tell stories of his own, he wrote five freeware interactive fiction games, and later founded the publishing imprint *Action Girl Books*.

His novels deliver fast-paced tales of action, suspense, and danger, including multi-faceted plots, high-intensity scenes, and cinematic storytelling. He thrives on creating strong heroines and complex villainesses, often pitted against each other. Drawing inspiration from books, TV, and film, he hopes to inspire others to be creative, too.